One Simple Journey
with Cee and Tee
AUSTRALIA as my COMPANION

CRAIG NELSON MAHON

To order additional copies of this book, contact:
Xlibris
AU TFN: 1 800 844 927 (Toll Free inside Australia)
AU Local: 0283 108 187 (+61 2 8310 8187 from outside Australia)
www.Xlibris.com.au
Orders@Xlibris.com.au
814738

Author's Note

There are a number of people who have come into my life and I would like to thank them all. Whether positive or negative they have all helped to form who I am today.

After years of grinding through life (even though to the outside world I was most probably seen as being reasonably successful – and had all my shit together), it was not until Tee came into my life that I truly found balance and happiness. So that said; my first thank you goes to Tee (my Wife) - for just being Tee! (oh, and for putting up with me).

The next person I would like to thank is Nanu (my grandfather) Joseph Spiteri who was my spiritual father and gave me most of my life skills. His philosophies are what I draw on every day of my life – A truly amazing man!

Then to my Mum – who through challenging times – took me from birth to adulthood safely and without fuss (not an easy task as I could be a ratbag at times). Thank you.

To my two boys Trent and Luke (Bruiser and Boof) – I say to you; my intentions for your lives didn't go to script and we have had some tough times over the years. But I know that deep down inside you understand how much I love you and how proud I am of your individuality.

Be the best you can be – as this is now enough for me.

To my biological father – Nelson – who I lost not long after writing this book. Even though you were missing from my life for 46 years, you were my father and I owe 50 per cent of my existence to you (thanks for the fat hands and the mean Mahon mouth). We had a laugh about how I was a "glass half full man" and you a" glass half empty guy". I always felt that you never achieved what you should have in life as you were so talented. You had the ability to be anything and yet were never truly at peace with yourself - RIP dad.

To everyone else, if you read this book then you will know who you are – Thank You!

About the Author

Craig Nelson Mahon is an everyday Australian fella who has always wanted a good simple life. Growing up in the Inner Melbourne suburbs, society dictated that to achieve a good life you needed to work hard. Craig did this, and for many years he did conform, but deep down there was something missing. Fortunately as a child Craig had the influence of his Nanu (Joe) who gave him some fundamental advice that would surface later in his life. This advise was cemented in place when Cee met Tee and their lives changed forever.

This Story – "One Simple Journey" is a part of that change!

Introduction

Life in Australian society today in general, is fast paced, with the need for people to be continually working. In fact, people now, more often than not work well past the old traditional retirement age of 65. With many struggling to make ends meet and most with little or no time to analyse or make sense of their life's journey. Tee and I felt that waiting until retirement to do this kind of travel is too late, as much of life has then passed by. Those that wait until retirement have had a fair chunk of their life happen as society demands, and don't get to use the experience of a long break to reflect and reset their lives.

This book was written to log our journey and our mission to slow down and discover more meaning to our lives. Both Tee and I felt that the only way to achieve this was to break away, almost completely, from everyday life and search for balance!

It is a simple story that takes you (the reader) on a journey across this great country of ours, and offers you an opportunity to see an ordinary Australian couple's perspective of that journey.

Readers will travel with Tee and I on our daily tour and we have set up an Internet based link so you can cross reference our destinations in picture form. (see back page for links). Alternatively, you can put the book down and research the areas through other means, which will give you a more vivid and pleasant way of joining Tee and I on our journey.

In addition to the "Simple Journey" we have added some personal experiences and a number of personal motto's and beliefs. These family experiences are part of our personal journey and are expressed purely for "us", as "One Simple Journey" has been penned for "us" and was never intended for widespread publication.

These personal beliefs are those that we have gathered over our lifetime, with many forming how both Tee and I approach life.

So please – Read On – and enjoy, but I ask that you don't expect too much, as this book is "Raw and Simple". It was written and is intended only to distract you from your daily existence and throw another perspective at you.

Note; There is always **a thousand** reasons not to take a long break from mainstream society – But only **one** reason why you should – "Choose Wisely!"

Day **1**

We dropped Whiskey (our fourteen-year-old black and white cat) off at Meo Meo Cat Manor which will be her home for the next 12 months – A bit sad but she loves it there.

We went from Beachmere to Dalby today and are staying at Lake Broadwater (Just outside Dalby). We are off to St George tomorrow

We have had a few minor problems:

- no Pillows – which we fixed at Big W in Dalby
- A few minor injuries (mainly me bumping into everything) I am too big for the Motorhome so I will need to adjust.
- Tamara also broke a nail and bent one right back cleaning the van floor by hand – apparently, I am a little mean as I wasn't sympathetic enough – I must admit the anxiety has got to me a bit and I am a little cranky.
- The biggest is a water leak in the main supply that I will have to fix tomorrow. No showers – confined space – not too good (sometimes deodorant does not cut it)
- Also, the bikes rattled apart (or one did) but stayed in the carry bag (Thank Christ) – a lovely man in Dalby pointed out that it seemed that the bike bag was nearly on the ground. I did not believe him at first but on inspection I saw something was amiss. I thanked him and he was on his way, but only after telling me a corny daddy joke. We put the bike back together after pulling the other one apart to work out how the heck it went back together.

- The weather on the first day has been stifling and it is only October – and shit we are heading west and into the desert – or so I hear.

That evening all my weather concerns were turned upside down when we were kept up half the night with a spectacular light show (performed not by pyrotechnics but by god) Then the rain came just as I nodded off. I know it was rain as my feet that hung out of the bed in the Motorhome, that I am too big for, were getting wet from the open roof vent. Not to be outdone Tamara awoke and slammed the side window just enough to ensure I knew about it – (or so I believe) I asked – what the hell was that and she explained that she was getting rained on. So, between Tamara – God and I we had quite a disrupted night sleep.

As the 90s hit by D. Ream goes "things can only get better". Great song and even better advice.

Day **2** - Day **4**

True to form things did get better – we awoke to a beautiful view of Lake Broadwater and as we started to travel to our next destination our troubles drifted away. We travelled trouble free until we got to St George then I realized that although my bumps and bruises had healed, along with Tamara's nail and the bike problem seemed solved, I still had the water problem. But first things first – with only a cuppa to sustain us so far this day and time rapidly approaching 1-00pm eating jumped to the top of our priority list.

We whipped out the cooker, which has a friend in the form of a rack on the side of our Motorhome, and proceeded to fry some Indian naan bread with an egg cracked on top – Yummy – with our view being the mighty Balonne River. Of course, me being me I could not help cracking the corny daddy joke "get that India". (As I passed Tee her Lunch/Breakfast.)

After filling our bellies my mind drifted back to the reality on fixing the water problem so we looked for a Hardware store and some level ground so I could crawl under the Motorhome.

We found such a place in St George central and it was also next door to a supermarket where Tamara went to top up our supplies. My first job was to buy a tarp as I don't enjoy getting filthy – especially when we have no water. I then proceeded to roll out the tarp and get under the Motorhome to take a closer look at the problem. I could see no obvious problem so I waited for Tamara to return and turn on the water pump while I viewed from under.

I knew that she would delight in soaking me so I kept myself well clear of the place I suspected the leak was. The water was in fact pumping out of a outlet and the problem was not that of a broken pipe but of the fact that we had stuffed so much into the storage area above the pipes that we had flipped a switch (that we didn't know was there) that drains the water supply if you want to empty the tanks. I must say I was relieved and now we could travel on with no "current" problems to worry about.

Our next point of travel was to a free camp area about 110klms west of St George in the town of Bollon. Along the road to Bollon we encountered numerous road kill which included – Goat – lizard – snake – kangaroo and wild pig and of course the mighty Road trains that apparently grow up to 53mts and I suspect are responsible for the production of the road kill. Our wish was not to be included in this long list of road kill and we proceeded with caution as they approached so not to make them angry. We also had a strong headwind which caused havoc with our fuel economy.

Upon arrival we saw a sleepy country town and on the edge of town there was the entry to an overnight camp spot that stretched along the river called Wallum Creek. It was absolutely done beautifully and was a credit to the town. We chose our spot by the River, set up for the evening and proceeded to stay a further two nights.

During our stay Tamara went on her first bike ride for many years and to my disappointment she was quite good at it. I wanted to tease her a bit if she fell off but I must admit I was really glad she could ride as you get to see a heck of a lot more scenery on the back of a pushbike. I think it is the perfect pace to enjoy what a place has to offer.

In town there was a heap of emus and many homes had wallabies and kangaroos in their yards alongside sheep and chickens (real country). There was a pub – post office – general store and produce store – police station and a church but not much more.

A fantastic place to relax though, as the camping facilities were both clean and pretty and it was a hard decision to move on. I must admit though I did check the attached cemetery to ensure there wasn't a pile of unmarked fresh graves and a local who collects Motorhomes and caravans.

Day 5

We got off to an early start this morning –too early to say good bye to Clem and Betty, the lovely couple from Bundaberg that we shared a yarn or two with. Turns out Clem was quite an artist and a very modest one at that, I emailed him a goodbye and a thank you for the yarns and let him know that I believed anyone would be proud to have his art hanging on their wall – especially me.

Our destination for today was Cunnamulla – the town known for Opals and the Cunnamulla Fella, who turns out was made in Texas, a little disappointing!

We arrived in the town on a Sunday and it was very quiet. We took our photos in front of the Cunnamulla Fella – turns out he was made of Bronze; lucky it wasn't Brass as it gets cold in Cunnamulla overnight and he may have lost his title (or titles).

We then visited the Robber Tree and took a peek at the mighty Warrego River that breathes life into the town. After this we then visited the Information centre to see what other attractions Cunnamulla had to offer and were greeted by the roar of the gentleman behind the counter who was **talking** to someone in front of him so loud that everyone else in the centre got all the information and then left. The noisy Information officer seemed bemused by this, but I for one don't know why, as I would have thought that it happened to him all the time. In fact, we were parked on the street having a cup of tea in our van and we could still hear him, so we classified him as one of Cunnamulla's attractions.

This was quite lucky for Cunnamulla as there were not many more, it was OK but it was a little disappointing to us so we continued our journey. (But if you are into Opals, I take this all back).

Bourke was our next point of call and as we crossed the Queensland / NSW border we were confronted by the town of Barringun, and I mean confronted. It had more meals on the pub menu than town's people - and by a long way. As we had not had a break for a while, we pulled over to have a bite to eat (in the Motorhome).

At this point I need to explain that we are on a budget and although not a super tight budget it is less than $100.00 per day, and when you include all things in this, including fuel, $500.00 per week is not a lot. What I am saying is that we are not tight arses, but we can't do our 12 months around Australia without making some sacrifices.

Just as we were finishing up our lunch, I heard a dull roaring noise approaching and said to Tamara – What the heck is that? As Tamara went to answer it became obvious as a group of 30 plus motorcycles started to pull in front of our parked Motorhome. We initially joked – "It's a gang!" – due to the recent publicity by the police force cracking down on these types of groups. And we soon realized that it was a gang, as such, as they were all members of the "Outlaw Motorcycle Club". I became very nervous as they were quite intimidating, although probably not intentionally, and I was keen to get out of there especially as they started using the wire paddock fence in front of us as a urinal. To my relief though they all proceeded to cross the road to the pub and we headed on our way shortly after.

Even though well behind us I still did not feel comfortable as my mind wondered back to the 80's movie Mad Max and the scene where the young couple drove out of town and although not as young as that couple my darling wife is much younger than me and extremely attractive. For the next 50 klm's I studied the rear-view mirror for signs of the gang. To my horror I saw them in my mirror and my heart started to race as they quickly caught up to our Van that doesn't run economically over 90 klm's per hour. They all passed with some passing within inches of the Motorhome, making me think that I was not the only one re-living the 80's hit movie. They took up the full width of the road both sides for as long as they stayed in view but there were no incidents.

We arrived at the outskirts of the town of Bourke shortly after and stayed at an oasis of a caravan park on the northern side of town. We set up the van and had a couple of drinks and I made a few phone calls as I had phone reception for a change. I rang my good friend Albert from Yarrawonga who has been my friend for over 30 years and was the best man at my first wedding (or what I call my practice wedding). I told him of the motorbike incident as he is also an avid motorcycle enthusiast and he proceeded to tell me that they are a bad group those Outlaws, who would Rape me while allowing Tamara to watch. Fortunately, I was on my third scotch by this time and my care factor level was low to numb.

Day 6

The next morning, we awoke to the pleasantries that our caravan park on the outskirts of Bourke provided us. It truly was a very attractive caravan park full of roses and shady trees and not one but two in ground swimming pools. But the same as us escaping the Outlaws when they arrived in Barringun, our pleasantries were only confined to a short space in time, reality hit when we entered the town of Bourke.

Although the outskirts of Bourke showed promise – the town itself was not attractive in any way shape or form and we had no hesitation in continuing our journey.

The next stop on our journey was the mining town of Cobar. Cobar was a tidy town and visiting the open cut mine lookout was well worth the journey. We had a pleasant lunch by the Cobar sign that is made from steel – concrete and looks very miney, and then we were on our way to find a free camp site for the evening.

Proving that my mind was not getting enough stimulation I broke into song singing "At the Cobar – Cobar Cabana" all the way out of town- much to the disgust of Tamara who kept telling me to "give it a rest!" We stopped at a rest stop called Meadow Glen which is famous for its wild goats and bull ants, but not much else. I am being harsh as it had basic facilities but was quite good for what it is intended and a number of people pulled up for the evening.

After watching the Ben Stiller movie Zoolander on my trusty laptop and having a pleasant night sleep we again set our sights on the road and the long journey of around 400klms to Broken Hill.

Day 7

We set off on the next leg of our journey with our first stop being Wilcannia, about 100klms on our way to Broken Hill. Wilcannia had it hey days in the 1880's and was an inland port that saw many steam ships and was the largest port for the distribution of wool in Northern NSW. It also benefited from local gold and opal discoveries. This explains the fantastic old architecture in the area. It went into decline apparently after the 1920's when road transport became more reliable.

On arrival in Wilcannia it is sad to see the level of decline, and these building deserve a better future than they have seen so far. There seems to be little pride in the town and tourists are not really made to feel welcome. There is no doubt that with a bit of pride and a pile of hard work this could be a beautiful town.

The rest of our journey to Broken Hill was filled with desolate open paddocks with dry river beds, an abundance of Road kill and a healthy supply of wild goats that seem to thrive in the conditions. On the outskirts of Broken Hill, we saw the first signs of civilization – A McDonalds signboard then a Hungry Jacks signboard and then a KFC signboard. This apparently is what Australians now believe defines a City from a town. But true to the signposts Broken Hill is a fully self-contained city where I believe you can get just about anything.

We bought some Diesel that was well priced and headed for a Caravan park for the evening. We were going to stay at a free camp along the way but they were not that crash hot and it was much easier in the hot conditions just to find a nice caravan park and pay the $30.00. This also allows us the luxury of our Air Conditioner – Woohoo!

Day **8**

The next morning, we awoke to the noisy old bugger in the caravan park next to us. Why is it that old people get up so early? I suppose I won't have to wait long until I find out for myself – although I WILL fight it.

Our plan for the day was to explore Broken Hill and then make our way south to the outskirts of Wentworth by sunset, and as we were up early (thanks old bugger) we would do this with ease. We left the Caravan Park in old Lizzie (the Motorhome - that was named by its previous owner – His Words "I named the Mazda "Lizzie" after my Mum Elizabeth, who had 10 children and couldn't travel much for that reason, so we took Mum with us on our travels, you extended her journey") and headed into town admiring the different architecture in the homes along the way. We went to the information centre and grabbed a map of the town and we went walking through the town.

The architecture in the buildings is stunning and is kept beautifully – a credit to its people – but the feature of the town that is most dominant is that every time you pass a street facing in a south-east direction you see the massive sides of the mine which towers over the town as if to say – I made this place so all you buggers better look after it. We had a great morning walking all over the town but when lunchtime came around, we were happy to be heading towards our next destination. Travelling is so exciting as you are always wondering what is around the next corner.

The landscape on the exit from Broken Hill soon returns to what it was like before we entered the town – dry and desolate. The only thing that did change was there seemed to be more goats and slightly less road kill, but that may just be a seasonal thing.

Our plan was to stay at Popiltah Rest area overlooking Lake Popiltah, and we did stop there for a bite to eat and a cuppa but we were not keen to sleep there as it was close to the main road and there seem to be a lot of Mining people using the toilet on a regular basis. So, we moved on and found a much nicer spot at Bunnerungee Bridge which was on a river bank and a lot quieter, a fact not lost on overnighters as there were quite a few. A point here is that the bible of travelling "Camps 6" would have you believe that it was the other way around. I am not having a go as some would see it as personal opinion.

Day 9

After a very good night sleep again, (this camping stuff does help me sleep well – unlike my stressful past life, which now seems a million miles away but is only really 2,000 Klms away) we were off to discover the town of Wentworth. Wentworth is the town where the Darling meets the mighty Murray.

Upon arriving at Wentworth, we were greeted by a charming country village type atmosphere where the streets were lined with multi coloured roses and charming old buildings. Tamara commented that the town reminded her of the town that Michael J Fox ended up in, in the movie Doc Hollywood. We pulled into town and had a walk through the main street up to the information centre where they were very helpful and gave us a brochure and map on all the local attractions.

As it was within an hour of lunchtime, we decided that we would drive to Perry Sandhill's (which was 5 Klm's out of town) and then find a caravan park close to town so we could ride our bikes to all the other points of interest in town. We arrived at Perry Sandhill's which in all honesty were quite spectacular, and the area seemed to be light on for tourists as when we got there around midday most of the sand hills still had no foot prints on them. In fact, if it was not for the magnificent gum trees in the area you could easily imagined that you were in the Sahara Desert.

We also noticed a number of paddy melons in the area and as they looked like a small water melon I said to Tee – "can ya eat that?" and Tee said "I think so, they are like a honey dew." I cracked the nicest looking one open and Tee had a taste, but quickly spat it out saying how horrible and bitter it was. I could not stop laughing as Tee could not stop spitting it out, and the look on her face. (I later looked them up on the internet and there have been cases of poisoning in humans from them.) A lucky escape as Tee had no such problem – thank goodness as I would have been in a heap of trouble for laughing at her, but the look on her face.

After taking photos and exploring a bit we went back into town and had "THE BEST" feed of fish and chips we have had in years. We then found a Caravan park, which was at the end of the main street and just over the town levy bank, and we quickly set up and got our pushbikes out for a ride around town.

Tee was really starting to improve on the pushie and we were taking in all the sights including the historic buildings and river views. We went to the Old Wentworth Goal and then headed to the point where the Darling meets the Murray, which was a park track that went on for about a kilometre of narrow track. We thought we were quite clever taking our bikes until we started to head back and I noticed that my front tyre had gone flat. So that's one klm of dirt track then one klm and two bridges back to town in 35-degree heat – I was not a happy camper, but at least Tee could ride on and one of us would be fresh.

As I crossed the first bridge, I noticed something stuck in the rear tyre so I pulled at it and sure enough soon followed that hissing noise that all bike riders dread. And ya can't push it back in – Shit two flat tyres – but what the heck I can't ride anyway. Tee also noticed the same things in her tyres, I said "leave them" and she was fortunate enough to make it all the way back without them going flat.

When we got back to the Caravan Park, we realized that all our tyres were full of these ugly looking thorns which we later found out via Wikipedia were called Tribulus *terrestris* nutlets and are a hazard to bicycle tyres and bare feet. And yes, all four tyres ended up flat.

But determined to enjoy the rest of our day we decided to put our head in the sand and we packed the bikes away and left the problem for another day.

Day **10**

We awoke the next morning to the sounds of ducks and ducklings on the Darling River and as we were parked backing onto the river, we peered out onto its morning splendor. Much more pleasant than waking up to the banging of some noisy old bugger that went to bed at 7-30pm. We had a bite to eat, went through all the routine required to get back on the road and we headed off.

Our next destination was the town of Mildura or actually just beyond to a place near the town of Gol Gol which is back in NSW if only marginally. On the way we stopped in the town of Merbein to get some supplies and have a walk around. The journey from Wentworth had been a picturesque one compared to the week or so that we had been traveling through near desert and very hot / dry conditions for the month of October.

Merbein is quite a nice rural working-class town again on the border of the two states, and we were able to stock up at the local IGA and receive a bonus of 4c per litre off our fuel for the privilege. We had a look through some second hand stores of which Merbein has quite a few and were disappointed that we did not have the capacity to purchase due to lack of storage in our Motorhome, as there were some bargains to be had.

We continued on our journey to Mildura and the landscape was dominated by two things – Oranges and Grapes – no surprise there! I had a hankering for some citrus so I stopped at one of the many roadside stalls and got me some Oranges – Mandarin's and even a bag of huge avocados. I popped a few oranges into the fridge so I could make a pig of myself at our next overnight stop and Tee said "are you going to eat all of them – what if they are not that nice?" I thought to myself, "they are bound to be better than the Paddy Melon" but I dare not say it as Tee- although only pushing 5 feet tall in heels packs some mean venom – and she cooks my dinner!

When we got to Mildura I was blown away as to how big it was, and as we are not city type of people, we were not keen to stay there too long. But reality had to kick in sometime, and there was the problem of the four flat tyres that were attached to our bicycles. Although hidden in a dust proof cover, they were still attached to the back of our Motorhome. Well – the laptop came out to hunt for the best price on bike tyres and tubes, with store availability in Mildura also a large consideration. I keep harping back to the budget, and this was not on it, so we needed to get out of it as cheap as possible. We decided on Big W and headed there to get what we required to get our push bike back on the road.

At this stage we had two alternatives; the first was to buy four new tyres and four new tubes and just fit them or just buy four new tubes and pick every single spike out of all four tyres. Our plan for this was that if the tyres were over $15.00 each we would be picking out the spikes – something neither of us were looking forward to. And you guessed it the tyres were $22.00 each, so happy days (not). We bought the four tubes and continued on our journey to Bottle Bend Forest Park which is a free camp on the northern banks of the mighty Murray and 18 klms past Gol Gol.

It was on a dirt track and because the weather has been so dry everywhere was just dirt and we were not keen to stay in those conditions – free or not. We just wanted some grass and a nice place to stop overnight and fix our bike problem, so we back tracked a little way to Trentham Cliffs Caravan Village and booked in for the evening. The site was lovely and with a healthy coating of green grass that we desperately wanted. We had a quiet afternoon and evening and an even better night sleep. (heads still in the sand)

Day 11

Well so far, we had avoided the task of the spike removal but today was maintenance day and there was no more avoiding. We got into the task and made a bit of a competition of it with Tee being the clear winner. It was all done in less than three hours; they were a worthy opponent though and we must have pulled out 150 spikes each. Confident we had removed them all I put them back together, cutting up the old tubes to use as extra protection for the new tubes while Tee cleaned out the Motorhome.

We did more washing and cleaning and just as we were finishing, I bashed my foot into the bike carrier and put a deep two inch cut into my left foot just below my ankle. But Nurse Tee was on the case and displayed skills that I had no idea she possessed. The cut was bad though and really needed stitches, but being somewhere we had no idea about we decided that if I took it easy and kept it clean it would heal OK, perhaps with just a larger amount of scarring.

We decided to stay at the caravan park for a further night and see what it looked like the next day. We had a great time relaxing and reading books, and this turned out to be the right choice as the wound was healing nicely and we were doing what we intended to do, "really enjoy our journey together".

Day 12

We left Trentham Cliffs this morning with only a short journey planned and arrived at the pleasant town of Euston at about 9-30am. Euston is on the NSW side of the Murray and is just seeing some development. We pulled up and decided to go directly to the Riverside Caravan Park and see if we could book in early as we were both keen to go on a bike ride. It was no problem for them so we parked the Motorhome and started getting ready for a bike ride to Robinvale which is on the Victorian side of the Murray and only 3 - 4 Kilometres away.

The ride was fantastic as it was away from the main road and followed beautiful Murray. In addition to this the track was bitumen and quite new, meaning those nasty *Tribulus terrestris* nutlets couldn't get us again. It did not take us too long to reach Robinvale and we explored the town for an hour or so. It was also quite a nice town but Tee and I enjoyed the solitude of Euston more. We bought a hot chook and a loaf of bread and headed back to our campsite for a bite to eat.

On returning to the campsite we got to appreciate the solitude of the Caravan Park, it was very quiet with no screaming brats – what a bonus!

We settled down for the afternoon each reaching for our favorite book and picking a corner of the Motorhome to enjoy the day. That evening was even quieter than the day had been and we both got excellent night's sleep.

Day 13

The next morning, we had brekkie and started the task of packing up for the day's journey. The evening before I had looked through the Camps 6 book and came to the conclusion that we should explore a bit more of Western Victoria rather than just following the Murray down to Yarrawonga, where we had planned to stay with Judy and Albert my lifetime friends. I spoke to Tee about it and she agreed as we may not get a chance when we head back this way heading to Adelaide. So, I plotted a journey that would take us through numerous country towns and also past many natural lakes.

The good news of the morning was that we must have got all the spikes out of our bicycle tyres as all four had stayed up – whoosh! – What a relief.

We set off early again – about 8-00am I believe, had a quick stop in Robinvale to top up our supplies and we were off. The first town on our journey was Manangatang – what a name, I should look it up to see what it means, or perhaps you will. The town showed no signs of oddities, apart from its name it looked like a typical Australian country town.

Today a typical Australian country town seems to be one of dilapidating older buildings and not many people under the age of sixty. This is sad to see and one can only hope that a back to basics society will see life pumped back into these places as they deserve better. We spent a short time in Manangatang and were soon on our way to Lake Tyrrell and the town of Sea Lake which was a short distance from its shores. The lake was almost dry and looked like one big salt pan, but was a unique and a beautiful sight.

The town of Sea Lake was a town holding its own and doing its best not to slip into decline. A big part of what helps the town to survive is the Sea Lake Mallee Rally which is the oldest currently running off road event in Australia and raced around Lake Tyrrell a distance of some 85 Kilometres. We spent some time walking around the town with our only purchase being a smelly thing from Tibet, or some god forsaken place, that Tee said would smell lovely in our Motorhome toilet. My only comment on this is that "you certainly know it is there!"

We have now got into the crazy habit of singing that song "Holiday Road" from the Chevy Chase movies every time we jump into the Motorhome to head to our next destination, a true indication that we are now really living the "simple life".

We drove through the town of Woomelang on our way to what would become our next overnight stay, the town of Hopetoun, and more specifically the Free Camp area of Lake Lascelles which is absolutely beautiful. We settled in quickly (after I stuffed around trying to find the perfect spot and level for 40 mins) and I cooked myself a steak by the waters edge prior to watching the sunset over the lake which was awesome. We slept well again – a pattern that is unfamiliar to me- and awoke to the calming beauty of the still lake and the chirping of the local birdlife - "it doesn't get better than this".

Day 14

We again got to the road after we performed all our duties and sung our Chevy Chase number. Our aim for the day was to travel past more lakes and towns and press marginally into SA and more specifically the town of Bordertown which was the birthplace of Bob Hawke.

This would take us over a lot of Kilometres but we may not get a chance to see the area when we eventually head through South Australia so we thought a fleeting trip was better than none.

We departed Hopetoun and headed for Lake Albacutya which was bone dry, but even dry it is an awesome site as it covers 5,850 hectares. It apparently fills from Lake Hindmarsh when the Wimmera River is in full flood and has a 20-year full/empty cycle. We headed off again stopping briefly at the town of Rainbow for a cuppa and then towards Lake Hindmarsh.

On the way we entered the town of Jeparit which I did not realize was the birthplace of Sir Robert Menzies – arguably Australia's greatest prime minister. They proudly displayed the fact on a sign at either end of town and on a memorial plaque in town. The signs, as does the town itself, show a low level of maintenance and follows the trend of many of our country towns.

We soon reached Lake Hindmarsh which was enormous compared to the lakes we had seen so far. It had its own beach on the side we entered from, and was probably as close to a seaside vacation as any of the locals would get, and quite a nice spot by anyone's standards.

As this was a quick trip to SA we had to move on and our next point of interest was the town of Nhill. On the way we saw many distance signposts saying 35 to Nhill etc – well you get the gist; I could not help the corny jokes. "That's a sad score line" and as we got closer to town each signpost of distance got the full cornball treatment much to Tee's disgust.

Nhill seemed to be a busy country town and with one exception seemed quite normal. The odd event that I am referring too was a man in his early to mid 40's running in a local park with a goat in pursuit – without a lead. I must admit though they both looked quite happy and did go some way to explaining the brightly painted farm animals proudly displayed on the entry and exit of the town. Actually, tell a lie, those farm animals were at Kaniva but it is the same district and maybe the man and his goat were just visiting Nhill from Kaniva.

We had a late lunch in Kaniva, close to the brightly painted animals before heading to Bordertown. On the way to Bordertown we were lured into a roadside store who offered a cuppa and a chat, along with fine produce for sale. We met Bevan, who was the owner, and his family. What a character Bevan was "and talk" – he could talk under water with a mouth full of gravel, and I should know being an ex Real estate agent as I could not get a word in. We bought some dry roasted almond and some four fruits marmalade; the almonds were sensational and the marmalade well I will let you know when I have some on my toast for brekkie.

We soon arrived at Bordertown with our interest not in the white Kangaroos, that are popular with the Brats, but in seeing Bob Hawks home of birth and the memorial for him that the town had compiled. The town was very attractive and extremely well maintained so we decided to walk to all the points of interest which turns out were not far from where we parked. First stop was Hawke House, as they called it, and it was a charming little cottage that now housed the local branch of Centrelink that Tee and I found a little amusing. We then took photos of the Bronze bust of Bob and the display that was created behind the library, it was nicely done. But us being us we much preferred the scenery and natural landscapes so it was back on the road and doing what we love, enjoying the scenery of the road.

From Bordertown we headed south to the small border town of Frances and then back into Victoria where we stopped overnight in the quiet town of Goroke. The loop that we had done had circled the Little Desert National Park and the scenery was magnificent, well worth any travellers' efforts to see.

Day **15**

The next morning, I cooked us both a big feed of Bacon and Eggs, the bacon was a smoked Italian variety and extremely yummy. I checked the navigator to see how far we were from Yarrawonga and with two days to get there we really needed to be around Bendigo by tonight.

Not long into our days driving we came across some exceptionally beautiful scenery in the form of a lake, rocky mountain and a rocky outcrop called Mitre Rock, located just East of the town of Mitre. We got out and climbed the rock and admired the scenery which stretched over the lake and out to the distant green pastures. Just as we were descending two eagles soared overhead hovering in the updraft, it was a truly magical place.

We proceeded to Horsham where we fuelled up and met an elderly gentleman who congratulated us on having the courage to leave our jobs and follow our dreams. He gave us his brief life experience of working hard, not seeing his family enough and the fact that his life had moved so quickly, and that we should live life to the fullest – Not bad advice. In fact, before we left to travel Australia, we took the Motorhome on a few trial runs and on one of those journeys we met a gentleman who had been around Australia four times. He gave me some lasting advice saying – "there are always a thousand reasons why you don't go a journey such as travelling around Australia, but only one reason why you should". If you don't know what the one reason is yet I will tell you later in my writing or in fact you may just start to get it before then.

The rest of our journey to Bendigo was a little uneventful apart from the fact that East of Warracknabeal was distinctly dryer and browner than the Western side. We are not sure if this is normal due to soil type and weather conditions or just a timing thing. We stopped overnight in a free camp just north east of Bendigo in the small town of Huntly.

Day **16**

The next morning, we awoke to the view of cows in a paddock which was amazing as on the other side of our Motorhome was a main road. Fortunately for us the road was not busy overnight so we slept well. We looked for a tap to fill up our water tank and I was excited when I saw a tamper proof tap, as it was my first chance to use the tap key that I had purchased from Bunning's for this very occasion. I filled up with water and we were on our way.

As we travelled towards Yarrawonga, to the east, the landscaped returned to green again so there was only a patch between Warracknabeal and Bendigo that was brown. There was no doubt that the Victorian countryside pre-summer 2012 is looking spectacular and we were privileged to see it at its grandest.

As we only had two hundred kilometres to travel to reach Albert and Judy in Yarrawonga, we had plenty of time as it was a Friday and they were working. We took our time and enjoyed the scenery and even had time to drop into an olive farm. The olive oil was very nice but Tee and I can't get into it, as much as we love Italian food and want to love it.

Anyway, we arrived at Yarrawonga around 3-00pm and to our surprise Albert was home on an RDO. It was great to catch up with them and we ordered in a pizza and chatted for hours, catching up with each others lives. Unfortunately, though they had both been asked to work over the weekend at the cracker factory and we were left to do stuff around town during the day until they got home.

This worked out well as my foot that I cut open was not healing all that well and in fact was infected. The doctor believed that it was Murray water from the caravan park that we stayed at that was the culprit, and after giving me a tetanus shot and a script for antibiotics I was on my way. I bought a few things in town before returning back to Albert and Judy's where Tee had been doing some cleaning and house duties on the Motorhome. We had a relaxing afternoon until Jude & Alb returned from work then we got back to chatting and catching up again while enjoying one of Albie's superb BBQ's.

Day **17**

The next morning after Jude & Alb went to work again, we decided to ride into town and look at the farmers market that is held on the foreshore of Lake Mulwala. It was a nice atmosphere with a beautiful location but the prices were a little touristy so we only purchased some homemade marmalade. We continued to ride through town and followed the lake for some kilometres before taking some photos and returning back to town. We then decided to go to the weir and have a look at that on the way back to A & J's. It was a good ride and one that was not marred by nasty plant spiking which although prevalent we managed to avoid.

Upon arrival back at A&J's we were very hungry as we had not had brekkie and it was almost 1-00pm by now. So, we pulled out the camp table and chairs and I cooked up a feed of Bacon and Eggs in A&J's garden. Sure, as anything when I started cooking A&J turned up as they had finished early at the cracker factory, we finished lunch and joined them in their home for a chat and decided to visit their daughter, partner and grand daughter.

We spent an afternoon with them and Matt (their son in law) filled us with beer while Alb doted over his grand daughter Charlotte. We then went back to town bought some Fish and chips and ate them by the weir where we had been that morning on our bike ride; it was a very pleasant day.

But we were travellers now and had a big country to explore so the next morning we were off to see the Alpine region of Victoria and were very excited to be on the move again.

Day **18**

Not long after A&J went to work Tee and I got our show on the road. We had to empty the shitter which is not a too terrific job – but when it's full it's full and it has ta be emptied. Luckily Yarrawonga is an RV friendly town and they have a dump point and "I have long rubber gloves". I will not give you a run down on how this is performed but you can look it up on U-Tube if you are that interested, anyway it got done and we headed towards Rutherglen.

We arrived in Rutherglen mid morning and we had a good look around all the antique and second hand stores, something we both enjoy. Again, we had not had brekkie so we went to a local bakery and had ourselves a steak, bacon and cheese pie each that was super yummy.

Before leaving A&J's I had jumped on the net to get a deal on the Spirit of Tasmania as with the Motorhome we thought it would pay to book early. Most of the fares were around $500 - $550 one way for Tee and I and the Motorhome but luckily, I had a win and found a fare at $439 – a big win on a tight budget. This locked us into a date of the 6th of Jan 2013 for us to sail to Tassie – which meant I would be spending my 50th birthday there.

It also meant that we could cruise for the next two months through the Alpine region – Mt Kosciuszko region - the east coast of Victoria and all the way down to Melbourne. We expect to be in Tassie for a couple of months to break the heat of summer and before embarking on the trip west.

Back to our trip – we left Rutherglen and had to do a stop in Wangaratta to get my doctors fee back from Medicare (or should I say a small portion of it back). Wangaratta is a lovely bustling country town – but Tee and

I just don't like those built up places and much prefer the quiet country towns and camping spots, so it was a case of do our business there and move on.

Our next stop was the town of Beechworth that we found to be lovely and much nicer than my memories of it from my youth. We spent a good few hours their looking at all the historic buildings before moving onto our camp spot for the night. The spot we chose for the evening was a spot on the Ovens River near the tiny town of Everton and when we arrived, we were not disappointed. We levelled the Motorhome in a spot that overlooked the river and a little bit away from the other four Vans that were there also.

The spot was a little close to the road but it was a very minor road so we didn't think it would be a problem. What was a problem was a Wanker who had to have a generator running. Do these people understand how intrusive this noise is and how much it dulls the tranquillity of the birds chirping and the river running? Do they know they are Wankers? We also had some clown who thought it was funny to beep his horn as he went past campers in the middle of the night. Now he knew he was a Wanker! Anyway, I did not hear any of this and it was Tee who heard it and it woke her up – a total role reversal and an indication that I am totally relaxed.

Day 19

The next morning, we decided to do a small amount of driving and just drive to Myrtleford and Bright. Also today is the last day of week three's budget and we are well in front. We are trying to put a few dollars aside for the crossing to Tasmania which will be close to the single biggest expense of the whole trip unless things go wrong with the Motorhome.

We drove to Myrtleford which is a lovely town, as most are in this part of the world, and we took a right turn to look at Nug Nug Reserve as an overnight spot to stay. It was very nice but it was a small charge campsite and we were watching every penny, so we decided against staying there.

The view along the road to Nug Nug Reserve was spectacular with tree covered mountains and lush green valleys, dotted with charming farmhouses and some trendy homes being built on the mountainsides. The only blot on the landscape was the cleared sections of pine forests which I believe go into the production of toilet paper, a horrible transition for the trees to go from rolling green hills to someone's **** (you know)!

We drove on and stopped for lunch in the town of Porepunkah, which is some 6 kilometres shy of the famous town of Bright. The spot we stopped at was a lovely little park and as it was quite warm the Weeping Willow over the Motorhome was just the ticket. We got lunch out, which consisted of a lovely Danish cured meat, Bega cheese and various things like Onion and tomato, all on lovely fresh crackers – Yummy. We sat and ate it and by the end were quite full and I decided to have a nap, "now that's living!"

When I woke it was getting on in the afternoon so we had better get going to find a free camp for our next evening. The next one was on the other side of Bright but only five or so kilometres, so we decided that we would drive through Bright, set up and stay the evening at Freeburgh Bridge and then explore Bright the next morning. As we drove through Bright, we realized immediately why people rave about it, from the tree canopied streets to the cottage style homes and shops, it truly is a postcard town.

We camped overnight and had a great sleep.

Day **20**

In the morning though we had a strange event, as we were preparing to leave a car (or small white 4WD) pulled up in front of us and the lone male inside seemed to be casing the Motorhome. As the Motorhome is quite dark inside and the windows reflective, I think he thought it was empty. He got out of his vehicle and approached, but I think he then saw me and jumped back in his vehicle and drove off. Tee and I are both sure he was looking to steal things from campers who had gone back into town and left their main vehicles behind, it was quite weird. Although not freaked out by the incident it changed our mind about staying for a second night in this location.

We then drove back into Bright and spent a lovely morning browsing the shops and admiring the scenery and architecture. The amazing thing about Bright is that when there you feel totally encased in nature and the shops and houses don't feel like they dominate the landscape, it is a must visit town!

With Lunchtime approaching we decided to hit the road again to find a spot for lunch and found a nice shady tree by the river about halfway between Bright and Harrietville. We pulled up and made ourselves another meat and cheese platter but this time Tee had a bit of a nod after lunch. Although not a long one as I didn't realize she was napping and yapped out "we should hit the road hey Tee" to which she sleepily replied "yeh what!"

We travelled to the town of Harrietville which is really just a small sleepy version of Bright, but we didn't stop as we realized that "Lizzie had to get Bizzie" as she had a mountain to climb all the way to Mt Hotham.

And what a climb it was as we never got past third gear all the way up. Halfway up our fridge came flying out of its hole and crashed into the shower – "never fear as Tee is here" and she rushed to right the fridge and held it in place until we fixed the retaining strap at the next place we could stop. The scenery was sensational and as we approached the top, we realized that there was still snow on the peaks, an amazing thing to us as it was over 30 degrees in the valley below and one day short of November.

The Village of Mt Hotham is strange to see as it is a swarm of accommodation in the middle of nowhere, but I suppose in winter and covered in snow it looks right. We continued over the mountain top past Dinner Plain (a classier looking mini version of Hotham) and onto our campsite for the next two nights at Cobungra, which adjoins Victoria Falls Historic Area. We ate dinner (Pasta Cabonara) and went to bed for the evening.

Day 21

For the first time in over three weeks I did not sleep that well last night and can only put it down to the fact that the Motorhome was on a bit of a lean. I have straightened it for tonight and I hope I sleep well. This area was the site of Victoria's first significant Hydro electricity scheme and was built in 1908 by the Cassilis Gold Mining Company but was short lived due to a dam wall collapse around 1916 which saw the company close down the gold mine. Today it is an isolated small river surrounded by rolling green hills and a few houses and a brilliant overnight camping spot. Today we are the only ones here and are loving the tranquillity, it is now 5-00 pm and we have not seen one person or one car. You can't beat that for Serenity and I am sure Bonnie Doon couldn't beat it for Serenity either.

We are really starting to get into a different mindset three weeks into our travels. It is really difficult to change years of habits – like having to be somewhere by a certain time – having to wake at a certain time – having a time constraint on completing a task. To step back and just do nothing sounds easy but when you have lived a lifetime of being conditioned by society it is extremely difficult. We don't want to be hippies but we want to live life with more meaning to us and not draw on other people or have them draw on us to survive, as today we believe society has gone beyond sharing and it is more dog eat dog wrapped in candy coating.

When your step off the treadmill society is not happy about it and it tries to hold you in its web, let me go back in time to explain to you how we got to where we are now and why where we are going is so special, as this is not simply a journey of two travellers in a Motorhome but of how life should be for all – **"One Simple Journey"**.

Tee and I have always been a little different and the story of how we became a couple is a story in itself as our lives crossed paths many times without us actually meeting. But as a couple we are searching for a simpler existence and our trip around Australia is part of that journey and it was a series of events that put us on this road.

A year or so ago we paid the mortgage off on our home and although happy with this it did not fulfil our dreams as something was missing. This is the trick with today's society, we are all so busy trying to pay bills and get ahead that we forget how to really live and we lose perspective on what is really important.

This phenomenon is often referred to as the Rat Race and for most people it goes like this; We grow up in a home where bills are paid and the general household is busy with numerous activities that revolve around education, work, social activities and sporting events etc. This is of course a generalization but a lot of other more specific activities can be loosely grouped within the above list. This means that to survive in today's society at least one parent and more often both have to work full time. Being kept busy, just to survive means that most people don't look outside the square as how life could be, and to make it more bearable, we get sucked into consumerism as a release from daily stress. But that in turn keeps us in the cycle of having to work and pretty soon you have a house full of "stuff" that is hardly used and you work harder and longer to pay for it all. In addition to that children become expectant and not appreciative as their values become entwined in "stuff" and they also head down the same road.

Don't be mistaken, this is not just something that happens but a detailed plan by society to extract your energy. Sounds sinister but what it is more simply is that because of the huge number of people on the planet to become wealthy all you need to do is extract a very small amount from a high proportion of the population. Example: you can't buy much with one dollar today, but get $1-00 out of 1,000,000 people and you are an instant millionaire. You may say, well a million isn't much these days, but remember there is now over seven billion people on the planet.

Now I could go on to talk about the problems of the world, but that is not where I am heading. I think we should all try to simplify our lives, enjoy what we have and take some of the stress off ourselves and the planet. What follows is how Tee and I got to break the cycle and question "normal living".

As said earlier, we had paid off our mortgage and were searching, but just up and leaving your life as you know it is not easy. Our story was that we were planning our trip around Australia, which we were going to do for twelve months, and doing the preparations for that. But I was getting sucked into my work and was starting to question the sensibility of leaving the good wage and security that I felt that bought.

A lot of my friends and colleagues were saying you won't go and I was looking for reasons as to why I had to stay. It was Tee who was resolute in her ambition and I was searching for a way to break that in her so I could stay in the Rat Race. Then a series of events that I will not go too deeply into led to me and my employer having a large argument and my resulting termination. Now I am still trying to figure out in my head whether this was my subconscious helping me break the cycle or just a coincidence but I am leaning towards my subconscious as I now firmly believe that without this event happening, we would not be on the road today.

To most people losing their job would be a disaster, but to me it was like a weight was lifted from my shoulders and the first thing Tee said when I told her I was sacked was "Good – now we can live our dreams". She then went on to say "oh shit – now I will have to quit my job also."

The logistics of living on the road for twelve months also takes a lot of effort as the bills still require payment and setting them up to be accessed from the road takes a bit of time. But as we can attest to now, it is time well spent and already we are feeling the benefits and sense of freedom that being a traveller brings.

Now - back to our travels.

Day 22

We awoke in Cobungra this morning and it was absolutely freezing, believe me in a Motorhome you really feel it. But outside the scenery was still magical and the cold weather made us move around quickly and by 8-15am we were on the road.

In no time at all we had reached the town of Omeo and on the way, we stopped at a lookout that gave us our first glimpse of Mt Kosciuszko, which we would visit in about a week from now, give or take. Omeo is a very old town and we stopped very briefly before continuing our journey.

The scenery after Omeo continued to get nicer and nicer until hunger overcame us at a place called Anglers Rest and I cooked Tee and I some yummy bacon and eggs for brekkie by the Cobungra River. This place was stunning like a page out of a fairytale book and it had fantastic free camping areas beside the River. After our feed and a few pictures, we were again on the road exploring new sights.

Not long after leaving Anglers Rest, we came to a fork in the road with the left road taking us over Falls Creek and the other taking us directly towards Tallangatta. The left road was steep and uninviting, especially to Lizzie who seemed to be pulling me towards the right road, but the promise of more snow-capped mountains and stunning high plain scenery forced me to pull to the left and guide Lizzie up the massively steep road. As she had shown climbing to Mt Hotham, she is a real stayer and this was a seriously steep road that seemed to go on and on, but how beautiful it was.

It seemed as though we were the only people on the planet as we did not pass another car for a long time, but we did pass a road closed boom gate and apparently this road is impassable most of winter. The next thing we saw was something that we did not expect; on the side of the road was a horse, not a domestic horse, but a wild Brumby. As we approached the Brumby retreated into a clearing where it re-joined another Brumby and they stayed there even though we stopped to photograph them. I am not sure whether or not it is common to sight them but we felt very special to have seen them.

The high plains are a very different and beautiful place and the air seems to breathe you - crisp and clean. We drove on to see pockets of snow, the beautiful dam at Falls Creek and the magical streams and waterfalls all down the mountainside. As we descended from Falls Creek, we saw cyclists climbing their way up the mountain, and we thought these fella's are extremely dedicated – what a climb they had.

We coasted all the way down the mountainside with the air brakes in full use to hold back Lizzie, (who is a heavy little lady), until we caught a glimpse of Mount Beauty. Mount Beauty is a quaint little town and the name says it all, it is a tidy town in a valley surrounded by huge mountains on all sided. In fact, from the sportsground we could see the snow caps of Falls Creek – and remember it is November now.

We went to the local convenience store to top our supply of groceries and we cooked some snags on our barbie for lunch, a late lunch at that, as we just finished as the local kids were getting out of school. We looked around town for a bit and then headed to find an overnight stop. We do this by 4-00pm each day so we have plenty of time to find a nice place and it has worked so far. We finally found a caravan park about ten or so Kilometres out of Mount Beauty called Mongans Bridge and although very pretty it was also quite busy. I asked the caretaker why it was so busy (to which she replied as if I was stupid) "it's Melbourne Cup Weekend" and to level the ledger I replied "but this is Mongans Bridge", we both smiled and she took my $20-00 and hand wrote a receipt.

The main reason we broke our successful string of free camps was because I broke the golden rule of budget camping – ALWAYS TOP UP YOUR WATER WHEN YOU SEE AN OPPORTUNITY. I failed and paid the price – twenty bucks!

Day **23**

Another lovely night's sleep and I awoke to wish Tee a happy Birthday – and a very special one at that as it was her 40th. We were going to stay at home and have a party for it but we were so excited about our trip around Australia that it seemed silly to delay it by a month for one event, as important as it was.

I had been anxious about today as I did not know how to make it special for her, and the best I could come up with was to take her to dinner in a major town and I had planned that for Albury / Wodonga for this evening. But as we approached Wodonga, we both expressed the fact that we disliked hanging around towns and we preferred to keep travelling. I was a little relieved about this, but I still feel that I haven't done enough for her birthday so I am going to get some surprises ready for her over the next few weeks.

We left Wodonga after getting fuel and putting air into the tyres. Travelling east we soon bumped into Lake Hume (it is massive) and we pulled into one of the day areas to make a cup of tea and as it was Tee's birthday, I was in charge of doing everything and she was in charge of doing nothing. It was the Melbourne Cup weekend and the weather was beautiful so the lake was quite busy with boating families who were both camping and day tripping. There were a number of boats on the water as Victorians are very fond of their high-powered vessels, almost as fond as they are of taking the Monday before the Melbourne Cup off as a sickie. We watched them for a while, finished our cuppa's and hit the road again. But it seemed like forever before we could shake off Lake Hume as it went on and on and on. Just as we thought we were at the end of it we crossed to the other side of it, did a full 180 degree turn and followed it some more. The only thing that could shake us from it was the town of Tallangatta where we stopped for lunch and for me to enjoy the task of emptying the shitter again.

I decided to do the shitter first as I did not want it to spoil my lunch, especially since we had not eaten since dinner last night and it was nearly 1-00pm. The Dump Point was at the showground and when we arrived there it was full of horse floats as there was some kind of event on. It was hard to get the Motorhome to the Dump Point but we managed to get close enough and the up side was that the smell of horse shit drowned out the shitter smell! As you can probably tell by now this is not my favourite task. With all that out of the way went headed into Tallangatta central to get our lunch.

Our favourite food on the road is Fish and Chips as we rarely have them at home and it just kinda makes it feel like a holiday when you are eating them in a park that is new to you. So, we did that exact thing – we got our Fish and Chips and went to the nearest park and sat on a park bench and starting eating. The one difference was that I grabbed the White Crow Tomato Sauce out of the Motorhome to have on my chips.

After a late lunch we took off to find a place for the evening. We were heading to a free camp but the two we saw were not very nice so we kept heading towards Corryong to the next free camp. Just before Corryong though we spotted a fantastic looking caravan park called Colac Colac Caravan Park and I went in to investigate the rates and found they were quite hefty at $36.00 for a powered site. At this stage I had had enough of driving for one day so I asked about un-powered site and was told they were $28.00 and with some further negotiating I got the price down to a reasonable $25.00. We took a spot just beside the river and began the task of relaxing for the rest of the day.

I must say the Caravan Park was very pretty and the river just set it right off, so $25.00 although high for an un-powered site turned out to be well worth stopping for.

While at the Caravan Park, we met a couple who had a Motorhome almost identical to ours and they were from Warburton in Victoria. We had a long chat and compared Motorhomes, swapping ideas and talking of our journeys. One thing that I was extremely grateful for was a tip on who to service our Motorhome while we were in Victoria. Sam put me onto someone in Lilydale and gave me their phone number. This was something that I was anxious about as finding a decent mechanic can be hard in your home town, let alone in a strange place.

Day 24

We left Colac Colac Caravan Park, after a few more tips from the owner on places to see on our journey, with our sights set on exploring Kosciuszko National Park. The first stop on our journey was to the town of Khancoban where we pulled into the National Parks office to get our Park permit. The lady there was extremely helpful, it was Sunday, and even pointed out which camping spots would be most suitable for our vehicle. (It was like she knew Lizzie). We started our accent of the mountain range with our first point of interest being the Murray 1 power station. We did not go into the power station itself but went to the viewing area which overlooked the massive white pipes that carry water to the power station from dams at higher elevation.

The climb up the mountain produced stunning scenery of valley, peaks and the odd glimpse of the massive pipes that carry the hydro water supply. We then passed another power station and not long after we approached snow on the highest peaks. The only distraction from the scenery was the hundred of motor cycles that continued to fly past Lizzie – no respect for an old girl, hey Lizzie! (Sunday, not a good day to travel up a windy road). We stopped at a roadside lookout to the sight of a spectacular mountain covered in Snow and just touching the cloud line, with a view across the ranges and valleys below.

We had a choice of two spots to stop for the evening, Geehi or Tom Groggin, so we decided to check them both out. Geehi was very pretty boasting a pristine, stone bottomed river, a stone historic cabin and heaps of cheeky Kangaroo's. We decided not to stay there for only one reason and that was that the Historic Stone Cabin was past the camping area on a dirt road and it was getting a lot of traffic (meaning dust). So, Tom Groggin it was, and we continued on our journey.

We arrived at Tom Groggin which is on the mighty Murray River, close to its headwater, and found a lovely little spot overlooking the river. The Murray is an amazing stretch of waterway and has been the dominant natural feature on our journey for about a month now. The water here is pristine and nothing like the cloudy wide girl that she is downstream, in fact we are using it to fill our water tank.

As we set up camp, we were confronted by a cranky Kangaroo who refused to leave the campfire he was standing in. Being a wild animal, I was apprehensive to approach too close but they all seemed quite timid so I waved him away which allowed us to walk to the river's edge. Turns out he was eating scraps out of the ash that past campers had thrown in the fireplace on their departure – not something I think us humans should do. The Kangaroos certainly seem to have it good here as it seemed there were two options for them – to be male or be carrying a Joey. We had a quiet night's sleep and heading off after a lazy morning with Thredbo in our sights and not many Kilometres away.

Day **25**

On the way to Thredbo we stopped at Dead Horse Gap about four Kilometres before the village. There was a gorgeous rocky stream beside the road which enticed us to get out for a short hike. We crossed the stream and started to climb towards the snow line and Dead Horse Gap, but short of halfway up the mountain Tee turned to me and said, "I think I will just do my stretching now" which is code for, "I have had enough of this mountain climbing shit, my legs are sore" and I continued alone. In fact, it was nice to be alone up there, not that I didn't want Tee there, but the solitude of nature is accentuated when you are alone with it. I climbed to the snow line when a storm started to come over and I decided that that was enough for today and started my decent. And no that is not code for "my legs are tired!" As I got over the ridge and started my way down, I spotted the Motorhome which looked tiny but was a welcome sight as it is always nice to know that you have followed the right path.

In life, as I said earlier, you get many opportunities with some being good and some being not so good. You are born as an energy cell with only so much you can do in a lifetime so it is important to put your precious energy into the right things. In life you see people who have boundless energy and this is because you will find they have a positive approach to life and thrive due to making clever choices.

I have an analogy that I will share with you and it is an observation that I have made after spending many years selling Real Estate. People who have a tidy home put less effort into their home than those who are untidy. Now you may say – and probably are – that is bullshit, but think about it. If you are tidy and organized you only have to spend a short time each day keeping it that way and don't waste time looking for things that untidy and unorganized people seem to always be doing. In addition, when it comes time to sell the home it achieves a better price and therefore allows the owner to be further ahead in life energy than those who have been less organized and received less for their home.

What I am trying to say is – use you time and energy wisely and work hard in the positive sector of your life and not in the negative sector. You will find then that you are not forever just trying to survive but in fact because you have that part of your life organized you can spend your time developing something that will make your life even better.

- Now back to our travels.

When I reached the bottom and got back to the Motorhome, we drove to Thredbo Village for a quick look. Thredbo is quite large and all the buildings are dark and a bit gloomy looking but not in an ugly way. It is difficult to come to Thredbo without recalling the Stuart Diver incident which saw devastation thrust upon this Village all those years ago – it was an amazing story of survival. We started descending into the Village but turned back as it was quite narrow and there was little activity in the summer months.

Onwards to Jindabyne which sits on a large lake, but we kept driving as it didn't do much for us. We stopped at Berridale which is a quiet country town that seems to be going backward and we had lunch in the Motorhome which consisted of a meat and cheese platter. Then onto Cooma where we stopped to get our Gas refilled.

This was an interesting spot and my introduction to the town was at the gas refill station where the gentleman who served me was a real misery guts. I asked him how his day was going, to which he replied, "Shithouse" and I said "that's no good, hopefully it will get better" to which he replied, "not before 5-00pm" which I presumed was his going home time. I said no more as he was depressing me and he had a horrible attitude to life, you could see it in his face, I paid him and left.

Now how the heck is this poor fella ever going to have a good life if he thinks like that? He was setting himself up for a life of misery. When if he talked his lot in life up, he could improve his attitude and outlook which in turn would create a life where he could see the opportunities that present themselves. Rest assured life does present opportunities to everyone who is looking for them.

Now even if you don't believe this what is the point in continuing to be miserable? It only makes you feel depressed and doesn't achieve anything in life. Nobody is going to come along with a magic wand and fix it for you as they too are looking for positive people in their lives. And if you are waiting for a lotto win you will be waiting longer than the fairy god mother with her magic wand, in fact even if you win lotto the chances of you keeping a wealthy and happy lifestyle is only about three to five percent. Statistics say that 95% of people who win lotto are back to their old wealth level within seven to ten years. It is all about "YOU" making your life better for yourself through a positive outlook.

- Now back to our travels.

We then went to the Woolworths in Cooma and bought some bottled water before heading towards Canberra and the free camp spot Numeralla River Rest Area which had a tick in the Camps6 book. When we arrived, we were less than impressed as the free camp area was on gravel, the grass was waist high and dead, the water wasn't working and the area was used by council to store mounds of gravel and dirt. Hey, but it was free – free or not the tick should be removed at the very least. But as it was 40klms away from its nearest alternative we stayed the night.

Day **26**

The next morning, we decided to head all the way to Eden, as we were keen to see the beach again after over a month of being away from it. On the way we stopped back in Cooma to top up our supplies of food, fuel and Tee's wine. We came down off the Great Dividing Range and decided to revisit the Bega Cheese Factory which is well worth a visit. They have cheese tasting and a sort of museum with educational stuff that would be good for kids, and adults too if you like that kind of stuff. We were keen to get our hands on some tinned cheese which is only produced for the export market and also some Smokey Cheese that is also only produced for the export market. Tee and I can't understand this as the Smokey cheese is sensational and the tinned cheese has some great advantages, especially if you are travelling like us with limited fridge space. We were in luck, as the tinned cheese was on special and we bought four tins of it. I took an iphone photo of Tee and the Bega cow, which Tee sent to her daughter back in Brissy.

While in the Bega Cheese car park I jumped on the net to hunt some cheap accommodation rates at Boydtown Caravan parks. I rang three and the Aspen Caravan Park at Boydtown gave me a week for $168.00 which was $52.00 cheaper than its closest competitor. I love a bargain and when we arrived, we were given a lovely spot right near the beach and on lovely green grass. It doesn't get much better than this!

Day **27** - Day **41**

We awoke to the beauty that Eden (Boydtown) provides; it has a natural beauty and stunning beaches unsurpassed anywhere in the world (personal opinion). The most amazing thing about it though is its lack of population, which is probably the main reason it is so naturally beautiful.

Tee and I have a soft spot for Boydtown as it was a standout on one of the first trips that we took together as a couple. Our first trip together was to Alice Springs, which came about when I asked her, "If there was anywhere that you would like to travel where would you go?" It was one of those questions that you ask a lady when you are trying to impress. Problem is that Tee said she would love to go to the Greek Islands – way out of my budget at the time as I was in the middle of a divorce, and we all know how expensive they are. So, I had to suck eggs and say "oh I meant within Australia" to which she said the Northern Territory – lucky escape!

But back to Eden (Boydtown) which we visited by chance on a trip back to Brissy from my original hometown of Melbourne some five years ago. I took Tee to show her all my old childhood stomping grounds and the homes that I had lived in prior to moving to Queensland about twenty years ago. We were just about to head home along the Hume highway when I said that we should take and extra day off and follow the coast to Sydney. Tee was happy with that as it would be new sights for her as she had never been that way before; in fact, it was her first trip to Melbourne. We followed the coast and somehow ended up visiting Ben Boyd's lodge (Seahorse Inn) in Boydtown.

What a magnificent building in such an isolated place, we stayed long enough to have a few drinks, have a walk on the beach and a general look around. We fell in love with the place and decided that we should holiday here when we had more time.

When we went to the front counter at the Seahorse inn to get some info on the place no one was there and the only brochure we could find was a Wedding brochure as the lodge specializes in weddings and functions. Turned out quite ironic as a few years later I popped the question and there was never any other option as to where the wedding would be. A year before we married while on holiday in Boydtown, we decided that we would eventually want to live here, so we put a deposit on a block of land metres from the beach. Unfortunately though, it didn't work out and we pulled the pin on that idea. We returned to Brissy and got stuck on the old treadmill again of work and paying bills – but with Tee and I life was always going to be different as there is a better way to live and eventually it would draw us to it.

We had always planned while travelling around Australia to end up in Eden around the time of our anniversary so it was no accident that we are again here now. What is amazing though is that the estate that we had nearly bought the land in some four years earlier had blocks with better ocean views for much less money. We have always had the intention of changing our lifestyle as this was part of our reasoning in travelling around Australia, but when we arrived in Eden and saw the land at such a discounted price, we started making further enquiries. We had brochures emailed to us by the local RE Agent and we rode our pushbikes from our campsite to the estate to choose a block. When we got their most of the blocks were not as good as the one we put a deposit on all those years ago, but the value was there and we were still keen.

Then just as we were about to leave, we went up to a block that was steep at the front and had a driveway cut into it. It was very well elevated, north facing and shelters from the cold south winds but it looked steep, - that was until we climbed the driveway and found a near flat block. We then turned around "OMG" what a sensational view, from Mt Imlay across the mountains to Boydtown beach and across Two-Fold bay to Eden, it was just spectacular.

We had not planned to live on a residential sized block again and had in fact decided to look at small acreage to be self sufficient but our attraction to this area and now to this block compelled us to purchase. It is a large block though (966 m2) and with the modest home that we intend to build we should have room enough to grow heaps of veggies, in addition to the fact that we can walk to numerous fishing spots. In fact, yesterday morning on a long beach walk we came across an elderly Greek couple who had caught half a dozen good sized flathead about 100mts from where our front door will be.

The next stumbling block would be to get a really long settlement so we could continue our travelling plans, as the funds would be seriously depleted if we bought this now and we would have to cut our travels short. After lengthy negotiations we got a six-month settlement which would allow us to do a full twelve months on the road.

All the plans are in place now for the purchase of the block of land but in New South Wales you have to exchange contracts that are prepared by solicitors. This meant that we would have to stay another week in Boydtown. Turns out it has been a great opportunity to enjoy the area more and do some fishing that Tee always says we are not doing enough of.

The next morning, we set off to where the elderly Greek couple had caught all those flatheads to try our luck. After an hour or so we had caught nothing other than a crab that even when brought onto the beach was guarding my bait and was not prepared to give it up without a fight. Luckily, I had closed shoes on and the fight lasted only a short time as I was able to get behind him and control him with my big hoof while dislodging the bait. He (or she) scampered off back to the water with a quick turn at the end as if to say "I'll be back". We continued to fish for another hour or so when finally, I got a bite.

The timing was funny though as by this stage we were getting a little bored and frustrated and started joking around a bit. There was a catamaran just off shore and the guy on it was just getting into a small shore boat and was leaning over when Tee decided to do a fart noise as he bent over. We were both laughing our heads off when I got the bite. It was a small flathead and was just a little undersize so we put him back in and not long after decided to call it a day.

Determined and motivated by my catch we returned the next day and finally we got a good-sized Salmon that we took home, cooked and shared before our dinner – there is nothing yummier than freshly caught fish – and we were well satisfied with the day. The most exciting part was that it was only 100mtrs from where our new home will be.

This meant that although we would not live on acreage, we could still provide for ourselves from our own effort, fishing and a small-scale veggie plot. It was a long way to living more simply.

It is now Monday evening and we are due to sign the contract tomorrow morning. The good thing is we are at ease with our decision as this place has always drawn us like a magnet and by going with our feelings, we will allow ourselves to see where life will take us and enjoy the rest of our journey on the road.

Day **42**

The morning started the same as many others on the road, that was until I took the Motorhome over to empty the shitter. I started the process and as I was emptying the canister into the black drain another camper turned up. Now I see this process as a rather personal one as most people would and was surprised when I turned around to see him standing almost directly behind me. To get him to give me some space I kindly said "I will be about five minutes mate" to which he responded "no problems". Then as I was going through my process, I felt him staring at me and then started the comments, "you've left the lid on mate" – "I've never seen anyone do it like that before".

All this time Tee was watching from inside the Motorhome and must have known this guy was skating on thin ice, she said "I have never seen anyone watching another person empty a shitter before" to which he made another comment "I have never seen anyone do it like that before". Tee was right this guy was pissing me off so I told him so. Then he pretended that it was all cool and started trying to make idle conversation. By this stage Tee and I were on the same page and we both ignored him. The odds aren't too bad though as this is only the second freak we have run into in six weeks on the road. Hey and you know who you are with your glasses and stupid long grey goatee, driving a fiat cab with Jayco back and from WA as you blurted out in some attempt to make decent conversation, after acceptances.

Well things are never what they seem and when we went to sign the contract with our solicitor this morning, we were advised of a number of problems that the block had. These included a covenant that we didn't know of, a bushfire overlay that could cause havoc to our building costs, a headwork's charge that could run into the tens of thousands of dollars and some other less aggressive problems. These problems were in addition to the concern that we were also dealing with in relation to the higher than normal building costs that the Eden area attracts, a problem that we were going to abate by our own labour and logistical input.

We were set aback by these issues as the resolution, if possible, would cost us in money terms or our time. As we had not signed up yet we decided, after lengthy discussion, to drop the purchase. That evening the Real Estate agent came to see us at our Motorhome to try and fix the issue. As not to be confrontational we allowed him to try and resolve the issues but as we were not prepared to stop our travels for a second time over this, we stuck with our decision not to purchase. We are sure now that it is best to leave it for now and continue our journey. I contacted my solicitor to cancel the proceedings and we are both happy with our decision as it was causing us stress that we did not need to have. So again, life twists and turns and we follow with it.

That evening we had a few drinks, to drown our sorrows, and then decided to have one last walk on the beach. As we headed towards the beach, we passed a number of campers and one lady who was chatting away with two empty wine bottles in front of her and she was quite animated. I quietly said to Tee, "boy she has had a few" and Tee replied in full voice "good for her". The funny thing is that I have no doubt that the lady and her friend heard this as they were quite close. I said to Tee "she would have heard that" and Tee said "So what, she won't know we were talking about her" – I have my doubts. But it was quite amusing.

Day **43**

We awoke for the last of our mornings in the Boydtown Caravan Park and were disappointed but content with our decision on the block. We then turned our focus on the road ahead and we turned left and headed in the Orbost direction.

The road ahead was beautiful to see as we had been in one spot now for about two weeks and it can get a bit cramped in the Motorhome when you are not doing new things. For about 100klms we saw national park after national park and we stopped at Cann River for some fuel which was about eight cents a litre cheaper than in Eden, everything seems very pricey there. Not long after we saw a turnoff to Bemm River and as it was rapidly approaching lunchtime, we decided to pay it a visit. The road in was very good and the scenery, especially as we came along side the Bemm River, was also very pleasant. But the bay itself was quite brackish so we had our lunch and moved on.

We took the tourist route not long before Orbost which looped us to the ocean and then towards the town of Marlo. Just before we got to Marlo, we saw a turning to a place called Salmon Rock Beach (I think) and it was absolutely beautiful there. We explored the rocks and beach for an hour or so and then headed to Marlo. We were surprised at how lovely Marlo was as we had never heard of it before and it is where the Snowy River meets the sea. There were beautiful estuaries in front of the open beach very similar to Lakes Entrance that is not all that far from here. Tee and I decided that we would stay beside the Snowy River overnight and then head back to

Marlo to explore it a bit more and do some fishing in the estuaries. We found a lovely free camp some 4 Klm's out of Marlo beside the road and we pulled up for the night. Tee made a lovely Indian dish which filled the van with its spices but I could not eat as I was not feeling the best and I went to bed quite early.

Day 44

The Snowy River here is wide and beautiful and it was quite a nice spot to stop even though it was right beside the roadway. That was until the middle of the night when the dairy cows decided to moo their little heads off. Never mind we were not on a schedule so we could sleep in. But no no the farmer's dog had other ideas and at 6-00am was checking out all the campers for any food and he decided to jump up at our door – little bugger!

We took off back to Marlo in the morning as it looked like it was going to be a lovely day and we headed towards the beach for a spot of fishing. But it was quite windy and a little cold; we tried fishing for a while without luck. As the weather was still not the best we decided to go and have a look at the town of Orbost that was about 14 Klm's away.

Orbost is a real country town and as such is shrinking in population like most others; we walked around town and had a feed of fish and chips before buying some supplies and heading back to the Snowy River for another afternoon and overnight stay. On the way back we saw another nice free camp spot and started to pull into it, but bugger me if it wasn't the Shitter bandit from WA parked in the same area. (The one that was annoying me at the Eden Caravan Park). Feeling the urge to kill or maim I decided it would be safer to move onto the spot we had stayed at the night before a few kilometres down the road.

As I was still feeling a little ill, I decided to have a midday nap while Tee tried her luck at fishing in the Snowy. No luck at fishing so it was back to sausages for tea – very nice though, and then a quiet evening. We were at the same campsite but we were in a spot that is closer to the rivers edge and slightly shielded from the traffic and the cows so we had a much better night's sleep.

Day **45**

We awoke again to the mighty Snowy River and this morning there was not a puff of wind so it was like a sheet of glass and proudly reflecting images of the mighty gum trees that studded the opposite bank of the river. Tee and I decided to go into Marlo today and try a spot of fishing on their fine jetty. The weather was much better than when we tried the other day as it was windy and quite cold on that occasion, but today the sun was lovely and the wind was down to a whisper. But when it came to catching fish the results were the same – a big fat zero and only a few nibbles. We did enjoy the atmosphere though and Marlo is a fantastic place not to catch fish.

To be fair though it is highly rated as a fishing location and our track record tends to show that it may have nothing to do with Marlo itself. We headed back to the campsite, had a bite to eat and spent the day reading and writing and emailing our family and friends. As we had been here for a number of days we decided to head off in the morning towards Sale and its surrounding beaches.

Day **46**

Again this morning we awoke to the mighty Snowy River and again the gods had produced a marvellous day for us with the sun shining and a tender breeze. This certainly is a magnificent part of the country. We set off after a corn flake brekkie and back through Orbost and onwards towards Lakes Entrance. Now we remember Lakes Entrance as a lovely town we admired on another trip some four or five years earlier, but today was a little different. It was a Saturday morning so one would expect it to be a little bit busier but what we headed into was chaotic, as it was the starting point for a push bike rally with over 4,000 participants.

Well didn't we pick a bad day to leave Marlo as we were stuck for over an hour behind bike after bike after bike who were taking up the whole road. All I can say is, thank goodness we were not on a schedule as it would be very easy for one to lose their patience. With the bike riders taking a turn off we headed towards Bairnsdale, but on the way, we saw that Metung was a few mins off the highway and turned to take a closer look.

I remember Metung from my younger days as a quiet fishing spot and was soon to be shocked as to how much it had grown up. But before we got there, we were handed a bigger shock as we were heading back into the bike riders OMG. As luck has it the road they turned off into earlier was a back road to Metung. No use turning back now though as it was a busy road and too narrow to turn easily, so we decided to press on and visit Metung.

As we arrived, we were glad we did push on as Metung was a picturesque spot and they had built a lovely boardwalk along a huge section of the foreshore. Tee suggested we pull up and have a bite to eat and we got a ripper spot right beside the boardwalk and near an old fella doing a spot of fishing. One of the greatest things about being a turtle is that you have everything at hand and while Tee was whipping up a culinary delight, I was whipping out the rods for a spot of fishing.

We spent a few hours fishing with a couple arriving not long after us to also try their luck. Fair dinkum we must be the worlds worst fishermen as the old fella was reeling them in and even the couple beside us were catching a heap, even though undersized, we didn't even get a serious bite. The only positive to come out of our few hours of fishing was that most of the bike riders had past and we had a clear run to Bairnsdale which was our next point of call.

They have everything in Bairnsdale which to us means it is like all other towns and we kept travelling though as we did not need any supplies at this point in time. We continued on to Sale where Tee spotted a Chemist Warehouse which is one of her favourite shops as she loves buying her Vitamins at a good price. While Tee was shopping, I bought a tow ball extension to lift the bikes a bit higher at the back of the Motorhome.

After a spot of shopping we looked at the map to pick a spot to stay near the beach somewhere as it had got quite warm and we thought it may be a bit nicer by the water. We headed towards the Loch Sport area and in particular the Paradise Beach camp spot took our fancy on the map. Unfortunately, we had a map reading error which turned into map anger that turned into not communicating for a period of time. But once we got that right we were on our way to Paradise Beach.

Now if you are thinking of going to Paradise Beach for anything but the beach our advice is, don't bother. We both looked at each other and said "No Way Are We Staying Here" and we turned around and started heading back to Sale.

While travelling we were looking at the map trying to find a free camp that looked half decent as they are thin on the ground around here which we are rapidly finding out. With time approaching six pm we saw a possibility at Rosedale some twenty or so kilometres out of Sale. We arrived to find a number of other free campers which made us feel safe and it did have a lot of green grass so we stopped for the evening.

Unfortunately, it was right beside the Latrobe river, which wasn't looking its best, and also almost under the highway bridge which made it very noisy. Neither of us had the best of sleeps but we did at least camp for free.

Day **47**

Disillusioned by the area, as it lacked the natural beauty of the East coast area, I asked Tee if we could go back to Marlo which was so beautiful. In addition, we were well ahead of schedule and would run out of sights in Victoria as we were not booked to go to Tassie until the 6th of January, over a month away. Tee agreed and we thought we could get in some more fishing and save a few bucks as the service on the Motorhome was due in the next few weeks.

On the way back to Marlo we took a more direct route to save a bit of time, but as it was a Sunday, we did keep our eyes peeled for a country market along the way. We did find one in the town of Stratford and though only a small produce market it was quite pleasant and we bought a few things including a salami to have on one of our yummy platters that we so enjoy.

As we planned to stay near Marlo for four or five days, we thought it best to stop at Bairnsdale to do a bit of grocery shopping and top up the fuel. After our food and fuel stop, we decided to go through Bruthen which is the inland route to Orbost and it proved to be a much quicker and quieter trip. Once we headed towards Bruthen the landscape changed for the better and we enjoyed the scenery all the way back to Marlo.

Once back in Marlo we headed to our familiar camp spot beside the Snowy and felt as much at home as one could being around two thousand kilometres from home. We met a couple there who were originally from Sale (just down the road) but had been on the road for eighteen months. They had sold their family home, invested their money and bought a beautiful caravan and new 4WD which we are seeing is very common out here on the road. Tee and Shirley swapped some books, as you tend to do a lot of reading when you are relaxing on the road, and Graham showed me all his gadgets and we traded travelling ideas. I must admit I did suffer from a bit of gadget envy.

That evening we retired quite early and our sleep was broken only by a clown who thought it was funny to beep his horn in the middle of the night at sleeping campers. It did though allow us to view the full moon that reflected over the Snowy and Tee even got up to photograph it. Funny isn't it how people view things, as we could have got cranky and tossed and turned all night cursing the beeping clown, but I think it is very important to your mental and physical health to look for the positive in everything. If nothing else it makes you feel better. But at this stage I can't help mentioning – You beeping Wanker in your small pale Toyota van (you know who you are) you are the only Wanker in the Marlo area and you must be so proud.

Day **48**

We were both so glad to wake up in a pretty spot and decided after heading into Orbost to empty the shitter we would go back into Marlo for a spot of fishing at the Jetty.

When we awoke there was another Motorhome at the site and the couple that were in it were from Glenrowan, in fact he was the Police officer from Glenrowan. We said hi as they were about to leave and felt it was a shame that we didn't have more time with them as they seemed a lovely couple.

At the Marlo Jetty we were having no luck again at this fishing caper but with the camp chairs out and our feet up it wasn't a bad way to spend a couple of hours. About lunchtime a couple came in to the jetty in a little tinny and we were having a chat. Turns out they were from Merimbula (near Eden) and were travelling around by boat. Tee and I were quite shocked by this as the boat was only about 3.7mtrs in length, but they said they just picked the weather and sailed on fine days. They were a lot braver than we were and good luck to them. They had stopped in Marlo to pick up a few bottles of wine and they were back off to their campsite on the ocean side of Marlo.

Soon after that we packed up and headed back to camp, Graham and Shirley were still there and we chatted for a while and then settled in our Motorhome reading and listening to the radio. One thing that we have not done in the past seven weeks is watch TV or listen to the news, and you know what? – we don't miss either. I think it is just a habit a lot of people get into and one that wastes a lot of valuable time. Anyway, this afternoon we did listen to the radio news which just confirmed that we really hadn't missed much.

Day **49**

They had forecast rain for today and Tee and I were looking forward to catching some fresh rainwater as we were a little low. In fact, we had just bought twelve litres in Bairnsdale a few days ago after three weeks without buying any. It was when we shopped in Cooma that we last purchased it and we had to get more as we were getting a little low. This isn't bad though as we only drink bought water and that includes our cooking, and in our tea and coffee. The fresh rainwater was even better than the bottled water and we decided we would stay at camp after lunch as that was when the rain was due. This meant that we had to come up with an activity for the morning and as we hadn't been on a good walk for two or three days, we decided to go past Marlo to French's Narrows for a walk on the surf beach and the estuary. Before we left though, we said goodbye to Graham and Shirley who were just about to head off travelling again.

French's Narrows is a naturally beautiful place and the walking tracks are fantastic. We went first past the natural lagoon to look at the surf beach which was stunning and unspoilt. Unfortunately, as we started walking it started to drizzle, but we pressed on as it was not heavy rain and the scenery was beautiful in any weather. We followed the walking track west along the lagoon and admired the scenery until we reached more sand dunes and decided to turn back and head back to our campsite.

We arrived back at the campsite where Graham and Shirley had still not left from yet so we said goodbye again and waited for the pending rain. Excited by the rain we got the awning out and set it on an angle to allow the water to drain to one end where we would place a bucket once all the dust was rinsed off. We then prepared the water containers to be filled and for about two hours it drizzled and we were able to bottle about thirty litres of pure unadulterated drinking water fresh from the sky. Sounds like not much but to us that is a saving of over twenty dollars in not having to buy bottled water.

Again, I go back to saying how you should look for small opportunities to improve your position in life and be rewarded for it. Twenty dollars sounds like a small amount but if you think that you are missing the point. We enjoyed doing this and we would have just been reading in that time, which we still did anyway, and we now had a bit of spare cash to use somewhere else. We were putting effort into the positive sector of our lives and achieving a part of our goal to make life simpler.

"One simple act in One Simple Journey"

We spent a quiet evening with me writing and Tee reading. Of course, we did a few chores along the way and Tee made Chicken and veggies for dinner. (Yum!)

Day **50**

The next morning, we awoke and got prepared to go into Orbost as I had to buy some brake fluid for the Motorhome. The day before the brake light on the dash had come on and even though we thought it may have been just some moisture from the rain in a contact, the light was still showing last evening. In addition to this I had to run the Motorhome for an hour or so last evening as I had got the batteries low by leaving the invertor on while charging our electronic gadgets.

Part of my routine in the morning is to open my emails as my bills come through there and I keep in contact with family and friends mainly this way. One of the emails was from my Bank CUA who were requesting my assets, liabilities and income stream to be supplied prior to extending my shop loan. I was bewildered by this and it made me very cranky as I had sent all the relevant documentation for the loan through a month ago and this was two days prior to when it supposed to happen. It was not a new loan but one to extend the fixed rate of interest for a further 12 months. This was ridiculous as I had never in all my loan dealings had to do this mid loan as it was always at a start of a loan that this occurred, for loan approval. In the email it mentioned my travelling, so now I was starting to get the picture.

I will not analyse this situation but will go on to say that in life it does not pay to tell people too much. Some people don't deserve information as they misuse it and others use it against you. Isn't it sad that we as human beings cannot be honest with each other? But when I confronted this issue with the company, they produced some bullshit line about the new

National Consumer Policy and as I was almost 2,000 Klms from home I was forced to provide the information.

We went into Orbost and bought the brake fluid for the Motorhome and on topping it up realized that it was a bit low and when I started it up again the light was no longer on – mission accomplished! We then decided that we would not just travel around East Gippsland but go back up to Cobungra and then Bright and come down onto Bonnie Doon as we did not like the Sale area.

I think we decided to move on because I was a bit cranky about the bank bullshit and driving would take my mind off it. In fact, just writing about it now has stirred me up a bit. We headed to the town of Bruthen that is the link town between Bairnsdale and the road to Mt Hotham / Omeo. We stopped at Bruthen and bought some fuel as the next well priced fuel in the area will probably be Myrtleford (near Bright).

Bruthen is a lovely town that is filled with old buildings and bric-a-brac shops and everything is well priced. We spent a few hours in the town and thoroughly enjoyed it before heading towards Omeo. Now when we get to Omeo, we will have completed a loop of Eastern Victoria that we have thoroughly enjoyed as this is one of the prettiest and naturally beautiful areas on the continent.

On the way to Omeo we stopped to have lunch on the site of the late Tambo Crossing pub which had burnt down many years prior. By the history displayed on their information board this place was pumping in the late 1800s. We had a feed of cheese, meats and nibbles before looking for a campsite in the town of Ensay. At Ensay we went to the showgrounds where the campsites were meant to be but when we arrived, we were met by long grass and neglected buildings so we kept moving on and decided that we will probably go all the way to Cobungra for the evening. By this stage we were starting to think that the whole Tambo Valley area was going to rack and ruin, but to our surprise the town of Swift Creek seemed quite nice with a number of businesses running.

We passed through Omeo again and onto the lovely camp spot at Cobungra on the Victoria River that we had stayed at about a month earlier. We set up camp and enjoyed the serenity. Soon after we cooked up dinner and settled in for the evening.

During the night we had a little visitor who carefully removed the corn cob that we had eaten for dinner from a sealed plastic rubbish bag and was just outside our Motorhome munching away. It was a lovely possum who was so gentle and not that scared of us at all eating by the light of a full moon. We took a photo and went back to sleep.

Day 51

The next morning, we awoke to try our hand at fishing in the Victoria River, we are certainly suckers for punishment. The river here looks as though it is not heavily fished and when we got down there you could hear fish jumping. In fact, even while we were fishing, they were jumping but none of them were jumping onto our lines. As we fished longer, we could see the fish physically jump out of the stream and most were under a foot long but there were heaps of them. We suspect that a good fisherman would catch heaps here. After fishing for about an hour or so (without luck) our serenity was shattered by a group of teenage school kids on a field trip. As you would expect they took over and we were forced to retreat to our Motorhome for lunch and an afternoon of reading and writing.

While in Bruthen yesterday we went to an Op Shop where we purchased some books and a Robert De Nero double DVD. The book I chose was called Jonestown and written by Chris Masters about the controversial Alan Jones. It is a very good book and I am enjoying many hours reading it. The best part is it was only one dollar.

We had a quiet afternoon as the temperature rose well into the 30's and it wasn't until eight pm that it started to cool down. During the late afternoon we met another traveller who we chatted to and he gave us a couple of flies to try our fishing with. We were a little excited about this especially Tee as she had spent a fair amount of time trying to construct a dragonfly out of local grasses and it wasn't too bad either (I had to put that in). We decided to have another crack at fishing and again without any luck. Although as it was quite warm it turned out to be quite a pleasant way to spend an early evening.

We went back to the Motorhome and I put out another corn cob for my furry friend and we read some more before going to bed. Well – during our non fish catching time I had been hammered by bugs and March flies around the ankles and of course, as they do, they became extremely itch when I was asleep. I awoke to a mad desire to scratch the shit out of them and when conscious decided I should try and find a remedy rather than end up with legs full of sores. This woke Tee who was less than impressed and we both had a much-disrupted night's sleep (my fault). I put some aftershave on my mauled ankles which seemed to work but before long, I was tossing and turning again, much to Tee's disgust. Tee got up and grabbed me some lavender oil which seemed to work a little better and I finally fell asleep again.

Later that night Tee woke me up saying that the Possum was by the tree eating the corn cob. I looked out the window to see him munching away and I said to Tee "I will get the torch" to which she said "no you will scare him away" but of course I did not listen and shined the torch on him to get a better look. Then Tee said OHHH see you scared him up the tree and now I can't watch him. OOOOPPPPPS! I said and quickly retreated to my side of the bed.

We had quite a broken sleep that night but did manage to sleep in a bit and we only had a quiet day planned for the next day.

Day **52**

The next day was cloudy, which was a relief, as yesterday was very warm and a little uncomfortable. We had planned to stay here for five days but our water will not last that long and the river that we planned to draw water from was dirty as they must have had some rain in the days prior.

We made plans to move on and decided that it may be nice to go to a caravan park in Bright and spend a few days there and as it was coming up to the weekend, they may have a few markets. We spent the rest of the day relaxing, reading and preparing for our next move.

That night as there was no corn left, we could not leave any cob out for our furry friend. The cheeky blighter must have got the cranks as we had a loud bang on our Motorhome door in the middle of the night.

Day **53**

I cannot believe it is now December and we are almost two months into our travels. The weather today is supposed to be hot but this will not affect us immediately as we had to climb to Mt Hotham then down to Harrietville and onto Bright and it should be quite cool up there.

On the climb to Mt Hotham we got signal back and my phone went off a dozen times. It was mainly family ringing as we had been out of range for about three days – we couldn't even get Telstra internet which was unusual. The top of Mt Hotham was different than when we went through a month or so ago as it was sunny that time. This time we basically drove into a cloud and on the decent to Harrietville we stopped at a clearing where we viewed the clouds being whipped up and over the peaks and swirled through the valleys, it was an awesome sight. It also gave me time to catch up with my emails which had reached seventy-three, (but mostly rubbish), and have a cuppa.

The decent to Harrietville was quite steep with numerous bends marked at 30 Kph, and with the Motorhome approaching five tonne it was very slow going. Harrietville is a very pretty place and is still lush green even after all this hot weather but when we got to Bright, we found it too commercialized and as it was Saturday morning it was also very busy. We decided not to stay there instead deciding to take a back road to Glenrowan and see where the road takes us. The countryside around this area, although dryer, is very beautiful and we ended up stopping at the tiny town of Milawa.

Milawa, as we later discovered, is the home of Brown Brothers wines and also has other wineries and a cheese factory. We saw a caravan park which was a bit run down but the grounds looked shady and decided to stay there the night. We had not been out very much so far in our travels and the budget was good so we decided we would have a night out at the pub and a good drink. We settled into the Caravan Park and Tee went to the pub to book our dinner for 7-00pm.

As we had not done washing for a while, we also got stuck into getting that done. The best thing about doing the washing here was that it was only $2-00 per load, some Caravan Parks charge up to $4-00 per load which can make a simple task quite expensive. Tee had got most of the washing done and then we heard the rumblings of an approaching thunder storm. As a fair amount of the washing was dry, we decided not to take the risk so we popped the rest into the dryer and with our towels still washing we decided to head to the pub for a few Carlton Draughts from the bar.

The pub was lovely and as we entered the bar there was a loud roar of laughter which turns out was at the Carlton Football shirt I was wearing. A few minutes before we walk in a one-eyed Collingwood supporter had put up a picture of Michael Malthouse on the pub wall which said "Just because I am here does not mean you guys will ever be as good as Collingwood". For those who don't know Michael Malthouse was the coach of Collingwood and after a few years of not coaching was asked to coach Carlton. One of the fellows in the bar explained this to us as he didn't want us to think they were taking the piss out of us personally.

We ordered a couple of schooners and started chatting with them and they said that the timing of me coming into the bar with a Carlton shirt on was amazing. We had a second schooner each and then went to the lounge area to order our meals. I ordered a surf and turf and Tee ordered a seafood platter and we also got another couple of schooners. While we were waiting for our Dinner Tee went back to the Caravan Park to put the towel onto a clothes airier that Joy "the caretaker of the park" offered us to use.

By the time Tee got back I had knocked off another Schooner and bought a replacement. We chatted about our travels and had a great time with our meals being absolutely top notch and the beer a notch above that. Alas I had too much to drink and was ready for bed by 9-30pm so we headed back to the Motorhome to sleep it off. And boy did we sleep it off as I didn't open my eyes before 8-30am.

Day **54**

Boy was I feeling seedy as I had not had more than one glass of beer in over two months and Tee was not feeling much better. She suggested Bacon & Eggs for breakfast which I thought was a fabulous idea. Tee shot over the road and bought a loaf of bread and the Sunday paper for me and then we had a yummy greasy breakfast together. We sat around most of the morning reading the paper and looking for things to do in towns around the area. Tee and I both decided to have a nap and we curled up for a short sleep.

In the early afternoon we decided to go for a walk, and as we did, we saw the sign for the Brown Brothers winery which was only a few minutes walk up the road. We had a look at the winery which was quite impressive before heading back to see what other attractions were around. On the way back we also saw the sign for the Milawa Cheese factory which showed it was two kilometres out of town. As this was a bit far to walk, we went back to the Motorhome and grabbed our pushbikes for a quiet ride. Turns out it was a lovely ride with nice homes, farm animals and finally the cheese factory.

We parked our bikes and entered the tasting area where we sampled some lovely cheeses before deciding to purchase a goat's milk blue vein cheese. Now what is a good cheese without a good wine and as luck has it there was also a winery attached to the cheese factory. We entered the tasting area and because it was late in the afternoon, we were the only ones there and the young gentleman serving gave us lots of samples and very good service. We purchased a semi sweet white and let it cuddle the cheese all the ride back to our Motorhome. We had a quiet evening and planned to go to Glenrowan in the morning.

Day 55

After a good night's sleep at the Milawa Caravan park we awoke and started preparing for our trip to Glenrowan. We decided to take our time and before leaving Milawa we had another look around the town where Tee found a shop that sold organic products and she purchased some organic moisturiser.

Upon travelling to Glenrowan, we then saw a winery turnoff and recognized the name from what Joy (Milawa Caravan Park) was telling us about the region. It was the John Gehrig winery and was about two kilometres off the main road. As we pulled up, we were surrounded by gum trees and a paddock full of cattle which is more what we imagined an Aussie winery to look like. The winery itself was also more of what we imagined and as soon as we stepped in you could smell the wine with the barrels in full view. It was not clean or tidy, but boy was it charming and real. The lovely gentleman behind the counter greeted us and even though it was just after 10-00am offered us some samples. We started with the whites and ended with a port some hour or so later, feeling totally relaxed we returned to the Motorhome with a dozen bottles of resiling under our arms.

We then headed towards Glenrowan and were in search of the Glenrowan Caravan Park that I had seen on the internet. The place looked great on the Net and more importantly had a dump point that we desperately needed. As Caravanning around Australia is so big now there is sadly not enough of these dump points for black waste and you need to plan this part of your travelling well.

When we got to Glenrowan it was not totally how I remembered it from my younger days, as it was very quiet with a lot of shops closed down. Then I realized that the main street use to be the main highway and was now diverted. I suppose people want to get to places quicker and a highway achieves that but I am not sure that small towns like Glenrowan are happy with that kind of progress. Never the less the giant statue of Ned Kelly was still standing and both Tee and I took turns in standing in front of him for our photo to be taken.

The Caravan Park that we were looking for was two kilometres out of town and when we arrived it looked a little dusty and not too inviting. But as we had no choice due to the Shitter situation we decided to stay anyway. When the owner came down from his man shed on the hill, we instantly felt welcome and at $22 per night it was super priced. We were allocated a site to park and with our three-square metres of fake grass beside our Motorhome we started to warm to the place. It was quite pretty once you were in the property and the dust did not blow around like I thought it might.

I now had my favourite task to do – empty the shitter – and with my long red rubber gloves on I performed my duty as quickly and efficiently as I could. That over with we decided to take our pushbikes off the back and ride into Glenrowan for a good look around. As it was only two Kilometres from town, we thought it would be a pleasant ride but the hill we came down before reaching the Caravan Park proved to be a bit of a killer and Tee struggled a bit (little legs). The rest of the trip into town was pretty good though and we had a bit of a look around but to be honest there was not all that much to see. We did find a shop though that was selling free-range eggs and we bought a dozen before gently riding back to the Caravan Park. The ride back was much easier and Tee was very pleased as the big hill into town turned into a coast back to the park.

When we got back, we decided to try out the pool, and as it was solar heated it was very pleasant and we spent much of the afternoon sunbaking and just loafing around. I did have a chat to some overseas backpackers who were picking cherries at the local farm to fund their travels around Australia. They said that things were very expensive though and they were struggling to compete for picking jobs with Asians who worked for less money. One of the couples was from Belgium and the other from France; they were lovely to talk to. The evening was pleasant and we got excellent nights sleep.

Day **56**

Off again for another day of adventure and it was to the town of Moyhu, which was not all that far. The intention of this week is to keep well under the budget and save towards our Motorhome service that is due in a few weeks. We have got heaps of drinking water thanks to the natural spring at the Glenrowan Caravan Park and we have supplies to carry us through the week if need be.

The countryside in the King Valley is very pretty and we finally found a lovely spot at Edi's Cutting beside the King River where we are just going to loaf around for a while.

Day **57**

We had a good sleep last night at Edi's Cutting and this morning we have decided to visit a few local spots in the King Valley region. The first town we went through was the town of Whitfield which looks like it is a bit of a time warp as it reminds me of country Victoria in the seventies. Not that there is anything wrong with that as it is very pretty.

We then went through the town of Cheshunt which looks like a miniature version of Whitfield. There are a couple of places that we wanted to look at up in this region and the first we went to was Lake William Hovell which is on the edge of the Alpine National Park and feeds into the King River. It was a partly cloudy day today and with light drizzle the area is very beautiful, it also keeps people indoors and we had the whole area to ourselves, or so it seemed. The lake was stunning and with its proximity the Alpine region the backdrop of tree covered mountains was spectacular as they extended right down to the waters edge.

The dam facilities were like a trip back to the seventies with a round brick toilet block and facility area that had built in windows to shield people from the wind and inbuilt wood barbeques. It was a very beautiful and quiet area that we really enjoyed as Tee and I both don't enjoy crowds. We had a cuppa while we sat back in our Motorhome and viewed the lake in the drizzling rain with the magnificent Alpine backdrop and stunning serenity.

Our next point of call was Paradise Falls that was on a different road than the road to Lake William Hovell, so we headed back towards Cheshunt and took a right turn and onto a dirt road. I am not so keen on travelling down dirt roads as it gets the Motorhome filthy and not being home it is quite difficult to wash, but as it was drizzling, we thought it won't be too bad with at least no dust. In fact, the road surface was very good and the dirt road changes the look of an area, giving a new dimension to the region.

It was about eleven Kilometres to Paradise Falls and we drove there quite slowly. When we arrived, we came to a dead end with a track on the right-hand side running down the mountain. It was quite steep but well formed in rock steps and the sign said it was about a 30 minute walk, which was good as we need to get as much exercise as possible as we are not in our regular routine and it is an easy trap to just laze around all the time. (Well it is for me anyway).

The first thing we noticed as we started our walk was how clean and crisp the air was, it was so refreshing. The track was good and mainly downhill, which while good on the way to the falls, means all uphill on the way back. But we barely had time to think of that as the scenery was magnificent, from the sweeping views of the King Valley below to the up-close rock formations and native fauna, it seemed like only minutes until we reached the falls. Now I know we haven't had too much rain but calling them a waterfall was a stretch – it was barely a trickle – in fact if I could drink water and urinate at the same time, I could have kept up with it. I am being mean though as you could see by the rock formations that when in full flight these falls would be huge and spectacular.

The trip back up the hill was not too bad also as it gave us a bit of a workout without exhausting us, bearing in mind that our fitness level would be in the average range- low for an athlete and high for a couch potato!

Back in the Motorhome we travelled back down the dirt road and meandered all the way back to Edi's Cutting for a quiet afternoon and a pleasant evening listening to the King river flow and the cicadas in the background. We really love this area as it fits in with what we see as an ideal place to live as it is quiet, close to major shopping, is reasonably priced and has great growing soil. With this in mind we decided that we would go into Wangaratta tomorrow to check it out and top up our supplies as we had not been shopping for eleven days.

Day 58

I woke up this morning not feeling the best as I think the Motorhome was on a bit of a downward angle. We got ready to go into Wangaratta with all the usual stuff we have to do and it does take a while – especially when you are a bit cranky.

Our first day of our new weekly budget was super but we had a lot of things to get today so that would soon change. We decided to travel to Wangaratta via Milawa as we love the area and we are considering it quite strongly as a place to move to for all the reasons that I listed earlier. On the way to Milawa we stopped at the Moyhu Caravan Park to check out their prices but they were not open until ten so I got back into the Motorhome.

While I was looking around the Caravan Park, which looked lovely, an old timer from the bowls club across the road had been watching us. As we got ready to start driving off, he came up to the Motorhome and said hello. His name was Max and he was a lovely old fella who was 74 years of age and had lived his whole life in Moyhu. He told us a lot about the area and invited us back to have a game of bowls that evening as they were practising tonight. Now after that meeting Tee and I just looked at each other and said how lovely that was and how welcoming a gentleman Max was. It is something that we as humans are losing and losing quite rapidly, the simple task of communicating and being friendly, it was another good reason why we should live in an area like this.

Between Milawa and the Milawa Cheese Factory we had seen a 2.5-acre block of land for sale that was of interest to us with lovely views of, I think, Mt Stanley. We stopped and looked at the block and thought to ourselves that it would suit us and the plans we had of becoming semi self sufficient. We then kept driving past the cheese factory and soon realized that we had found a back road to Wangaratta and that the block we were considering was only 12 or 13 Kilometres from "Wang" as they call it.

This was great news and as we entered Wang, we realized that Tee could easily find a job in a town this size and it would only be a 10-minute country drive from home. This area is really growing in appeal to both of us. In Wang we went to Coles to do some shopping and as it was attached to K-mart we decided to see if we could find a 4Kg gas bottle and some water filters. We found the water filters but no 4 Kg gas bottle so we went to Coles to do our food shopping. We ended up spending just under $100 on shopping and we can now say with some confidence that we are averaging about $50 per week on groceries which isn't too bad.

On the way to Coles I spotted a KFC and said to Tee "I need to get some junk food into me" as it had been eight weeks on the road and we had only had Fish and Chips three times I was very keen to get some greasy chicken into my veins. After the food shopping we stopped in at KFC and gorged ourselves on greasy chicken and salty chips, IT WAS SENSATIONAL!!!

Then with full tummies and full food supplies we headed to the Shell servo armed with our 8c off per litre fuel docket to fill up Lizzie who needed fuel as much as we did. We then saw a Super Cheap Auto store so I thought I would try my luck and see if they stocked 4 Kg gas bottles. As luck had it, they did have them so I bought one and we were now finished with Wang and we could go for a bit of a tour and do what we really liked and that is to explore the countryside.

I was still not feeling the best though and as we were driving around, I was getting crankier and had a headache. We decided to turn off near Moyhu and head towards the town of Myrrhee which was about 17 Kilometres off the main track to Edi's Cutting. On the way there we got a little confused with directions and we took a wrong turn only to see that road turn to gravel. So, I turned in a driveway and unknown to me picked up a huge rock between the driver's side rear tyres. When we got speed up on the bitumen the rock came flying out and crashed into the underside of the Motorhome. Now I was really cranky and was quiet all the way back to our camp spot. I was really concerned that I had damaged the tyres and when I got back to the campsite I was in a foul mood.

Even after inspecting the tyres to find no damage I was still cranky and not feeling well at all. This was the first time on our trip that I was not enjoying it and would have loved to be home. Poor Tee could not do anything right and must have wanted to kill me in the mood I was in. Tee suggested I take it easy and take some Panadol and she would do the chores, but even with her being supportive I was still a grumpy pain in the arse. Though about an hour after taking her advice I was feeling a fair bit better and we shared some wine and had a quiet evening. I was really cranky and I realized that it was me that was making it that way, sure I had a headache and didn't get a good nights sleep but I had nothing urgent to do and nowhere urgent to be so I should just go with it and stop my "stinkin thinkin"!

That night I had a pretty good sleep and was only woken by a wild pig who was snorting and banging around the bush on his way to getting a drink in the river. This only kept me up for a short time as we tried to see him in the darkness and we slept in until after 8-00am which was fabulous.

Day **59**

Tee and I have decided that we will hang around Edi for a few days and get a bit more savings together for the Motorhome service. Today we have not got any plans other than our reading and writing activities. Turns out we had a relaxing quiet day that was quite uneventful. That evening we had a few wines and a lovely night's sleep.

Day **60**

We had planned a quiet day for today and it started off well as before I sat down to breakfast, I had done all my chores which included filling the water tank from the creek, which I do by hand. But that was all about to change! Now from time to time you get campers who do silly and strange things and as it turns out today was a silly day for not only the camper who set fire to the bush but all the campers who had to get out because of him.

Tee and I had just finished our brekkie when we herd a loud bang and a heap of yelling. At first, we just thought it was kids doing something stupid but as the smoke got thicker, I thought I should go and see what was going on. When I got closer, I noticed a young man on a mobile and his mates frantically trying to stop the bush from burning by getting and throwing buckets of water over the flames. But I could clearly see that they were fighting a losing battle and as he was calling the fire brigade, I decided we should get the heck out of there.

On the way back to the Motorhome I told a family who were camping not far from us what was going on and that we were going to get out of there in case it spread rapidly. Our main concern was that it was in a valley and with one exit blocked by the fire, if someone broke down trying to get out on the rough track the other way then we all may get stuck. As much as we were annoyed to leave this pleasant place, we were confident in our decision to just move on, as it was the safe option.

Today was shaping up to be stinking hot with the forecast of 36 degrees and low winds. When we went back to the township of Edi to camp, we felt it looked nice but it was not as comfortable as Edi's Cutting, even though it was shadier. That's where we incurred another problem as we had been on the computer all day with the inverter on and forgot that we were in the shade. Some good news though as we saw the fire trucks heading back to town and they had obviously sorted the teenager's fire out – I hope they had a serious talk to those boys as it really did look like it was a prank that got out of hand. With the inverter on all day we had flattened the battery and as it was so hot, we were in a bit of a predicament. By this stage it was only 5-00pm so I decided to back the Motorhome into a sunny spot and get three hours of charge. We had also been sampling the locally purchased wine and were extremely relaxed so all this was a big hassle.

Tee had got out a lamb chop to cook for my dinner and we were both cursing those young fire bugs as it had thrown out our routine and because of that we flattened our batteries, something that did not happen at the other site. After dinner I grabbed some of the dishes to rinse them in the creek as Tee had been busy all day and I wanted to help her.

As I approached the river, I slipped down the embankment scraping the back of my legs and arms and bruising my bottom – but on the positive side I did not drop a single plate. This was not turning out to be the best of days! It is quite amazing actually as I don't think there has been a single week where I haven't done some sort of damage to myself. I suppose breaking from your normal environment and living in such a confined space will do that. I have this week for the first time thought that living in a home is quite lovely. I think that is human nature though and you can't have everything, if you want to see Australia like we do then you have to make some sacrifices.

Later that evening we moved the Motorhome back to under the trees and tried to get some sleep but it was still thirty plus degrees and it took some time for us to get comfortable. Not long after we fell asleep the warning light for low battery came on and I had to get up and see what I could do. The only option I had was to turn the fan off above our bed and turn the fridge right down. Fortunately, by 11-00pm it had cooled down quite a bit and the fan was not a problem, we just hoped that the fridge would last until the morning.

At that time another vehicle pulled in to Edi free camp and did two laps of the whole area before stopping to camp. This woke the local dogs who, like us, were not impressed with this late-night intrusion. Tee told me that not only that but they were walking past our Motorhome and everywhere with a flashlight like they were in search of something which she thought was quite weird. Fortunately for me I was fast asleep at that stage and missed the light show, but I did get re-awoken a few hours later by the fridge trying to come on every few minutes and the power light flashing again. My only option was to turn the fridge off and trust that it did not defrost too much and leak all over the floor.

Day **61**

The morning hit us before we knew it and the plan for the day was to go to the Milawa Produce Market and then onto the town of Eldorado and stay at the Gemstone Caravan Park. Although not having much sleep neither of us were too cranky as I think we both were starting to realize that with the lifestyle we were living we could catch up with sleep at any time. No where we had to be – no time we have to be there – nobody is let down if we don't meet a schedule.

The Milawa Produce Market was lovely but a little small and we were not there long. We did buy some lovely fresh cherries though and Tee bought some Jam also – Yummy! – Oh, and a fresh Avocado.

It also gave us an opportunity to look at the 2.5-acre block that we liked in Milawa before heading to Eldorado. This block is really growing on us and does meet our criteria for what we envision as the perfect lifestyle, but it is early in our travels and we may find other areas that do the same or better. I think because we both kind of miss being in our home that we are trying to nest, which is probably a natural reaction in these circumstances. Not ever being in this circumstance before we don't know, so I think the best thing to do is just keep travelling and enjoy the fact that we are so lucky to be able to do this at a young age.

The countryside just out of Milawa was very pretty and was in fact lovely all the way to Eldorado but markedly drier. We arrived at the Gemstone Caravan Park and were greeted by Joy the owner who picked a spot that was shady for us as it was still quite warm. The spot she had picked though was still occupied at 11-00am even though they should have been out at ten. I said to Joy that we would go into town for a while and come back in an hour or so.

Tee and I decided that we should go for a walk in this time and we found a track called Reid's walk that lead to a suspension bridge over a small river. It was a lovely walk of just over two kilometres which was enough as we were still both a little tired from lack of sleep. We encountered a red bellied black snake on the track that was quick to disappear as we approached, much to our delight.

We returned to the Caravan Park about 12-00 noon and the people were still packing up, I think Joy was a little embarrassed and offered us another site that we thought was nicer anyway. We set up camp, which takes us all of ten minutes now, and both decided a bit of lunch followed by a nap was in order. Tee made a lovely Bacon & Egg toasty for me with fresh tomato, onion and carrot – it was a credit to her culinary skills! We then had a nap for an hour or so and awoke to a lovely summer breeze and a very lovely and quiet Caravan Park.

The reason we came to this area was that I had seen this particular Caravan Park for sale on the internet and it intrigued me. In the past I have always thought it would be lovely to own a caravan park as you could potter around and live where you worked and if you liked the area what more would you want. But in all honesty after taking a closer look I think it is a bit of a fairytale actually as it is a lot of work and it keeps you quite tied down. The main reason that I would not do it though is because it does not fit into our criteria of living more simply and not relying on other people or have them rely on us to survive.

We had a lovely afternoon and evening at the Caravan Park which is so peaceful and quiet. We went to bed early after not sleeping well last evening and had a marvellous sleep, almost 10 hours.

Day **62**

The next morning, we awoke to part sunshine and the tune of the birds singing in the trees. Slowly we got ready for our travels and decided that we would do a few things in Wang before heading to Moyhu where we had planned to spend a few nights.

I dropped into Super Cheap Auto and bought a gas attachment for a gas bottle we bought a few weeks ago. We had to buy a new one as the old one was out of date and we would not be able to take it on the Ferry to Tasmania next month. I got the last one there and we then went to a hardware store where I purchased some screw covers for the Motorhome to tidy it up as some had broken off. Tee said she would like to buy some KFC again and because we had a voucher it would not be too expensive. While Tee went into KFC to buy lunch, I fixed the few screws that needed new covers on. Then in the tune of the original KFC tune, When Tee got back - then Cee hit the track - with the KFC in the back - we felt better inside! You will have to look on YouTube to understand that one – just type in original Kentucky Fried Chicken Ad and look for the old-fashioned cartoon.

We headed back towards Moyhu where we camped near a few nights ago and stopped in Oxley to eat our KFC as it is not the same cold. But when we stopped the strangest thing happened, I turned off the ignition but the engine kept running. I must admit I panicked a bit at first as I did not know what to do but then I though well I will just manually stall it, as all the electricals had stopped and it was just the engine running. I restarted the Motorhome a minute or so later in the hope that it was a one-off thing but the same thing happened again. So, I drove a bit further and down a side street again hoping for a miracle. But it was not to be and I had to stall it again at which point I said to Tee, "we will just have to eat and then I will ring my mechanic" and as we both were starving Tee said that was a great plan.

We ate in the back and soon after I rang my mechanic who said that it could be the ignition relay or the fuel pump relay playing up, to which I asked if it was OK to stall it? He told me that although not ideal for the clutch it would not cause too much damage in the short term. As we were booked in with him for 10 days time for a service, I asked him if we could bring the service forward, and we did that by two days. The whole episode was a shock at first but I felt better after speaking to my mechanic.

We then set the radar for Moyhu and headed to the Caravan Park there. When we got to the Moyhu Caravan Park Tee and I looked through the manuals to see if we could fix the problem ourselves but as we did we soon realized that even if we found the problem (highly unlikely anyway) then we did not have the parts to fix the problem. It was now only eight days until we would reach the mechanics workshop so it would be best to just minimize the stopping and starting and leave the repairs to the experts.

We settled in the Caravan Park for a quiet afternoon and did our usual reading and writing with a glass or two of Wine.

Day **63**

The next morning after a fantastic night's sleep we decided to look around the area a bit more and to look at a block of land that a local agent had emailed through to us. I also worked out that if I stalled the Motorhome in forth gear it seemed to be less harsh on the clutch. We drove around the Tarawingee area and went back into Wang to pick up a new fan for the Motorhome as the old one had all but stopped turning.

While in Wang Tee spent time on the computer making a calendar for her daughter for Christmas and I fitted the new fan. We then travelled around the area until lunchtime and returned to the Moyhu Caravan Park to cook lunch and do a few chores.

As it was stinking hot again, I decided to make use of the facilities and have a dip in their lovely swimming pool. I did not stay in too long though as the temperature contrast was vast (the pool was f**ken freezing). I went and had a lovely long shower and returned to the Motorhome to plot our travels for the next few days and to do the weekly budget that ended today.

We had another good week with low spending and have now managed to save nearly $300.00 towards the Motorhome service. With another good week of budgeting we may even be able to pay for the entire service. As far as plotting our travelling for the next week I have picked out a few free camp spots that I think look OK. Our intention is to spend the next four days in the Mansfield Bonnie Doon area, and we want to go to Bonnie

Doon purely because of the Australian Movie "The Castle". In particular the scene where the family is in the car travelling to Bonnie Doon and the father is singing – "Were going to Bonnie Doon!" - So cornball – we love it.

We had another lovely evening and a good sleep that was only broken by a cheeky possum that flipped the lid off the metal garbage bin to see what was for supper.

Day 64

We woke this morning and after another shower and some Brekkie, we hit the road. Now it may seem like we shower a lot, but this is because when we are in Caravan parks, we take full advantage of a BIG shower – and if you showered once in our Motorhome you would instantly get an understanding for why we do this.

Anyway – we started or journey for the day and quickly came to the town of Whitfield which we had visited about a week ago. Straight after Whitfield we started climbing a mountain range, something that Lizzie hasn't had to worry about for a while and she took it well. At the top of the range we came across some fresh Jams and Chutney's, but as with a lot of this produce it was very pricey. We think that paying eight dollars for a jar of Marmalade is a bit excessive so we let them keep it.

We then came to a signpost that showed Powers Lookout and pointing down a dirt track. We normally don't travel down dirt roads if we can avoid them but as the next few free camps were down dirt roads then Lizzie was going to need a bath soon anyway. We followed the dirt road for three kilometres to Powers Lookout and we were not disappointed with the journey as the view from the viewing platform here is extraordinary. Powers Lookout was named after the Bushranger Harry Power who is said to be the mentor of the more infamous Ned Kelly, and used this area to keep an eye out for the police if they came looking for him. When you visit the area, you can see why as it has sweeping views over the King Valley and the mountains beyond and is definitely 'a must visit place'.

A little further on today's journey we came to the town of Tolmie where we found the service station closed down and the Pub for sale, so not a big go-ahead area. In all fairness though there were some very pretty properties in the area and because it was very close to Mansfield the local shops probably just could not compete. Bridge Creek was the next tiny town that we came to and the first campsite on my list to check out was four kilometres down Blue Range Road on the outskirts of town. Again, it was a dirt road but for free camping in this area there is not a lot to choose from so off we went.

When we arrived at Blue Range Creek Campground, we were pleasantly surprised as the day visiting area was quite lovely and they had a good quality drop toilet set up. The camping area was also well maintained and with not a soul around we thought it would be a lovely place to stay for a night or two. We set up camp and settled in to what was proving to be a very hot day. We weathered the heat but could not stomach to eat in this heat, so we skipped dinner and stuck with a few glasses of wine. At our last campsite in Moyhu we had used the town water, which was very good, and filtered heaps to take to our free camps over the next week or so. It proved to be a good move as the weather is very hot and we are drinking heaps.

The other problem we have with free camping is the Motorhome water totals only fifty-five litres. This is supposed to last four to five days but we have trouble keeping it for three. Even though we like roughing it a bit we both draw the line at showering with neither Tee or I missing a shower a day – it's a bare minimum for us. So, after three days at a free camp we have to move on, unless of course there is another water source. The temperature did drop down quite a bit after the sun went down so we luckily had a good night's sleep.

Day **65**

Even though we both had good nights sleep Tee woke up with a migraine and was feeling pretty ordinary. She said she had a stiff neck and must have slept funny – (which is code for – I would like a neck massage) so I went to work on her neck and shoulders. But after a while she was still not feeling better so she asked for some Panadol and said she would rest for a while. I let her sleep and decided to plot our journey over the next week.

As Tee was still not right about lunchtime, we decided that we would stay in this camp area for at least one more night and probably two more. I had planned on one more so my plan of visiting Mansfield and Bonnie Doon would just be delayed and instead of spending two nights at the next free camp site at Toolangi we would just stay one. This would then give us a day to get to Lilydale and find a Caravan Park before getting the Motorhome serviced on the 18th. As Tee was not feeling that well most of the day, we did not do much today but we did have a nice meal of pasta for lunch and again not much for dinner – just some steamed veggies.

Day **66**

We both woke up again this morning not feeling fantastic and I now put it down to sleeping on a downward angle causing the blood to rush to our heads. It is not enough to stop you from getting to sleep but it does cause a very restless nights sleep and you wake up feeling shithouse. We are learning all this as we go, as normally in your own home you get to go to bed that is on level ground and has plenty of space. When we first left on our journey, we thought it would be all easy to deal with, but you soon find that every lifestyle has its difficulties and its rewards.

As we felt the way we did and that the heat had passed we thought we should stay here another night, with the first priority being to get the bed (Motorhome) on the correct angle. After we did this, we spent the day pretty much feeling ordinary and to make matters worse I had finished my last book and was not keen on reading gardening books so I just chatted with Tee and relaxed. Again, when dinner time came around, we were not that hungry and decided to have some instant cheese noodles for a meal.

We went to bed around 8-30pm and I fell asleep immediately. Around midnight I felt Tee tossing and turning and woke up to ask if she was OK, to which she replied she had had a nightmare. A few hours later I heard the wind pick up and I had not put the awning away so I was a little concerned it may get damaged. But as I was half asleep, I just lay there for quite a while thinking to myself that I should get up and wind it in. I was a little annoyed with myself as that evening I had packed everything up and the awning was the only thing that I didn't put away. Which is a bit silly really as we were the only campers in what seemed to be the middle of nowhere and if we were harassed, I could not just drive away because of the awning.

As I have said before it seems that this lifestyle is hassle free, but in fact there are heaps of things you have to think about and all situations and all places are different. For example, when you are free camping you have to watch your power consumption as you are on your own and that in turn means different things to different campers depending on their power sources. In our case it is mainly Solar, so no sun – no power and this may limit your days at free camp. If you have a generator this can fix that problem but it may create others like carrying fuel, annoying other campers with generator hum- and it is just not other campers you disturb as it spoils the bush experience for yourself also. This is just one issue that has a hundred different angles and there are many more as we are finding out. Now this does not mean to say that it is not worth it but to me I think the term free camp is a bit of a myth, as my grandad use to say to me Craig "The only free cheese - is the one in the trap"

As by that last paragraph you can tell I am a little tired and quite frazzled. I am writing this on the 15/12/12 (evening) that hasn't happened yet and I will give you a little tip – It gets better for us today!

I finally got up and wound the awning in with the lantern blaring and quickly getting covered in bugs, the wind howling and the rain smacking into me while I toiled away in my red underpants and cranky attitude. I went back to bed wet and a bit pissed off, but I managed to get a bit more sleep before the Kookaburras started up. Funny thing, when you have slept well the sound of the Kookaburras in the morning is lovely but if you haven't slept well you just want to strangle them. (Lucky I can't climb trees☺)

Day **67**

After another ordinary night's sleep, we awoke and quickly prepared to head to out next location which was going to be a free camp near Alexandra. I had a shave and washed my face in the cold creek water to give myself a bit of a kick start. Overnight because we had no power the fridge had defrosted but not too much and the freezer items were still frozen. After a quick mop it was all good to go. Tee made a cuppa and I packed up the last of the Motorhome, drank my yummy cuppa and we were off.

The rain was good in a way as the four-kilometre road into this campsite was dirt, the rain was enough to stop the dust but not enough to make it slippery and with a creek crossing we did not want to get stuck, but that was fine also.

On the road we were heading to – Bonnie Doon – so time to crank out the lines from the movie "The Castle" and Tee was soon belting out the tune – "we're going to Bonnie Doon; we're going to Bonnie Doon." I think Tee had a bit more sleep than I did as she was loving it and I was just struggling to keep the cranks at bay.

The first town we came to was the town of Mansfield which is quite old but seems to be pretty active – no Macca's or KFC but they seemed to be chugging along OK. The weather probably helped also as there was huge black clouds in the sky and the dry brown mountains probably would have looked ordinary if it wasn't for the black backdrop. We were planning to get supplies in Mansfield but we thought it was a bit small, which usually means higher prices in the local supermarket, so we pressed on.

Next stop Bonnie Doon and we were there before we knew it. The town of Bonnie Doon is very small and is more a pub and a few shops rather than a town, but with the water levels high and the scattering of nice homes in the area it was quite pleasant. We headed off around the lakes edge and took some pictures before heading towards Alexandra where we planned to free camp.

Being a Saturday, we kept our eyes out for local markets to see if we could pick up some produce and it was not long before we found one in the town of Yarck. The market was being held in the local hall in the main street with "Con the Fruiterer" taking pride of place out front. He bailed us up and within five minutes had sold us $14-00 worth of Fruit and Veg. Inside the hall there was various handicrafts, fresh baked bread and free-range eggs, of which we purchased the eggs and we were off.

Next stop Alexandra where we thought we would find our free camp spot first and then head into town to do some grocery shopping. The free camp spot was right by the river and very nice indeed so we went into town. When we got into town, we had a bit of a Barney while filling up our water supplies and I said to Tee in the end – babe I just want to go to a Caravan Park and relax. So, after shopping we had a feed of hotdogs in the Motorhome for lunch and I searched the internet for a local Caravan Park. I found one that looked good about six kilometres out of town, so I booked it and said we would be there about two o'clock.

With a couple of hours to kill we decided to walk through town (Alexandra) and look at the shops. I found fuses that I needed in the hardware store and we then headed to the local Op Shop that Tee and I love to browse through, as the usually have great cheap books. It worked out fabulously also as Tee found a great laundry bag, a nice scarf and three books (one of which she said was exceptional) and I found two good books with the total cost being ten dollars. How good is that! With our new purchases loaded into the laundry bag we continued through town and then back to the Motorhome and onto our Caravan site.

The Caravan Park was located at Ackron and was on the creek that is a spillway for Lake Eildon. It was a very pretty spot and was almost an island with the fast-flowing creek doing close to a full circle around the Caravan Park. We were given a lovely spot by the creek (90% of the sites were) and set ourselves up for a relaxing afternoon and evening. By this time though

I had got my second wind and decided to wash the Motorhome, which was now looking quite grubby. And what a stupendous job I did also as the old girl (sorry Lizzie) was now shining like a polished gemstone. Although by the end of washing her I was over it as she is a big girl to clean and awkward without a ladder. We had a lovely evening and enjoyed the power to burn that the Park has provided us.

Day 68

The next morning after a lovely sleep we awoke to the bang of a local farmers gas gun that they use to keep the cockatoos off their crops (well I think it was a gas gun!). It was nearly 8-30am though and I was glad to be awake as I had promised Tee a cooked breakfast. At Alexandra yesterday in the deli I got some Chorizo's and armed with fresh free-range eggs I whipped up a spanking breakfast of fried Chorizo's and Omelette. I must say it was a credit to the chef – if I do say so myself. It was lovely to enjoy the surrounds and not have to think much about anything else, so I asked Tee if we could stay another night here as I was really enjoying it. Tee was more than happy to do that and I ask as more of a courtesy as Tee is always accommodating and understanding (I put that in there for her to read – Shhhhh!).

During the day we didn't do much at all and I even had a little nap to charge up my batteries, while Lizzie was gleaming and having hers topped up also. I did get a chance to watch a bit of cricket on the camp TV and time to catch up with my budget and writing this. Tomorrow we are off to Toolangi, which is about an hour from where we are getting Lizzie serviced on Wednesday in Lilydale.

Day **69**

This morning we awoke to the sounds of screeching cockatoos and they seem to be quite a menace around here with other campers complaining about them. But for us it was probably a good thing as we both wanted to tidy up the Motorhome and do a few bits and pieces before heading to Toolangi.

We watched the campers near us busily packing up their tent and camper trailer set up while we slowly prepared Lizzie for the road. The poor buggers were at it for over two hours and as Tee was continually hinting at a cooked brekkie again, I was thinking how time-consuming tents and camper trailers are. I finally said "OK Tee I will fry up some tomato and eggs for brekkie" to which she replied "well if you are doing that you might as well do those two other Chorizos also!" She is good I tell ya! But I didn't mind as we were in no hurry and they are very yummy. After brekkie I pulled the awning in while Tee did the dishes and then we were off. It was now just after 11-00am and the people with the tent and camper trailer were still at it.

On the way out of the Caravan Park we stopped to take a photo of the eight feet tall trout that the owners had commissioned to be carved out of an old tree that they were removing. They told me that a local fellow from Yarra Junction had done it and I must say it was quite impressive.

I got the gate and typed in my code to lift the boom gate but it wouldn't open. I followed the instructions that the owner had given me by pressing the hash key to clear the code and start again but on four attempts it still would not open. I was a little pissed off and had to back up the Motorhome and get out and walk to the office to ask to be let out.

Then what happened next infuriated me as I was treated like an idiot by the owner (she will know who she is). I requested to be let out and said that the gate wasn't functioning correctly, to which she replied that I had to press the hash button and start again. I told her that I had done this three times and it still didn't work and I saw her do something on her computer which I believed was clear it and then all smart arsey she came out and pinned in the code and it opened. I repeated that I had done that three extra times without success, and that I knew she had cleared it on the computer screen. At this point right or wrong she should have just agreed and left it at that, but being a F**ken smart ass Kiwi, she had to go on with it saying that I had typed in the wrong code. I was so pissed of that I said 'OK whatever' and drove off.

The countryside between Ackron and Healesville is lovely especially though the black spur, so beautiful that it can quickly cure the crankiest of travellers. In fact, I was over the stupid Kiwi by the first bend out of Ackron.

We arrived in Healesville around lunchtime and I showed Tee my old home which was in Stanley Rd, just off Don Rd and was the last Melbourne home I owned prior to moving to Queensland. We had been there on previous trips to Melbourne but it was still nice to see. From there I rang the mechanic in Lilydale and suggested that we drop in so he could check which relay was crook in the Motorhome and it would give him a chance to order the part as it was booked in for a service tomorrow. He said that was a good idea, so we headed down the Maroondah Hwy to his workshop. When we got there, he had a look and found that it was not even a relay but a screw holding the release cable had come loose and that was all it was. He screwed it back into place and it was good as gold.

With that fixed we thought we would treat ourselves to a Caravan Park stay rather than drive all the way back to Toolangi as it would cost in fuel and we had saved a bit by not having to put in a new relay. We headed off again and kept our eye out for a Caravan Park on the way to looking at my old home in Seville which was where I lived before moving to Healesville.

When we got there, I was amazed at how the place had hardly changed. All my landscaping from 27 years ago was still in place including fencing, shed and carport. I was always proud of my garden in Seville which was in the front purely all varieties of conifers with the Blue Spruce being a standout. In fact, the home in Healesville was also relatively unchanged also, and both properties stood out nicely – well I thought so (and that's all that matters).

After my bragging to Tee at how wonderful a landscaper I was we went to a local park where Tee whipped up another superb platter that we ate with vigour as it was now after 2-30pm. After lunch we headed back to Healesville as I could not find any Caravan Parks closer and I knew the one in Don Rd Healesville was quite lovely.

We went the back way to Healesville through Woori Yallock and past the Healesville Sanctuary which is a lovely drive with very little traffic. Well the traffic was ten times what I use to encounter when I travelled it over twenty years ago but was still light compared to the Maroondah Highway. We arrived at the caravan park by late afternoon and after chatting to one of the local park residences had Dinner and an early night as we had to be up at six the next more to take Lizzie in for her service.

Day **70**

The traffic in the morning travelling to Lilydale was crazy compared to my days of working in Melbourne and commuting over twenty years ago. Lizzie was not impressed at being pushed to speeds in excess of eighty kilometres per hour and having cars buzzing all around her. I must admit though it is great to know that I am not travelling to work and that after the service we have no schedule until Christmas Day and even that was a social appointment.

Upon arriving at the Mechanics, I was told that the service would take about two hours so we decided, as we had only had a cuppa for brekkie, that we would treat ourselves to a Subway brekkie and have a walk around Lilydale. After our brekkie and walk around town we decided to go back to the Mechanics to check the progress and I wanted to have a look at the underside of Lizzie while she was on the hoist.

When we arrived back at the Mechanics, we were immediately hit with the bad news that all the brake cylinders where leaking and that the wheel bearings were quite dangerous. They also recommended that the shock absorbers be replaced but they were not critical to safety if money was a problem. This was quite a shock as we had only had Lizzie about 12 months and she had passed a roadworthy then. But it was not worth taking risks especially with Brakes and bearings and if they failed us while we were crossing the Nullarbor the costs would be double.

They told us that they would get a quote on all the parts and get me a price in about an hour, so Tee and I decided to catch a bus to a bigger shopping centre and kill some time looking around there. The Mechanics rang me back with a price of $2,100.00 approximately which was quite a shock but that price did include the shock absorbers. What could we do? We really had no choice with the bearings and brakes so I told him to go ahead with the lot. As we had budgeted only $500.00 for the service this has now blown our budget out of the water and will be very hard to reel it back in. But as it was a safety issue, we decided there was no option and we will just have to find the money some how – maybe get some work for a few weeks or something.

Armed with an extra bill we looked around the shops and were very mindful of the new budget and kept our spending to a bare minimum. We were lucky with on thing though and that was finding the Eddie Murphy movie Norbit that we had been searching for in heaps of stores. Not only did we find it but it was only five dollars, a super bargain in our books.

By 4-00pm we had had enough of the shopping so we decided to catch the bus back to Lilydale to see how Lizzie was doing. The mechanics had progressed nicely and said it should be ready by about 5-30pm so we decided to go for another walk around Lilydale. But this time of the day in Victoria always seems to be the hottest time of the day and after walking a few back streets of Lilydale we soon realized that there were not too many more shops and that we should get some liquid into us.

Fortunately, right next to the Mechanics shop is a place that produces my favourite type of liquid – Beer – and not satisfied with any beer our favourite is Carlton Draught on tap. We entered though the bar area as we did not know where the lounge was and I walked straight bang into an old work colleague from over twenty years ago, a mister John Gaskell. I recognized him straight away and he I, but I also remembered his name where John did not remember mine. We were on different shifts at Bowater Tissue but were both Winder men so we took over each others job on a rotational work roster in a 24-hour operation.

Now John and I were totally different people and in everyday life would not associate with each other. Nothing wrong with that as John is 20 plus years older than I am and from a different school of thought. But as I had not heard much about the people I use to work with and John went to all the 20-year club reunions I was keen to hear his stories. And stories he had, and as I was quite young compared with many of my workmates in those days a lot of the stories were about colleagues who had died. It was an informative hour or so that I talked to John, but by the end of the conversations the dominance of our different perspectives on life made me grow tired of listening to him. We said our good-byes and Tee and I went back to the Mechanics to hopefully pick up Lizzie.

When we got there Lizzie was nearly ready but the head mechanic was keen for us to bring her back in the morning to make sure the oil and fluid levels were OK and that there were no problems with the brakes at all, so we decided to re-visit the Healesville Caravan Park which we knew was clean and accommodating. The trip back to Healesville was great as the new shock absorbers were making the handling and cornering much better and stopping a lot of the body roll that I thought was normal on these types of vehicles and especially of Lizzie's vintage (sorry old girl). The brakes were not exactly perfect as they were spongy but the mechanic said they would be like that and that's one of the reasons why he wanted it back in the morning. It was going faster though which I thought was great, but Tee said "don't get excited, that is only because our pockets are lighter".

When we arrived back at the Caravan Park it was almost 7-00pm and it had been a very long day in a strange place in the middle of the Christmas shopping rush season. We were very tired but relieved that we at least had a place to sleep tonight and did not have the added expense of having to get a motel room for the night. I met the owner of the Caravan Park when I booked in for the night and she gave us a small discount for coming back which I thought was nice and we were given a spot near the amenities block. Actually, this was because of Tee's clear instructions to be located close to them. We parked next to a couple of ladies who were in a caravan and had just travelled from the eastern side of Melbourne for a short break. I introduced myself and we all started chatting – in fact we all got along so well that we broke out the wine and the nibbles and chatted until tenish, when I said to Tee, we better get ready for bed as we had to get up early again in the morning for Lizzie's check up.

Day **71**

We jumped in the Motorhome after rushing to get ready and packed up for the Mechanics. As we were just about to head off, I thought I better pump the brakes a bit as they may have dropped a bit overnight. But there was a slight problem as when I did this the brakes locked up and it would not release. I immediately thought, what the heck are we going to do now, and at the same time Monica had come out to say goodbye. I tried to force the brakes loose by accelerating and moving forward but it seemed to be quite locked, but on the third attempt there was a cracking sound and it broke free. We said our goodbyes with a promise to catch up when we passed their place on the way to Gippsland.

Lizzie lead us to the Mechanics shop as we are both a bit tired today and we were not there too long with all the required adjustment taking less than an hour. They did also find one more problem that we will address when we come back from Tassie, but for now we just wanted to hit the road.

Our sights were set on getting to the free camp near the town of Norjee and to get there we would travel through Seville, Launching Place and Lysterfield which are all very pretty places and with that in mind we thought the campsite would be lovely. But upon arriving at the campsite we were quite disappointed as it was right near a logging area and there seemed to be some freaky people camping there. As we had three nights to stay somewhere before heading to family for Christmas, we decided to put up with it. Not long after we decided to stay, we started getting a lot of four-wheel drive traffic and they were flying, causing heaps of dust that seemed to just sit in the air. This was the final straw for me and I said to Tee, lets get out of here, and even though we had to now pay for a caravan park it would be well and truly worth it.

Heading off we found a Caravan Park in the Camps 6 book at Neerim South and we set sail for it. The landscape around the Neerim area is lovely as it is quite elevated and boasts beautiful pasture and rolling hills. We arrived at the Caravan Park that was well out of town, very pretty and reasonably priced so we booked in for three nights.

Day **72**

After a lovely night sleep, we awoke to raindrops falling on the Motorhome roof which is lovely when you are still warm and cosy in bed. I was keen to get a few chores done today as the Caravan Park was very neat and well laid out which would make it easy to clean some of the outdoor items and check in the boot. We had parked right next to the camp kitchen and as we were the only campers there it was like our own personal living area and we didn't even bother to get the awning out.

After Brekkie I started pulling the bikes off the back of the Motorhome so I could check under it for that water leak. Tee decided to clean out some of the cupboards and generally clean up inside while I was working on the outside items. After I removed the bikes, I realized that it would be easier to search under the Motorhome with the spare tyre removed so I proceeded to do that. Once the spare tyre was removed, I could clearly see the water pipes and I asked Tee to turn on the pump so I could find the leak. Tee did this and I was extremely mindful that she would love to get me soaking wet, so I kept back a bit. Tee turned on the pump but only a bit and although I thought I saw where the water was coming from, I was not sure so I asked her to turn it on again. This time though she left it on longer and I was closer to the leak and she got me good and proper. The thing is when you are in a confined space you can't move naturally as you will bang into something so I just had to cop it sweet – much to the delight of Tee who was giggling her head off. The good news for me was that it was not a leak but the release valve and it only leaked when the pump came on and no water was running, so if we just turned the pump off when we didn't need it all would be fine.

While I had the entire outside of the Motorhome apart, I thought I may as well wash everything as I put it all back together. My first job was to put our completed books into the boot and then wash the spare tyre and put it away. After this I washed the two bikes, the bike cover and the back of the Motorhome – beauty all done! Now all there was to do was to relax for the afternoon reading, writing and enjoying the scenery as the sun begins to make its appearance after a cloudy morning.

Tee made up some yummy salmon patties that we ate and, in the evening, we watched the Eddie Murphy movie that we bought earlier in the week, Norbit, which was hilarious. We went to bed early and I thought I would be awake half the night but we both had a super night's sleep and were fresh in the morning.

Day **73**

After a great night sleep, I awoke and started preparing to fulfil my promise of making Tee bacon, egg and fried tomato for brekkie. I thought I might as well start as she would never let me forget a promise like that. It was so easy with the camp kitchen right next to us as we didn't have to set up tables and chairs and washing up in a sink is much easier than in the Motorhome. We ate brekkie on the outdoor tables soaking in the fresh crisp air and light, bright sunshine. After Brekkie we cleaned out the fridge and defrosted it, as we would be staying with family after tonight for a few days and we wanted to get everything fresh for when we travelled to Wilson's Prom and then over to Tassie.

For our last day at the Neerim South Caravan Park we continued reading and I continued my writing. I am reading a good book at the moment about James Packer – called "who wants to be a Billionaire" and it is one that I picked up in Alexandra for two dollars.

Day **74**

We awoke this morning and prepared for our journey to Cranbourne where we would spend a few days over Christmas. The journey from Neerim down the mountain range was quite pretty but once we got to Drouin it started to get flat and a little uninteresting. We had a few items to get on the way and decided to go into the township of Drouin as it may be quieter than Fountain Gate especially at this time of year. We found a Home Hardware store and dropped in to look for a tool bit that would take the security screens off the Motorhome and allow us to replace the flyscreens.

But at the Home Hardware store we got no service for ages and when we did were made to feel like we were annoying them, and as they had limited stock, they didn't have what we wanted anyway. There were other things we could have bought there that we needed but as we were made to feel horrible in the store, we left to try our luck at Fountain Gate.

As we thought when we arrived at Fountain Gate it was totally packed there but we were lucky to find a double car spot to park the Motorhome that was within a reasonable walking distance of the shops. We parked the Motorhome then decided to ring Monica & Christine (the ladies we met in Healesville) to see if they wanted to catch up for Coffee. They said they would love to catch up and we would meet later that day around 2-30pm. This gave us about four hours at Fountain Gate to shop and have a bite to eat. We had organized a Calender for my dad for Christmas that we designed online and had delivered to Big W Fountain Gate, so we picked that up first and bought some well priced wine that we took back to the Motorhome prior to Lunch. This would be a treat for us as we did not have take away that often and we were spoilt for choice at Fountain Gate so we had some serious decisions to make.

The decision for Tee was quite easy as she had spotted a Sushi place earlier but I was a little confused as to what to have, but as I feel better on straight protein, I thought chicken would be better than a burger and settled on Nando's. We sat at the Sushi place and enjoyed our yummy lunch together.

We continued shopping buying another Eddie Murphy DVD and some chocolates etc for the family at Christmas. The place was packed with people and Fountain Gate is one of the biggest shopping centres that we have ever been in, it is massive. Time flew and before we knew it it was 2-30pm and time to meet with Christine and Monica for a cuppa. We rang them to see where to meet and we decided on a Coffee shop just outside Big W, which was good as we knew where that was. It was great to catch up with the girls and we chatted for over an hour before we had to be on our way to my Dad's place.

My dad (Nelson) is not a well man who has had two heart attacks, has lung problems and is bed bound which means that we had to arrive at his place in a specific time window. I rang him just before we arrived and he was sitting up in the family room when we got there. But I immediately recognized that he was not well as he was a very grey colour. Until recently I thought there was only one grey but as Tee tells me there are fifty shades of grey! Nelsons shade was one of a man who was not too well and I think he was sitting up just to greet us as it was less than one hour before he had to go back to his bed. His wife Leonie had told us that they had a party organized for Maddie who was seven today and coming over for a birthday barbeque.

That was about all we saw of Nelson for the next four days other than when he was awake and we had a chance to go in and speak with him.

After the birthday barbeque Tee and I went out to the Motorhome to get our gear out as Dad had insisted that we sleep inside the home with them. We didn't mind this as it would be the first time we slept in a real bed since we left home. When I saw the Motorhome, I could not help but think of the Chevy Chase movie – Christmas Vacations when his brother in law turned up in the Motorhome and pulled up in his driveway. I turned to Tee and said "The Shitters Broke"! and Tee got it straight away and we both had a laugh to ourselves.

Day **75**

It was great to get a bed to sleep in and Leonie had done a lovely job of making us feel welcome.

At this point I should give you a bit of a history about my dad and I. The thing is I don't talk freely about this as I don't like upsetting any of my family, but in a forum like this I feel able to express how I feel more openly. I think this is because I can get it all out there and if my family read this then they will listen to (or read) the whole story and not get as emotional as in direct conversation. For any of my family who read this – this is my story and my interpretation of events.

It all started for me almost fifty years ago – actually the twentieth of January 1963. I was born in Melbourne to two loving parents, Pee and eeN, (obviously not their real names). Mum was very young and born to ethnic parents coming to Australia around 1947 – 1948 which was very common for that time in Melbourne. My father I believe did the same from Ireland and is about four years older. They met when mum was about eighteen and dad was about twenty-two (both very young) and after getting married I was born. This is a light lead up but you get the gist.

Without knowing the details (and not fussed about the details) when I was two years old, they split up. I believe it was a horrible time for both of them and they have both told me different versions of the events. So, it is best for me to state now that it is of no interest to me now, as I grew up not knowing any different. My childhood was fantastic – and I had the world's best grandfather who gave me fantastic life skills that I believe make me who I am today. I spent what seemed like endless amounts of time with him in his garage as he made fantastic works of art out of copper, old artillery shells and many other metals. And always in the background I remember hearing the AFL (VFL in those days) on the radio and more specifically the Carlton Football Club who he loved so dearly – names like Alex Jesaulenko (Jezza), John Nichols (big Nic), Sergio Silvagni, Wes Lofts and Ron Barassi – etc etc.

It is funny how these things stick with you, as at the time I thought nothing of it but I still hold those skills today even though my contact with Nanu (my grandad) was scaled down around the age of five. Up until then we lived with my grandparents, and even though I loved my Nana – Nanu was very special to me.

I grew up in the developing area of Preston / Reservoir, which in those days was a pretty rough and ready area and very working class. I went to school in East Preston and with my mum, who was extremely strong and independent we moved around a bit as I think mum was trying to get into better and better forms of accommodation. All of those moves and mums attitude seemed to have jelled in me as I was also extremely independent and very capable of handling myself at a young age.

You know, even as I am writing this now, I am understanding myself more and more as I have lived my whole life with a "just get on with it" attitude. My secondary school life was also in Preston, in fact at the Marist Brothers School near the old PANCH hospital which I hear is a Christian Brothers school now and the PANCH hospital is gone also.

My primary school days were full of good memories and even though I was bullied a bit my attitude of "just get on with it" was firmly entrenched.

At my secondary school of Marist Brothers my stature grew and I was especially good on a football field and excelled at Technical Drawing, which I loved. At around twelve years of age mum bought our first home in the outer northern suburb of Bundoora and a year later I got into Parade College (Christian Brothers) in the same suburb. This meant that I no longer had to walk to the bus – catch the bus – walk to the tram – catch the tram – then walk to school and back every day.

The problem was that I struggled at Parade, as my football wasn't the same and my Technical Drawing class was cancelled after the teacher left in the first week of the first term and not replaced. The bullying was also quite bad and seemed to be more accepted than at Marist Brothers. The headmaster was also a prick, and I think as my confidence dropped a bit

I started to rebel. But my rebellion didn't get too intense and the "just get on with it" me shone through.

The most difficult time of my life came when I was just sixteen and Nanu was diagnosed with terminal cancer. Now even though I was only on visiting terms with my grandparents prior to this event we always remained very close. This brought us even closer together and at seventeen I left Parade College and did my HSC at night school. The extra time I had I spent trying to understand myself and taking Nanu to the Peter Mac Cancer Clinic for chemotherapy, when I was needed to. Mum was working and Nana didn't drive. Now I didn't leave school because of that but it did give me more time with him.

The most emotional time I knew with him was when he told me he was dying and I broke down. But when I saw Nanu break down and cry, which I had never seen him do before, the "just get on with it" Craig set in. Not long after his death I met my first wife and moved out of home with her.

Now back to my biological father, who after the age of two was never in the picture. In fact, I had not even seen a picture of him and that never changed until the day we met some **46 years later.** To keep things in perspective though I will have to go on with my life story as (obviously) it ties it all together. But I promise I will keep it brief.

My "just get on with it" attitude to life gave me reasonable success financially, but "awareness" of my true self was never allowed to raise itself. In the early days my first marriage was good and we had two strapping boys – Bruiser and Boof – that was the name the nurses in hospital gave them and at 9lb 14oz and 10lb 1oz - you can understand why. Problems in my first marriage started early but again with my "just get on with it" attitude and my youth I didn't have a clue. My first wife was also struggling to find herself and, in hindsight, saw me more as a father figure than a life partner.

As I stated earlier, and mainly because of my huge inner drive we were quite successful, and to the outside world we must have looked like we had all our shit together. In fact, I had a good profile job and we owned (us and the bank) our own home and eight other rental properties at one stage. I think my first wife thought that she should have been happy as our home was lovely and our assets were huge but clearly, she was not.

Just before the 2003 real estate boom though I was doing it tough and we downgraded our family home for a property that had subdivision potential but was not too flash. This to me was a smart move as our cash flow was a problem and even though asset rich the cash flow was killing us. As I did all the finances my first wife knew none of this and only saw the overworked and stressed husband that struggled to spend time with his family. We did not have open communication in our relationship.

The downsizing of our family home saved us from bankruptcy long enough for the boom to hit and for me to get all financially sweet again. When the boom hit, I was forty years old and as I do every ten years, I took a year off work to reinvent myself. As our new home needed renovations, I used the year off work to renovate and make a start on the subdivision. But in hindsight I should have spent it on my family, especially my two boys.

I am probably being a bit hard on myself here as I am sure my first marriage was stuffed five years prior to that and the warning was given to me – BUT- with my "just get on with it" attitude and my head squarely up my arse I didn't see it. I am referring to the counselling session that we had some five years earlier when the councillor asked us both a pertinent question – which was – "What do you want for your children in life". I said – "I want them to be educated, disciplined and prepared for life". My first wife said – "she wanted them to be happy and to be her friend". Clearly our parenting skills were not aligned and the boys suffered for that, and all I can say is - Bruiser and Boof - "I am truly sorry for that".

After the renovating was completed my first wife still seemed unhappy and began drifting away. The subdivision was proving to be a nightmare due to some contractual arrangements with interested parties who defaulted on their agreement and I started feeling like I had no support anywhere. Bruiser who was now almost eighteen was giving us heaps of grief and Boof had just isolated himself from the rest of the family. I made a decision that because the financial strain was back on again, I had to go back to work and that is when I started work as a Real Estate Agent.

I also sold a few rental properties which took the financial pressure off, but the rest of my life was pretty much turning to shit. At this point I must add that although I knew this I was in no way "aware" as to how to really fix it and even with my "just get on with it" attitude my self esteem and self worth was virtually zero. To the rest of the world I was a make it happen guy, but I was dying inside. In fact, when I look at old pictures of myself, I can see the huge stress in my face and my posture.

Then an amazing thing happened to me, and at first, I thought it was what everybody else thought, (and probably still do think). I met a young lady through work who turned my world upside down. Let me call her eM, and at first, I was attracted to her but it seemed different and as I was as "aware" as a lamppost I was confused. We spent a lot of time together and she taught me enough about "awareness" for me to start seeing what I really was.

She told me that I was a good-looking fella, and at first, I thought she meant to her, but she took me to our local shopping mall and pointed out other women looking at me and explained that they were checking me out. I slowly started to believe this to be true and more to the point "awareness" entered my life. I then was completely blown away when I found out that she was born a few days after my Nanu had died. To the "unaware" this will mean shit, but to me it is my Nanu helping me when I was at breaking point.

To the "unaware" it is just me wanting to bone a younger chick, but the reality is that eM and I were, and still are, great friends and my first wife now had her free pass – and took it. We tried to keep the marriage going – or I did – as we had been through a lot together and our boys would prefer it that way. But in the end, she left stating that she was choosing "happiness over financial security" – "says it all really".

Of course, now everyone "non aware" thought eM and I would get together, but to the "aware" you know we wouldn't. eM actually left and went to work for another real estate office that was closer to her home and about three months later I switched agencies also.

Now with the divorce happening my finances would hit strains that made the past look like a picnic. But with my new "awareness" I was earning a fortune as a Real Estate Agent and my life seemed great. Not long after this and about six months after my separation I met Tee, and my "Life became Living". I will go through how we met at a later stage but for now it will suffice to know that Tee took my "awareness" to a whole another level.

Back to my Dad.

By this stage I had been made aware of my dad by my mum, as some five years or so earlier (about when I was forty) she gave me a slip of paper with dad's brothers and sisters name on it. She said she was cool if I wanted to find him and the extra names may help. You know I had those names in my wallet then in my car centre console for at least four years but with my "just get on with it" attitude I didn't give a shit.

But not long after Tee and I became a thing she said that maybe I should look for him as in a few more years he may not be around. (How right she was). I said to Tee, "I would like to" and asked her if she would do the groundwork for me. Tee did that and engaged the Salvation Army who do that 'find your family' type stuff. After eight months and on my birthday, dad sent me an e-card. I was at work at the time and was overwhelmed by an odd emotional feeling. I rang Tee who was excited for me and we arranged for me to go to Melbourne to meet with him, with Tee by my side.

Now to the "aware" this is how things happen, but to the "unaware" they call it luck or a fluke.

To me "aware" people make life happen and "unaware" people life happens to them.

Back to our travels.

The next morning we awoke refreshed and ready for a new day. We had brekkie which was yummy raisin toast and tea and then took their dog Toby for a walk which we have done on previous visits. We spent the morning and early afternoon chatting to Leonie and occasionally Nelson in between his sleeps. That afternoon we accompanied Leonie to the airport where she was picking up her friend Olga who came down from Sydney almost every Christmas to spend a few weeks together while Leonie was on holidays from work. They both loved playing golf and at 92 years of age Olga is a remarkable lady who is still very sharp and quite an inspiration. We had a quiet evening watching movies and again enjoyed the luxury of a real bed.

Day **76**

Just a quiet day relaxing and preparing for Christmas day.

Day 77

Christmas day and still Nelson was bed bound, he seemed to be getting better one minute then bad the next. Leonie's son and family came over for brekkie which included pancakes and fruit followed by opening presents in the lounge near the Christmas tree. I had never before spent a Christmas with my father and although there in mind his body was not allowing him to participate in the festivities which was sad really.

Rod and his family left just before lunch and as we were all not that hungry, we decided to put off lunch until mid afternoon. When that time did arrive, we were treated to a lovely table full of seafood and salads which would definitely be Tee's favourite meal and close to my favourite also. There was oysters, lobster, prawns and also huge king prawns that were spectacular. We lazed around for the rest of the afternoon as we were stuffed full and even had a bit of a nap which has now become a common occurrence for me as I get older.

Day **78**

Today is Dad's birthday so we had decided to make it our last day with the family, but unfortunately Nelson is still not good and it is another day of festivities that he is not able to participate in. It has been disappointing to me personally as even though Leonie and her family are lovely, they are not why I am here and Dad, who I am here to see, is not able to spend any length of time with me. We decided to leave in the morning.

Day **79**

This morning we were awoken by a knock on our bedroom door and what Tee and I were expecting to happen happened. Overnight Dad had not slept at all due to his inability to breathe freely and had requested to see me. When I did go and see him in his bedroom, he was a deeper shade of grey than before and said he had to go into hospital as he was not improving, in fact, he was severely deteriorating. Leonie rang the Ambulance and they arrived within fifteen minutes to start preparing him for the trip to hospital. They were fantastic and had him stabilized within thirty minutes and soon after he was off to the local hospital.

We were left to look after Olga and after a text from Leonie from hospital we decided that there was not much more we could do and we should continue our travelling this afternoon. About lunchtime Leonie got back from the hospital and advised us that Dad was improving quickly and his problem was a lung infection which they had stabilized and were quickly eliminating.

We said our goodbyes, got in the Motorhome and onto the open road. But first was a quick stop at Coles to restock the Motorhome with supplies as we had emptied right out prior to spending time at my Dads.

Our plan was to drive East on the Princess Fwy to Traralgon and then head South to the town of Gormandale where we had planned a stay at the Free camp there. The Journey as we headed East changed as the landscape went from dead flat to views of rolling hills, and when we turned South at Traralgon, we started climbing those rolling hills. Nice country up here but a little bit hillbilly and a long way from civilization. It also lacks the privacy that normally would come with this distance from a major city but quite pleasant all the same.

We got to Gormandale and with the free camp located in their sportsground it was OK but Tee and I decided to try our luck at the next marked free camp which was only ten or so Kilometres away. Unfortunately, though when we got there it was also a bit ordinary so we thought we would just go to a Caravan Park in Yarram. On the way to Yarram Tee spotted another free camp spot in the Camps 6 book at Port Albert but it said it had only six free camp bays and we didn't think we would get one as by this stage it was after 5-00pm. As we went through Yarram, which was a lovely little town, we spotted two Caravan Parks one of which looked particularly nice. So, with that as a back up plan we headed to try our luck at Port Albert with our fingers crossed that we could secure one of the six prime waterfront Caravan spots. As we entered Port Albert, we were amazed how pretty the place was and our desire to secure a spot was sky high. To our surprise there was only one vehicle there and we slotted into a bay that was next to grass and looked directly over the bay and marina – what most people would call million-dollar views. We had to pinch ourselves as we felt privileged to stay here for free.

At Port Albert there were heaps of fishermen going out in their boats and it was quite busy. But they were quiet and we liked staying somewhere where there was a lot of people and houses as it made us feel secure. We had a light meal, a glass of wine and went to bed about nine or so. I got a text from Leonie that evening saying that Dad was a lot better which was a great relief as it was hard to leave under those circumstances but I was quietly confident that in hospital and with good care things would improve for him.

Day **80**

We awoke the next morning at 6-30am, or should I say Tee did, so I had to, and although early we had a great night's sleep. In fact, going back to sleeping in the Motorhome was like getting back into our own bed again after being in a motel or another strange bed.

Port Albert was looking beautiful as the tide was in and although cloudy the overnight rain had ceased. Our plan for today was to take a walk around Port Albert and then head in to Yarram for a look around also. Port Albert was very pretty with its multiple jetties, historic buildings and quiet country lanes. We walked for about an hour and dropped into a gift shop that was closing down and having a 50% off sale. We got some lovely gifts at fantastic prices and were disappointed that we could not purchase more, but it was not sensible with the Motorhome as we simply didn't have the room to put a lot of stuff.

After a cuppa we set off for Yarram in the hope of finding somewhere that fills gas bottles as most now just do that swap and go thing. On the outskirts of Yarram, we found a hardware store that did fill them so we achieved what we planned to do in Yarram and headed beachside again.

The places we were going to allowed us to do a bit of a loop back to Port Albert as we thought we would stay there for a second night. The first stop on our round trip was to Woodside Beach and because it was about lunchtime, we thought a local park there would make a great place to eat. Tee made up some chicken and salad sandwiches and she had the same on rice cakes. We then had a cuppa and wondered over the sand dune to have a look at the beach which is apparently the start of ninety-mile beach.

It was nice, but we have been a little spoilt and we would now only rate it as average. But to a kid with a surfboard it may be heaven. (Not my thing – city boy!)

Our next stop was to another free camp spot called Reeves Beach and unfortunately it was on a dirt road. But our curiosity got the better of us and we thought if it was nice, we would stay there the night rather than go back to Port Albert. We hate dirt roads as it dirties the Motorhome and the bikes on the back get filthy even though they are in a cover. After about five kilometres of dirt road we finally reached the campsite but it was a little like Paradise Beach and although not as feral it was stacked full of campers.

We kept driving though the camp site road hoping to find a place to turn without much luck, and then when we came to a soft sand area, we were not sure whether or not to proceed. As we had not seen a place to turn, we assumed the road must loop back onto the main track again – WRONG! – and when we got to the other side of the soft sand we were confronted with a dead end. Now under normal circumstances this would not be too much of a problem but at Christmas every square inch of this place is covered with a tent. So, I was confronted with the task of either backing out or – (well I had no "or" at this stage!) The thought of backing though the soft sand was not a good one as there was a real chance we would get bogged and at nearly five tonne there was no vehicle there that would pull us out in a hurry. WHAT THE FUCK COULD I DO NOW!

I toyed with the idea of asking someone to pull down their tent and let me use that space to turn but the closer you got to the dead end the narrower the overall space to turn was. The best spot was near the soft sand as there was only a car parked there, it seemed to be the easiest choice. I thought the tent was empty though until the people in the next tent along said that the bloke was in there and when I asked what his name was, they said Dave (they thought). I called out to him and he eventually came out. He was quite a scruffy looking bloke and by his set up it almost looked as though he lived there, with wind, solar and petrol generators. But he was a lovely fella and realized that we were quite stuck without his help.

He had a little panel van type vehicle but the battery was not in it and I think he was running stuff off it, so it was going to take a bit longer than we first thought. In addition to that his alarm system remote was broken and we were in for a bit of a show while he tried to get it all happening for us. But after thirty minutes of hearing the alarm going off I said to him perhaps we could just push the vehicle to the side of his tent and I could turn my Motorhome and then we could push his car back. He was cool with this, as he was with the whole episode, and after a twenty-five-point turn while my heart was in my throat, I got Lizzie facing the way we wanted her.

When I had turned the Motorhome around Tee got a bit of a fright as I raced through the soft sand as not to get bogged, leaving her fifty metres behind. She rushed after the Motorhome with her little legs and understood fully when I explained why I kept going (I think/hope). As we approached the bitumen road again, we were both so relieved to be out of there, vowing that we would not go down a dirt road again. After hitting the road again, we did drop into McLaughlan's Beach but we both thought it a little ugly and couldn't wait to get back to Port Albert and our little beachside patch. After a yummy dinner we relaxed and had another sound night's sleep.

Day **81**

The next morning, we awoke and when we went to boil another cuppa, we realized that the other gas bottle was now empty. (At least we knew where to go to get it filled and Yarram was just down the road). So, I popped out the trusty Butane burner and we had our precious morning cup of tea.

Today we intended to set sail for Wilson's Prom, which promises to be a great day on the road and even though the weather was not fantastic we were brimming with expectation. We arrived at the Yarram hardware store a few minutes after 9-00am to get our second gas bottle filled and were able to get this done in a few minutes as it was very quiet there even though it was a Saturday. What Tee and I have discovered is that in Victoria not much happens before 10-30am and it is after lunch before most places get busy. We put this down to the fact that they have daylight savings over summer and it does not get dark until around 9-00pm.

The road from Port Albert to Wilson's Prom was quiet until we got to Foster where they were having their monthly Saturday markets and the place was packed. Before we got to Foster though we took a slight detour to Port Welshpool, where I use to go fishing with mates in my younger days. Port Welshpool had not changed that much in my memories but I do recall hearing that they used the area for a short time to launch a rival to the Spirit of Tasmania in the form of a huge Catamaran that would do the journey in a much shorter time than the Spirit of Tasmania's ten hours. It obviously went bust though as there was no sign of an operation of this size in the area, and the only thing I saw that I didn't remember was a large car park. There was no free camping at Port Welshpool which is crazy really as they could easily convert the car park and pump dollars into the area.

It amazes us why country towns that are struggling don't do this as 99% of the campers that we have met leave the place as tidy as or even tidier than when they arrive. Not only that but the locals would capture the dollars that these people have to spend. At worst they would buy petrol and supplies. Anyway, there was no free camp so we could not come back here after our visit to Wilson's Promontory.

As I said earlier Foster was packed with people and even though the town was lovely, we had trouble finding a spot to park the Motorhome so we continued our journey to Wilson's Promontory. After Foster we passed through the town of Yanakie which is like the gateway to the Prom and the last spot to buy fuel and supplies if you were running low on either, not much there but pleasant enough.

Not long after Yanakie we entered the National Park area and as day travellers, we did not have to pay a fee. We were given a map and information brochure on the area which was quite handy and we were on our way to explore this beautiful place. The road was very busy and we were amazed at the number of vehicles coming in and out of the park, but they tell me it is a favoured camping area mainly with Victorian families.

The landscape was mountainous and pristine in contrast with the surrounding coastline which tends to be quite flat and apart from the beaches a little uninteresting. But as we had seen it is also extremely windy, a natural occurrence that does not rate that highly with Tee, as she likes her hair to be in order.

The sky was overcast and the mountain tops were being tickled by the low-lying clouds creating a mystical feeling that was only dominated by the stunning ocean views when the sun broke over it. If anyone ever tells you that this area is only nice on sunny days believe me, they are not looking at it in the right manner. We were ore struck by its natural beauty and were enjoying the cool climate that is so refreshing compared to our Queensland humidity.

Our fist stop was to a place called Whiskey Bay that was again stunning. We parked the Motorhome in the car park carefully as with a bigger vehicle you always have to anticipate how you are going to get out in the event of other vehicles parking near you (or in front of you as some dickheads do!).

As it was now after 1-00pm we were quite hungry and had only had a cuppa for breakfast mainly due to our gas running out. We decided to have another platter of meat, cheese and crackers etc before braving the cold wind on a walk through the area.

After some yummy lunch and a cuppa, we were greeted by glimpses of sunshine over the ocean and as we approached the beach we were amazed by the stunning scenery. There were huge rounded rocks that looked like they were tumbling into the ocean and the sand was pristine against the brilliant Blue Ocean and wild surf. We walked along the beach and then over a hilltop area to the left which boasted sweeping views over the bay we had just left and into the next bay called Picnic Bay. The sun was bursting through on occasions adding brilliance to the colours of the area, but a few minutes after we arrived at the viewing platform the weather started turning and we could see the rain clouds heading in. With this we calculated that if lucky we may make it back to the Motorhome without getting saturated if we left immediately, and so we did. Only slightly damp we beat the best of the rain and were both pleased we had taken a pile of photos before the rains came. On the positive side the rain brought in the low clouds that looked stunning as they danced around the surrounding mountain ranges.

We hit the road again and headed to Tidal River, and its camping area, to find it chock full of people. This explained to us where all the vehicles that we had seen on the way in were coming from and going to. But both Tee and I don't like big crowded places and decided not to get out and look around, and as the weather was also against us, we opted instead to keep driving and exploring the area in the warmth and comfort that Lizzie was providing. We would have liked to have seen the river but it was not the kind of atmosphere that we enjoy so off we went.

As Tidal River is as far south as you can go, we headed back and, on the way, took a right turn which took us to the top of Mt Oberon. (Now don't quote me on the name of this mountain as I think the road stops at a place called Telegraph Saddle). The scenery was awesome and with the clouds becoming lighter we got great views on our decent. By this stage it was getting late in the afternoon and we decided to head back to the Foster area and a Free camp area just on its eastern outskirts.

By the time we reached Foster most of the market crowd had dispersed and after filling up with fuel we headed up the mountain range to the free camp area. But upon arrival we were confronted with a no camping sign and were confused as to whether it was just that part or the whole area. But the beauty of being fully self contained is that we don't need facilities and we decided that around the corner in an open grassed area we would be fine. The area was also very quiet so we felt quite safe and not long after we arrived another small van pulled up so we felt even more secure.

With our Motorhome we have security screens all around and access straight to the driving cabin, so if someone is threatening outside, we can pull out of the area within a few seconds. That is why I always point Lizzie in the direction I would escape into and never nose into an area for that very reason. This gives us greater security than in a Caravan as in a Caravan you have to get out of the Van and into the vehicle, putting you at risk if you have a freak or freaks annoying you outside.

Day **82**

Even though we were in what we thought was a less than ideal location it turned out to be extremely quiet and we had a great night's sleep. After cooking Tee a feed of bacon and eggs we again set off to explore the southern coastal region of this garden state.

The first town we would come to would be Fish Creek but on the way there we would travel along a lovely country road that meandered through the hillsides with beautiful rural views to each side. Fish Creek was not a stopping point on our list and when we travelled through it, we saw no reason to change our plans. Quaint but uninteresting would best describe it.

Tee and I have always been avid viewers of lifestyle and travel programs but we both enjoy honesty, thus to be genuine I am not writing that every place is wonderful as many of those programs do. I think most people would rather hear and see it as it is.

We continued our journey travelling through Waratah North where we saw lovely rural properties many of which had ocean views and views of Wilson's Promontory, which continues to dominate the landscape. As we headed to the coast again, we were spoilt for choice with beach locations, and decided to go to as many of them as possible.

The first place we went to was Shallows Inlet that proved to be quite unusual. We stopped in the car park there, and as is the case with most beaches in the area you have to trek through a section of Teatree to reach the sand and ocean. As we broke through the Teatree we were greeted by a small car (not a 4WD) driving along the beach at slow speed. This was quite freaky as all the beaches in this area so far have been heavy surf beaches and we hadn't looked at the map prior to arriving. If we had of looked at the map it would have made sense as the area was directly opposite Yanakie and was what its name suggested – "a shallow inlet". When we looked further and to the right, we realized it was a very popular fishing spot also, as parked beside the dunes were about forty cars with most having boat trailers attached and the bay was just full of boats. We had a quick look around but as this was really a boaties place there was not so much for us to do.

Sandy Point was close to Shallows Inlet but was completely different as it was a surf beach and looked as though it had a fair-sized population with heaps of beach houses and many that looked like permanent residences. We happened to stumble across a fruit and veggie stall among these homes and purchased some yummy little tomatoes that would go great on our platters that we love so much. We then travelled to Waratah Bay which was very busy and a bit trendy, and on to Walkerville (Bell Point) further around the coast which was quite similar.

The area that was of great interest to me though, and yet to come, was Venus Bay where 25 years earlier I had owned a block of land and my mum had a holiday home. All those years ago my practice wife, my two boys and I spent a number of weekends and holidays at mum's holiday home, and Venus Bay was then a sleepy little place with more Teatree than holiday homes and a string of lovely beaches.

To get to Venus Bay we had to travel through the sleepy but shabby town of Tarwin Lower, and in those days it only had a Pub, a General Store and a few houses. What I loved about Tarwin Lower in those days though was the river and the abundant amount of young trevally that my son and I caught there. I also use to surf fish off the beach, with fresh pippies at your toes and with the Teatree flowering you were almost guaranteed a catch of good-sized salmon. Which when bled immediately and eaten fresh were great tucker. Here I go again telling fishing stories, but if you take 20% off for good story telling that was about how good it was.

To my surprise Tarwin Lower was pumping and was not as shabby as I remembered it, and it also seemed to have a lot healthier population number and a lot more facilities. This is more than I can say for Venus Bay. As we reached Venus Bay, I was shocked to see that it was now full of houses and although twenty-five years ago the houses weren't flash, at least they weren't on top of each other. The place to me felt like a seaside ghetto and Tee, who had never been there before, thought it was yuck and she didn't like the vibe of the place.

I drove Tee past mum's old place which looked as though it had not had a cent spent on it in twenty years, and my block, that had a fibro box on it as interesting as watching paint dry. With no further interest in the area and a feeling as though I should not have come here but held onto my fond memories we headed for Inverloch.

Now I might add here that the intention for the day was sightseeing and not looking for a place to stay, but if we did find somewhere nice, we would stop overnight.

Inverloch to us was clean and tidy but it lacked the appeal of many of the smaller seaside locations that we had stopped at in the past – Marlo for instance, and even Boydtown. From Inverloch we travelled inland through Leongatha – Korumburra and finally to Poowong where we found our free camp area and then headed into the town before settling into the campsite for the night. Poowong (bad name) was a town that didn't seem to have much to offer and although no further to Melbourne than Drouin had seen none of the growth that Drouin has.

At Poowong we found a general store that sold fish and chips with a second hand store right next door. As it was dinner time, we bought some fish and chips and while waiting for them we had a browse in the second hand store. Lucky, we did as what a collection of bargains we came out with – two good books, a power monitor and three trendy candles all for ten dollars. We sat out front of the fish and chip shop to eat dinner and then headed to the free camp site to settle in for the evening.

Day **83**

We had a great sleep at Poowong free camp as it was a lovely setting and very quiet. I checked the weather forecast on the internet last night which made us change our plans for the day. We had intended to just chill out and travel to a few local towns but the day promised low winds, sunny sky's and a temperature of 23 – 25 degrees which would be perfect for our trip to Phillip Island, so that's was what we would do.

Upon visiting my dad over Christmas, and in his ill state, he requested that I visit my grandparents (his parents) grave at Cowes (Phillip Island) cemetery. I told him that I would do this and thought that I could catch up with Dads brother, who lives on the island (and works there) so he could help me with directions to the gravesite. But upon his visit over the same period he seemed pre-occupied with keeping us from going to Phillip Island, as he seemed worried we would try and freeload off him. I canned that idea and turned to the internet instead. I located a site that offered photos of headstones and I sent them off an email with a request for directions to Cowes cemetery, as I could not find directions on Google. The very next day I received an email from them with a gravesite picture and the name of the road that the cemetery was located on. (much more help than my long-lost uncle).

BACK TO OUR TRAVELS

We left the campsite and decided as it was not far out of our way that we would return here this evening. We decided to head to Phillip Island via Wonthaggi and again the country scenery to the coast was lovely. Wonthaggi was quite a thriving town, quite large and it seemed very tidy. We got a full tank of fuel there as it was very well priced (8c a litre off voucher) and while in the servo a lady on a motorbike asked us about the Motorhome as she was about to buy one. We chatted for a bit and invited her in to have a look. We get a lot of this, as many people seem to want to do what we are doing.

From Wonthaggi we sailed towards Phillip Island and before we knew it, we were in San Remo and crossing the bridge onto PI. PI is quite a large Island and the farmland there seems quite arid, indicating that the soil is not over fertile. But with some of the best surf beaches on the planet all around it, it is not the farmers getting top billing.

We travelled to our first destination (and the major reason for our trip here), quickly finding the Cowes cemetery – the resting place of the grandparents that I had never met. It was a lovely cemetery, yet unusual, in the fact that you drove through wetlands to get to it and it would definitely not be classified as your typical cemetery entrance.

The finding of the cemetery proved easier than finding the grave itself, but after splitting up and searching for 15 – 20 mins Tee finally found the grave. Covered in Lavender bushes, Tee had done a great job locating it and after a few words (said to myself) and a photo session which had Tee smirking, we achieved the results we were looking for and left.

In the car park I rang Dad and told him where I was and he seemed pleased, as I was, at the news that he was coming out of hospital today and starting to take some medical advice (for a change).

The rest of the day we spent exploring PI, which included Cowes (packed with people – New Years Eve), visiting the Nobbies and a general look around. PI is a nice place to visit but by late afternoon we had seen enough and headed back to Poowong via Grantville and Nyora. We were pleased when we got back to camp as we had done a fair amount of driving for the day. No plans for New Years Eve was good news for us as a few drinks and a late night usually wipes us out for the next day or two.

But not long after we got back to camp Alan (who was the only other camper on site) came over and invited us to their campfire for the evening. We said "that would be great" and ended up almost making it to midnight and also having quite a few white wines along the way. Alan and Gloria were a lovely couple from Musslebrook near Newcastle in NSW and we had a very pleasant evening.

Alan and Gloria were travelling as Alan had gone through a pretty horrible health scare and they wanted to live life NOW! It is amazing that people need this event to shake them up, and some even leave it too late. I was made aware of this by a client I had who owned a Caravan manufacturing company back home. He told me that one in eight of his customers who ordered a caravan through him did not pick the caravan up, as they either got too sick or died before living their dream. I said to him – is that because you are too slow at building them? – but seriously – that is amazing isn't it.

It was also a guiding factor in my wanting to travel "now" as you never know what curveball life might throw at you. Not only that but it makes more sense to do it when you are still fit and active. We saw an example of this on the road one time, there was this amazing huge Motorhome with swish paintwork and all the bells and whistles. Positioned next to the auto doors was a walking frame that belonged to the owner. Tee and I were amazed as the gentleman looked about ninety and needed the frame to get around. We both said to each other that we were privileged to travel now, as it was not worth waiting until you could afford a $400,000 Motorhome. We are travelling in a $35,000 unit and are having the time of our lives. "A serious lesson here!"

Day **84**

Happy New Year – and as predicted we were both wiped out today and spent all day relaxing and doing odd jobs around the Motorhome. But I did manage to make a lovely pasta sauce for dinner and we are looking forward to visiting the Mornington Peninsula tomorrow. During the course of the day though the camp area quickly filled up with people and to our surprise it was nearly full by evening.

One guy turned up with the biggest fifth wheeler that I have seen on the road and at a small campsite like this it looks enormous. He turned out to be quite the tosser also, walking around the campsites spruiking to anyone that would listen about his fantastic rig. He was deliberately looking to get energy from other people while his wife was back at the Rig looking quite miserable. Anyway, to each there own. There was also another group who set up a caravan and annexe and then a tent also, spending the whole afternoon doing so. They also became a nuisance when they lit a barbeque with scented heat beads and the smoke came gushing in our direction. The smell was very overpowering and the next morning we both woke up with throat and nose problems.

At about 11-00pm I was awoken by a van that pulled in right behind us and with those sliding door that make a hell of a racket when they are shut. But eventually I fell back to sleep and did manage to get six or so hours in.

Day **85**

A little sleep deprived and feeling nasally from the smoke we prepared for a lovely day on the Mornington Peninsula. Then to our amazement when we started the Motorhome to leave Sedrick appeared at my driver's side window. Now I think I have spoken about Sedrick before, he and Marree were the French couple that we first met at Glenrowan where they were cherry picking with a Belgian couple to help fund their travels around Australia (I don't think I mentioned their names though). We also met them at Port Albert where I made a bet with Tee that we would never run into them again, and Tee said we would. Guess who just lost that bet! They had met another French couple and were travelling together – four of them sleeping in a Hi-ace van – very cosy, but they are young so they do that shit.

I gave him one of my business cards and said I hoped we would catch up again soon, but I knew that if we did, I would cop a heap of ribbing from Tee as she would have more to spruik about.

We left the Poowong Campsite and headed towards Koo-Wee-Rup which is on the way to the Mornington Peninsula, as we wanted to check out what the Free-camp spot was like out there. It was on the opposite side of the highway and as we approached it, we realized that it was too exposed to the highway and would be noisy, (not to mention dangerous) as it was a high traffic area. This left us in a horrible position as I knew that the Mornington Peninsula would be packed with campers and we may have to go back to Poowong for the evening. Not an ideal option as it was a fair distance but a great "Plan B".

We continued past Koo-Wee-Rup and as we got to Tooradin Tee said that this is where Leonie (Dad's Wife) had brought her to pick up the Seafood for Christmas. Tee said it was very pretty there especially down the side street that lead to the boat ramp. We just stopped in time to turn down that road and when we got to the parking area, we discovered it was beautiful and to top it off they had overnight camping there for $10.00. We booked in straight away and after a cuppa we headed back on the road to the Mornington Peninsula that was now only a short distance away.

We decided to go right out to the point of Western Port Bay via Hastings and then Flinders. The area around Hastings was a bit ordinary but as we continued towards Flinders it got nicer and nicer. We pulled up at a jetty near Flinders where we took a few pictures and had a bit of a stroll before heading towards Rosebud on the Port Phillip Bay side. Amazingly from Flinders we had a clear view of the Nobbies (Phillip Island).

Not too long out of Flinders we came to Cape Schanck which was absolutely stunning and we got out to go for a long walk around the Lighthouse and along the boardwalks that meandered around the cliff faces and spilled onto the rocky beaches. We took a number of photos before continuing to the Port Phillip Bay side of this peninsula. We hit Rosebud in no time and turned left to get us to the western most point of this area which is Portsea. We found our way to Portsea back beach and to the elevated car park from which we could see for miles either way down this stunning surf beach. In fact, we were just in time to see and photograph a huge cargo ship sail in through the heads. It was so big that at first glance it looked like part of the landscape was moving and it wasn't until you worked out what it was that you could focus on it and work out the shape of it.

As we left Portsea back beach, we saw a small sign that pointed to London Bridge which use to connect to the mainland but broke away many years ago. It was a place that my grandparents had brought me as a child and in those days, you could walk across it. The road to London Bridge now backed onto a stunning golf course that is the play toy of the mega wealthy and their stunning homes that have now swamped this area. In fact, Portsea had always had grand homes but just not as many.

We then kept on to see how far west we could travel and soon discovered that the old army area that was blocked off was now a growing tourist attraction. This allowed us to drive a fair distance towards the heads where we had a little look around before heading east again past Sorrento and onto Rye where I had spent a number of summers as a young boy. In my memories it was always a busy place but now it seemed to have doubled in numbers and we could not even find a place to pull up the Motorhome. As a young fella I have fond memories of catching flathead off the jetty and going to the carnival that was set up there every year – both of which are past memories that don't exist any more. But to my surprise the carnival was there, which made me wonder if the flathead were also. I reckon not, so one out of two isn't bad.

Another thing that I recall from my childhood summers here was the large number of mini golf centres and wondered if they were still here, but alas it was down to one out of three now as we only saw one crazy golf centre and that was in Rosebud. No wonder kids get up to no good these days as their activities revolve around indoor games in a lot of cases. But at least here they have heaps of outdoor stuff to do with the beach and all its water sports if they choose to.

The beach in this area is even more beautiful than I remember it from my childhood and if it weren't so crowded, I would like to camp here and spend some time on it. But it is so busy that it makes it unpleasant for us as we both enjoy the quiet locations. So, we slowly cruised through McCrae and Dromana before heading inland again and back to our lucky camp find of Tooradin.

We got back to Tooradin mid afternoon and were undecided where to park the Motorhome for the evening as we had a choice of the general car park (which was near the toilet block) or on the grass around the back that was near the boat ramp. We were leaning towards staying in the car park area as it felt safe and it was nearer the amenities. That was until after 5-00pm when it seemed like half of Melbourne decided to visit Tooradin and the car park became chocked with cars. By the time we decided to move around to the grassed area it was too late as we could not get out. In fact, we had to wait until after nine before we had enough space to get out, which we did. When we got around the back it felt a lot better and we got a very restful nights sleep as a result.

Day **86** – Day **89**

The next morning, we awoke and found ourselves almost blocked in by boat trailers as there had been about fifty cars pull in with their boats in the early hour of the morning while we were sleeping. Before we had brekkie, I moved Lizzie to the edge of the roadway to ensure we were not blocked in and as we had brekkie the boats continued to arrive. (Smart move).

Today we had planned to visit Rodney (my step brother) and his family. This was a little awkward for us as we were not sure if they were just being polite when they invited us to stay with them or they were genuine. So, I thought that it would be best to visit them and if they weren't genuine, we would soon find out. Upon arriving we felt more than welcome and in fact it gave us all some time to get to know each other and how we all felt about me arriving on the scene 46 years after my Mum and Nelson split up. We all got on fabulously and ended up staying two nights with them. We both agreed that it had been a great experience and that regardless of what happened in the family we would continue our friendship.

We slept in our Motorhome in their driveway so as not to crowd them but spent the full two days in their company and we all seemed to thoroughly enjoy it. In fact, it was a shame that we had booked a caravan park for the next evening as they had invited us to the horse racing that they were going to in Cranbourne on the Saturday night.

But sensibly thinking it did turn out for the best as we had to weave our way through to Port Melbourne and to be there by seven in the morning would have been pushing it. After leaving Rod and Cindy's home we did a trial run to find where the Spirit of Tassie's dock was, and after finding it we went to the Caravan Park in Braybrook that we had booked. We had a hell of a time finding our way around and Karen (our navigator) seems to get us further in trouble when we really need her. By the time we arrived at the Caravan Park we were exhausted as the last few days had been forty degrees and over and the city area had been a nightmare.

My first chore was to empty the shitter that had not been emptied in over two weeks and we were surprised that even though the weather had been so hot it didn't smell too bad. After this I had a shower while Tee made up a fabulous Souvlaki that we ate before settling in for a quick movie (The Nutty Professor – Eddie Murphy) and an early night.

The Caravan Park was surprisingly quiet even though it was only a few minutes from the city, and although over priced at $52.00 for a powered site we did get a good night's sleep.

Day **90**

We awoke at 5-30am which was 30 minutes before the time that I had set the alarm for and I had deliberately booked the Tassie crossing for a Sunday so the roads were quiet. This proved to be a great move as we had quite a relaxed journey to Port Melbourne's Station Pier and we got there quite early. It was to be a long day today and we were a little concerned that the fires that Tassie were experiencing would spoil the trip, but it was too late for all that now and we boarded the Spirit of Tasmania.

The trip to Tassie, although long (10.5 Hours) was quite pleasant as the weather was clear and calm. The view from the decks was fabulous and we took heaps of photos, especially when going through the heads. We had taken heaps of stuff in two bags including heaps of water which we didn't need. But on a positive note we didn't go hungry and we know better for our return journey which will be a night sailing and we have booked recliners for. (Smart move).

Upon arriving it took us, for what seemed to be forever, to get onto dry land and then we were held up in a long que for customs. In the end it was 7-30pm before Lizzie touched down on Tassie soil. As we had not eaten properly all day, we decided to go to the Devonport central to get a decent feed. As it was Sunday though the options were limited and the decent feed was conjectural as we ended up having McDonald – one of the few places open on a Sunday evening in Tassie.

We then headed for the free camp spot that I had picked out about seven kilometres West of the town of Lower Barrington, near Sheffield.

We had a hell of a time with trying to find this place and our troubles were compounded by the fact that it was rapidly getting dark.

When we did locate where the free camp was supposed to be, we were confronted with a No Camping sign. This was extremely frustrating as it is the second time this has occurred and it will now be the second time, we ignore it. We were both extremely tired and us being there would affect no-one so we stayed put and fell asleep about ten after a quick tidy of the Motorhome.

Day 91

This illegal camping must be good for us as we slept in until 8-30am with the intention of a casual trip to Sheffield planned and a quiet day for me as I was five days behind in my Journal / Book writing. We stopped at Sheffield for a brief time and Tee went and bought a few supplies while I got stuck into writing.

After an hour or so it got a bit too hot so we decided to head to a free camp area on Lake Paloona. It was a beautiful drive there and we stayed for most of the day while I wrote some more and Tee whipped up another one of her yummy Souvlaki's. But as it was quite crowded and a little noisy, we decided to move on and find a quieter free camp for the evening.

The best option that we could find on the map was at a place called Gowrie Park which is an old hydro town. When we arrived there, we found a number of campers already set up and the place was very nicely laid out on a massive old concrete slab. We set up for the evening and we are both looking forward to another great night's sleep.

Day **92**

We woke the next morning and checked the Tasmanian Fire website as there had been some very large fires burning in the state over the past few days. In fact, at one point we were not sure whether to make the trip over. Fortunately, though the fires had started to die down a bit and the temperatures forecast were cooler, so we stuck to our original plans. But when I checked the Tas fire map it showed that the fire in the North West on the road to Stanley was flaring up again. As this was the direction we had planned on heading to first we had to decide what to do, and where to go next. With all the uncertainty we decided that we would be best off spending the day and night here and just monitor the conditions.

They were pretty bad fires with the town of Donnelly hit the hardest and basically the whole town was wiped out.

The place we were staying in was surrounded by bush but clear where we were and as I said earlier, we were located on a massive concrete slab. I felt comfortable that in the unlikely event that a fire did come this way we could shelter it out here. One concern though was that it was very Smokey and on the Tas fire map the closest small fire was near Cradle Mountain which was a long way from here. But we soon heard on the radio that most of Tassie was suffering from smoke coverage and that put our minds at rest. We monitored both the internet and the radio all day for updates in the hope that the North West fire would abate and we could stick to our original plans of heading to Stanley.

We spent the day reading and writing and I even read the Steve Waugh book "Never Say Die" cover to cover in the one day. To be honest he probably took the same amount of time to write it – it was a bit ordinary. By late in the evening the status of that fire had got worse due to the increased winds that were gusting up to one hundred kilometres per hour. Although the weather was cooler this made it very hard for the fire-fighters to contain the fire. We plotted a new journey and decided we would check one more time in the morning to see how things were then.

Day **93**

After a sensational nights sleep we awoke and I checked the Tas fire site again, and although it had improved we decided it was still better not to go near that area and go with Plan B. Plan B was to head towards Deloraine via Mole Creek and on the way we would have a look at Lake Parangana which is 29 Klms South of Mole Creek.

The trip to Lake Parangana took us through some sensational Tassie scenery with a huge climb up a mountain range with its rocky mountains and then down to it rainforest gullies. The area is truly stunning and is another one of our must sees. When we arrived at Lake Parangana, we immediately decided that we should camp here for the evening as it is amazing and the free camp area is right beside the lake. Even better it was quiet and we were the only campers in this section.

We set up for the day and with the temperature struggling to reach eighteen degrees we revelled in the cool climate and watched in amazement as the sky changed from sunshine to cloudy rain and back again over this stunning lake. The water was so clear that we were able to fill up our tank out of it and Tee cooked another Souvlaki for dinner as it has now become her favourite new meal. I was happy with that though as the wog in me is always up for a Souvlaki.

I even managed to drop in a power nap "AND" get a solid night's sleep.

Day **94**

After a brilliant night's sleep, we slowly prepared for our journey to Mole Creek and onto Deloraine. We stopped briefly in Mole Creek but we were both happy to just slowly drive to Deloraine and continue to enjoy the lovely scenery.

When we arrived at Deloraine, we decided to find the free camp area first as it looked as though it was not too far from town and we could walk back to town once we secured a spot. We figured that because it was the Christmas holidays and the East Coast was a bit burnt then these types of areas may be packed. When we arrived at the free camp spot there were a few campers there but it was by no means packed. We levelled the Motorhome, locked it up and walked towards town.

The walk back to town was invigorating and even included a river crossing via a suspension bridge. The old buildings in this town are lovely and we did a bit of browsing before buying some local fish and chips for lunch. After lunch we continued browsing in the local shops and bought a lovely homemade date loaf for afternoon tea. On the way back to the free camp spot we also bought a few bottles of wine as the ones we got in Victoria were all gone now. At the free camp spot, we settled in for the evening and as we did the place started to fill up with campers. In fact, by the time night fell it was quite full.

In the late afternoon I had a call from my step daughter who was leasing a flat from me with her new boyfriend. Some weeks earlier they had split up and he had moved out. When she rang me, she was all upset, as he had been hassling her over money. One thing I have found while you are travelling is that the two things you can't get away from are bills and family problems. She explained to me the situation and I gave him a call and was expecting him to be a smartass. He was younger than my step daughter but thought he was a little bit special, and didn't treat her too well. I laid it down to him when he started talking over the top of me and told him what to do and when to do it or I would deal with him. I then hung up on him as he was ranting and I could not believe how a boy of eighteen could be so disrespectful after I helped them both so much in setting up the flat. He text me a few minutes later with a note saying he would do it. But he had wrapped it in a few smartass comments. He must have thought I did not get the message as a few minutes later he rang me. I told him to do the right thing and walk away. I added that if he didn't, I would ensure he did. I think it has all settled down now but only time will tell. We had a great night's sleep and were prepared for the next leg of our journey.

Day **95**

The next spot that we had planned to travel to was Lilydale which was on the Eastern side of Launceston and about one to two hours drive from Deloraine. The countryside was again very pretty, as is most of Tassie, and in no time, we arrived at Launceston. We had taken the back roads there rather than the highway and it was good that we had as we found a Shell servo that took vouchers saving us eight cents a litre on our fuel. The lady in the store was lovely and, on our way out, said "enjoy your stay in Tassie" which we both thought was a lovely thing to say.

We travelled along the huge Tamar River for a while until we started heading inland to Lilydale. If you are wondering why we didn't spend a lot of time in Launceston, it is not because there isn't a fair bit to see there, it is because we have been to Tassie a few other times in the past four years and we have done heaps here. Our trip this time was mainly to go to all the little places that we haven't seen before.

We arrived in the town of Lilydale about lunchtime and visited the IGA supermarket there to buy a hot chook for lunch, as we hadn't even had any breakfast today. The ladies in the store were lovely and all in their late forties plus, so it was a bit of a surprise to Tee and I to here Acca Dacca playing on the store speakers. But the ladies there loved it and seemed to be having a great time in their work – "good on them".

The free camp site that we were going to was only two kilometres north of town and when we arrived there the place was packed. It was mainly packed because it was a day picnic area as well as the camping area, plus there was one way in and one way out. The only spot that I could find was one that Tee thought I would not get into, but I was determined and executed a stunning reverse park to nail it on the first attempt. Now if Tee was impressed, she wasn't showing it. The area was also a car park for the Lilydale falls and after a yummy lunch of hot (free-range) chook we went for a walk to the falls.

When we got back to the Motorhome Tee read a book while I had a power nap that ended up lasting over an hour. When I awoke it was nearly dinner time and we decided to have some fat sausages and packaged pasta. After dinner I did a heap of writing and did not go to bed until after 10-30pm, which is very late for me, while Tee had gone to bed about an hour earlier.

We had another one of those shit wits that think they are funny by beeping their car horn at campers in the middle of the night. This time though he was in the car park and beeped all the way out of the car park within metres of all the campers. Still a gutless wonder though as he did on the way out and not the way in. I would quote the date and time now if I thought this would be published but, in all honesty, I am sure the dickhead couldn't read anyway. To all non campers out there think about it – if you live in a small town campers can be a good boost to your community as most will at least buy food supplies in your town. Anyway, I didn't hear the beeping which amazed Tee as I am normally a very light sleeper, but it must have been that I went to bed later than normal.

Day 96

Today we are planning to head to Derby which is halfway between Launceston and the East coast. But we have some domestic choirs to attend to on the way in the form of Laundry that we haven't done for a week or so now. Over the past month or so we have been fortunate as we have been able to do it at relative's places. Looking at the map the best chance of finding a Laundromat would be in Scottsdale and sure enough we found one pretty quickly and did our washing. Prices vary heaps at Laundromat's, anywhere from two to six dollars per load but we have found that three to four is the average.

After getting the washing all done and filling up our drinking water, we headed to the main shopping area in Scottsdale to get a few more supplies. On the way back to the Motorhome with our shopping I saw a pub and asked Tee if she would mind if I got myself a slab of beer, and quicker than she could say "of course not" I was in there. I got myself a slab of Carlsberg as I don't remember ever having it before and I had heard of it so I thought that will do. I was so excited as we have been on the road for three months now and I haven't had a beer other than once or twice in a pub.

As we started heading out of Scottsdale on the way to Derby, I saw a sign that said one kilometre to a camping park. We thought we would have a look and when we got there, we decided we would stay the night as it was very pretty and the toilet block even had hot showers via a donation. This would alter our plans for the day but it looks like a great spot. We had a walk through the charming park and because the weather was lovely, we set up outside with our awning and chairs and enjoyed the sunny day that Tassie was turning on for us. As to being a bit behind schedule with our travelling we knew that we could always catch up tomorrow by heading directly to the coast.

Over the afternoon the free camp filled up quite rapidly as we are noticing they do, especially between four and seven in the afternoon. By the end of the afternoon it was quite full, but not uncomfortably full, and all the campers seemed quite friendly. We met a couple from Georgetown and they brought their chairs over and we had a great chat for the evening and of course I was in heaven drinking my Carlsberg. We had been chatting for so long that we didn't notice the time until it started to get dark, which is 9-00pm in these parts in summer. Not like home where it is dark by 7-30pm.

At first, we liked this getting dark late gig but we both now feel as though it robs you of your evening which when you are working is good wind down time. I suppose it depends what your hobbies are as in one spot in Victoria we saw a couple of young blokes getting their motorbikes off a trailer at 6-30pm to go for a ride in the forest where we were camped. We ate the rest of the free-range chicken we had bought in Lilydale and after a shower we went to bed.

Day **97**

E ven though the camp park was full it was quite quiet and we got a lovely night's sleep, although Tee said she was awoken by a few campers who left about five in the morning. Today we planned to head to the East Coast and then back to St Mary's to stay overnight.

The trip from Scottsdale took us through some mountainous and winding terrain with the rainforests and views making the hard Motorhome driving all worthwhile. We travelled though Branxholm where we saw another lovely camp site near their pubic swimming pool, and although our stop in Derby was just to use the public toilets the camp by the river here didn't look too bad either.

As we approached the East Coast and more specifically St Helens the landscape got dryer and dryer and on the outskirts of St Helens it was bone dry. We had originally planned to travel through Bicheno and down the East Coast but for two reasons we will not go there now. The main reason is out of respect for the people who have lost their homes there in the recent fires. Even though they are asking tourists to come back in, with barely a week gone by since the fires, I think it is more the shopkeepers that are saying that, as I am sure if my house had just burnt down I wouldn't want tourists sticky nosing. We had a cuppa on the wharf at St Helens and a piece of that yummy date loaf we bought in Deloraine. Oh, and the second reason is, as I have said earlier, we have been to Tassie many times and we spent a fair bit of time in St Helens last trip.

We then followed the lovely East Coast until the road diverted us inland and rapidly up a steep mountain range to the country town of St

Mary's. Lot of saints in this area! We have fond memories of St Mary's from our last trip to Tassie as we camped here and had a fabulous breakfast two days in a row in a little café in the main street. But Tee said she found another place in the Camp 6 book that had free power and it was only about fifteen minutes up the road in the town of Fingal.

Fingal is a quiet little town about half way between the East Coast and the Midlands. When we found the camp spot, which was more a car park and park really, we were thrilled to see that it did indeed have power. We got there about three in the afternoon and as we had not eaten lunch, we decided to have an early dinner and I fried up come Italian sausages and eggs while Tee made me a fresh salad (Yum).

Not long after dinner and minutes after I packed away the outdoor cooking gear it started to rain. This would be good news for the fire-fighters in Tassie and it was nice for us also as it got quite cool and we were nice and snug in our lovely little Motorhome (Thanks Lizzie).

Day 98

Another nice sleep and we awoke to bright sunshine, after a bit of toast and a cuppa I did my rounds of the Motorhome and was excited to see that our batteries were on full charge and that we had access to water to fill our tank. After buying some bits and pieces in town (to thank them for the free site) we hit the road again.

The objective of today was to have a look at the countryside around the southern end of Ben Lomond National Park and then cruise down the midlands highway to stop at Oatlands or Kempton overnight. The countryside, although dry, promised to be spectacular and immediately after the town of Mangana (hide your sister) the road went almost vertically upwards. In fact, I would go so far as to say it was steeper than the back-road climb to Falls Creek. But when we got there, we were treated to some stunning views of Fishers Tiers and Frogmore Ridge.

The town of Rossarden was unique also, as it was pretty much located in Bumfuck Shitsville but had views to die for and in winter one could only imagine how beautiful those views would be. From Rossarden it was all downhill and that is in the physical sense, as the trip down to Avoca was as steep, if not steeper than our climb from Mangana.

When we reached the base of the mountain range we got into a bit of a panic as the road turned to dirt – "we don't do dirt roads". For a minute or so I thought we had taken a wrong turn and would have to re-climb the mountain range. And Karen the Nav Bitch was no help as all the way down the range she was telling us to do a U-turn and before we reached the dirt road, she just said nothing. The only thing that gave us hope was that we were heading South and Avoca was south of Rossarden. Finally, the trees thinned out and we saw a town in the distance and could only hope that it was Avoca. Another Kilometre further on and the road turned to bitumen again which brought smiles to our faces.

Turns out it was Avoca and we continued our journey to the midlands highway where we stopped at the small town of Conara and cooked up a feed of Bacon & Eggs which we wrapped in Pita bread and added some salad. There was a free camp area here but it was very noisy as the midland highway is very busy with truck traffic. We decided to try Campbell Town free camp area and when we arrived it was quite full. If we had not been to the area many times before we probably would have stayed there and explored the town. But this trip is more about going to places we haven't been to so we thought Kempton would be better for us.

When we arrived at Kempton, we were not disappointed as the free camp area was quite nice and bugger me if they didn't have free power also – what a bargain. After we settled Lizzie we decided to walk into town and spend a few dollars. But although lovely to walk through there was not a lot open, and what was did not have much of what we would like to buy. We headed back to the free camp and settled in for the evening, planning to watch a DVD (Eddie Murphy – The Klump's).

While watching the movie a Motorhome pulled up and proceeded to park in between us and the fellow beside us. Normally this wouldn't bother us too much but the gap he was going into was less than a metre from us and the same on the other side. This just confirms the fact that nothing is free as you have to put up with some shit in these places on occasions. To take it further at 9-00pm he knocked on our Motorhome door to ask if he could share the power outlet I was using. What a fuckwit this bloke was and I just said "whatever mate" and ignored him trying to stay in touch with the movie we were watching.

Day **99**

Both Tee and I woke up this morning not feeling too flash. We are not sure whether it is because it was really cold last night or Tee's theory that the power plugged into the Motorhome was the cause. I have noticed though that the cold seeps into the underside of the mattress as there is not much to protect it from the breeze that would flow under the Motorhome. We will monitor it now to see if we can find the cause of our lack of sleep when it occurs. Today we want to get from Kempton to Gordon which is about three hours of Motorhome driving in a straight line. But I decided after studying the map that if we went back up to Bothwell, we could cover territory that neither Tee nor I had seen before, so it was settled.

The road to Bothwell was another climb, but nothing like we have done in the past week, as it was quite mild a climb in comparison. The landscape in Tassie seems to be brown and crispy everywhere and nothing like what you would expect when you think of Tassie and the way it is advertised. I must say it is a little disappointing as its beauty is well hidden by the current heatwave and lack of rain, not to mention the bushfires.

Bothwell was ordinary and we continued on to Hamilton via a lightly used sealed back road. Again, the scenery was extremely dry and even though there was rolling hills, they are not the same when they are not green. At Hamilton we stopped at the information centre and had a cuppa before heading directly south towards Hobart. Hamilton has a lot of historic buildings but they are all in average condition with one or two exceptions that have been well preserved. We passed thorough the town of New Norfolk which is heavily populated in comparison to the towns

159

we have been through and how can I say, "scrappy" is the best way to describe it.

We continued towards Hobart following the mighty Derwent River for a considerable amount of time. Hobart is another place that Tee and I have spent a fair bit of time in and the Botanical Gardens there are stunning, a bit like Tivoli style gardens and very old fashioned. This said we sailed thorough Hobart with minimal fuss or delay and have planned to visit the Salamanca Markets their next Saturday.

Once safely over the large mountain range that flanks Hobart to the South the landscape tried its hardest to show us it still had some green in it and the further South we travelled, the harder it tried. The coastline along the Channel Highway is very pretty and it is always a toss up which side is prettier – the bush or the beach - and for a fair length of its shores the beautiful Bruny Island stares in waiting for those who wish to ferry to her shores.

We finally reached our evening destination at Gordon and both decided to have a bit of a power nap as we both did not wake up too flash and were getting a bit snappy with each other. After a bit of a nap we got up to prepare dinner and were keen to ensure that we slept well this evening. The campsite at Gordon though is lovely and we are both keen to appreciate it more in the morning after a good night's sleep.

Day **100**

Well a good night sleep evaded us again and it was due mainly to noisy campers. At 9-40pm it was still a bit light and some ferrel tenters who were not far from our Motorhome let their children run around until almost 10-00pm, which ruled out an early night for us. A few hours earlier a group of four boys who were having trouble getting tent pegs into the ground over the other side of the free camp area decided that the soil was softer near our Motorhome and moved their whole shindig near us. Now this was OK for the evening as they went to bed by nightfall and the swearing for sixteen-year old's was quite light. But for some unknown reason they started chatting at 4-00am, and it was not quiet chatting either. I could not make out what they were talking about but they were quite loud – who knows what boys of that age talk about at 4-00am – probably who has the biggest dick or some shit. Tee was pissed off and got out of the Motorhome and yelled at them to shut up – I thought to myself, go Tee. They did quieten down for a while but you could still hear them talking.

We both fell back to sleep and didn't wake until about 8-00am. Of course, the little shits had gone back to sleep and were still asleep at 10-30am when we left the campsite. I felt like running over the tent or beeping the horn, but I composed myself and did neither as we headed quietly on our way. Last evening, we were impressed with the place and thought we may use it as a base camp to come back to each evening but that crap soon changed our minds.

We continued our journey south following the coastline all the way to Cygnet and further to Huonville. The coastline all the way round is lovely and we especially enjoyed the area around Randall's Bay and Eggs & Bacon Bay. This area is especially nice due its light population and unspoilt beauty.

Cygnet had grown a fair bit since we came here last and we didn't enjoy it as much this time around. Huonville was pumping and it always seems quite busy here. We topped up our supplies and our fuel before heading to Franklin just down the road a bit to camp overnight. We bought some prawns and some fresh salad stuff in preparation of a quiet evening.

The campsite at Franklin was right on the Huon River and at $10.00 we thought it was great as it seemed very quiet here (fingers crossed).

Day **101**

Our instincts were right and Franklin was a lovely Cheap camp area, we had a lovely night's sleep. I had the unenviable task now to empty the shitter and just the thought of it fills me with such joy. There was a bloke at the water tap when I got there and with the dump point just behind it, I waited for him to finish. He gave me a nod and he was on his way. I moved the Motorhome up to line up with the dump point; I do this to save every possible inch of carrying it, and started the task. While I was doing this another guy in a Motorhome pulled around in front of me and backed up to the tap, blocking me in. I was pissed off thinking "can't you just wait two minutes until I finish". I quickly connected the freshwater tap and started filling my Motorhome and made him wait anyway. I have no idea why people do this as they just succeed in pissing people off. What pissed me off even more was the fact that I was so nice during the whole process. I vowed then and there that I would be more decisive and less pleasant when situations like that occurred again. It made me quite agitated and it took me an hour or so to get over it – he won didn't he!

We had planned to follow the coast all the way to Southport today, which is close to the most southern point in Australia. We could travel further down but none of those places further south interest us. Our first stop was at Geeveston which is an old logging town and home to the logging of the famous Huon Pine. We had a look in the Information centre and the museum and then went to a craft store in the main street where we met a couple of lovely people who had their artwork for sale in the store.

From there we hugged the coast all the way to Dover with a stop at Roaring Beach which was very pretty and we went for a short walk.

That entire coastline is quite beautiful as again the population is low and it is reasonably unspoilt. We then stopped at Dover and had a cuppa overlooking the bay and all the birdlife etc.

After Dover we went to Strathblane where we found a block that we had been eying off on the internet some months earlier. The area was lovely but the block looked like hard work so again we were glad that we did not pursue to purchase it. From there the road moves away from the coast and doesn't reconnect with the beach until you reach Southport. We spent a short amount of time in Southport but as we had visited here before we only stayed a short time. The day had been forecast to reach twenty-nine degrees but by one in the arvo it had barely cracked twenty degrees. What amazed Tee and I more than that was the fact that kids were swimming at Southport beach – crazy little buggers. We decided to go back to Dover and shout ourselves a treat in the form of a café or pub lunch.

The café we chose was a lovely little converted post office that had done a lovely redecorating job. We chose the beer battered flathead with scallops and fat chips. When it came out, we were a little surprised as it was in a bowl and contained more chips than anything. At $44.00 it was a week's groceries to us and although nice quality it was not what we expected. If I was working, I would not have given it a second thought, but as we are limited in funds, we will have to choose wiser in the future. At Southport we were going to stay at a Caravan Park but decided that Franklin would be a better spot as it was cheaper and quite good.

After our café lunch we headed back to Franklin and as we did the temperature started to climb and by three thirty it was twenty-five degrees. We found a spot in the Camp area and after words with a dickhead who was trying to reserve parking area for a mate who was on his way we settled in for the afternoon. The temperature climbed to over thirty degrees in the next few hours and stayed at that until about eight thirty in the evening. It was quite amazing really as until two in the arvo it barely reached twenty degrees and in the next three hours it jumped from twenty to thirty degrees. We had a comfortable afternoon reading our books under the awning and Tee made me another yummy Souvlaki for dinner. The town had a shindig for the Tassie fire victims and one of the townspeople even came down to the camp area to invite everyone. That was lovely.

Day **102**

Again, it is time to move on as we are heading west now and the plan is to get to Lake Meadowbank on the outskirts of Hamilton. There is a free camp there and plan B is that if it is no good, we will go to a cheap Caravan Park in Hamilton that only charges $12.00 per night. I spotted it when we were in Hamilton about four days ago. The way we intend to go is via Westerway as it is a back road and we are endeavouring to visit areas that we have not been to before.

We decided to stop in Huonville again to pick up some more prawns as we really enjoyed them the other night and they are easy to digest when, like us, you don't get enough exercise. When buying these we grabbed a few extra supplies as the West is light on shopping districts, and as a bonus we got a shopper docket that had a KFC voucher on it. We had not had a fast food feed for a few weeks now apart from the café meal in Dover and as we were passing through Kingston in about half an hour it was a great chance to pick up a feed. Not only that but with the family pack we get two meals each out of it for twenty bucks (great for the budget).

We stopped just after Kingston and just before Hobart to eat it, and boy did we enjoy it. While we were stopped on a roadside area, we noticed a family of chickens and as we have seen a few of these with no houses around them we presume that there are a number of them running wild in groups around Tasmania. Watch out guys, the Colonel is just down the road! After our feed (and warning the chickens) we sailed through Hobart without much fuss, in fact I would say that it is one of the easiest cities or even country town in Australia to get through.

We were going to go to the Salamanca markets here on Saturday but timing our travels is often a problem and we have done it before anyway. So, decision made and in line with our policy of not hanging around the cities too much we continued our exploring of the beautiful Tassie countryside. We followed the mighty Derwent again and veered towards Westerway not long after New Norfolk.

When we got to Westerway, we changed our plans of not going to Strathgordon as the countryside looked spectacular. The main reason I said not to go was because it is almost 100 klms in and then 100 klms back out again. I had been there about fifteen years ago and my memory was only of the dam and not the scenery on the way in, and on that basis, I thought it not worthwhile. But boy was I wrong, the scenery was stunning, and it also helped that Tee had not been there before and was far better company than my ex wife. We also passed the site of Miranda Gibson who has been sitting almost 200 feet up a tree for 410 days in protest against logging of the area which was home to old growth trees – some of the largest in Australia. What is amazing is that it was also suppose to be a protected area – which in Tassie doesn't seem to affect the loggers who can cry that they need jobs and then do as they please. Good for her and you can see her website at http://observertree.org. Another amazing fact is that less than twenty minutes drive from here is World Heritage Listed and I might add that the forest Miranda is protecting is even more stunning in natural beauty.

We continued our journey towards Strathgordon, but about twenty kilometres from there we decided to turn around as we had consumed more fuel than I calculated and we wanted to get to Lake Meadowbank with good light to find it. I have been pretty good at working out the fuel so far and it was the hills and bends that messed me up this time. In reality we may have had enough fuel but it was not worth the risk and we had seen most of this stunning area by now. If you want to see a place that is close to total wilderness and on a sealed road then this is a journey that you must make – just take enough fuel! Truly special!

Back in Westerway we turned left and headed to the tiny town of Ellendale where we had a toilet stop. In fact, it was a unique toilet as it had the boys and girls in one door that had one cubical for the boys (to the right) and one for the girls (to the left) and Tee was not overly impressed with that. From Ellendale we only had to travel about ten kilometres to our destination of Lake Meadowbank, but we were in for one more amazing sight. We did not realize that the recent Tassie fires had burnt through here and that in fact we had to travel though the same path as the Lake Repulse fire. As we travelled through, we saw the scarred landscape and were stopped at roadworks where the Electricity boys were replacing all the fire damaged electricity poles. At that point we were a little concerned that there would be no campsite, but the lake area was unaffected and we found the campground quite easily.

We quickly set up and as it was after seven, we cooked up the prawns and made a lovely salad rather than having Souvlaki like we had planned. The campground was lovely, quiet and sited right beside the lake.

Day **103**

We were going to keep going with our travels today but even though I had a superb nights sleep the driving yesterday had taken its toll on my shoulder. Lizzie is a great Motorhome but she is quite heavy on the steering and with all those windy roads and gear changing through the hills my shoulder was very tender. Even after a great shoulder massage from Tee we decided to spend another day here. This was yet another reminder of the pending disaster that was to occur tomorrow, MY 50TH BIRTHDAY, something I was trying to forget as I knew I could not put it off.

We didn't do much for the day but we did enjoy the serenity of the area and with not many campers here we relaxed in near silence. A day to reflect on the horrors of tomorrow.

Day **104**

I woke up this morning hoping that I wasn't crippled with arthritis or suddenly had grey hair or/and wrinkles – yes, I am turning fifty. But to my surprise I feel no different and most say I look early to mid forties – "they are the only people I talk to". The truth is though that no matter how I sugar it up if you count all the years that I have lived on the planet they add up to fifty.

Today will be like any other on the road though as we are out west and there is not much here. This suits me, as I don't like making a fuss about birthdays. We left Lake Meadowbank and intend to continue westerly towards Derwent Bridge. Last time we came to Tassie we stayed at Derwent Bridge in a cabin there, I remember it as it was September and freezing. Today promises to be warm but who knows what the evening will bring.

The countryside turned to forest about twenty minutes out of Ouse and we stopped not long after that in the Hydro town of Tarraleah. The view from there to the Hydro stations at the base was superb and off to the right we saw a walking track to a waterfall. We didn't expect stunning scenery but were both eager to go for a walk, and as it had not warmed up too much yet it was a great opportunity. To our surprise though it was quite lovely with huge old growth gum trees and gullies filled with tree ferns and fallen timbers covered in moss. There had been a fire through here in the last few years with a lot of damage to the landscape. But nature, the clever girl that she is, was hard at work making the place beautiful again and may I add "doing a fine job". We went back to the Motorhome after our walk, did a few stretches, and then had a yummy cup of tea.

The first free camp that we wanted to check out was Brady's Lake and was only about fifteen minutes drive from here. We thought even if the place was no good to camp at, we could at least have some lunch there. Turns out though that the place was lovely and well away from the road making it very quiet. Not only that but there were bugger all people here, meaning I could spend my fiftieth birthday suffering in silence. We had some leftovers for lunch and we even slipped in a power nap that we took in the heat of the afternoon. Although not everyone's idea of a great birthday I have really enjoyed it, as I am the whole trip after the hectic life that I have always led.

Day **105**

We had a fabulous night's sleep and are looking forward to the day's travels. I made us an egg and bacon wrap for brekkie, cooking it outside in the brilliant sunshine, and to my surprise it was about twenty degrees, quite warm for eight thirty in the morning. I had expected it to be quite cool in the morning as we were in the highlands lakes area which I thought got very cold in the evenings no matter what the day temperature was.

Today we plan to travel across country to around the Queenstown area. I do not have high expectations of the area as we just want to be close to the west coast so we can explore the region over the next few days. In all my previous trips to Tassie, and the latest two with Tee, I/we have sped through this area on our way to somewhere else. I think this was mainly because in the past all of Tassie was so green and this area didn't seem as appealing. But as we approached Derwent Bridge, we started to appreciate the true beauty of this place and were really getting into it. The landscape was quite unique and similar to the high plains of the Victorian Alpine Region which we enjoyed immensely.

Just before Derwent Bridge was a turning to Lake St Claire which we took, but part of the way there we saw that it was National Parks controlled and we didn't have a permit so we turned back. It was not only the fact that we resent paying to see our own country but last time we were here we visited it and to be honest it rates as average to me compared with other lakes in Tassie. Last time we were here and visited the lake I am sure it also was no charge to enter.

Derwent Bridge is a shitty little place and I saw no reason to stop there so we continued. The countryside continued to amaze us with its rugged beauty and another thing that amazed us was an entry fee to picnic at the Franklin River – seriously! Fortunately, Nelsons Falls was still free to enter and we did the forty-minute walk there and back and thoroughly enjoyed it. Nelson Falls are well worth looking at.

We planned to camp at Lake Burbury and as it was only ten or so minutes down the road we would be there by lunchtime. We saw a sign that said Lake Burbury camping area but it was now a pay site, so we went in to have a look. The area was a bit ordinary but it was only six dollars overnight. If it wasn't so early in the day we probably would have stayed there, but because it was early and we didn't think it was the free camp area in the Camps6 book we kept travelling. And boy where we glad we did, as after a fluke in finding the road into the free camp area we had a view and a spot that was quiet and truly stunning. The best way I can describe it is it looked like we were on an ocean liner sailing into Milford Sounds in New Zealand – and remember we are fifteen minutes drive from Queenstown.

The road to this campsite and to the boat ramp on the way to this campsite look like they use to be the main road into Queenstown and they both disappear into the lake. We suspect that Lake Burbury is not that old (less than forty years) and that they built a new road when they dammed the area. We will Google it when we get into range, as both Telstra and Optus don't work here and I suspect Optus hasn't heard of Tasmania.

This campsite, although having no facilities, would rate as the one with the best views on our trip so far and when you are fully self contained you don't need facilities. We had a great day – reading and writing and after brilliant sunshine all day a cold front rolled in at about six and changed the view completely – truly lovely.

Today has given me time to reflect on our trip so far and one of the habits that I always had at home was never missing the news. I would sometimes watch the morning news but Never – I mean Never miss the evening news. I truly thought I could not live without knowing what was going on at home and overseas. On this trip we have not bothered with any of that and I could only tell you about a half a dozen news items that I have heard of in over three months. And you know what? I don't think I have missed much at all. They say ignorance is bliss and I am tending to agree as you get caught up in all that shit and it invades your brain. I think it is a negative influence to a lot of people as most of the news tends to be negative (more news worthy).

All of these positive experiences that we are having have also made me reflect on my life in general and more specifically how lucky I have been. The greatest gift has only come to me recently and that was meeting Tee. I spoke earlier about eM and how she made me "aware" of myself, now I would like to describe my interpretation on "awareness" to you and how Tee made me discover it. But first I would like to tell you of the amazing story of how Tee and I met, or in fact did not meet until it was time to meet. It all started when I was still in my first marriage but I didn't know it had started! Confused? Well I will take you on my journey and clear the picture for you – in fact it may even help you look at things a little differently so just go with it.

I had just started working in my new career with my first agency and was desperately trying to establish a new career (Real Estate), although at this stage finances were good again and I was reasonably relaxed in an industry that runs on commission only (only paid upon sale). Part of the process was to get yourself out there in the community and one thing that I did was to produce a small magazine that was area specific and related to a particular market. The specific one that brought me to the edge of the Tee Circle (OT -1) was one on rural properties. I would deliver these brochures / magazines to shop keepers in the area for people to grab a copy. One of these shop keepers in a place called Wamuran (funny name – pretty place) eventual became my in-laws. At this stage there was no use meeting Tee as we were both married and both living completely different lives.

(OT-2) I was living in our renovated property and directly across the road lived Tee's best friend where she spent more time than in her own home. This was because she was having marriage difficulties, as I was. The difference was she had "Awareness" and I still had my head up my arse. So still no use meeting Tee as eM was still yet to happen. If you have forgotten eM well you can refresh your thoughts on page 117.

(OT-3) I soon met eM and started to find myself and as described earlier she helped me immensely and I became "aware" that my marriage was shit and I had to do something about it. What happened next I have spoke about earlier, but to touch on it again things at home went from bad to worse and my now ex-wife looked elsewhere for whatever she was looking for. eM and I both changed agencies and for me it was a bonanza as I found my straps and was beginning to earn big bucks. In this new agency I had a visit from Tee's parents (they were the Wamuran Shopkeepers) who wanted me to list their rental property for sale. The amazing thing is that Tee had been living in the property just prior to me listing it as she was having trouble with her ex also. Again, we didn't meet as we both had unfinished business elsewhere.

(OT-4) Around the time I started separating from my ex-wife Tee's best friend from across the road put her home on the market with the agency that I was working for. Part of the process of new listing of properties is what we call a caravan or stock run, where the listing agents show the properties that they have listed for the week to all the agents in the office. On our stock run to Tee's best friends house, as was usual for her, Tee was there but again we didn't meet. In fact, Tee met all the other agents but I was in the rear yard at that time. Still we both had unfinished business.

(OT-5) A few months later Tee came into the agency I worked for and asked to list her property with me as her parents had given me a big wrap after achieving a good result on their property. But when she came in, I was not in the office and as the industry can be quite sharky another agent broke etiquette and took the listing.

(OT-6) On the stock run to Tee's home I meet her ex but she was not home.

(OT-7) The day the circle was cracked and we finally met.

I was working the window (client walk ins etc) when a lady asked about properties with privacy and within a certain budget range. The thing she wanted was unique as the pricing was low and most small acreage had reasonably close neighbours. The only property that fit the bill was Tee's and we arranged an inspection.

This was the first time that I met Tee and instantly was drawn to her. By this stage I was very much single and with my wads of cash coming in and my freedom I was having a ball. In fact, it was now six or so months since my ex had left the family home and after the grieving period and so on, I was just starting to enjoy my freedom. Our first meeting was on an inspection and we spoke very little but this would soon change as the client was keen to make an offer and we went back to the office to draft a contract. Later that evening I went back to Tee's place and this time we got a chance to chat. To be honest with you I have no recollection of how the offer process went other than to say that I got it sold for her. I do however remember the fact that I was so keen on her that I asked her on a date. In fact, I also remember ringing my boss to see if I could ask her out on a date as I thought it may breach a code of ethics or something. I remember him saying "for fucks sake you're not a doctor", which I translated to "go for it". Tee said she would think about it." Fucken think about it" – I was shattered.

I rang her late the next day to have another crack and added that if she wasn't comfortable going out alone, we could go in a group with friends. Again, she said she would think about it. Now my ego was getting a little dinted. I can't remember if Tee rang me or I rang her but it was probably me as I would have made an excuse that I had to discuss the contract or some shit. I asked her what she thought about going out in a group and she said No, but before I could beg she said "she would go just with me".

Turns out that the day I had asked her out she had said "Oh Shit" very loud after I left and her daughter who was twelve said "what's wrong mum" to which Tee replied, "that guy just asked me out" and her daughter said "about time someone put their foot forward". It was not that she wasn't interested either; it was just that she had planned to do things in a particular order and meeting someone else was a fair way down that list. MY LIFE WOULD NEVER BE THE SAME AGAIN.

Day **106**

We had a fantastic nights sleep last night and got up quite early, in fact we were on the road before 8-00am. After navigating our way through the bushes that have now almost encompassed the old main road, we were surprised as to how quickly we reached the outskirts of Queenstown. The sad part is that before the copper mining Queenstown would have been exactly like the Lake Burbury region.

Just before climbing the mountain range on the edge of Queenstown we bumped into the dilapidated town of Linda which now comprised a General Store a house or two and the shell of a magnificent pub built in 1910. The pub was right on the brink of not being repairable and by the look of a lot of the old buildings around Australia it is unlikely that it will have a saviour. In fact, it only seems like certain areas of old dwellings get saved, and it is usually in groups as prices increase and tourists flock in.

As we rose the range and onto the ridge above Queenstown the mining scars look horrendous. But if you look past that you start to see its unusual beauty as it is not too dissimilar to Queenstown in New Zealand. Sure, the outskirt ranges look like they have been nuked, but the town itself has got some real character and is sort of the "Wild West" of Australia where you would not be surprised to see a gunfight in the main street.

As we arrived in Queenstown, I spotted a dump point and thought although not a weeks worth it could do with being emptied and I pulled in. As luck has it there was also town water there so I could get two jobs done at once. There was even internet access so I got the trifecta and searched for my e cards that I expected for my birthday. Alas I am not overly loved and only received two, one from Mum and one from Dad. I still had phone messages when Optus decides to come to the party and my hopes hinge on receiving heaps of those.

Tee noticed a creek nearby and after giving me a bit of help she wondered over to have a look. She came back to say that there was an AFL footy oval on the other side of the creek that was all gravel. I had heard of this oval years ago but had no idea it was in Queenstown. We went to have a look and our thoughts were that these guys must be slightly crazy to play on this surface. I said to Tee that the Italian Soccer team should train here, and she laughed. But the truth is she hates all footy and probably had no idea what I was talking about.

In Queenstown we spent a fair bit of time walking around the shops and Tee scored a heap of books which will keep her occupied for hours while I am writing. We enjoyed Queenstown this time round and we thought it had greatly improved from when we were here about two or three years ago.

Our next port of call was Strahan but unfortunately it was raining so hard we didn't stop too long. It is very touristy there and Tee and I don't have the budget or inclination to participate on River Cruises or the likes. Last time we were in Tassie though we spent a day here and it is a lovely spot, (when the weather is good). From Strahan we took the coast road to Zeehan and along the way we spotted a picnic area that seemed to be close to the beach. As we had not seen a West Coast ocean beach yet we pulled in. There was a mini bus there also and it looked as though they had gone down to the beach. I said to Tee, "do you want to go and have a look?" and even though it was still raining she agreed and we prepared to get wet. Just as we were about to head off two guys from the mini bus arrived back and they were soaking wet and covered in sand. I decided to ask them how far it was to the beach, to which they replied about two hours round trip. OMG – thank god I asked them and as we got back into our Motorhome others from the mini bus were arriving back – they were all saturated and sandy – and none of them looked happy at all.

Zeehan prides itself as an old train town and it too has picked up its act a bit, but is still very shabby. We had a lovely lunch there at a café before heading to our destination of Reece Dam where we planned to spend the night.

Reece Dam was both pretty and quiet and we spent another relaxing evening reading and enjoying the scenery.

Day **107**

After a peaceful night's sleep, we awoke to a blanket of fog over Reece Dam. As we had parked directly alongside the lake the view from the bedroom window was stunning. Over the next half an hour or so the sun exposed the lake to us with its far bank reflecting in the still water and the fog floating in a mist that was slowly being eaten up by the sun's rays.

We are heading to Tullah today which isn't too far and plan to camp in Tullah or nearby Lake Mackintosh. The journey was again very pretty and the Meredith Range area was unlike anywhere else we had seen. In fact, I commented to Tee that here we were on a planet of seven billion people and we had not passed one car in an hour of driving and we could not see a house, person or animal in any direction. The spot we were standing at had 360-degree views for miles and we could not see a soul – amazing!

Further along we saw a sign for a forest walk and we did stop and have a walk for about a kilometre before again heading towards Tullah. Tullah was a quiet little town and like a lot of West Coast towns was looking tidier than I had seen them on previous visits. The thought to stay here did cross our minds but it was generally prettier near dams and lakes so we headed towards Lake Mackintosh.

True to form it was pretty at Lake Mackintosh but we had been spoilt at Reece Dam and were not sure if we would stay or not. It was getting warmer and about lunchtime so we decided to stay while we had lunch and then decide if we stayed the night or not. As we ate lunch more Motorhomes started rolling in and because we were in a great spot and I had a few chores to do we decided to stay.

After lunch I decided to tackle the job of replacing all the flywire on the Motorhome. This was quite a big job but the weather was nice and I hadn't done much tinkering for a while and thought it would be pleasant. It took me over four hours to complete, but at the end it was satisfying and Lizzie was looking as fresh as a daisy again. During my chores Tee was cleaning and making the windows that I was re-screening all clean and shiny. We also had a visit from a couple who had pulled in beside us, they were from Perth. Turns out they were both Real Estate agents from there and we had a lovely chat. They were doing what we were doing in that, as the Real Estate Market is soft it was a great time to travel and were taking advantage of it. Also like me they were undecided if they would do Real Estate again and being on the road was making them lean away from getting back into it, as it was for me.

We had a pleasant evening with a few drinks and a pasta meal followed by a good night's sleep.

Day **108**

We even slept in this morning as it was after eight before we got out of bed. The next leg of our journey was to Waratah which I remember from about ten years ago. Back then it was very ratty and it always seems to rain there. Well today it was a fair bit different as there was no rain and the place was looking heaps nicer these days, which is the form of lots of these West Coasts towns. We went to look at the campsite there but it was $27.00 per night for basic facilities which we thought was too steep, and with free camps not far away we decided not to stay. We had a look around town for a few hours before locking Hellyer Gorge into the NavBitch (sorry Karen).

The road to the Gorge started off ordinary with a lot of messy forestry plantations and cleared paddocks of tree stumps, but once we reached the edge of the Hellyer Gorge State Reserve it got instantly pretty. We arrived at the Free camp area here and were lucky enough to find the prettiest of spots that was level and private as it only had room for one Motorhome and was totally surrounded by bush and tree ferns. We went on a forest walk here that was very pretty as there was a stream and a lovely canopy of trees and ferns for the entire walk (Great Spot). Didn't do much else here but it was a lovely peaceful place for a good night's sleep.

Day **109**

Today we had planned to go to Burnie which on a direct run isn't too far but we decided to go to Ulverstone instead as we would be able to go there via a heap of back roads. Our first turnoff was to be a dirt road that went for about five to seven kilometres, but as it had rained overnight, we didn't see that being a problem as there would be no dust. Turned out great as the road was very good quality (as far as dirt roads go), and it took us through some very interesting country. There is a little trick that Forestry Tasmania do here and that is to heavily tree the sides of the road and log from about twenty or so feet in. This gives the tourists the "beautiful Tassie Experience" while they go full steam ahead with their logging. The side roads show a different picture where we saw huge sections of cleared trees and large plantations being put in. The land seems to get knocked around a bit, but I am not going to get into the politics of logging other than to say that as much as they say they manage the land I did not see examples of new forests that looked anything like forests that hadn't been touched.

On these back roads we also saw how isolated some people live and we were amazed at how run down some of these places were – but to each there own. We passed the town of South Riana and had a look at a free camp just past there which was very nicely done and a credit to the committee that maintain it. It had all the facilities and took donations for its upkeep. I also think that it is a good idea as it keeps places like this on the map and I am sure that the local IGA and bottle shop get some steady business out of it.

We continued on our Journey and soon reached a ridge that looked over the area known as Gunns Plains. It was a beautiful looking valley that reminded Tee and I of Kings Valley in Victoria. We explored the area for a while and then headed into Ulverstone to do some shopping and get some phone reception (we bloody hope).

As we went over the range near the town of Gawler my phone stated going off like a cracker as we had not had phone reception since before my birthday (20th Jan). I had a stack of birthday wishes (text's) – about eight in all and six phone messages, some of which were related to my birthday and others that were business. With this and all the things I had to catch up with it ended up being quite a hectic day.

We stopped in Ulverstone outside our favourite take away (KFC) and we bought ourselves a lovely feed which we ate there and then. The main reason we did this was that Ulverstone was so busy that we didn't want to look for another place to park and it was reasonably central where we were. A second bonus was that there was a camping store just over the road where I got the toilet chemicals that I needed (to do my favourite chore in the world). We then walked a few blocks to the Coles supermarket and got all our supplies for the next week or so, in fact it should last us until we get back to Melbourne on the Ferry next Sunday. Ulverstone looked like a very much thriving town and as so was not our favourite place to be, but by now I was a bit tired and we looked around the area for the free camp that was in the Camps6 book. But unfortunately, it had been turned into the entrance for a new bridge, so we would have to travel further to the town of Penguin to try our luck there.

When we reached Penguin, it seemed nicer than other times that we had visited and after a quick stop off at the local information centre, we were given directions to the free camp area in the local Lions Park. Wow, what a spot and we were fortunate enough to get a site overlooking the beach and back over the town to the left. We could not believe how nice the spot was and it was right in the heart of Penguin. Earlier that day we had rung ahead to the Penguin Caravan Park and they had quoted us $35-00 for a beachside spot and I couldn't imagine it was as nice as this. We were so lucky and we enjoyed every minute of it with another yummy Souvlaki for dinner and a few evening beers – life doesn't get much better. Even the goods train that sailed past our Motorhome within ten feet of us in the late evening was an experience (an unusual one at that).

Day **110**

I had not levelled the Motorhome all that good yesterday which in turn gave me a bit of a restless night's sleep. I got enough sleep but it wasn't the best of quality and I was a bit off in the morning. Shame really as the spot was so quiet and if I had of done a better levelling job I would have slept like a baby – never mind it was a new day and a new adventure.

One of the calls I made last evening was to a friend of my mums who we were going to catch up with while in Tassie. But we had all got so busy travelling that it didn't happen and they were going back to Queensland in the morning. We spoke for a while about where each of us had been and she told me they had free camped on the foreshore at Stanley, which was interesting as that was where we were heading today. We were actually going to free camp outside Stanley and travel in there each day, but this new information allowed us to plan better.

Armed with this new knowledge we headed off and the plan was to fill up with fuel in Burnie, about ten minutes up the road. We did this and Lizzie had quite a drink of her expensive liquor with the bowser stopping at $99.00, the highest we had spent in one filling. Never mind we had to get it and as we don't know the area, we could waste more money looking for cheaper petrol than we save.

From Burnie it was off to Wynyard to see if there were any tulips up on Table Cape and on the way, we spotted a seafood place that had Crayfish and Oysters so we pulled in. The Oysters were huge and we bought a dozen that we quickly devoured in the Motorhome before climbing Table Cape. Seems the tulips have got new competition with poppies being grown here in large quantities, and I suspect there must be a better market for poppies at the moment as we have seen them heaps around Tassie. We stopped at the lookout at Table Cape and after taking some photos of the scenery, including the very few tulips we could find and the majestic lighthouse, we tucked into the cold KFC that we had in the fridge for lunch.

A bit further down the road we passed another of the Tassie fires that was south of the Sisters Beach area and it appeared to still be smouldering a bit. Soon after we spotted a farm that had eggs for sale and we bought a dozen before cruising into Stanley and straight onto the foreshore where we would spend the next day or two. The conditions at Stanley were very windy but by late afternoon they had died down a bit and we looked forward to a pleasant evening with the waves breaking only metres from Lizzie's windows.

Day **111**

Well I did it again thinking that I could get away with sleeping sideways in the Motorhome. Old Lizzie has a fundamental flaw in the fact that to get the best sleeping position (slightly up at the back), the shower doesn't drain properly. So last night I thought after our showers I would move the Motor home to a sleeping position. Thing is I got lazy and said to Tee, "why don't we sleep sideways. The problem is that I am too long for the Motorhome sideways and I get all bunched up. The previous owners were not as tall as me so it wasn't an issue. Add to that that the shower tray on the wrong angle not only doesn't fill but it overflows, and we don't want that. Over the next few days, I am going to look for other solutions, maybe like changing the pipe work under the Motorhome. Today we planned on just going for walks in the area so I could always have a power nap in the afternoon ☺

After Brekkie I checked my emails of which I had one from my mum. Now mum is looking out for our home while we are away as we had toyed with the idea of selling it but the Real Estate market in our area (and most of Australia) is pretty ordinary at present. Since we had left there had been very little rain in our home region which was good in the fact that I didn't need to pay the mower man as often but the garden was now seriously drying out (according to mum). The email sounded all doom and gloom as there was huge rains happening which had been caused by Cyclone Oswald and winds to match. I checked the BOM (Bureau of Meteorology) site and there was a warning out for low level flooding. I then checked the Moreton Bay Regional Council site and it also showed a warning and our area was in the group of "at risk" areas. Our home is significantly higher than a lot in our area, but it was still a concern.

We drove Lizzie into town, now we could have walked but I still don't feel comfortable leaving the Motorhome where there are not too many people. I am concerned that someone may get into it and steal our memories. Now you cannot go to Stanley without visiting "the nut" and the best way to appreciate it is to climb it.

When we arrived in "The Nut" car park I noticed I had mobile phone reception and I decided to ring my neighbour Brian for an update on how things were back home. Unfortunately, he wasn't home so I left a message then rang Mum. Mum was concerned about the winds mostly and I was concerned about the flooding. By now it was 9-30am Brizzy time with high tide due at 10-00am. I spoke to mum and asked her to ring Wayne (our mower guy) as he lived in the area and could check our place for us. Mum lives close but there is a low-lying area between our homes, that is always one of the first to flood, so we decided it was not safe for her to check our home. We also decided to talk after the high tide which would be after we had a walk on "the nut".

Tee wasn't feeling too well this morning and from the start of the climb she was struggling, which is strange really as I thought I would be the one struggling after the sleep I had last night. To be honest though it is a serious climb that only people of moderate to high fitness should do and for the rest "there is a chairlift!" Last time we were here we decided to take the chairlift as a novelty and on the way down it was so cold and windy, I thought Tee's nose would snap off. In fact, she got a bad ear ache from it and it took her the rest of the day to get over it. We climbed to the top and after a short rest on the bench at the top Tee was starting to feel better and we decided to also walk the full circuit around the top. It is a lovely walk and the view is to die for. More importantly the weather was superb and the wind was only moderate – which is a "good day" for Stanley. We took a heap of photos and then tackled the decent which is nearly as hard as the climb.

Not long after we reached the car park mum called me to tell me that our mower guy had reported to her that the area was OK and that only very low properties had any issues. This was a great relief to us as we were not sure, and it is always a bit stressful when you can't see for yourself. He also told mum that he would check our home and that if she didn't hear from him; she should assume all was good. I said to her that both our homes were very well built and that the winds would not blow the roofs off them.

We then drove into the centre of Stanley to look around the shops there. It is a lovely town with 90% of the homes being restored and in pristine condition which really adds to its already natural beauty. It was now after lunchtime so we decided to go back to our campsite on the beachfront, have a feed, then enjoy the glorious sunshine. I also managed to slip in a power nap that lasted over an hour, that's what all that exercise and fresh air will do to you. In the evening we went for another walk on the beach with my mind still wondering how our home was doing. Fortunately, when we got back, I had an email from our lovely neighbour Brian who informed us that all was well with our place and as I hadn't heard from Mum, I assumed that our mower guy had also checked and all was good. Gee Whiz what a relief! So now with our minds at rest and the Motorhome parked in a good sleeping position we could get a great night's sleep.

Day **112**

A new day begins and our hopes are that the flood issue is past its highest point and we are spared anymore scary moments. Apparently, Bundaberg and Brisbane are coping a flogging and it hasn't reached its peak in either area. Bundaberg is where Clem and Betty are from, one of the first couples we got to meet and get to know on our journey. We will send them an email in the hope that they have been spared the floodwaters.

Our journey for today will take us a short distance to the town of Smithton where we will check out a base camp for travelling to the two far North West points of Woolnorth and Green point. We got to the town of Smithton in less than an hour and it is quite a big place with a small shopping district and an array of all types of homes. Some homes were a bit run down but other hilltop homes had lovely ocean views and again others were large homes on acreage. It certainly looked like a healthy town and even on this Australia Day public holiday it was quite busy. We searched for, and quickly found, the dump point and I got to again perform my favourite chore. The fresh water tap was close by so I filled up our tank for our everyday use. With our drinking water we are checking water in various towns, and when we get a good one, we fill up three ten litre tanks which we store in the Motorhome and filter as needed. We have not had to buy water since Cooma I think, which has been a great saving.

Around the corner from the Dump Point we found the free camp area that was a small car park near a lovely park and a small marina. As small as it was the area was level and right near the water so we gave it a tick and started on our trip out to the far North West area of Tassie called Woolnorth. The road out to Woolnorth took us through some nice country that resembled Northern Victoria more than it did the rest of Tassie. It was fairly flat and good grass cover that is well suited to cattle, not that most of Tassie isn't, it was just that this place was different. Not a lot of people seem to populate this area and the journey for the most was a little dull.

We passed the turnoff to Montagu Park which we will explore on the way back from Woolnorth. As we approached Woolnorth, we saw a number of wind farms and the size of these are not apparent until you get closer to them, they are huge, making trees look tiny. When we got to Woolnorth, we were quite disappointed as we could not get to the beach as it becomes private property well before the ocean. I had not done my homework, as if I had, I would have found that the land was granted to the Van Diemens Land company in the eighteen hundreds, some 25,000 acres or so, and included Robbins Island as well as some other smaller Islands.

We had been travelling along a stretch of dirt road (four or so Kilometres in fact) which I had expected as the Camp6 book showed this. But it was a disappointment to be confronted by a "Keep Out Private Property Sign" at the end of it. As we had been travelling on the dirt section, I noticed a four-wheel drive approaching from behind. I tried to speed up a bit as I didn't want Lizzie to be covered in dust, or worse still, receive a broken windscreen. Neither of these things was going to happen as the Keep Out Sign put an end to the excitement.

As we pulled up though the driver stopped and asked if we wanted to look at the place, to which we replied "that would be lovely". He told us to follow him to the village where he would ask the caretaker if we could look around. Tee and I were so impressed with this gesture and we followed in anticipation. But unfortunately, when we got there, we were refused entry as they had a tourist deal with a local company and this company had exclusive tourist rights. We thanked the guy who had been so wonderful in trying to get us in, and with that we headed back to Smithton. Later that day I checked the Internet to see how much the tours were and a half day tour cost $77-50 per person which was way out of our meagre budget.

On the way back to Smithton we still had a chance to glimpse the ocean at Stony Point, or Montagu Park as it was called. We travelled to the turnoff and then onto the short section of dirt road prior to reaching the Ocean. But again, the only way to see the beach was via a property.

Fortunately, this time it was a Council Caravan Park and we decided to look at it for a possible stay overnight or at least it gave as an opportunity to see the beach. The campsite was quite well priced at $10.50 overnight and they even had a figure for a stay of six months, which was $420.00 for two people. This works out at $2.31 per night for two people, and must be the cheapest accommodation on the planet. It is half the price we pay just for council rates back home. We headed towards the marked boat ramp and the colour of the ocean there was sensational, but for us there was little else to do. If we had a boat with us, I think we would have stayed and explored the local Islands but we didn't so we headed off back to Smithton.

When we arrived back at Smithton, I looked at the map to discover that basically from Smithton all the way around the coast to Green Point, Montagu Park is the only spot you can reach the beach. We both found this quite amazing. We settled into our Free camp area and enjoyed a peaceful and quiet late afternoon and evening.

Day **113**

We awoke to bright sunshine this morning and contrary to its reputation, Tassie has turned on a fantastic string of good days weatherwise, for almost our entire time here. As town was close and there were a number of vehicles in the free camp area, we decided to go for a morning walk. In fact, it turned out to be quite a long walk as we went back through town and up a huge hill which brought us to a heap of lovely homes that had stunning views all over Duck Bay. On the way back we visited a local green grocer that we had spotted on the way in and bought some lovely fruit and veg. Both Tee and I were surprised that all over Tassie the price of fruit and veg has been quite high and substantially higher than home in Queensland, it was not what we expected.

The plan for today was to have a day trip to Green Point and again return to here (Smithton) for another night. The weather was superb, about twenty-one degrees and with a light wind we knew we were in for a lovely day. Feeling fit after our walk we set off for Green Point only stopping briefly at the entrance to the free camp to say goodbye to an elderly couple from Victoria that we had chatted with last evening. The drive to Green Point was a little nicer than to Woolnorth with some patches of forest area and more undulation to the countryside.

As we reached the ridge above Green Point, we spotted the ocean which was basking in the superb sunshine that it had been graced with. The place looked stunning with its crystal blue water and its rolling white waves gently breaking on the shoreline. The only blot on the landscape was the Wind Turbines which are not what I would call offensive looking but are not exactly natural looking either. There is a free camp here near the picnic and day area but we have to go back through Smithton anyway and time was not restricting our return today.

There were people surfing and surf fishing, but not a heap of people, it was lovely here. Tee and I decided to go for a walk along the beach where she looked for sea sponges and I took photos of seagulls, which were in huge numbers, along with lovely rock formations and pretty bays. Tee didn't walk for long as it was a little windy for her even though it was mild in comparison to other time I had been here. I continued for my adventure, climbing rocks and taking photos of all the areas natural beauty. When I got back the Motorhome was surrounded by cars and most were people going for a surf, so we decided to head off slowly as we did not want to get blocked in. We headed back to Smithton at a casual pace and arrived back about two which we decided was a good time to have some Linner. Linner – what the hell is that you say? Well Tee and I like to think that we invented it. It is the meal you have when every day is your own and you don't have to answer to anyone or be anywhere at a certain time. It also allows you to have a light snack in the evening and not be too full when you go to sleep.

We had a quiet afternoon and evening with Tee reading and I writing. Late afternoon we had a visitor from town, his name was Huey and he turned up at the free camp area on his pushbike. He proceeded to knock on our door and invite us to the local RSL club for lunch tomorrow. He was a friendly chap and we said we would make an effort to get there. He proceeded to tell us that the RSL club had just reopened and they were trying hard to promote it and get it financial again. He also told us that his wife Joy was the cook there and she would look after us. With that he was off. We thought – what a great fella, and felt that more small towns should do this to bring people into their town. He had a great community spirit and we were keen to support that. We went to bed thinking what a lovely place Smithton had been, it wasn't overly pretty but it had a good feel about it and the vibe was good – we all know how important the vibe is!

Day **114**

ast night some clown had a crack at ruining the reputation of Smithton in our eyes by speeding out of the area we were camped in and doing a burnout. It was 2-00am and although annoyed by this we still woke up in a positive frame of mind. As both of us did not feel hungry we skipped brekkie and decided to go for a walk through town.

We wanted to top up our supplies in town and maybe check out the second hand stores. It wasn't quite 10-00am by the time we reached the shops so the second hand store had not yet opened – most shops open at 10-00am here – so we hunted around to see if we could locate the RSL club. The brochure that Huey had given us had all the info about the club, except the address. We spotted a lady getting out of her car who looked like a local and we asked her where the RSL was located, and as is often the way, it was across the road and just out of our immediate sight. We thanked her before heading off to the second hand store again as it had just ticked over ten.

As is the case with many of these Tassie towns the second hand stores are a treasure trove of fantastic items. We bought some lovely Royal Dolton plates, some more good books and a host of other items. We have to start taking care of what we buy from now on as at this rate we will have to start throwing our clothes away to fit everything into our Motorhome. Never mind we are having a great time. We then strode off to Woollies where we found the grocery prices very reasonable compared to many other towns in Tassie.

With all our nick knacks and all our groceries, I was not looking forward to the walk back to our Motorhome and Tee said I more resembled a pack horse than a husband. She always knew what to say to make me feel good! We finally got back to the Motorhome and I rubbed my hands with vigour trying to get the grove marks out and blood back into my fingers. Tee was right onto it though and asked me if I wanted a cuppa, funny how I forget things when I think about my stomach.

After a cuppa we did a few chores around the Motorhome and before we knew it, it was a little after twelve and the RSL would be serving up lunch. We were going to walk down again but it had started raining. We were not staying in Smithton after lunch as we had planned to go back to Stanley for a few nights before heading to Penguin and then onto the Spirit of Tassie back to Melbourne, so we drove Lizzie to the RSL.

It was a quaint little place that was immaculate in presentation even though it was old in years. There were already a number of people having lunch, most of them oldies.

Both Tee and I were very hungry as we had had nothing to eat so far today and we raced up to the counter, almost obviously, and we ordered the Chicken Parma which is a specialty in many Aussie institutions. I spotted the lady who I presumed was Huey's wife and asked her if she was Huey's better half, to which she answered "yes I am". I followed by telling her that Huey had asked us to come down and that he was doing a fabulous job drumming up business. She laughed and said "I have to keep him useful".

As all the meals were ready, we got ours served up immediately, which in no way disappointed us as we were both starving. We sat down at one of the numerous tables with all of them being covered in fresh white table clothes. It was a lovely touch. Tee and I made short work of lunch and when we finished Joy (Huey's wife) came over and asked "how did you know I was Huey's wife; did he say that I was the short fat one!" I had to fix this one up so I replied "Don't be silly it was easy to pick you out as Huey said you were the cheerful one that could light up a room instantly". To which she replied "bullshit, you blokes always cover up for each other!" We all had a laugh but by the look in her eyes I could tell Joy wasn't sure what Huey had said. Hopefully he could still ride a pushbike in the morning.

We left the RSL both satisfied and happy, and we now only had to fill up with fuel before heading to Stanley. I had plotted a path to Stanley that would take us thorough some country towns, and although nearly doubling the distance it would make the journey a lot more interesting. We found the Shell Servo we wanted that would honour our 8c per litre discount voucher and headed off on my plotted path. The countryside was again lovely and ever changing, as much of Tasmania is, and even though I had doubled the distance to Stanley we arrived there quite quickly.

The weather was not so good but as the afternoon wore on it got more promising. We had parked Lizzie on the foreshore again and as the weather improved, we decided to go for a walk. We had a quiet evening and only had a light dinner as Lunch had done the trick and that Chicken Parma hit the spot.

Day **115**

Overnight it just pissed down almost all night and although no good for tourists I am sure that the rain had killed off the last of the fires and there would be some very happy fire-fighters around Tassie. Basically, we did nothing today as it drizzled on and off all day and the temperature was very cool also. Tee finished her Jackie Collins book and started the Lindy Chamberlain book "Through my eyes" and I finished Gallipoli and started "Bad Ground" the book about the Beaconsfield mine disaster.

Day **116**

Today started maturely for me as I woke and tuned to Tee giving her a pinch and a punch and saying "first of the month!" Tee was so impressed; I could see it in her eyes! Last night we heard some strange sounds and quickly identified them as penguins feeding their young in the burrows that were within metres of our Motorhome.

The weather here is so changeable as we woke up this morning to brilliant sunshine. We went for a walk up to "The Nut" as they call it, and we went as far as the car park to check our mobiles, no messages cool. We walked back to the Motorhome and prepared to head to Penguin for our last full day and night in Tassie. It is always nice to travel on a sunny day and as it was so cold and wet yesterday, we were going to just drive straight to Penguin without stopping, but the sun changed our plans. We looked at the map and decided that we would take a detour through a little town called Flowerdale and then stop at Wynyard for lunch and a walk through its town centre.

On our way to Stanley a week or so ago we had picked up some farm eggs from a home on the side of the highway, and as we were running low on eggs again, we kept our eyes open for it. We found it shortly after and got the loveliest big fresh eggs you could imagine. Going by the last batch they should be very tasty. Not long after that we found the turnoff to Flowerdale and went for a lovely short country drive. It is amazing how quickly the place had greened up, as last week it was brown and dry. Although it was by no means lush yet the whole area was green again and looking more like the postcard Tassie.

We drove into Wynyard and through the main street to a park where we decided to have lunch. I had a hankering for a bacon and egg wrap which would be mainly due to the yummy looking eggs that we had just purchased. I set up the cooker outside and Tee sliced up some tomato and lettuce to go with it. That hit the spot, now off to Wynyard to pick up a few things and check out the second hand stores. The town was charming and reminded us of what our area around home was like about twenty years ago. After we picked up some butter from the supermarket, we found a couple of second hand stores and tried without luck NOT to buy anything. I found Steve Waugh's autobiography – I thought I would give him a second chance and Tee found a book called "Why men don't listen and women can't read maps" – how ironic – but I am sure all couples say that when they see the book. Tee also bought a couple of berets and you wouldn't believe it but one of them was a reddish colour. What a cliché – she bought a raspberry beret, from a second hand store – you could write a song about it!

We strolled back to the Motorhome and off to Penguin for the day and our last night in Tassie. When we got to Penguin, we headed for the Lions Park in the hope it was not full, as we had a great spot there overlooking the ocean when here last week. There were only a few cars and one Motorhome with the best news being that our special spot was free. We filled Lizzie up with water and went for a brief walk before settling in and enjoying the charming view.

Day **117**

Today is the day we go back to Australia, just kidding Tasmanians; we all know you are part of Australia like New Zealand. I am quite happy to upset a Kiwi though so I won't be apologizing for that. We enjoyed our time in Tassie but we did feel a little trapped and as we had been here many times before we started to run out of things to see. If we had a four-wheel drive and a boat it would be a different story as we could have then added another month to our trip here.

Penguin was lovely this morning and we have really enjoyed the North West and West coast but today we have a ferry to catch. Our ferry doesn't depart until 7-30pm so we decided to stay in Penguin until about lunch time catching up with emails and doing some more reading. Before doing that though we went for a walk around town and I dropped into the local Information centre to collect a key for the local Dump Point. Some places lock their dump points as they believe their shit may be stolen; apparently there has been a spate of shit stealers operating in the area. They told me that there was no key and they had no idea it was locked. I told them I hadn't been there yet so I would check and let them know, but if I didn't return, they would know it was open.

After our walk we read for a while and then started doing our checks for departure, which included filtering drinking water – topping up the drinking water and – topping up the water tanks. Then we could leave to do my favourite task; "empty the shitter". We left and went to find the dump point, which we discovered had its cover completely ripped off. Perhaps there was a shit thief after all.

It was now a little after twelve noon so we decided to head for Devonport and stop at Ulverstone on the way for some lunch. The plan was to get some KFC which we could eat for lunch and then take the rest on the Ferry for Dinner. We stopped for lunch and a cuppa then continued along the coast to Devonport. We arrived at Devonport at two thirty so we had over two hours to kill before the ferry was loaded. More reading and good Internet reception helped us pass the time and then we were loaded.

When we came to Tassie, we did it on a day sail and it was quite boring as there is only so much you can do, so we decided on the way back we would get a recliner lounge on a night sail and sleep all the way back. But during our stay in Tassie I was speaking to a fella from the Q (Queensland) and he said that you get brats running around and the recliners are quite close together. Well that sealed the deal for us and we upgraded to a cabin. Not that we are snobs, we just hate crowds almost as much as we hate brats.

We were slowly loaded onto the Ferry, and I mean slowly, as we were parked in a car park for an hour and a half before loaded. In fact, the Devonport operation seems less sophisticated than the Melbourne end and the crew don't seem that happy. Maybe we just got them on a bad day. Eventually we made it to our cabin and it was lovely to have our privacy and A BIG SHOWER – I even got to have a shave with A BIG MIRROR and HOT WATER – OMG it was heaven on the high seas. We ate our KFC and then lay down to watch a movie before bed. I was soooo lucky; I got to watch Steel Magnolias what a treat. Well at least it set me up for my next task – SLEEPING.

Day **118**

Before we knew it, the loudspeaker was going and a lady, who was obviously half asleep, was welcoming us into Devonport where she said we would arrive in forty-five minutes. Now we couldn't have slept through landing in Melbourne and gone all the way back to Tassie, could we? All jokes aside, it is the only way to travel on the Spirit of Tasmania unless you haven't been before. In that case I would recommend one day sailing and best out of Melbourne as there is a lot to see in the bay before leaving the heads.

We had arrived at 6-00am which was fifteen minutes early and we were actually on the freeway to Geelong at 6-03am. It was amazing and proved my theory that the Melbourne end of the operation seemed more streamline. We got to Geelong where we stopped for a cuppa and some brekkie in a local park before heading for Torquay.

When Tee went to heat the water for a cuppa, she discovered that the gas had run out – and this time it really run out, it was just not me forgetting to turn the gas on (who me never!). This meant that although we thought our chores list was complete for our trip on the Great Ocean Road, we now had to fill our gas bottle. Keep in mind that it is now 8-00am on a Sunday morning.

We searched through a fair bit of Geelong looking for a place that filled gas bottles, with no success, mainly due to the time and day and the fact that most places do swap and go. On the outskirts of Geelong, we found an Anaconda store where they fill them but it was only 8-30am and they didn't open until 10-00am. In hindsight we should have had a nap and waited but we headed off to Torquay.

By the time we got to Torquay it was almost 9-00am and the Mitre 10 was opening at 9-00am. I took the bottle in and had it filled by a gentleman that was less than helpful (lets call him Ross – his real name) and when I got it back I was shocked to be charged $23.99 for the fill and I am sure it was not completely full either. When I put it back into the Motorhome, I also noticed that the tap was bent – something I hadn't noticed before. By this stage I was totally pissed off as the last place I filled at it cost me $16.00 which was also a Mitre 10 near Port Albert Victoria. Anyway, as you do as a consumer in Australia, you take it and move on. I got five weeks use out of the last fill so I will wait to see how long this lasts before making a complaint to Mitre 10. I wonder if Scott Cam would help me out, I bet Jamie Durie would. (FYI – Scott does the Mitre 10 ads).

I would not mention this but Ross of Torquay really pissed me off; "Torquay is not the start of the Great Ocean Road" as they claim and in fact is probably not even worth visiting as there are far more less cluttered areas on the real Great Ocean Road. As you can tell I wasn't having the best of days and as we started our tour of the Great Ocean Road, I soon realized that we should find a place to camp as it was a Sunday and the traffic was crazy.

We got to Lorne which was crowded with people and this sealed it for us so we headed inland to the Great Otway National Park and a free camp there which was only twelve kilometres from the Great Ocean Road. We could relax, have a nap and prepare for a relaxing trip tomorrow and besides we have no place to be and are in no hurry to get there.

As we travelled inland the crowds disappeared and the area got prettier and prettier until we reached our free camp area. We had a nap and a yummy dinner of sausages and veggies then a fabulous nine-hour sleep.

Day **119**

After our fabulous sleep we both felt much better and yet we still pondered why we so tired yesterday. Never mind today was a new day and we had new adventures and places to explore. But unfortunately, Mother Nature had other ideas and gave us a cloudy and drizzly morning. As we had no place to be and all the time in the world to get there we decided to stay put for the day and enjoy the bush of the Great Otway National Park.

The day was lovely and relaxing, and for most of it we were the only ones in the free camp area. But as usually happens we got a surge of people around four in the afternoon. On the weather front by 4-00pm the sun was out again and we could be optimistic that the next day would also be sunny. It was exciting as we were now well rested and with the weather looking promising the Great Ocean Road was going to be a great day tomorrow.

All this anticipation for a great day tomorrow was put in to jeopardy within the next few hours as camper after camper of overseas backpackers started swarming in. Our experience with these types has been mixed and we have found that they are OK if there are not too many of them, but tonight the place would have over fifty of them and our sleep was in serious jeopardy of being disrupted. First up went an outside shower strung up on the toilet block that they all used until the whole water tank was emptied (no running water left for anyone else). Then the fires were lit and the carry on went well into the night, in fact it was close to 11-30pm when a group of French girls near our van went to bed and they ensured that we had no hope of sleeping before then. In fact, even when they went to their van, they were banking doors and making a ruckus until around midnight.

Now you may say oh you old fuddy duddy, but if this happens night after night it really affects you. And to those who still think I am a fuddy duddy well I rarely see any of these people out of their vans or tents before 9-00am, so they shouldn't have any problem with me returning the favour to them at 7-00am.

Day **120**

This is exactly what I did this morning, as I returned all the respect that they had given me the night before. I banged every door ten times each on the Motorhome to ensure they got the message and I was pleased to see the curtains on their van open and shut on many occasions. This is not normally something I would do but they had really pissed me off and even Tee gave them a door bang as we drove alongside their camper on our way out. There was an elderly couple just near us and as we left the gentleman was returning from the toilet. The poor bugger looked zonked with his eyes hanging out of his head as we waved goodbye to him.

I believe that the behaviour of these young adults is what gives campers a bad name and my experience with 99% of caravaner's and Motorhomers is that they leave a place cleaner than when they got there and that many oversees ex-students are abusing the privilege of visiting our country. My proof of this came as we got back into Lorne on our way to the Great Ocean Road.

We pulled into a beach area to take some photos and we were met with another wall of campers that lined the front of the beach car park. Most of these ex-students were bathing in the surf and having breakfast on the picnic tables and there was rubbish everywhere. There was also about five or six council workers cleaning up. I said to one of them that I thought it was disgraceful how the Council workers looked like these people's servants. His reply to me was "I agree, and this is a good day as the weekends are much worse!"

Now on with our travels – I have had my whinge now and the scenery is helping me forget how tired I am. But Tee and I are niggling at each other a bit and I decided to be extra nice as I did not want our tiredness to spoil the rest of the day. Our plan was to travel about half the Great Ocean Road and stop just past the Cape Otway lighthouse. The journey from Lorne to Apollo Bay was superb with all the twists and turns that you expect to see with the reputation that this road has.

The goshes and OMG's were flying think and fast as this coastline rivals any that we have seen.

We saw one guy driving a Ferrari which he had obviously hired, as all you could here was it jerking though its low gears at high pitch, and Tee spotted that his girlfriend looked suitably unimpressed by the whole ordeal as her hair resembled an eagle's nest.

We arrived at Apollo Bay to find it a lot quieter and less "sophisticated" than Lorne, which Tee and I think is a good thing. It seemed to scream – if you are here just for the café lattes - Fuck Off. It is more of what I think most people expect from a seaside town and it certainly hadn't attracted the camper riff raff like Lorne. Tee and I thought it was lovely.

Not long after Apollo Bay we took a left turn to look at the Cape Otway lighthouse which is located about twelve Kilometres off the Great Ocean road. It was a nice but narrow stretch of road and when we got about eight or so kilometres in, we saw people pulling over to the side of the road everywhere. It took us a few minutes to realize that they were all looking at Koalas that were scattered in large numbers down this narrow stretch of road to the lighthouse. We soon spotted another in front of us that had a nice clearing beside him where we could pull over safely, something that was not done by many other vehicles who just stopped in the middle of the road. It was not too much of a problem though as the road was quite quiet and everyone seemed aware of the constant stopping.

The fella we stopped to look at was quite a show off and was lazing there with one leg and one arm daggling from the tree, and he had one eye shut and the other firmly placed on our movements. He was adorable! We took a heap of photos and continued on our way.

The Cape Otway lighthouse was a bit disappointing though as there was a charge to go and see it. Tee and I are adamant that we won't go to paid attractions as we are not on holidays for a short time and these fees would chew up our budget in no time, if we allowed them to. So instead we went for a walk along the coastline to where we got a great view of the lighthouse from a distance and we took a few photos before returning to our Motorhome.

Now we had a bit of a dilemma, as we were getting close to our intended campsite but it was not even lunchtime yet. After a short discussion Tee and I decided we would continue through to Warrnambool which would complete our whole journey of the Great Ocean Road in one day instead of two. We probably could have stopped anyway but the weather was so good and there was no guarantee that it would be this good tomorrow. It was also only another 100 klm's so we are not talking marathon driving either.

We carried on driving until the small town of Princetown where we stopped for lunch. We were tempted to stop there for the day but with the sun shining and the Twelve Apostles very close we pushed on. And when we spotted the first rock formation, we were glad we did as it was spectacular. Soon after we pulled into the car park of the Twelve Apostles that is on the other side of the road, and they have tunnelled under the road for safety. It also stops the car park detracting from the area's natural beauty, which is a great idea. We walked amongst the hundred or so lookers and marvelled at the stunning formation that Mother Nature had created. This is another of my "must see" places – no excuses.

Over the next ten kilometres there was formation after formation that required our viewing with each taking a reasonable walk to reach. Over the course of the next few hours we viewed most of these until they started to look the same and our tired legs started to object. We briefly stopped in Port Campbell that is unusual in the fact that it surrounds a narrow beach that has been carved out of the high cliffs, but again with the camper army taking over front row and centre of the beach we moved on.

The rest of our trip to Warrnambool was pleasant but uneventful with only a petrol stop before arriving in town and looking for our next campsite. We found the showgrounds where we planned to stay and paid the $20-00 for a powered site. But with poor facilities that were old and dirty it is certainly not going on my recommended campsite list; in fact, I would recommend you avoid it as it is also noisy in the early morning with a scrap yard right next door.

Now Warrnambool is nothing like I remember it from my childhood as it is huge, but it did allow me to pick up some butane and a new camp cooker, as the old one is nearly stuffed. We settled in for the evening and had a reasonable sleep that was cut a bit short by the scrap yard next door that I mentioned earlier.

Day **121**

oday will be a gentle day for us as we did a lot of driving yesterday and it is supposed to get to 34 degrees. In fact, by the time we left the campsite it was already over 25 degrees. We dropped back into Warrnambool as we needed food supplies and would not be in a major town for the next week or so. Tee likes Coles for certain things so we went there. With just over fifty dollars worth that included four bottles of White Crow tomato sauce we were on the road again. As we are not big town fans, we spent little time in Warrnambool and on reflection we probably should have spent another day there. But too late now as we were approaching Tower Hill which is the remnants of a collapsed volcano that is now like a sanctuary for native animals and from my memory had a lovely picnic area. The last time I was here I could not have been more that ten years old and all I remember are the Emus trying to steal my lunch and the beauty of the area.

I was on the phone last night to Rodney my step brother and he told me to take the road on the right before Tower Hill which takes you up onto the rim of the crater and gives a panoramic view of the area. We did this but what we saw was a little ordinary and we hoped it was not like that when we got in there. Unfortunately, though it was not much better inside the crater and there were hardly any native animals to be seen. We saw one Koala, one echidna and three emus which I thought was sad and I would have liked to keep my childhood memory of the place instead of this. The picnic area was OK but again not as nice as I remembered it. I will try and make excuses for it now and say that it was hot and the summer had been very dry, but I believe in my heart that this place is not well managed and has gone downhill big-time.

What a shame, but onwards we travel to our next destination of Port Fairy. On the way to Port Fairy we spotted a turnoff to the Crags, which we saw in the brochure and we went to have a look. The view was fantastic from the viewing platform and if we hadn't seen the Twelve Apostles the day before we would have thought the view was stunning. My memories of Port Fairy are of a big shark strung up on a jetty and not much else. We arrived to see a charming seaside town of lovingly restored historic buildings and a heap of houseproud residents. After a look around the town of Port Fairy we went down to the to the small Wharf area for a look at the only place I remember in Port Fairy from my childhood. But it had completely changed and the Jetty where I saw the strung-up shark was no longer there, it had been replaced by many other jetties and some flash new homes.

It was now about lunchtime and we found a lovely fish and chip shop right on the water where we decided to buy lunch. It was a little pricey but the position was lovely and we placed our order of flake and chips. I noticed when the older gentleman spoke to the young lad, he had a Maltese accent and I said to him – you are Maltese hey! Turns out he came to Australia as an orphan in 1964, one year after I was born. I may not have mentioned this but my mother was born in Malta and came to Australia as a five-year-old after WW2. We chatted for a while and when our order was ready, he brought it out to us and said "there is another piece of fish for you as you are Maltese". My grandad always told me that Maltese look after each other and we thought the gesture was lovely, and we knew the Fish and chips were Yummy.

We left Port Fairy and continued our journey along the coast towards Portland with our intended destination being at a free camp just north of Narrawong on the road to Portland. This place had a tick in the Camps6 book and we really hoped this time it lived up to it as it was very hot with the mercury tipping 36 degrees. We found the turning to the campsite and although at the start of the way in it looked a bit dodgy, when we got there it was quite nice. In fact, being quite treed and elevated the camp area felt four to five degrees cooler than the coastline we had been travelling.

We settled in for the afternoon and evening an even got to view some wildlife in the form of Kangaroo's and Parrots that were so friendly we could hand feed them.

Day **122**

Today we are off to the base of the Grampians and in addition we need to do some domestic choirs and pick up a few bibs and bobs. We thought while we were down this way though we would go and look at Portland before heading inland again. We reached Portland in a short amount of time and although it was OK it felt very industrial and there was an odd odour in the air. This stopped us from staying too long and we were soon heading inland. We drove through Heywood and a few other towns before arriving in Hamilton.

Now Hamilton it turns out was a very easy town to navigate by foot and we did most of our chores on foot, which included some personal shopping and to search for an electrical store and a Laundromat. We completed all of these chores including doing all the washing, buying petrol and all the other bits and pieces by 2-00pm. Problem was we hadn't had lunch and it was a bit late to start searching for a park and cook. Never fear KFC was a block away, so I walked there and bought some lunch that we ate in front of the Laundromat.

After lunch we had a challenging experience with the navigator and this time (Karen) the navigator was right. We eventually headed in the right direction and arrived at the southern tip of the Grampians by mid afternoon to our free camp spot which was just before the town of Dunkeld. It was right next to the highway and a bit noisy as at the moment there are a lot of trucks passing, but we hope they die down by this evening. The view though to the North is fabulous so we have parked our Motorhome to take full advantage of it.

Day **123**

Well it was a little noisy at this roadside free camp but we didn't sleep to bad. It was cloudy when we woke up so we slept in until 8-00am. Today is "G" Day, we are heading to the Grampians, and we are looking forward to this as it looks like a lovely place. We headed to Dunkeld which was only one or two kilometres up the road, it is also the southern end of the road to Halls Gap and dissects the Grampians. We stopped at the Information Centre in town and went to the toilets there, which were immaculate I might add. The lady at the counter of the Information Centre was busy with another couple but we had found the brochures we needed and were off. The day started cloudy as we started into the Grampians but there were patches of blue sky ahead which looked promising.

We drove at a snail's pace admiring all the rock formations, mainly to the West but the East was also quite attractive. Even though the scenery was nice and the lack of traffic was even nicer we were starting to wonder why people go on about the Grampians. I remember the almond nut farmer, where we stopped on the Victorian side of Bordertown South Australia, was raving about it and so were a number of travellers that we met on the road. Again, it was nice but not – set your socks on fire – fabulous. At least the sun was starting to win its battle with the clouds by now and we could see all the mountain tops in a more effective light.

A fair way into our journey towards Halls Gap we came to a turnoff to Mt William and as it didn't look too impressive, we were not going to turn up there and have a look. But I looked at our map and realized that we were not far from Halls Gap now and we hadn't taken a single turnoff or gone on a single walk so we decided to have a look. It was 12 kilometres in and 12 out so it wasn't a too expensive gamble, in either time or fuel.

As we drove along the road to Mt William, we started to rapidly climb a mountain range which looked promising from a viewing perspective, as up until now the view had been restricted by trees and no turn-ins to stop and view. In fact, that would be one criticism that I had for the whole Grampians experience and that was the lack of pull over areas. Once we started to get some elevation the whole place just lit up with fantastic scenery and amazing rock formations. We got to view the mountains, including Cathedral Rock, which we had driven past but not been able to appreciate fully due to the restricted viewing from the road and lack of pull over spots. So, if you are going to the Grampians then Mt William is a "must see" area as you will be able to view the Grampians from a wonderful perspective as well as see Mt William itself. There is a two kilometre walk at the end of the road that we didn't do but I am sure would be lovely.

After we slowly descended from Mt William, we continued our journey to Halls Gap and stopped, or turned off, at Silverband Road to view the Silverband Falls. The road had been severely damaged by recent floods but you could still access the Falls area. I think it was about a one kilometre walk from the car park to the falls themselves and on the walk there we witnessed a huge amount of damage that the flood had caused to the area. In fact, it really shows how diverse the weather is in our country as when we arrived at the falls it was more what you would call a Watertrickle not a Waterfall. Nice but more water would have helped its appeal. We had lunch in the car park there before heading to Halls Gap.

Now I suppose Halls Gap is what you would call the capital of the Grampians, a term that over emphasises it size, but we did see people and cars which is more than we can say for our journey today. In fact, if you are into bushwalking and like a quiet place then this place in February is ideal as you will have found your utopia. Not being attracted to groups of people we travelled through Halls Gap along the road to Horsham. In fact, if you were to head towards Stawell from Halls Gap you would be out of the Grampians immediately.

We saw a number of campsites in the Grampians but we decided not to use them as they are charge sites and we did not intend to stay in the area more than the one day. I think if you were into tenting and bushwalking, they would be worthwhile but with free camps all around the edges of the Grampians there is no need to pay for camping otherwise.

Along the Road to Horsham we stopped and went on a number of walks. We did MacKenzie Falls (a must see), Reeds Lookout and the Balconies (another must see) and Boroka Lookout (another must see). At Boroka Lookout we saw a couple who were out on the viewing deck having a nap on the ground (or deck). This was weird to Tee and I and Tee's comment was that they were attention seekers as they could have had a nap anywhere in the car park area and they would not have been in the way of other people wanting to use the viewing platform. Worked out Tee had their number as when we went back to the car park, we realized they were driving a pretty red Mercedes Benz. (Wankers).

By this time, we were almost out of the Grampians National Park and we now had a choice of two or three free camp areas reasonably close by. But as we were soon heading to Mt Gambier the free camp at Cheerypool was not only the closest but would save us on fuel, as it was closer to Hamilton (on the way to Mt Gambier). It seemed like no time at all until we reached Cherrypool and found the free camp area. The area was next to a river and had good camp sites but it wasn't all that attractive even though it had a tick in the Camps6 book. There was also suppose to be toilets there but they had obviously been removed as they were now gone. We half expected other campers to stop there later in the evening but we ended up being the only people to stay there the night. We were OK with this as it would make it quieter and we would get a good night sleep – but then things went sour.

When we arrived at Cherrypool I had used my computer for about half an hour and we had filtered sunlight feeding the solar panels – and then the unthinkable happened – our batteries went flat in the Motorhome. This was impossible as we had been driving most of the day and unless something was wrong, we should have had a strong charge. This meant that we had to turn off the fridge at 8-30pm and hope that the freezer didn't thaw out. The problem could have been only one of two things (a) the Motorhome batteries were dying or (b) the charger that is meant to isolate the main battery and charge the house batteries first is not working.

Either way the problem would have to be fixed and an Auto Electrician would have to be sort. In addition to this my laptop battery that has been crook for weeks is now only lasting 15 minutes from a full charge and also needs replacing. We decided that we would ring an auto electrician in the morning and get him to look the Motorhome system.

Day **124**

The stress of these problems has made me a little cranky and it has also interfered with my sleeping which is making me crankier. It is times like these that the confined space of a Motorhome (at least the size one we are in) starts to get to you. It took a huge effort from me to get over it and get on with it, which I knew I had to do. I had 15 mins of battery time to look up auto electricians in Hamilton and check my emails.

Fortunately, I found the numbers quickly and as we had decided to pull into a caravan park until we had this sorted, I got their numbers also.

I rang the only Auto Electrician in Hamilton on their landline without success which is not surprising as it was a Saturday, but fortunately I did get through to the Caravan Park and Shirley at the Hamilton Caravan Park got the auto electricians mobile number for me. I rang David (Auto Elect) and he told me he was out of town until Monday. He was nice about it but I was still frustrated at my inability to get things straight. Tee and I talked about it for a while and decided that we should book in to Shirley's Caravan Park for a week and get all our problems sorted out properly. We went into Hamilton central to see if we could get a battery check at one of the retail outlets but none had good testing equipment for Deep Cycle Batteries and recommended that I see an Auto Electrician. With all our avenues exhausted we decided to go to the Caravan Park and unwind. This would mean also that we could plug in to the mains power and all our troubles would be gone (as long as we didn't travel that is).

Shirley was a great help to us and even gave us a great weekly rate – so if you need a Caravan Park in Hamilton (cnr Dickens and Shakespeare

Street) you know where I will recommend. I also asked Shirley if I could have my laptop battery delivered here and she said "of course", so I jumped online and ordered one immediately. This is another one of those hard things when you are travelling, as you have no fixed address for deliveries. Which is OK until you need that item delivered to you personally. With the laptop battery I could not buy one in any retail outlet and if I ordered it in store it would take a minimum of two weeks.

This stop in Hamilton was a must stop for us as we also needed to recharge our batteries. This can only be done effectively when you are in one place for a while – well it is for us anyway.

Day **125**

The caravan park we are staying in is super quiet and we both had a fabulous night's sleep. Today there was not much we could do to fix the Motorhome, being a Sunday, so we decided to go for a long walk through town and check it out. Hamilton is a mid sized town that we have found to be very easy to get around in, so finding what we need has been a breeze. I knew that the Auto Pro store was open 7 days a week and I have been meaning to change the curtain configuration around in the front of the Motorhome so we can divide the driving cabin from the back. It was a simple job and I had already purchased the cupboard hook I needed, but silly me I had forgotten to bring drill bits.

We went into the Auto Pro shop but they had very limited tools and the drill bits they had were all too big. They helped us with directions to a Hardware store and we continued our walk through town and soon came to the Home Hardware store. We went into the trade section at first and when we finally did get service, we were told the drill bits were in the main store so we went back out and soon realized that we had entered the wrong section of the store. No harm done though as we were served immediately and we were on our way within two minutes thanks to the great service from the young fella working as a greeter.

We continued our walk through the town and really enjoyed looking at all the lovely old homes and how many of them had been kept immaculate. There were huge churches, lovely timber cottages and modern homes all close to each other with most seeming to be on generous sized blocks. We turned one corner and spotted a lake, so we changed direction and headed for a walk around it. Hamilton is a very liveable and pretty town and we are enjoying it immensely. We must have covered a fair bit of it as we would have walked about ten kilometres.

Back at the Motorhome I fitted the new curtain hook and our idea to split the cab from the rear is looking great, it lets in a little more light but it looks a lot tidier and we still have the flexibility to set it up either way each time we stop. We ate dinner and had a quiet evening before hitting the sack as tomorrow was the big day when we would be getting the electrical problem fixed in the Motorhome.

Day **126**

Again, last night it was really quiet at the Hamilton Caravan Park and we both had a great sleep. We awoke about 6-30am and had a cuppa and some brekkie before I rang the Auto Electrician to arrange a time to take Lizzie there. I rang David at about 7-50am hoping to catch him as he opened up his workshop. He answered his phone and told me he had just opened up his workshop and he would walk in and check his book for a time. He gave me a time of 2-00pm THURSDAY – and I said he had to be kidding as he gave me the impression he would do it today, Monday. We had booked into the caravan park for a week but did not expect to wait until the day before we left just for him to look at it. I was furious and let him know we were stuck here waiting to see him but he said the best he could do was Tuesday afternoon and if it was a big job, he wouldn't be able to finish it until Thursday.

Well as angry as I was, I had to suck it up and accept the Tuesday at 2-00pm inspection and I left it at that. I felt as though he had put his local customers in and left me until last, which I could have dealt with if he hadn't indicated that he would look at on Monday when I first called him. A lot of Tradesmen seem to do this as it holds work to them and if fronted, they can say "I didn't promise Monday" even though they implied it. Fucking mind games – I was really pissed off.

I said to Tee that I was going to look at alternatives as I had the booking but if I could do better I would. So, I jumped onto Yellow Pages. com and looked for other Auto Electrician in the area. There were plenty at Warrnambool and Portland but both locations were over an hour drive away and chances are they couldn't now see me before tomorrow either. I said to Tee, fuck it, I am going to fix it myself and after resting a fair bit yesterday I was in the mood to have a go.

I looked through the maze of wires and was starting to get a little spaced out by how complicated it seemed. I searched for loose wiring around the Alternator without success and then went over all the wiring going in and out of the Rotronics devise, but it all looked OK. For some reason I decided to look at the solar unit and discovered a schematic diagram of the whole Motorhome that Ken (the previous owner) had drawn up. On the diagram it showed a fuse on the intake side of the Rotronics devise which I could not find. I had found two fuses on the House battery side of it but they were both OK so I presumed it was not a fuse. For the life of me I could not find this third fuse and thought Ken may not have put it in and neglected to erased it from his drawings. But there was one area I hadn't checked which Tee and I presumed had nothing in it as Ken had said not to worry about it when we asked what it was. We thought that it may have been replaced by the Rotronics devise and was no longer in use. But I decided to open up its case and guess what I found? – "You are so clever" – yes it was a fuse – and yes when I opened up the fuse case it was blown. OMG, I had found the problem and I was so excited and now just to buy another fuse.

It was only 8-45 am and I had found the problem in less than one hour – Tee now had a new superhero – a better one than her old favourite John Travolta – who is said to be gay anyway! We quickly got ready and walked down to the Auto Pro shop where we bought 5 fuses of each size and I even shouted myself some caravan chocks so I didn't have to keep using chunks of wood, then back to the Motorhome we went. In fact, we went to the Information centre first, (the young girl there was fantastic), as we thought once I had replaced the fuse, we could go on a day trip.

Back at the Motorhome I replaced the fuse and immediately the orange charge light came on and we were 100% functional again. By 11-30am we were on the road heading to the Byaduk Caves and the other attractions that the young lady at the Information Centre had recommended as a good day trip. But as usual when we get over excited about having a win, we end up going blindly and not checking maps properly. This time it caused us to turn into the wrong area and we ended up in the Mt Napier State Park.

I can't blame Tee for this one as the map that we obtained from the Information Centre was a little broad and it did look as though the areas were connected. Now if anyone has been into this area, they will tell you that it is more of a track than a road and would be considered a low level 4WD track at that. The problem was that we could not turn around and by the time we could we were over four kilometres into it and just under four kilometres to drive forwards to get out of it. The second problem was that it wasn't until we couldn't turn around again that the track got worse.

But Lizzie stood up and ploughed through it with only minor scratching to her sides as the bracken tried to devour our path. As we got closer to the end of this goat track, we passed a side track that had a ranger's 4WD stationary facing our track. We gave him a wave and he waved back with the most puzzled look you could imagine. I must admit though we must have been a sight ploughing through the bracken on a goat track in an almost five tonne Motorhome. I suspect he must have thought that Chevy Chase was at the wheel. All jokes aside though we were fairly pissed off as the Motorhome was filthy with light scratches to the side, and without care it could have been a lot worse as it was quite rocky.

The lava areas that we travelled to were OK but the dirt roads are a turnoff and very dusty. The Byaduk caves which were on the dirt road were the best, but if you don't want a dirty vehicle then I am not sure you are going to be impressed by what your see. Harman's Valley Lookout is on the main road and worth a stop but the Lava Blisters are not what we imagined; in fact, we didn't know we had passed them as we thought they were part of an old scoria quarry. Never mind, all in all, the day was pretty good and with one more chore to go we headed to Heywood to empty the shitter.

A straight run to Haywood, a smooth shitter emptying and it was on the road back to Hamilton. As we started to leave Hamilton a logging truck (there are heaps in this area) pulled out of a side road right in front of us. I could see him edging to go but we were very close to him and I thought there is no way he would pull out right in front of us. That's where I was wrong as he did do exactly that and Tee and I were just bewildered. Under normal circumstances I would have gone off but I was so relaxed by this time of the day that I just shook my head in disbelief.

What happened next was even more unbelievable as a dark blue Ford overtook us on the inside and quickly flashed his police lights and went after the log truck. We thought to ourselves how unbelievable, and this guy was going to get his just rewards for being an asshole. The police car seemed to be going to pull him over, but then we thought he was not as he was following him for a long way with nothing happening. We lost sight of them and then when we rounded the next bend, there they both were, with one officer at the cab of the truck and the other about 50 metres on directing us to pull over. We did pull over and the officer asked us if we had flashed our lights at the truck to let him in or something to which I replied "I did not" and that we were both bewildered as to why he pulled out in front of us. He took our details and I gave him one of my old business cards in case he needed to contact us and we were on our way.

I noticed on his name tag the name T. Glasl which is a very unusual name. I remembered a Thomas Glasl from when I was at Parade College back in the late 70's but I thought he had died in a house fire. I told Tee that I knew a Thomas Glasl from school and she said it must be him as he looked about my age. But then when I told her that he died in a house fire I remembered that he was in a house fire and was injured but a Michael O'Shea was killed and Thomas was injured. This was freaking me out so I goggle searched his name and in fact T. Glasl was Thomas but I don't know if it is the same Thomas so I am going to email the local police station here and find out. It would be amazing if it was him.

By this time, it was getting close to 3-00pm and I said to Tee we should clean the Motorhome when we got back to the Caravan Park and then I would take her out for dinner. We got back to the Caravan Park at 3-30pm and it took us until after 6-00pm to get Lizzie all scrubbed up with me giving the outside a good clean and Tee cleaning the inside top to bottom. But all the hard work was worth it as she is a good Motorhome and now looks stunning.

We quickly got ready and were down at the Alexandra House Hotel by a little after 7-00pm. Tee was excited about the oysters and I was watering at the mouth about a steak and after we ordered I went to the bar and got us a beer each (Carlton Draught of coarse) and we toasted an unusual mixed day of success and mystery. The beer was free, as Paul at the Caravan Park had given us a couple of complimentary vouchers that came with a meal purchase. After the beers I go us a carafe of house white wine. We really enjoyed the meal as it was only our second night out to a sit-down meal in over four months of travelling. We were also not that use to all that alcohol either as we were quite tipsy by the end of the evening. We walked (or staggered) back to the Caravan Park and soon we were in bed fast asleep. What an amazing day.

Day **127**

Amazingly we slept in until almost 10-00am and I cannot remember the last time we did that. All those drinks really knock us around and the relief of the Motorhome being fixed and cleaned gave us pleasant dreams. I was quite seedy all day today and I have been reading and writing most of the day while Tee has done some clothes washing and cooked a yummy dinner for us. The only other thing that happened was that I got the delivery of my new laptop batteries so really, we are ready to travel. But the rest of the week here will do us good as we can relax and maybe catch a movie and discover more about the lovely town of Hamilton.

Late in the afternoon I started researching T. Glasl to see if they were one in the same. I rang the Heywood Police Station and they said he must be Highway Patrol from either Hamilton or Warrnambool. I then rang the Hamilton Police Station and they said he must be from Warrnambool, and when I rang Warrnambool, they said they did not know him. I spoke further to the female office at Warrnambool and she looked him up for me and said he was from State Highway Patrol that operated out of the Brunswick Head Office. She also said that she could not give out any of his details. I thanked her and left it at that for the evening.

I also tried my new laptop batteries and found that one worked and one didn't so I emailed the company I bought them from and they sent me a problem-solving sheet. These batteries were generic and I was hoping this type of problem didn't happen, but the fact that Toshiba didn't have a replacement battery in the country left me with no option but to get a generic battery, or batteries as it turned out.

I had another idea of how to find out if the Thomas Glasl was in fact the same Thomas Glasl that I went to school with. I emailed another schoolmate from the same year, Tony DeBolfo who wrote for the Old Paradians and also for the Carlton Football club. He was always in touch with ex students and getting stories for his newsletter. In the email I asked Tony if he remembered Thomas Glasl and Michael O'Shea who were in that cabin fire while we were at school. But I did not mention the fact that a Thomas Glasl had pulled me over near Heywood.

My efforts to fix the battery via the company's problem-solving sheet had failed and with a few loose ends for the day we both had an early night.

Day **128**

Suppose to be a warm day today, in the low to mid thirties, so we decided to do a bit of walking around Hamilton. The Information Centre girl had given us a group of points of interest that were in a reasonable walking distance from town. We thought if we left early, we could beat the heat but I had to check my emails first and see if I had anything from Tony. I also had to email the Battery Company and see what they were going to do about my faulty battery. After I finished my emails, we started our morning walk.

The first place on our list to visit was the Ansett Museum, as Hamilton was where Ansett Airlines was created back in 1931. This was the furthest most point of our walk and was about two kilometres from our Caravan Park. We arrived there just after 10-00am but although the opening hours were from 10-00am to 4-00pm there was no one there so we headed of to the second place on our list – the Botanical Gardens.

Not as far to walk this time and what we found when we got there was just lovely. The gardens were fantastic and equal to the standards that you find in capital cities like Melbourne and Hobart but on a smaller scale. By this stage the day has started to heat up and the Botanical Gardens with all its shade offered some welcome relief. We spent about an hour walking around and I would highly recommend that if you are in Hamilton that you take a picnic rug and basket and enjoy this place. We then took a detour to a local second hand shop where we picked up a couple of books before heading to the Art Gallery that is located in the centre of Hamilton. The Art Gallery was also of a very high standard but not really our thing, in saying that if you are into art it is well worth a visit.

We were tempted to go back to the Ansett Museum but by now the weather was really heating up and we were still over a kilometre from our Motorhome. We thought it best to go back and avoid the hottest part of the day.

When we arrived back at the Motorhome, I checked my emails and I had one from Tony and one from the Battery Company. The Battery Company told me to return the battery and they would replace it – good news – and Tony had responded to my email by saying that he had contacted Thomas Glasl's father. He also confirmed what Tee and I had suspected, that Thomas was in the Police Force. With this information I am positive that Thomas Glasl the police officer that I met in Heywood is the same Thomas Glasl that I went to school with – how freaky is that! I then emailed back Tony the story of Thomas pulling me up in Heywood after the Logging Truck incident and how I had given him one of my business cards.

We spent most of the day avoiding the heat apart from my bike ride to the Post Office to post back the faulty battery.

Day **129**

Another day that is meant to rise into the mid thirties and we have decided to stay in the air conditioning of our Motorhome most of the day and then venture out for dinner at the Alexandra House Hotel this evening. We read our new books and did a few chores in the Motorhome while the temperature outside raced into the mid thirties.

Just after lunchtime we had a knock on our Motorhome door and it was Shirley bringing me over my replacement Laptop Battery. The service from this company has been second to none and I quickly plugged it in to ensure that it was functioning correctly. No problems this time and my issues with the Laptop were now at an end. About 5-00pm we got ready to go to dinner and were on our way for our Valentines Dinner by 6-30pm. I did do a detour into the Caravan Park office to thank Shirley for bringing the Battery over and asked her if she received my email on who I bought the batteries from. She said she had and I said that I did not want to recommend them until I knew that they would fix the problem with the dodgy battery promptly. Just so happened that we mentioned we were off to the pub for dinner and Paul gave us another couple of drinks vouchers. (A total coincidence as to why we went to the office.)

We had a great time again at the Alexandra House Hotel and would highly recommend the place to anyone travelling in or around Hamilton. After dinner we walked home and were in bed and asleep by 10-00pm.

Day 130

Now that we have finished all the business we needed sorted in Hamilton (Laptop Batteries and Auto Electrical problem fixed) we didn't really have much reason to stay. But we had paid until Saturday at the Caravan Park and we decided to do some shopping in the morning and do some more chores around the Motorhome.

With the weather again threatening mid thirties we decided to do the shopping early and as we walked home with all our bags of shopping, we were glad we did as it was now only 10-00am but already quite hot. I had not heard from Tony D about T Glasl as yet and was hoping that an email from him was awaiting, but if not, I may give him a call this arvo.

Spent the evening with Paul and Shirley who run the Caravan Park here and they showed us some pictures from when they travelled through the centre of Australia towards Darwin. They are a lovely couple and it has been great staying at this Caravan Park in Hamilton and our visit to the Alexandra House Hotel was especially nice.

Day **131**

Today we are off from Hamilton and heading towards Dartmoor which is suppose to be a really good free camp spot. But first we are going to Mt Eccles National Park to look at the Volcano crater there. It was a pleasant drive to Mt Eccles and we stopped at a roadside market in Macarthur on the way. It was a very small market with very few things of interest to us so we continued to Mt Eccles.

We arrived at Mt Eccles which was a crater containing a body of water and from the lookout it was very pretty with the whole area in a very natural state. There was a walking track that promised to take us to the summit of Mt Eccles so we took off for a morning stroll. In fact, it turned into quite a strenuous hill climb, but when we reached the peak the view from the top rim of the crater was well worth the effort. In fact, going down the hill turned out to be more challenging as the slope was extreme and the surface was quite loose so it was a slow decent. Back at the Motorhome we grabbed a water each before heading towards Heywood.

It was now about 11-00am and the weather was getting quite hot and we were starting to think that maybe we should head towards the coast where it should be cooler. We passed Heywood (the place where I met Officer T Glasl – still haven't heard back from Tony on that yet) and thought it would be silly to go inland now to Dartmoor as we would be there in an hour and we would have to spend a hot afternoon there. So, we decided to proceed to Portland and then onto Nelson.

We arrived in Portland just before midday and thought a good feed of KFC would be nice, as we would be able to have cold chicken for dinner if we were travelling all day today. I grabbed a voucher and was soon back with a feed of chicken and chips that we enjoyed outside in the Motorhome before heading towards Nelson. The weather was a lot cooler by the ocean, as we had hoped, which made travelling a lot more pleasant.

Now we had heard from a number of people that Nelson was a pretty little place and when we arrived, we thought it was OK, but not what we expected. Nelson itself was not on the ocean but more at the end of an inlet that was fed by the Glenelg River. We went to the information centre where we found a "where the hell is Nelson sticker" that I bought for my dad Nelson, and asked about accommodation. The Caravan Parks were a bit ordinary and with time on our hands we decided to push on to Port MacDonnell.

This part of the Journey pushed us into South Australia and after spending such a lovely time in Victoria before and after out Tassie odyssey it was nice to be into a new faze of our travels. Neither Tee nor I had seen all that much of South Australia so this time for us was quite exciting.

On the approach to Port MacDonnell the landscape changed significantly with the Limestone being very dominant and when we approached the coast the ocean was a brilliant shade of blue. Port MacDonnell was very pretty, with its white sandy beaches and onto its rugged rocky outcrops, it was a place built to enjoy. We travelled through town slowly to look at all the facilities available, and then onto the rocky outcrops where we went for a walk to enjoy the lookouts that were scattered everywhere. We were even lucky enough to see a baby penguin and its mother, and although hard to see at the time we took a zoom shot on the camera that captured the little fella in his full glory.

We went to the local Information Centre to ask about accommodation and were told there was only one Caravan Park in town. The young girl who served us seemed to lack any skills in customer service and was totally different than the lovely girl in Hamilton and they would have been about the same age. She didn't even give us any brochures or talk about any of the features or attractions in the town – not much of an Information Centre!

When we got back into the Motorhome, we noticed that it had cooled down considerably and that if we couldn't find anywhere nice here to free camp, we would be OK to head inland now. As we approached the Esplanade, we noticed a Power and Water point similar to the ones used in Caravan Parks. There was another Motorhome sitting there and I decided to ask the lady if this was a camping spot. She was arrogant and rude saying she didn't know and getting quite agitated – I smiled and walked away. The site was right opposite a Take Away Store, and as in other towns the local store looks after camp spots, I thought it would be worth asking them. Well wasn't that a mistake as the lady who ran the store was rude and argumentative and yet still didn't give a definitive answer. I will not go into what she said but it was obvious that they were not an RV friendly town and that was that. So, if you are looking to spend your Tourist dollars on the limestone coast, I would not recommend Port MacDonnell to do it in, but it is a pretty place to do some sightseeing.

By this stage we were only thirty or so kilometres from Mount Gambier and it was tempting just to head to the Caravan Park that I had pre-booked for Sunday night, but with a free camp located between the two areas we thought it would be worth a look. The Free camp area was called Mt Schank and when we arrived there, we knew it was a great place to stay as a number of campers were already there, in addition to the fact it was elevated and there was a lovely breeze. We found a nice spot where the breeze was coming through a gap in the mountains and set up for the evening. By this stage it was almost 6-00pm so we broke out the cold KFC and got stuck into it.

After Dinner we were just kind of sitting around and enjoying the cool breeze when a free camper's worst nightmare occurred. Yes, a Wicked van turned up – and the contents were worse still – Young French Backpacker. I am generalizing of course but they tend to be Feral and quite noisy. They parked a bit away from us so hopefully they won't be disruptive this evening.

Tee piped up and said "seeing it is cooler now why don't we go for a walk to the top of the Volcano crater". At first, I wasn't so keen but it would mean if it was hot in the morning, we would still have seen the Volcano. It was after 8-00pm by this stage and I said to Tee that we would have to go straight away as it would start getting dark in an hour or so, so off we went.

After we walked about a hundred yards or so we realized that it was a fairly steep walk from here to the top and we were soon confronted by a mile of steps. But the temperature was mild now and in fact we should reach the top and get to see a sunset over the Volcano – this motivated us to go on. Another good thing about walking in the late evening, as we were about to find out, is that you are more likely to see wildlife and it wasn't too far up the path that a Wallaby skipped by to say hello.

Twenty or so minutes later we reached the top and WOW what an awesome crater did we see before us. Unlike other craters Mt Schank was a dry crater, which meant you could see deeper into it, this made for spectacular viewing. After taking a pile of photos we realized that if we hurried, we could catch the sun setting over the Volcano. This meant a brisk walk all the way around the crater rim to the other side as we were currently on the Western rim. The brisk walk ended in me jogging to catch a photo before the sun disappeared. We made it in time to get some stunning photo's but that paled into insignificance as to the what we saw next.

We decided to walk the other half of the crater rim completing the full circumference of Mt Schank. We got about fifty metres from where we photographed the sunset and were startled by a Wedge Tailed Eagle that was obviously as startled as we were. It was awesome as he flew into the centre of the crater and then caught a thermal updraft and soared above our heads. Then we looked back to where he flew from to see his lady friend still perched in a dead tree about forty metres into the crater from where we were standing. I took a photo of her and as I approached slowly to get another shot, she too took off. We then had a pair of majestic Eagles soaring above us and Tee and I were in no doubt that they were putting on a show for us as they hovered to great height before pulling in their wings to rapidly drop altitude. With the fading light, stunning views and our two performers we both agreed it was one of the most amazing experiences either of us had ever encountered.

With a renewed feeling and smiles from ear to ear we completed the circuit of the Volcano rim and descended back to our Motorhome. Excited by the experience I was keen to get a look at the photos, so I fired up the laptop and uploaded them for a good view. The photos of the Sunset and the Crater were fantastic but because of the fading light and the movement of the Eagles in flight the Eagle photos were a little blurry.

Tee had a shower while I was doing the photos and when she finished, I turned on the invertor to charge the laptop while I showered. When I got out of the shower Tee said she had to turn the invertor off as the low battery light had come on. We couldn't believe it as we were both sure that the problem had been rectified. Well it got worse as we again had to turn off the fridge and hope that it didn't thaw out by the morning. Our troubles were not confined to the power either as those bloody French Backpackers kept us awake until well after midnight.

Day **132**

Amazed at the highs and lows of yesterday we stayed positive and both agreed that we would at least be now heading into a major town where the problem of the Auxiliary power could be solved. In addition, we were going to a paid site so we wouldn't have ferals interrupting our sleep.

The time it would take to get to Mount Gambier was minimal as it was less than twenty kilometres from Mt Schank. This meant that we could take things slowly and as it was Sunday; we could do nothing about the Auxiliary power problem until Monday anyway. A rest day, and with forty degrees forecast going to a Caravan Park where we could run the air conditioner was a god sent. As luck has it there is a god and as we were prepared to leave Mt Schank a garbage truck arrived and awoke the poor little sleeping Ferals, oohhh – they say god takes many forms – today it was a garbage truck!

We arrived in Mount Gambier about 10-30am which was too early to go to the Caravan Park so we went to Umpherston Sinkhole which was lovely, and at noon we went to the Caravan Park. By this time the mercury had already risen to 35 degrees and we were super keen to get that air con running. We had tried the Auxiliary power under different conditions and by different charging conditions, without success.

When we arrived at the Caravan Park, I asked the owner if they knew of any good auto electrician in town. I got a few leads and with the help of Google I got a few more. By this stage I was convinced that the house batteries must be dying and not able to hold a charge. So, my plan of attack was to get them tested by a battery shop first and if they were OK,

I would then have to see an auto electrician. I was dreading seeing an auto electrician as they know how to present a hefty bill.

While I went to pay for the campsite Tee was setting up our site. I asked the Caravan Park owner if there was a bottle shop around as I wanted to buy Tee some wine and me some beer as we needed to relax with this entire battery problem. He told me there was a Dan Murphy's around the corner and as I got back to the campsite with the booze Tee was more than set up and even happier than normal to see me. We had a couple of drinks and by late afternoon with the weather cooling down a bit I decided to read all the manuals on the Battery system and have a crack at fixing it again. I soon discovered that the C-Tec charger was on the wrong setting which would explain why the batteries were still low after being plugged into a campsite all last week. This coupled with the fact that even though we had travelled a bit my usage before the batteries went flat could have well accounted for the charge that the house batteries did get. We decided to test it out by charging it on the correct setting for a few hours and then unhooking the main power and seeing how long the batteries would last with everything running. It would mean that if it still wasn't fixed, we hadn't lost any time, as tomorrow was the first day that we could see an auto electrician after the weekend (obviously). And what a great success with everything still running strong after an hour. I had got so confused with all the wiring in the Motorhome that I forgot to just check the settings.

Again tomorrow was set to be in the high 30s, so the fact that we didn't have to go all over town trying to fix a problem was a great relief. Sleeping just got a whole lot easier with – NO FERAL'S – AIR CONDITIONING – NO AUTO ELECTRICIANS BILL.

Day **133**

After a great night's sleep, we awoke at about 6-00am and I talked Tee into going for a bike ride around the Blue Lake. I showed her on the map that it was just up the road and if we went soon, we would avoid all the heat. Tee agreed and we had a lovely bike ride around Mount Gambier's nicest natural feature. On the way back to the Motorhome we stopped at Target, as I needed some new thongs, and it helped us to cool down as the store was like an ice block with the air conditioning running full tilt.

We got back to the Motorhome at about 9-30am and it was really starting to heat up. We decided it would be silly to try and do anything in the heat of the day so we cranked up the air con and both relaxed with a good book. At about 7-00pm the weather had cooled down considerably with the wind picking up and the temperature plummeting. I suppose that was a cool change but not the kind you would expect as it normally involves rain, but never the less we were able to have a shower and head out for a walk around town.

Mount Gambier is a lovely town and we enjoyed the central park area and the Town Hall buildings that were beautifully lit up. There is a large amount of pride in the town and it seems to be one of the thriving towns. Again, with the temperature down we had a great night's sleep and as the temperature had dropped so significantly, we didn't even need the air con, in fact if anything, it was a little chilly.

Day 134

The heat must have really taken it out of us yesterday as we slept in until 9-00am. There was no panic though as we had "No place to be, and All the time in the world to get there". In fact, we had planned to look at a few natural features around Mount Shank before spending the evening there. We needed a few supplies and we set about getting them. First we went to Dan Murphy's to grab some more wine for Tee. I had only bought a few bottles for her the other day, as it was so cheap that I thought it may not be too nice. In fact, Tee loved it and we went back to buy her a half dozen for the road. While parking in front of Dan Murphy's Tee spotted another second hand shop and before I knew it, she was in and out with a new handbag to add to her collection – amazing!

After Dan Murphy's we headed to Coles to pick up a few supplies and then we grabbed a new clothes line as I had broken the old one with the automatic Motorhome door. Finally, we started to head to Mount Shank, but as we were approaching the Blue Lake on the outskirts of Mount Gambier Tee said she was getting hungry. I checked the time and bugger me if it wasn't 12-30pm already. We were just in a roundabout when I spotted a picnic area overlooking the Blue Lake, and as I had passed the turning, I did a full circle in the roundabout and pulled in there for lunch. At Coles we had bought a Danish Salami, so we (or Tee) decided we were would have a cheese and veggie platter with crackers.

With yummy lunch in our tummies we headed for some of the attractions around Mt Shank which included Hells Hole Sinkhole and the Little Blue Lake. As we were going past the Little Blue Lake on our way to

Southend tomorrow, we thought we would just go to Hells Hole Sinkhole before heading to Mt Shank for a quiet afternoon. We followed the Nelson road out of Mt Gambier which would take us to the road that Hells Hole Sinkhole was on, but as we reached the road to Hells Hole Sinkhole, we discovered it was dirt. We have had so many dramas on dirt roads that we have now created a NO DIRT ROAD POLICY which states that unless the dirt road is less than one kilometre long "we don't do it". So, we then decided that we would go and look at the Little Blue Lake before heading to our free camp spot at Mount Shank.

The Little Blue Lake was more of a sinkhole full of water that was used as a local swimming hole and when we arrived there a group of students were having a swim. Three of the boys were showing off on a high cliff saying that they were going to jump in. I thought they were full of shit but one of them did actually jump in and hit the water pretty hard. He was curled up in pain when he surfaced and the others were laughing at him. The only two that were not laughing at him were the two others on the cliff that were too chicken to jump. We didn't stay there too long as there wasn't much to see and we reached Mt Shank by about 3-30pm.

We had been to Mount Shank three days earlier and were kept awake by bloody French kids in those Wicked type vans. When we got there though there was none of them there. But as they normally arrive late, we were dreading their arrival. In fact, two of their vans arrived but it was so windy at Mt Shank that they hardly got out of their vans and we got a very pleasant night sleep. More importantly we had no issues with the Auxiliary power in our Motorhome, the first night after our discovery of the wrong setting and not plugged in to Mains.

Day **135**

We headed off early from Mount Shank with our plans to travel the back roads to Millicent and then onto Southend where we had been recommended a place to stay there called Lynnies. Not too much excitement on the way to Millicent but pleasant enough. Although on the outskirts of Millicent we spotted a huge factory which turned out to be the Kimberley Clarke factory that makes Kleenex tissues. This was of interest to me as they were our main competition when I worked for Bowater Scott Paper Mill in Melbourne, twenty odd years ago.

We arrived in Millicent and went directly to the Information Centre where we were greeted by two lovely ladies and a pleasant gentleman who told us of the attractions in Millicent. I asked them about the Kimberly Clarke Mill and they told me that it was struggling and most townspeople expected it to be closed within two years. I thought this might be the case as I had heard the same of Bowater from one of my old workmates, and on our recent trip to Tassie the Burnie Pulp Mill there had already closed down.

The problem is that they cannot now compete with the Chinese who have less strict environmental guidelines and with international freight now being so cheap it has changed the game. Shame, as Kimberley Clarke is Millicent's largest single employer.

From the Information Centre we travelled to Lake McIntyre which was a little ordinary and we had a cuppa before shooting off to Southend. We had planned to stay at Southend in a place called Lynnies Caravan Park. We arrived around lunchtime and found Lynnies almost immediately. With our sleeping destination discovered we went for a tour around Southend and found a lovely little fishing village that specialized in Crayfish (yummy). We want for a walk along the cliffs overlooking the bay and then for a walk on the jetty where a number of crayfish fisherman were arriving with their catch.

After our long walks we were starting to get hungry and with it approaching 1-00pm we headed back to Lynnies to secure our camp spot. But when we arrived at Lynnies there was nobody there and only a mobile number written on a chalkboard. I rang this number only to get a recorded message, so I left my number for a return call. By this stage we were very hungry so we went around the corner from Lynnies to the beach where there was a small sheltered parking area. We again had a platter of cheese, salami, cracker and veggies and waited for a call from Lynnies Caravan Park – a call that never happened.

Annoyed by this we decided to push on to Beachport and then to a free camp area just south of Robe. Beachport is kind of Southend's big sister and when we arrived there, we discovered a charming seaside town. Unfortunately, although a sunny day the wind was unbearable. Our first stop at Beachport was at a lookout on its southern approach that had a toilet and a tap. Tee was first to use the toilet while I filled the Motorhome with water. When Tee got back, I went to the toilet which turned out to be an interesting adventure as the wind was blowing that hard that it came into the toilet block and blew my own urine all over my legs – how impressive! In fact, the wind was so strong that when I used the outside tap to try and wash it off, I had to stand two feet downwind from the tap for it to wash my lower legs – thank God I had thongs on!

We took a number of photos of Beachport but had to do it from the cover of our Motorhome as the wind was just impossible. With no free camp available in Beachport we headed towards Robe where we had circled a campsite just South of it to stay at. We arrived at Springs Road Roadside Stop and although it was close to the highway it was quite pleasant. We set up for our stay and did a few chores around the Motorhome. For some reason we were both a bit grumpy and had a little bit of a tiff. I decided it was best for me to stay outside the Motorhome as we were both getting on each other's nerves.

I noticed that the outside passenger rear tyre was a bit flat so I got the compressor out of the boot and pumped up all the Motorhome tyres. Sounds easy hey, but to get to the boot I have to take the bike cover off – remove the bike locks – remove the two bikes – remove the bike carrier and then dig through all the stuff in the boot to get to the compressor. I pumped up all the tyres and was quite concerned with the rear passenger tyre that had dropped from 70 psi to 50 psi. Tee and I soon made up and promised to try and be nice to each other. It is difficult in the Motorhome and occasionally it boils over but as we normally get along so well it never gets too serious. Then the unthinkable happened – the fucken auxiliary power fucked up again – unbelievable! So, we have now no choice but to take Lizzie to an Auto Electrician and sort out this problem once and for all.

Day **136**

oly Shit, we woke up this morning and that tyre that I was concerned about was completely flat. So now I had to go through the whole process again of getting into the boot. But as I had "no place to be, and all the time in the world to get there" I decided to take my time and not to rush. Generally, when this sort of thing happens, I rush around and get myself into a bad mood, but I was determined that this was not going to happen today.

I took the bike cover off - unlocked the bikes – took the bikes off – undid the bike rack – got into the boot – found all the tools I needed and then started to remove the offending flat tyre. Fortunately, it was the outside tyre that was flat which meant I could just chock the inside wheel up onto a lump of wood and remove the flat wheel without a jack. I removed the spare and pumped it up to the correct pressure before putting it onto Lizzie and putting the flat tyre onto the spare carrier. I was very proud of myself as I had it all done and we were ready to travel by 9-30am, which is often what time we leave a campsite anyway.

I had got it done so quickly that we really didn't have to change our plans for the day and with another spare on board we could wait until Adelaide to replace the tyre. We looked at the situation from a positive aspect and observed that it was an easy wheel to change (outside rear) and the tyre that was flat was the low tread one that we would have had to replace in the next few months anyway. So off to Robe we went.

We arrived in Robe at about 10-30am and had a good look around. It is a nice little village but was quite touristy so we decided we would see the main sights and head off. Robe has lovely historic buildings and both surf and calm beaches, which is why I suppose it is so popular. Our next port of call was Kingston and, on the map, it looked bigger than Robe so we expected it to also be touristy with huge beachfront homes like Robe. But in fact, Kingston was more country and far less touristy than Robe. There is a free camp here and we were keen to find it and then hunt down where the Auto Electrician in town was. Ended up we found the Auto Electricians shop first and he was able to book us in for 1-00pm. As it was now only 11-45am we decided to head to the foreshore and have some lunch before our appointment.

On our way to the Auto Electricians shop we spotted the free camp and were well pleased with our morning's efforts. The Auto Electricians confirmed what we really didn't want to hear and that was that the house batteries were both shot and needed replacing. The good news was that the rest of the system was running fine, but unfortunately even though they had a fairly good supply of Deep Cell batteries they didn't have the size we needed. This was a little annoying but at least we now knew for sure what was wrong, and we could find a place in Adelaide that would have the right batteries.

The Auto Electricians shop was being run by two young boys who did an excellent job and it only cost me a half hour labour for the whole check-up, a grand total of $44-00. This was cheap peace of mind and we could now organize the supply of two new batteries and a new tyre when we got to Adelaide. The Auto Electricians had quoted me $400.00 for each battery in a good quality American made battery or $250.00 for reasonably good Chinese made batteries. This meant that we would be up for about $1,100.00 in Adelaide for the two batteries and a tyre (good quality) or $800.00 if we went with the Chinese made batteries that still had a two-year warranty on them.

On our way back to the free camp area we had some thinking to do and as we were not going to keep Lizzie more than two more years, we didn't see the point in going overboard on new batteries that would last eight years or so. The free camp area was very nice and that evening after dinner we went for a long walk on the jetty and had peaceful nights sleep.

Day **137**

Unfortunately, the batteries went flat again half way through the night and it has prompted me to ensure that I get organized with new batteries in case they had to be ordered. But first things first it was brekkie time and we had our usual cuppa and a piece of toast with Marmalade, Tee has a twist on this by having a rice cake with Marmalade instead.

The area around Kingston is very flat which makes it ideal for bike riding and Tee had commented last night that there are numerous bike paths in the area. After Brekkie I got the bikes off the back (I am getting very good at this) and we went on a twenty-kilometre bike ride through town and right along the esplanade. We were so impressed how well we were riding and it wasn't until we came to the end of the path and started heading back to the Motorhome that we realized we had been riding with the wind at our tails. This made the ride back quite strenuous and Tee was worn out by the time we got back and I must admit I had had enough also. But it was good exercise and at least it wasn't too hot yet.

This gave me a good amount of time to ring around and get the best price on both tyres and batteries. The best place, that was on our travels, was Murray Bridge and I ended up getting some super prices especially on the batteries. The total for the two batteries and the new tyre and tube was $639.00 and I thought it would cost me at least $800.00 but probably more. (Pays to shop around). Also, it was good that I rang as both the tyre and the batteries had to be ordered in and would take four days to get there. With this news we thought that we would stay in Kingston for one or two more nights as it was free, and quite a nice place. We could then cruise up the coast at a gentle pace as it was only two hundred and twenty kilometres form Kingston to Murray Bridge.

Day **138**

Today it was supposed to get to 36 degrees and we had planned to go for a walk through town in the morning before it got too hot. Yesterday evening I had gone and filled the Motorhome with water and on the way back I bought a loaf of bread so we were set up for today at the same camp spot.

On our walk through town we ran into a local named Rex who lived in the old courthouse / police station and he invited us in to have a look. Rex was a funny character in his mid eighties who did a bit of Blacksmith work and his wife sold antiques from their home. He gave us a wonderful tour of his home that still contained the gaol cells which held the hoodlums of the late 1800's and he told us of the officer who was fatally wounded by a bandit and died at the station. He said he had never seen any ghosts but his son said he had, with Rex believing it to be more of a big night on the grog.

Rex then showed us where he worked in the Men's Shed down the road and also many of his endless number of unfinished projects – a real character and a credit to Kingston. He even took us on a guided tour of his town and out to the Cape Jaffa lighthouse where he told us of its entire history – Good On Ya Rex! We had walked and talked with Rex for over three hours and by this stage the mercury had risen to 34 degrees.

We walked back to the Motorhome and had a bottle of water each before Tee heated me up some leftovers for lunch. No plans for the rest of the day as we just tried to keep cool. Tomorrow we will be off up the coast towards Adelaide and our only required appointment will be at Murray Bridge in three days time to get the Batteries and Tyre fitted.

Day **139**

Last night was a really hot night and when we woke this morning it was already 27 degrees. But at least today we would be back on the road and seeing new sights, with the plan to be at least half way to Murray Bridge by this evening. The first stop was at a place called Granite Rocks which gave us a look at the SA coast in its full isolation. In fact, from Kingston all the way up to just before Meningie the coast is quite the same. There are hardly any people on the beach and very few homes for about 100 Kilometres or so. We had a brief stop at Salt Creek that has a general store / camping ground, a replica Oil Well and a half a dozen houses – that's it! And this is about the biggest town for over one hundred kilometres; it is a very desolate and unusual area. This is presuming it is always this dry as the weather had been extremely cruel to this area over the past month or so with exceptionally hot weather. It may be a different story if it gets good rainfall, but we both feel that the area would be like this most of the time.

About twenty or so kilometres before Meningie we had our first view of Lake Albert which added water to the equation, as most of the lakes that we have viewed since Kingston have been salt lakes. These salt lakes are in abundance here and quite amazing to look at, but not too good if you are a farmer I suspect. Lake Albert is an unusual lake and also looks quite salty and shallow, but as it seems to be feed by the Murray River and the ocean it unlikely to suffer the same fate as the smaller lakes south of it.

Meningie seems to be the town that tells the traveller that is heading north that civilization is close at hand and to the traveller heading south that the harsh Aussie coastline will be your companion for the next few hours. The town itself is quite lovely and they have built a lovely park on the banks of Lake Albert that is a great stop off for travellers heading in either direction. We were going to go out to Narrung but the weather is so hot that we have decided to head to a caravan park and get some air con action happening. We had a cuppa in Meningie and even though it was after lunchtime it was so hot that we both didn't feel like anything to eat. I made a few phone calls to a couple of Caravan Parks and we decided to stay at the Wellington Caravan Park that is the last town on the Murray before it spills into the lake system and onto the ocean.

The drinking water so far in South Australia has been horrendous, with the drinking water in Kingston tasting like spat out tooth paste. One of the criteria's that I picked the Caravan Park with was that it had good drinking water, and Wellington Caravan park had tank water for drinking – a winner for Tee. Even though we could have stayed at a free camp close to Wellington it made economic sense to go to the Caravan Park as we could fill up our drinking water supplies and make use of the power to run our air con. The caravan park was $25.00 per night and if we were to fill up our drinking water supplies it would cost us $30.00 in the supermarket.

As we approached Wellington, we were surprized to see a group of cars stopped at the rivers edge and we thought at first that there must have been a ship going upriver and the bridge was raised for it. Turns out there was no ship – and no bridge – and the group of cars were waiting for the Ferry to take them across to Wellington. Initially, we thought, great there goes the budget, but the ferry ride was free and turned out to be a nice little experience. We arrived at the Wellington Caravan Park and although it was quite an old park it was clean and tidy and more importantly quiet. We quickly found our site and plugged into the power to crank up the air con – WOW – how good is This! We filled up some drinking water and then settled in for a quiet afternoon.

About 4-00pm we had an early Dinner / very late Lunch of Steak, Sausages and salad – Yummy - before having a bit of a nap. In the evening as it cooled down, we decided to go for a walk around town and to check out the local pub and see what their meals were like. With tomorrow night being schnitzel night, we may even stay another night at Wellington Caravan Park.

Day **140**

We had a pretty late night last night as we watched a movie before going to bed at 11-30pm. Because we were so tired yesterday, I let my guard down a bit and didn't do all my chores properly. Turns out the Motorhome was on a bit of a lean backwards (bad for sleeping) and I left the awning out which started flapping a half hour after I went to bed. As I was so tired, I tried to convince myself that the wind would die down and the awning would stop flapping. No such luck and by 1-30am I was still awake and the flapping got worse so I had to bring it in. Then at 5-00am Tee awoke (so I had to) as she was being attacked by ants that had accessed Lizzie via our electrical cord. This meant both of us getting up and spraying the ants inside and out. After about a half an hour of getting rid of the little buggers we had it beat and went back to bed, only to be awoken at 6-30am by rain.

Normally rain is not a problem, but because I had the awning set up, we had the cooking gear and the tables and chairs out that were now getting wet. So up I got again and instead of trying to put all the gear away I put the awning out again instead. There was no wind with the rain so we should be fine and we both went back to sleep for about an hour. What a comedy show last evening was, and in the morning when we did get up, we were both exhausted.

As we didn't have to be anywhere today and we were so tired we decided to just stay here for another night. This would allow us to rest for the day and with the temperature now much cooler we may even slip in a nap this arvo. About 9-30am the fellow from the tyre shop rang me to say that my tyre was in and ready to be filled and later that day I confirmed with the Battery place that our two house batteries were also in and ready to install.

We had a quiet day as we had planned, and this evening we are going to the local pub for a meal. I think we will also have an early night as I didn't get a nap and we have a big day tomorrow getting Lizzie all fixed up for the Adelaide leg of our journey.

Day **141**

We had moved the Motorhome yesterday to a grassy site to get away from the ants and it seemed to have done the trick. We both had a fabulous sleep last night and were ready to get all the work done on Lizzie. As we were not too far from Murray Bridge, we had plenty of time to get on the road and we got going a little after 10-00am.

The drive to Murray Bridge followed the Mighty Murray River which we have done a fair bit of on this trip, mainly in Victoria. It only took us about forty minutes to reach Murray Bridge and even though I told the battery guys that we would be there at lunchtime we thought we would try our luck. They were cool with us being there early and they had the batteries fitted in under an hour. We thought well we are on a roll so let's try and get in early for the tyre also as it was still not yet lunchtime and we were booked in for 2-30pm. Again, we were fortunate as they did the tyre straight away, which gave us the whole afternoon to explore the coast on the way to Victor Harbor. We had initially thought that the process of getting Lizzie fixed up was going to be a whole day affair but it was all done in an hour and a half, we were having a great day.

I forgot to mention that we had decided to hire a car in Victor Harbor so we could zip around the city a lot quicker. We also could do Adelaide, the Adelaide Hills and the Fleurieu Peninsula and use a Victor Harbor Caravan Park as a base camp to leave Lizzie in. I had booked the car hire as they seemed to be quite busy and we secured a Hyundai i20 for four days. But the Caravan Parks were not so busy so I wanted to wait until I had more time to compare prices.

The trip to Victor Harbor started a little boring as once we left Murray Bridge, we were straight onto a Highway. But we soon turned off and headed towards Goolwa and with the old stone buildings scattered along the road to Goolwa our heads were turning from left to right admiring them all. We arrived at Goolwa a little after lunchtime and Tee whipped me up a couple of Peanut Butter sandwiches which I ate as we parked by the lake.

After lunch we followed the lake road which took us to a dead end and a path which went over sand dunes and appeared to be going to the ocean. We were not sure as to if the path was going to lead us to the ocean, as our map was not detailed and we didn't know exactly where we were. But having just had a feed we were keen to go for a walk anyway and even if there were only sand dunes it was a lovely looking walk, so off we went. We climbed over two or three dunes until we heard the roar of the ocean and after walking about two kilometres, we arrived on a stunning wild ocean beach with not a soul in site (despite the fabulous sunny weather). Photo time and as Tee has the longest arms (monkey arms) she has taken the role of camera holder as we tried valiantly to look our best for the camera. An easy task for Tee but I had to get the angle right to avoid the second chin look (not a good look). We walked back to where Lizzie awaited and headed off towards Victor Harbor.

About half way between Goolwa and Victor Harbor we came across the stunning town of Port Elliot and by accident we ended up in an area that they call the Strand. Being elevated over the whole area this place looks as though it was the pick of the places to live in the early days, and you can see why. It has granite outcrops with large waves crashing into it and a lovely horseshoe shaped bay that looks perfect for swimming. All this surrounded by lovely gardens and stunning stone buildings that are all individual works of art. This place is one of the nicest seaside towns we have seen so far and we spent a few hours enjoying its beauty.

I also seized the chance to find a well priced Caravan Park and as we wanted to stay for about a week, I negotiated the best deal I could and ended getting a place close to the centre of Victor Harbor for $168.00. ($24.00 per day) what a bargain. We pulled into Victor Harbor in the late afternoon and decided to go straight to our Caravan Park as we had a few days free to explore the town before we got the hire car. The Caravan Park was lovely and quiet and we were really looking forward to exploring the place, especially as we had got Lizzie's problems all attended to and we were now free to enjoy the journey again.

Day 142

This Caravan Park was not only a good economical choice but it is also super quiet so we both had another lovely sleep last night. We had planned to explore Granite Island today but unfortunately; we woke to rain. I have spent the morning writing and Tee has been looking through the tourist's books for places to see. Hopefully after lunch it will clear up and we can get out and about.

We were very fortunate and the rain didn't continue after lunch so we were able to fulfil our plans and go out to Granite Rock. The walk to the Jetty from the Caravan Park was about a kilometre and on the way, we found an IGA and a butcher shop just around the corner from the caravan park. This would be handy as we need supplies and were going to wait until we got the car, but supplies are low and we will carry them this short distance rather than spend our car hire time shopping.

In South Australia they don't hand out shopping bags and you have to buy them if you want them. I think it is supposed to be for the environment but it is very inconvenient if you don't live here and are a tourist. Hard to work out if being totally inefficient in the workplace is better for the environment than plastic bags, and I don't believe there are many people left on the planet who are so irresponsible that they would drop their old plastic bags into the street or the ocean. But hey it floats the croweater's boat – so be it.

We dropped into a second hand shop where Tee got a book and I bought a DVD (Mission Impossible) still in its wrapper for $3-00 – Bargain. Before we knew it, we were at the Jetty that goes over to Granite

Island and we soon spotted the horse drawn tram that runs tourists over to the Island. The jetty is an easy walk of 650 metres and you can circumnavigate the whole island with a 1.5-kilometre walk. The Tram ride is only eight dollars return and would be great for a family but Tee and I (on our no tourist shit policy) decided to walk it. But it was good value, and is one of the few things touristy that we seriously considered going on.

The walk around Granite Island was fantastic and reminded us a little of the Nut (Stanley) in Tasmania, and like the Nut you would be wise to avoid it on a very windy day. But today was perfect as it was cool and not windy, the only thing missing was the sun but the weather was still clear and the photos still looked good. The granite boulders here are enormous and the place is a serious "must see" for any traveller. There is a Kiosk and Penguin Centre on the Island and again would be a fabulous family outing.

We returned to the mainland and decided to have a walk around town as I was keen to sight where the hire car mob was located and we could maybe do a bit of shopping. The shopping district of Victor Harbor is lovely with an open Mall type feel and lovely tree lined streets. I needed some shorts and a T-shirt and Tee just likes a bit of shopping. I got a T-shirt in Target and we found a Rivers store where I got some shorts and Tee found a nice pair of casual pants. Now it's off to the Butchers and the IGA for supplies and then to the Motorhome for some dinner as it is now after 5-00pm.

Back at the Motorhome Tee cooked me a fresh steak that we had just bought and a plate of veggies also freshly purchased (Yummy). We then did a few chores before heading to bed to watch our new movie which we had also freshly purchased. All in all, quite a big day where we walked over ten kilometres and saw some beautiful places.

Day **143**

Great sleep again and today it was off with the bikes for a ride out to the Bluff, an outcrop off the mainland that helps protect Victor Harbor from those huge Southerly Winds. After Brekkie I got the bikes off the back of the Motorhome and we were off on our ride. The first kilometre of the ride was OK but as soon as we hit the foreshore we were riding almost directly into a headwind. Well at least we were doing it on the way there and not on the way back like we did in Kingston. So, if we got too tired, we could turn back and have the wind at our backs. But we took it easy and it wasn't too bad. Like many towns near the beach in the summer months there were many people walking their dog, which made us keen to get home a bit as we now plan to get a Golden Retriever puppy when we get back.

The foreshore was lovely with a mix of new huge homes and little stone cottages all with views of the Bluff and Granite Island. We toured the area and climbed to the lookout with our bikes to take in the lovely ocean view all the way back to the township itself. The contrasting grey clouds looked stunning against the wild ocean and we marvelled at its beauty.

As I hinted before the trip back was a doddle and we got back to our Motorhome in half the time that it took to get to the Bluff. It was still not lunchtime but we ate anyway as the sea air and the exercise had given us a healthy appetite, in fact we had ridden almost 20 kilometres which surprised me a bit as it didn't seem that far. I had a nap after lunch and we spent the rest of the day planning the next four days travel that we would be doing in the hire car.

Day **144**

Hard to believe it is March already and we are into our fifth month on the road. Today is to be our first day with a hire car and it will be interesting to see if it works out better than just getting around in Lizzie. We had another peaceful night's sleep and awoke at about 7-30am.

I have to pick the hire car up at 10-00am and will have to walk into town to get it, about 1.5 Kilometres. I had a bite to eat and we organized what we would need to put into the car for our daytrip today, in list form. I then started off on my walk to town and planned to buy a pair of jeans while I was there from Rivers. Tee stayed at the Motorhome and started getting the gear ready for our day trip and because it was going to be windy on the coast we decided to go to the Adelaide Hills. We were going to make our lunch on the road in the form of sandwiches and we took the Butane cooker to make cups of Tea for ourselves. It is times like this that I wished we had a bigger budget as I would love nothing more than to take Tee out for lunch in a German pub in Hahndorf. But we are set on a plan and if we faultier then we won't be able to travel for the whole twelve months, and this is more important to us than a meal out here and there, I think!

Back to my walk into town, and I arrived there in heaps of time to buy a pair of jeans at Rivers and still be at the Car place by 10-00am. The place where I got the car was a sub agency of Europcar and the fella (Bruce) told me that the car was unmarked and had a full tank of fuel – neither of which turned out to be factual. The hubcaps on the passenger side were both scratched and the fuel gauge was reading a touch under full. With the fuel gauge it is hard to judge where they should sit in a car you have never driven before, but as I found out a day later when I filled it up, full was over the full tank mark like my car at home. My hope is that the car hire company don't penalize me when I return the car with the same amount of fuel and the hubcaps the way I received them. (We will see).

Anyway, the car was great, a little Hyundai i20 and I returned to the Caravan Park to pick up Tee and head off on our day trip to the Adelaide Hills. It was really freaky driving what seemed to be two inches off the road compared to three feet off the ground in Lizzie, but the zippy little Hyundai was a welcome change. While I was away Tee had been very busy and had done some washing as well as getting all the travel gear ready. She was glad to see me when I pulled up in the i20 and we took only a few minutes to pack the car, check off the list and be on our way. Big effort as we were on the road by 10-30am which is a similar time to when we set off without all the organizing.

Our plan was to look at a number of Adelaide Hills towns that Tee had marked on the list, with the first being Echunga and more specifically the Jupiter Creek Gold diggings on the outskirts of town. We arrived in the town of Echunga which was a bit ordinary and run down, and within a few minutes we spotted the tourist signs that would take us to the Gold Diggings. When we got to the car park of the Gold Diggings, we were a bit shocked to find that it was a three kilometre walk each way to the open shaft that you could walk into (named Phoenix Tunnel).

As it was about lunchtime and we had found a picnic table in the car park of the Jupiter Creek we decided to have a bite to eat before our six Kilometre walk. We were soon accompanied by a family of hungry Magpies who sang to us from the trees before acting like they were starving to death as we feed them the crusts of our lunch. (They were cute though).

The weather was quite warm but not yet hot and just about perfect for a stroll in the bush. It was not long before we came across the first of many shafts that had been dug at times from the mid 1850's though to the 1930's. All the ones that we saw had been fenced around but there were some areas that had warning signs that there were open shafts in the area. From what we saw of the fenced shafts you would not want to go wondering too far off the tracks in this place. Not only were the open shafts a concern but because there were so many tracks it would be quite easy to get lost around here.

After we had walked about 2.5 kilometres, we came across our first structure called Beatrice Chimney which was constructed in 1869 and amazingly was still in quite good condition. I am not sure what it was used for but I will Google it when I remember. A short distance after that we came to the Phoenix Tunnel which is a horizontal shaft that was open to walk into (at your own risk). I braved the walk into the tunnel but the bugs soon gave me the shits and it was quite scary in there by myself. Shit now I could get a slight feeling as to how those two boys from Beaconsfield Mine felt, "and I could walk out". Tee stayed on the edge of the mine opening ensuring that her hair was not messed up and we laughed on the way back that her Coco Channel handbag (real or fake) would have definitely been the first to travel to this location. I got some great photos all the way through this area and especially in the Phoenix Tunnel.

On the way back we nearly got lost as the tracks are quite confusing, in fact without the named / fenced shafts along the way I am sure we would have lost our way. On two occasions we took the wrong track and had to back track. As we got within a kilometre of the car park, we passed another couple going for a walk and we told them to be careful to remember where they walked as it was easy to get lost. They thanked us and we were both on our way. We arrived back at our car safely and were soon on our way to the most famous of the Adelaide Hills towns, Hahndorf.

We arrived in Hahndorf and the place was packed (remember it was Friday) and we were not overly impressed as we thought we may be able to see the place quietly. No chance of that as we could not even get a car park in the main street, so we just drove up and down the street a couple of times and headed to the next town. The place had semi trailer trucks trying to squeeze through the main street and the town was so commercialized that we knew it would not be pleasant. It was a nice place but there were so many people we had to leave.

Fortunately, the other towns that we went to were quiet and we saw a number of lovely heritage stone buildings. Mt Lofty had a fantastic Botanical Garden but it closed at four, and as we arrived at 3-30pm we didn't get a heck of a lot of time to enjoy it. On the way back to Victor Harbor we spotted a farm selling fresh corn and we stopped to buy some as well as some fresh garlic. We had quite a nice day and the drive was pleasant enough but we both felt that the Adelaide Hills were a little over rated. All I can say in its defence is that it was very dry and brown and when green it would be a lot more beautiful, I am sure.

Back at the Camp site Tee cooked up the fresh corn which we had with Sausages and potato for a yummy dinner. It was quite a pleasant day.

Day **145**

Today we were doing the Fleurieu Peninsula that we had planned to do yesterday but swapped as the winds were strong yesterday on the coast. We were on the road by 9-00am and our first stop was at Waitpinga Beach. On the way we passed the Victor Harbor Bluff area that we had rode to a few days ago. It was here that we got some lovely morning photos from a lookout high above. Waitpinga Beach was lovely and there was a National Park campground there within walking distance of the beach. Not a lot of people and a lovely stop on this very attractive coastline.

After Waitpinga Beach the road took us slightly inland and we passed some quiet farmland on our way to Cape Jervis. Cape Jervis is where the ferry goes across to Kangaroo Island and we had looked at doing a day trip there but the Ferry ride made it too expensive. The return trip for Tee and I and our hire car would have been $376.00, a figure that we could not justify. I think if you were going there for a couple of weeks it would be OK but for the average traveller going around Australia or even part of it, the price is not justified or more to the point affordable. I got some lovely photos from Cape Jervis with KI being quite visible from the mainland. We took advantage of a picnic table at Cape Jervis and had an early lunch (it was 11-15am) and while dining on our sandwiches and crackers the Ferry pulled in. We watched it unload as in the water it did not look big enough to hold cars let alone Motorhomes and boats. But as the boom door dropped its belly exposed a number of vehicles including Motorhomes, boats, trailers and multiple cars – we were amazed!

We left Cape Jervis shortly after and headed up the North West coast of the Fleurieu which takes you to Adelaide. We took a turnoff to the small coastal village of Second Valley which was quite pretty. It contained a Caravan Park, a small jetty, a few homes and a very lovely beach area. We went for a short walk, took a few happy snaps and moved on. Back on the road with the next planned stop being Normanville, and when we arrived there the beach area was just beautiful. They had a small Kiosk there, and a food van that had a menu that would rival most restaurants – in length anyway. We spent a bit of time here and had a chat to some people from Cleveland (near Brisbane) in Queensland – about two hours from where our home is.

Back on the road we took another turnoff arriving at a place called Sellicks Beach. This place also had a stunning beach and was quite unique also. The amazing thing about this place was that from the elevated town area there was a road that went out onto the beach. There were cars all over the beach which is not a sight you see every day, as most beaches that you drive on are in remote areas – this was 30 minutes or less from Adelaide. We drove all the way to Christies Beach, which is on the outskirts of Adelaide and as we did, we faced more and more traffic. Christies Beach was lovely but a bit busy and at 3-00pm we decide to set off inland back to our campsite at Victor Harbor. By 4-00 pm we were home and by 4-30pm we were sipping wine and chatting about how lovely the drive today was.

Day **146**

Today is Sunday and we thought today would be the best day to visit Adelaide as there would be no business traffic. The problem was that the Clipsal 500 motor racing was on. We thought about doing Adelaide on Monday instead but thought, as Adelaide is not a huge city, the Motor racing may take people away from the places we wanted to visit. I read on Google later that 95,000 people went to the Clipsal 500 today – I got that wrong!

But all in all, Adelaide was not that busy and it is quite a simple town (or City) to navigate around. We had found some places that we were keen on looking at and by the time we reached Adelaide it was over 30 degrees. The first place we went to visit was the Old Adelaide Gaol and we walked around there for a while taking a few happy snaps along the way. We then went for a drive through the city area taking note of the stunning churches that are dotted around the city. We then went for a look at the Adelaide Botanical Gardens that were very nice indeed. Inside the Botanical Gardens we visited the Palm House, the Giant Lily display and an odd Museum that was full of Apples, Pears and Mushrooms – they called it the Santos Museum – it was definitely different. It was a good thing that we went to Adelaide on a Sunday as the parking all over the city was free on only this day. This made getting around and seeing the sites a hell of a lot easier.

After we spent a couple of hours exploring the Botanical Gardens we went and had a picnic on the grass in the same grounds. It was a lovely spot full of gum trees and yet close to the centre of the city, we really enjoyed it. We again drove around the city after lunch and soon thought we had seen enough. The last place I wanted to look at was Glenelg Beach where I had gone as a child of eight or nine. This was the last time I had been to Adelaide and with over a forty-year gap I was in for some surprises. Upon arriving at Glenelg Beach, the place was totally unrecognizable to me and looked more like Maroochydore than the Glenelg I once visited. I suppose that was to be expected as it was the closest beach to Adelaide and all the Ritchie Rich people would have flocked there when the seaside became popular twenty odd years ago. There certainly were some spectacular homes on the waterfront. We then headed along the coastline south to Christies Beach and then inland and across to Victor Harbor.

In our opinion Adelaide is more for a fly in holiday where you would walk around the city or enjoy one of the many festivals. But I suppose most cities are like that and visiting these types of places is not what we are about as we both far more enjoy the small country towns and the remarkable scenery that Australia has to offer.

Day **147**

We both didn't sleep all that well last night but we did go back to sleep early in the morning and didn't wake until almost 9-00am. Last night Tee had dropped her mobile into the washing machine and we are pretty sure it fried. Luckily the Sim card was OK, so we planned to pick a new phone today for Tee and if the old one comes good it will be a bonus. We were going to head inland today towards Renmark, but we both did not feel up to it. We decided that we would take it easy and just do something locally. Tee came up with a brilliant idea to go snorkelling and as we hadn't done it yet it would be a great way to beat the heat of the day.

We did not leave the campsite until after 11-00am and by that time it was starting to heat up, in fact it had reached 28 degrees. Our first stop was to Big W where we got an old-fashioned Samsung phone for $38.00 and we also grabbed a box of Butane cylinders for our camp cooking. As far as snorkelling spots around the area they were only average and The Bluff area was supposed to be the best. But it was not as nice a swimming place as Port Elliot (Horseshoe Bay) and if the water wasn't clear then Port Elliot would be a better option as we could just go swimming. We decided on Port Elliot and we had a ball. The snorkelling was poor but we had a great time swimming and enjoying the beach – it turned out to be a fantastic day.

Back at the Motorhome by three we both had a laugh at Tee trying to use her new mobile phone to send a text. It was one of those phones that you press the #2 key three times for C, etc and it took her ages to send one text. How did we ever survive without technology? We started packing up all the gear as we were off tomorrow with Lizzie on our way to the Yorke Peninsula, but only after dropping off the hire car at 10-00 am. This means that we will probably end up staying at a free camp area just North of Adelaide and we are both looking forward to being on the move again.

The use of the hire car has been a mild success, but the cost has meant that we blew the budget this week, something that we don't like doing. So, I suspect it will be a while before we try the car hire thing again – perhaps it might work in Perth – we will see.

Day **148**

Today was the day we were to leave Victor Harbor and head towards the Yorke Peninsula, and we headed off after dropping the Hyundai back at the Hire Company. The plan was to get to a free camp area at Parham which would put us within an easy driving distance of the Yorke Peninsula, but if it was no good at Parham, we could go to a local caravan park in the area. It was such a change driving Lizzie again after have the Hyundai for four days, and it was even weirder as we travelled towards Adelaide in her as we did in the Hyundai a few days earlier. We were a lot higher up, moving considerably slower and we were noticing hills that we didn't even see in the Hyundai. But we can't live in the Hyundai so Lizzie has no worries about being replaced; in fact, the slower pace means we see a lot more of the Journey.

The trip to Adelaide was tedious as we had done it a number of times this week. Just after Adelaide we ran into a heap of roadwork's so it was a relief when we got to a motorway on the other side and were again surrounded by countryside. Very uninteresting scenery continued, as the whole way from the outskirts of Adelaide to Port Parham was very brown and very flat.

When we arrived at Port Parham it didn't look too promising as it looked very arid and quite isolated, but we soon spotted the free camp area and it was a different story. There were a number of Caravans already there and it was quite an OK spot, so we both nodded in acceptance to one another and found a private spot to set up.

By this stage we were really tired from driving most of the day and the temperature reaching a crazy 43 degrees. Even though we had set up camp we had not yet looked at the beach to see what it was like, so we decided before dinner to have a look. The track to the beach was right beside our Motorhome and we were set up so we were facing no other van or Motorhome. When we got onto the track to the beach it was only about 10 steps to the sand, but to reach the water we were in for a hike. The tide was out and it was close to 700mtrs from the high tide line to the water line. As it was so hot, we still decided to walk out there and the breeze was much cooler once we got onto the beach meaning that the long walk to the water would be a pleasant one. It was amazing how far the tide went out here and I later found out, reading a local tourist book, that it is one of the best crabbing beaches in SA. They do thing a bit different here and crabbing involves a thing called raking. I am not sure how they do it but I did see a rake near one of the traveller's caravans and it looked like a garden rake but only had about six blades (or prongs).

When we reached the water line, we splashed our feet around a bit and then turned to walk back. Wow the sand looked even further away than the water did on the way out, but with the day fading and the temperature dropping it was a pleasant walk back. With the weather still topping 30 degrees neither of us felt like much for Dinner and Tee had some Sardines while I ate some peanut butter out of the jar. Late in the evening though, just before sunset, I said to Tee that I wanted to look at the beach now as the tide should be in. Tee said she was making a cuppa and not to be too long, so I quickly went to investigate the tide. Well what a difference the tide made to this place and with us facing the west and the sun about to set the place looked fabulous. I quickly went back to the Motorhome and grabbed the two camp chairs and asked Tee to meet me on the foreshore with the cups of Tea, and before she could ask why I said "it will be worth it".

I set up the chairs on the beach and started to photograph the most amazing sunset, with Tee arriving a few minutes later saying what a great idea this was. We could not believe that we were the only people on the beach to see this, as the free camp area must have had over 50 people staying in it and the town must have had a similar amount of people living there. But believe it or not in the coolest and most beautiful part of Port

Parham, Tee and I were the only ones witnessing this magnificent sunset. We took photos of every stage of the sunset and numerous photos of the local birdlife who were also busy on the beach.

For a place that has a reputation of being ugly but good for crabbing we were witnessing a thing of beauty, and would highly recommend it to anyone who is travelling the area. Not quite a must see but well worth the short drive in off the main highway. The evening was stifling hot but with the fan going all night we ended up having quite a good night's sleep.

Day **149**

First day of the new weekly budget today and with the full week in the Caravan Park at Victor Harbor and the hire car for four day we went $150.00 over budget. In fact, for the trip to date we are a grand total of $151.00 over budget. Not bad considering we had to replace our house batteries and a new tyre last week. We hope to be back on budget or under in a week or two. (Our budget is $500.00p/w for everything on the Road).

After a fairly long drive and a stinking hot day yesterday we plan to be a bit kinder to ourselves today and last night I booked a Caravan Park in Stansbury for two nights. This would mean an easy drive of only 150 kilometres for the day and we thought we may do a bit of swimming or snorkelling for the afternoon when it heated up. On the way to Stansbury our first stop was to a place called Port Wakerfield which was lovely and full of historic buildings and homes. Tee and I felt it was very much like Alice Springs as it was very dry and almost void of any grass cover.

As we turned off to the Yorke Peninsula, we made our second stop and this time we had a cup of tea and a bite to eat. The stop was a wayside stop that had a metal Emu that I rode and a metal Kangaroo which Tee cuddled each while being photographed by the other. Then I noticed a Stump Jump Plough displayed on the other side of the rest stop and read about its history on the plaque in front of it. Quite a unique and interesting invention that I now know was conceived and produced in this very area.

After Lunch we set off to Ardrossan for some supplies as it seemed to be the biggest town in these parts and it would probably be the cheapest. On the way there Tee got a text message from her daughter saying that she had got back together with her old boyfriend. This enraged me as he had turned out to be a little smartass and was quite verbally abusive to me when I tried to straighten out their affairs last time. I won't go into any details other than to say that the only times Tee and I don't see eye to eye is when reading a map or discussing our daughter.

It was a quiet shopping expedition as my ears were steaming as Tee was defending her daughter's actions. In the end we both got over it and decided it was her life to live and her choices to make and at the end of the day she was now an adult. We visited a few beachside towns on the way to Stansbury but decided to skip Port Vincent as it was getting on and we would not do it justice by only spending a short time there.

We arrived at the Stansbury Caravan Park in plenty of time to set up and spend a wonderful afternoon snorkelling. It is amazing how many fish you see when you put on snorkelling gear and it doesn't seem to matter where you go. To be honest it was just great to go for a swim in a place with a half decent beach and get out of this disgusting heat. We had a yummy dinner before retiring for the evening with a Robert De Niro Movie (Showtime).

Day **150**

We had picked to stay at Stansbury for a couple of nights as it was the centre of most sights on the Yorke Peninsula, plus the fact that this weekend was a long weekend in Adelaide and everywhere here was booked out after tonight. We didn't see this as a problem as two days here was probably going to be enough for us anyway. The plan for today was to follow the coast south to Edithburgh, west to Marion Bay, north to Corny Point, east to Warooka, north again to Parsons Beach and then back across the inland to Stansbury. I had read that Parsons Beach was a good place to snorkel so the rest of the trip was just going to be sightseeing, and with over 300klms of travelling it would be short stops in each area before a cool off in Parsons Beach.

To be honest the area didn't do that much for us and with the heat the way it was it was just uncomfortable. The coastal towns were all pretty similar with the water being almost waveless everywhere. We flicked from town to town hoping that we would find a lovely spot, or at least a place that was uniquely different. The only time this occurred was when we ran into a huge rain cloud that dumped a heap of rain at Hardwick's Bay. This at least cooled things down, if only temporarily.

We stopped at Parsons Beach which was at least one of the nicest spots and had planned to do a bit of snorkelling here, but as Tee said it was similar to where we snorkelled at Stansbury so we might as well go back there. At least at Stansbury we could wash down in fresh water after our snorkelling, so off we went.

Amazingly when we got back to the Caravan Park, we were confronted by a tractor which had just backed a caravan into our campsite. I told the guy that we were parked here and he moved it straight away, but if we were ten minutes later, we would have had to go to the office and get it all sorted. Funnily enough Tee said she had fully expected this to happen when we left this morning. Later on, one of the people in a spot nearby told us that the old guy had a hell of a time backing the Caravan into the spot and that he had just finished when we arrived. And you know what they say "it's all in the timing!"

We spent the rest of the afternoon snorkelling twenty metres from our campsite and had a great afternoon. It made us feel as though we should have just put the $35.00 of fuel money in our pocket and stayed here for the day. But of course, we didn't know what the southern tip of the Yorke Peninsula would be like and now at least we could proclaim that we had visited it all. Dare to say it does not rate well on my "must see list", but for local families wanting a holiday not far from Adelaide it would be perfect.

I must say that South Australia so far has not set our socks on fire. I say that not as an ex-Victorian but as a traveller who has been to a few places now. The other thing is that South Australia does not seem to work hard for the tourist dollar as the parks and roadside facilities are few and far between. I may be being a little tough, but when you compare the facilities for tourist here against Victoria and Tassie – SA comes in a distant third. My exceptions to these have so far been – Mt Gambier, Kingston / Robe area and the Victor Harbor region.

Day **151**

I would like to say that we will miss the Yorke Peninsula but it would be easier to say that we are looking forward to the Eyre Peninsula and crossing the Nullarbor to Perth. We still have a bit to see of the Yorke Peninsula as we have done the East and South coasts but will be travelling up the West coast today. This will give the area a chance to redeem itself with us. Our first stop will be Port Vincent as we missed it on the way to Stansbury a couple of days ago and it is only a short drive away.

Port Vincent is quite nice and is probably a better choice of places to stay than Stansbury with a lot more activities and a few more facilities. Again, the architecture of the old homes here is stunning but we are just looking on our way to the North of the Yorke Peninsula on route to the Eyre Peninsula. We now will cross country from East to West with Port Victoria on our radar. The Yorke Peninsula road structure is a little odd as you seem to zig zag on the East coast to head South or North.

Port Victoria was also not a bad little town that is well elevated to the ocean and we had a cuppa on the green grass near their timber jetty and spotted a number of dolphins enjoying the bay. We had a walk on the jetty before again zig zagging inland to Maitland, where we bought a few things, and then onto Moonta on the coast. Nothing more to say about these areas as we were now more focussed on driving as far as possible out of the Yorke before finding a place to sleep. We got all the way up to Port Germein as the temperature again soared to 38 degrees.

Just prior to Port Germein we found a free camp site that was really ordinary and we decided to go and stay in a Caravan Park in Port Germein because of the heat. Unfortunately, though the Caravan Park was booked out because of the long weekend and we decided to go back to the free camp area and sweat it out. It was amazingly hot but we really had no choice as I was buggered driving in this heat (no air -conditioner in the driver's cab of Lizzie) and we could have the same problem all the way up the coast finding a Caravan Park that had vacancies.

We parked the Motorhome in what can only be described as a highly littered truck stop and made the best of it. It was within view of the ocean and about an hour after we stopped, we were blessed with a strong sea breeze. It meant that we could at least get to sleep even though we were sweaty and uncomfortable.

We got a reasonable night's sleep but I think it was more because we were exhausted than anything else. The only interruption was at about midnight when a road train pulled in and woke us briefly, but we were glad for the company as up until then we were the only people there and it felt quite isolated.

Day **152**

I forgot to mention Port Pirie which is apparently the sixth largest city in South Australia, and in a line from the movie "The Castle" "What do you know about Lead". As Port Pirie is home to the worlds largest Lead Smelter. NICE!

Today we are out of the Yorke for sure and by mid morning we had reached the turning point from the Yorke to the Eyre in the form of Port Augusta. Driving in from the Yorke side of Port Augusta we didn't think much of it but we stopped at the old water tower which is located on the Western side of town for a look. This offered sweeping views of the town and as we were able to climb the water tower, we got even better views. From this aspect Port Augusta looked OK but it was not earmarked as a stop for us and we continued our Journey.

Almost immediately we entered the Eyre Peninsula we felt good about travelling again and the scenery was quite different. The land was more in its natural state and not parched farmland. We saw Emus within the towns limits and the countryside was rugged and more mountainous, making it more interesting. Our next stop was Whyalla about 60 kilometres from Port Augusta. When we arrived, we were confronted with another heavily industrialized town but unlike Port Pirie Whyalla township was a bit away from its industrial hub. We headed towards a lookout first to get an overview of the town and were greeted by great views over the town and harbour. We toured around the town for an hour or so and were tempted to stay the night, but as there were no free camps here and our budget was tight this week we decided to keep travelling. The beach at Whyalla looked lovely and with a large shallow area it looked like it would be good for snorkelling and for family swimming. The parks around the foreshore were also impressive.

Off again with a free camp spot about 40 kilometres south of Cowell in our sights. When we got about 15 kilometres shy of Cowell, we hit a freak rain storm which was a blessing as prior to that we had been hit with a tonne of bugs that had made a mess of Lizzie's windscreen. The rain was so heavy it completely removed all the bugs and the storm was so isolated that Lizzie was dry by the time we reached Cowell.

Cowell looked like a lovely little town and we explored the possibility of staying here for the night. Tee checked the Camps6 book to see what was available and said there was a Motorhome park that was a charged site but was for self contained vehicles only and might not be too expensive. We finally found the site in town but it had a sign saying that the Motorhome Park was now on Beach Road. Well we had been on beach road and we couldn't see it, only a Caravan Park that was on a side road. We decided to go back and buy fuel as we may have to keep driving, but on the way found the Dump Point where we filled up with water. Tee said we should go to the Caravan Park and ask about the Motorhome Park but I wasn't keen as I was embarrassed to ask. I gave in though when she said she would ask and we headed back, minus the fuel.

Tee came out of the Caravan Park with a smile on her face and said that it was just a bit further up Beach Road and just passed where the road turned to dirt. We have this no dirt policy but thought we would investigate how far up the dirt road it was. As soon as we touched the dirt, we saw it and turns out it was free as well. We both turned to each other and said "this will do" as the town was nice and we were both sick of driving in the heat. The area was dry and had no facilities but we didn't mind as we could at least explore the town tomorrow and get a bit of a rest. The afternoon cooled down and we got great nights sleep.

Day **153**

The morning was cool and dry and we were looking forward to having a bit of a look around Cowell. We needed a few grocery items so we decided to walk the one kilometre back into town and visit the local IGA. We secretly hoped for a Sunday Market to be on but we seem to luck out on these, as we have always been in the wrong areas. But today was our lucky day because as we approached the main street of Cowell, we could see a lot of activity and then we spotted the street stalls. It was not a huge market but it looked lovely and they even had live entertainment. We looked around for some bargains and came across some good books and a DVD. This time there was boy books and I got to buy some, I now have enough reading material for the rest of our trip, I think.

There were lovely cake stalls and all the old-fashioned stuff that you don't see much of anymore like homemade jams and pickles, different nuts, food and two headed oysters. Yes, they had two headed oysters for $7.50 per dozen, but I am not sure if that price was per head or per double head. I must admit I had more expected double headed oysters in Tasmania than South Australia – but times change!

After browsing the market stalls, we headed to the IGA as it closed at 12-00 noon and we needed a few things. The prices were very expensive but we only needed a few things, and what we got was reasonable in price with most being on special. The eggs were a huge price and I remembered seeing some at the market so I said to Tee that we should go back and grab those. We did that and, on the way, back through the market Tee said she would like to look at the Art Gallery.

The art was housed in a lovely old building with the works of a number of local artists who all had them priced so well. The ladies that were on hand to direct people were lovely and they even had feedback forms to try and gauge what people liked for future works of art. That was a great idea as it kept people looking and really appreciating what they saw. Tee and I both seemed to like one particular artist as we both wrote down her work for a number of the three favourites that we were asked to nominate on the form. There was more art upstairs and the works even lined the stairwell. I think the winter months here must be cold and windy as these artists seemed to have a lot of time for their hobby.

Upstairs was a studio where it seemed all the artists came together to do their works and it was not long before Tee spotted her favourite painting. When she pointed it out to me from across the room it stood out from all the other paintings in its fine detail and classic style. It was a painting of an old MG motor vehicle on a dirt road with gum trees in the background. The detail was superb and we loved it straight away with both of us nominating it as our favourite. It was one of the only ones that were framed and when we saw the price we nearly fell over; it was only $25.00. But our problem is space in the Motorhome and even though we loved it we were not sure how to transport it. Tee came up with a solution to store it behind the hanging clothes in the small wardrobe and said she was sure it would fit. Armed with this knowledge I asked the lady how we could purchase it and she told us to take it downstairs where the ladies would wrap it for us and we could pay them for it. We could not believe our luck that this painting was so good and yet so remarkably cheap.

We took the painting downstairs to the ladies and one of them took it away to wrap while the other told us the history of the painting. She told us that the lady who painted it was a 77-year-old woman who had a life full of men, having two husbands and three further boyfriends – it was a wonder she had time to paint! These local ladies seem to love the gossip stuff. She went on to say that the car was her first boyfriend's car that she had a photo of and painted it from that. An unusual story but it mattered little to Tee and I as we both loved the painting. Armed and loaded with all our purchases we struggled back to the Motorhome in the midday sun.

Back at the Motorhome we unloaded our gear and decided to cook up a bit of lunch. With the awning out and a slight cool breeze it was quite pleasant sitting outside. The flies were down in numbers so we sat out there for the afternoon reading and patting the dogs of the other campers who all kept coming over to visit. But we love animals so we didn't mind and the atmosphere at the campsite was reasonably pleasant, even though we kept to ourselves.

There were though the Chinchilla feral's who spent the whole day drinking and were fairly noisy into the late evening. But we have to learn to deal with this sort of shit as the free camps tend to attract these sorts from time to time and at least there were no whiz bangers here. I must explain the term "whiz bangers" as it is a new term to me also, which we heard in the town of Normanville from some Queensland travellers. The term "Whiz Bangers" comes from the noise that those vans make when their side doors are pulled shut – Whiiiiizzzzzz – Bang! And the people who sleep and live in them are generally feral tourists with the biggest group hiring "Wicked Vans". They come to the free camps or foreshores late in the evening and stay up making noises or partying until the early hours of the morning. They are in and out of the vans constantly and they don't leave the door open. They continue to open and shut the door creating the constant "Whiz Bang" noise all evening. They are extremely selfish and care little about other campers or for the environment.

We had a good afternoon and have decided we may stay here a third night as the weather is again forecast to be hot for a few more days before cooling off on Wednesday. If we stay here until Tuesday morning, we will be able to balance the budget and have full budgets to work on until we have to service the Motorhome in about four weeks. We had a late Dinner of Sausages and Veg, and the evening was clear and cool with the night sky full of stars. The Chinchilla feral bunch did keep us awake for a while but we slept quite well all in all.

Day **154**

Short on Motorhome water we decided to take Lizzie into town and do some domestic chores. We had neglected to check if there was any Laundromat's in town yesterday and decided that if there was, we would do a spot of washing. The trusty shitter needed to be emptied and we were also getting low on drinking water. I also had just run out of bread so the first stop would be the local IGA to grab a loaf as they had none there on Sunday.

As we pulled Lizzie in to town we immediately spotted the Laundromat, and while Tee sorted the washing, I ducked over to the IGA to grab a loaf of bread. Unbelievable – it's a public holiday here today – Adelaide Cup- and I nearly walked straight into the un-opening automatic doors. Bread will have to wait, so while Tee was doing the clothes washing, I took Lizzie to the Dump Point down the road to empty the shitter and fill up with general water. As I pulled in, I also noticed they had tank water – now that was a bonus as I hadn't seen it there when we passed here a few days ago. Drinking water is a big thing in SA as the tap water is not real flash, but fortunately a lot of places have good quality tank water and both Tee and I love tank water.

After doing all the domestic chores on Lizzie I drove back to Tee who was reading magazines and chatting to a lady who was from Tassie. I snuck over to the pub while Tee was chatting and bought a slab of beer (to help us cope with the hot weather). When the washing was finished, we drove back to the free camp site to hang up all the freshly washed clothes to dry. When we arrived back, we soon realized that the wind was too strong to put the awning out and we would have to use a rope clothesline which we could tie to the mirror of Lizzie and across to the only ratty dead tree close to the Motorhome. This turned out to be quite an ordeal as the wind was so strong that it threatened to rip the poor ratty tree out of the ground and send all of our fresh washing into the red dirt. I stood with the washing to ensure that the wish of the wind did not come true and as luck had it the washing was all dry in less than an hour. We spent the rest of the afternoon trying to stay cool and without the wind I don't think we would have survived (I am such a drama queen) but shit it was hot.

That evening we had a few of those lovely beers and looked forward more to two day's time than merely tomorrow, as the weather had promised to cool down by then and we could enjoy the countryside in more bearable terms. Tomorrow we were off to Tumby Bay with a couple of stops on the way. I have emailed the Modra's Apartments accommodation to try and secure a powered site for the next few nights as we would then be able to run the air-conditioning and abate some of this heat.

Day **155**

ore dramas on the home front as the new lease on one of our rental properties started late last week and the tenant had failed to increase their direct credit amount or to add to the Bond as the lease required. This would mean chasing up and the anxiety of trying to manage affairs from a long distance. Some good news though as I received an email from Modra's Apartments who have a powered site ready and waiting for us.

Today the mercury has promised to reach 40 degrees and it was almost 30 degrees by the time we left the Cowell free camp site at 9-00am. The trip to Tumby Bay from Cowell is only 110 klms and with only two stops planned along the way we should be at Tumby Bay by 12-00 noon or so. Our first stop was to be Arno Bay and as we turned off the highway to Arno Bay, we noticed that the mercury had already reached 40 degrees and it was barely 10-00am.

Arno Bay was a lovely little town and they had gone to a lot of effort to present the town at its best, with a lovely display at the highway exit to town which had a little sailor in a boat and a dolphin statue floating among flowering red roses. Arno Bay itself looked lovely also with beautiful facilities and a very well-presented little town. We stopped for a cuppa at the foreshore park but did not walk around much as it was quite windy. The next town was Port Neill, which was equalled as well presented as Arno Bay but with a slightly larger population and more interesting coastline. It would probably make a better choice to stop at if you were only going to stop at one, but we were glad we saw both.

This heat is unbelievable and it is very energy sapping, so even though we were keen to see as much as we can, the heat is forcing us to take shelter. We decided to drive straight to Modra's Apartments and check out our site before looking in the town of Tumby Bay.

We arrived at the Modra's Apartments at about 12-30pm and the place looked fantastic as it was surrounded by palms and lovely native trees, (something you don't see a lot of in SA). It was like a little oasis and at $15.00 p/n for a powered site and only $5.00 p/n unpowered it was exceptional value. We met with Damien and he showed us the sites available and we said we would just slip into town and be back in an hour or so. We couldn't believe our good fortune and the plan was to spend three nights here with the first night powered and the last two unpowered.

So, it was off to the town area of Tumby Bay and what a charming little town it was. We had a bit of shopping to get and fully expected to find that the prices would be quite high. But we found them to be extremely well priced and even cheaper than a lot of the larger towns along the way. The lady who ran the shop was lovely and the fruit and veggies were so so fresh. We bought the things we needed, had a quick look around the town then headed back to Modra's where we could enjoy the air conditioner and top up Lizzie's batteries.

We spent the rest of the afternoon trying to keep cool as the outside temperature hovered around 40 degrees all the day long. Then at about 6-00pm a lovely cool changed rocked through and the temperature plummeted to 28 degrees in less than an hour. By the time we went to sleep after watching a movie we had turned off the air con and enjoyed a natural cool breeze from our open windows. We were so pleased with the drop in temperature and we looked forward to spending the next week or so exploring the area in kinder conditions.

Day **156**

Wow what a sleep we had last night, that heat had really knocked us about, and we didn't wake until 9-00am. We set off about 10-00am for a walk on the foreshore and planned to do a bit of fishing this arvo on the turn of the high tide at about 3-30pm or so. The town of Tumby Bay is lovely and the townsfolk all wave to you as you go by. They are revegetating the sand banks with native plants and have lovely green grass that is meticulously maintained all along the foreshore. We went for a long walk and then went back to the Motorhome to enjoy some reading and writing before our fishing adventure.

At about 3-00pm we headed off to the jetty which was about a kilometre from where we were staying and were hopeful for a catch or two. The weather was quite blustery but not cold so we were still hopeful we may have some luck. Whatever the outcome of the fishing the walk to and on the jetty was lovely and we checked in with a few old salties on the jetty to see how the fishing was. They were after squid and had light luck with only a couple caught.

Now fishing is a frustrating pastime for Tee and I as we both love it but are not very successful at it. We have to remember that it is "all about the journey" and not the result. This was good advice to adhere to as without one bite let alone a catch, we would be very cranky if we relied on fishing to survive. We had a great relaxing time though as the sun was lovely, the temperature mild and the company grand. We took photos of each other and named them "this is what people who don't catch fish look like while fishing" and we had become experts at it. We walked back to the Motorhome with an empty bucket and smiles on our faces, happy that we could afford to buy fish if we were so inclined.

That evening we did a few chores which included defrosting the fridge before retiring early to read.

Day **157**

Today would be our last day in Tumby Bay and this morning I restocked and restarted the fridge while Tee did her hair and makeup. We didn't have much planned for the day but I have checked all the camp spots and shopping areas in and around Port Lincoln as we will have to do a big shopping there tomorrow. There are no major towns between Port Lincoln and Ceduna, and Ceduna will probably be pricey. So, the supplies that we do have will have to last us at least two weeks until we reach Western Australia.

We went for another walk into town today and bought a few supplies including some farm eggs from a gift shop in town. The weather today is lovely with the sun shinning and a mild top of 25 degrees forecast. We walked back from town via the back streets as we had been on the beach road numerous times now and we wanted to look at some of the older homes. It was a nice walk and the area was full of character homes, nothing flash but with plenty of character. When we got back to the Motorhome, we filled up our water supplies and I sat in the sun reading while Tee sent off some emails to family and friends. Tee made me some sandwiches for lunch and came and joined me at the outdoor tables with some of her crackers and condiments.

After lunch I checked over the Motorhome to ensure we were all ready to leave early in the morning. I checked the new batteries to ensure that the didn't need topping up, (which they didn't), and I also checked the oil and fluid levels which were also all good. We gave the Motorhome a spruce up and while I was putting away the fishing rods, I broke one of the eyelets. No matter as I had super glue and would fix it straight away, (or so I thought), but soon discovered that the super glue had gone hard in the tube. Don't you just hate that, and I cannot remember a time when I have got a second use out of those silly little tubes.

Looking at the rough schedule that I have produced we are due to cross the Nullarbor late this week but we are a bit behind, not that it matters. I have checked the wind directions and at present the wind is blowing East to West, (which is what we want), and will do so for at least the next five days. If we just cruise, we should get most of the way across the Nullarbor with a tailwind and we can just hope that the wind continues in that direction for three or four more days after that to give us a tailwind all the way across.

A hamburger for dinner as the cloud cover increases and so comes to an end what has been a lovely day.

Day **158**

O ff we go this morning leaving the lovely sleepy town of Tumby Bay behind. We have had a great few days here and it has been a good rest spot for us after the long heat wave of late last week and the start of this week. We decided to shoot back into the town of Tumby bay to pick up some of those yummy hamburger patties that we had last night as they were superb. When we got into the shop, we found that the price had been marked down and we bought all four packets that they had on the shelf and a few other items they had on special.

Port Lincoln was where we wanted to do the major shopping and we were off in that direction by 10-00am, after our little detour. On the way we did another little detour to the town of Louth Bay, which turned out to be a lovely spot. We went for a walk on their southern foreshore where we found a lovely rock outcrop that stretched into the ocean and on the way back, I almost stood on a Blue Tongue Lizard who had wrapped himself around a small shrub and was close to invisible. We took a photo of him before returning to the Motorhome and then onto Port Lincoln we went.

We arrived in Port Lincoln some fifteen or so minutes later and were greeted with the hustle and bustle of a busy town. In fact, it was more like a small city. We decided to do what we had to here and move on as soon as possible as Tee and I both don't like hustle and bustle. The first stop was to a Coles supermarket that we almost drove into upon entering town, which was handy. They had great prices there and we were lucky enough to get a lot of what we wanted on special.

Next was to buy petrol, and the Shell was just around the corner from the Coles and not by accident as they are often close to each other offering discount fuel vouchers to their shopping customers. The servo was very tight and not at all designed to cater for Motorhomes. I had a tight squeeze getting Lizzie onto the right side of the Diesel pump. I commented to an old dude who was parked on the other side of the pump but he was a dead set prude and just looked at me stupid. Tee had the same result with the gentleman's wife who, when Tee said hello to her, just pulled a stupid face. These two honestly thought their shit didn't stink, so we just smiled at them, smiled at each other and had a good laugh about it when we left the servo.

We had planned to go to a curtain shop also, as we had broken a few curtain clips in the Motorhome, but the place was so busy we decided to just get the heck out of there. I am sure Port Lincoln has some nice places to visit but it was too busy for us. We spotted a KFC and could not help ourselves and we stopped for a yummy lunch – thanks Colonel! On the way out of town we spotted a Liquorland and we stopped to buy some more beer for our trip across the Nullarbor.

The next leg of our journey took us past Lincoln National Park and also past Coffin Bay. We decided that we would not go to either of these places, even though they seemed to be good destinations. The reason for this was that I had checked the wind patterns over the Nullarbor and until Tuesday they blew from East to West and after that would turn West to East. This gave us four days to cross the rest of the Eyre Peninsula and the Nullarbor with favourable winds. In a car this would perhaps not be too much of an issue but with the size of Lizzie and her being a little overweight (not her good living but ours) it would be a fair bit extra in fuel and a strain on poor old Lizzie.

The road moved away from the coast for a considerable distance making the scenery a little dull. But this all changed when we got to Lake Hamilton and more specifically Cummins Lookout. The lake was stunning as it was a pale blue colour with salt pan edges and desert surroundings. We pulled up to the Information board / Rest area not thinking that the beach was so close or at all nice. Boy were we in for a surprise as even though the road was dirt we decided to go and have a look. As we climbed the road the view of Lake Hamilton got better and better. We took photos as we travelled and even spotted a group of Emus enjoying a farmer's paddock. When we arrived at the top of the range, we could see that we had climbed onto huge cliff tops that towered over the wild ocean below. We walked to the lookout where we saw a magnificent coastline that was hungrily being devoured by the enormous waves and had produced caves, cliff collapses and pillars similar to those that we witnessed at the Twelve Apostles. This place was absolutely superb and goes straight onto our "must see list".

Soon after Cummins Lookout we reached Elliston which was charming and a place that we considered staying at. But with a few free camps just up the road and a budget that would be savaged by fuel costs over the next few days we decided to press on. We did spend enough time there though to explore its coastline and it is definitely a great place to stay if you are a Caravan Park type person.

By this stage of our journey it was after 5-00pm and we were getting a little tired. With the free camp area only about forty minutes drive away we were looking forward to pulling up for the day. But as we arrived where the free camp should have been, NOTHING, and we were starting to get a bit pissed off that we didn't stop earlier. We carried on to where another free camp was supposed to be and again, NOTHING. It was now a little after 7-00pm and with Streaky Bay only about fifty kilometres away we decided to make it our destination and stay in a paid Caravan Park. This was really not what we wanted to do and with one more free camp before Streaky Bay it was our last chance to stop somewhere free of charge.

Just before we were to find our last free camp area Tee spotted a signpost to Murphy's Haystacks that we really wanted to see. Now a dilemma! As if we didn't go there and went on and the free camp area and it was again not there, we would travel all the way into Streaky Bay. Then if we wanted to see Murphy's Haystacks, we would have to drive back the 40 kilometres to see them and waste a total of 80 kilometres of fuel. We decided to go to Murphy's Haystack and take the risk!

Now Murphy's Law is not normally a favourable one, but perhaps because I am half Irish, he shined his light on me and produced a favour to which Tee and I likened to a miracle. Murphy's Haystack parking area WAS A FREE CAMP. And not just any free camp but an ultra quiet free camp with no Wicked Vans or French tourists – alleluia!!!!

Day **159**

Wow! What a great night's sleep, with the temperature being very mild, a cool breeze and a sky full of stars. This morning we plan to get another fair bit of driving done but first it was off to look at Murphy's Haystacks. There was no need to look at them last evening once we knew we had a place to sleep. We walked up to them and were greeted by quite an awesome natural wonder. We saw them in the distance from our Motorhome but did not realize there was so many and how unusual their shapes were. We walked around them for over an hour taking heaps of photos and enjoying their beauty from every angle.

After our little adventure we were off "on the road again" with our first place of interest being Streaky Bay. We arrived there at about 10-00am and it was the first time in a day or so that we had mobile reception so we both checked our messages after pulling up on the foreshore area. I had a message from my best mate Albert (from Yarrawonga) who had just completed a motorcycle tour of Tasmania. I rang him back and we had a chat for a while before he told that he had come off his bike while he was there. I was quite concerned as I know how he loves his bike riding and we spoke at length about how it was shit getting older. I said to him that it was difficult to comprehend but our reflexes are not the same as when we are young and that it is not a crime to "live your age". I think it is a very hard age for a guy (50ish) as you still think you can conquer the world but the truth is that your reflexes and movements are not as sharp and you just have to accept it.

I am really lucky as Tee is good about this and tells me all the time to take it easier. In the end he said to me that this was a good warning to him as he knew that if it wasn't for his leathers, he would have been seriously injured. He went on to say that "between him and I", this would be his last tour of this type and that he will just cruise on his bike now and not push things like he has. This was very nice to hear as he is a very important person in my life and one that has been a friend for over 30 years and attended both my weddings.

Streaky Bay was a lovely town but it was a little commercialized and once you have seen it, you have seen it. I am sure it is a great holiday destination for South Australians.

Off again and just passed Streaky Bay we saw an acreage subdivision where one-acre blocks were for sale directly on the waterfront (amazing) as we didn't think there were still places like this. Off again and off to the left we saw the most amazing group of white Sandhill's which Tee photographed in large quantity. Then we pulled into the small town of Smokey Bay where we saw heaps of industrial sheds that were all Oyster processing sheds, there must have been forty of them! Smokey Bay Township was quite pretty and very old fashioned and it looks as though they had resisted the temptation to commercialize. It had a long jetty and a lovely foreshore area where they had planted a number of palm trees (very nice little place).

Now off to Ceduna which Tee remembers from her childhood, and her family trip to Western Australia (not so many years ago ☺). When we pulled into Smokey Bay, we had spotted what we called the dual vans that were parked side by side at Murphy's Haystack. We called them that as these couples had bought identical vans and were travelling together. Tee and I have found that generally oldies are quite quiet when on their own but when they travel in groups they act like kids and get quite noisy. They must feel more comfortable and generally are knocking over a wine or two most evenings, good on em! We have learnt to park away from them though as we are on a year's journey and need our sleep whereas most of these oldies are just taking a short break and kicking up their heels.

We arrived in Ceduna and Tee could remember it even though it had got a bit trendy and the grass had been replaced with shrubs in the middle of the main street. She remembers the grass as she said that the Aborigines were sitting on it drinking out of brown paper bags (cordial I guess). There were still a lot of Aborigines in town but they were on the foreshore and were not drinking, with their kids running about having fun. Tee gave them a wave as we went past and they all waved back which was lovely. We pulled up in a foreshore parking area where Tee whipped up another yummy platter and we ate it overlooking the Ceduna jetty and beach area, it was lovely. On the way out of Ceduna we filled up with fuel and plan to top up at every opportunity.

After Ceduna and over the next 150 kilometres there were about five free camp areas that I had circled so surely, we would find on of these (not like yesterday). The first two were a bit ordinary as they were right next to the highway, which is OK but with the trucks can be quite noisy. We then topped up the fuel again in the town of Penong, which was an interesting little outback town and onwards we went. The next free camp area was also ordinary and we were starting to think we would not find a good spot and decided that we would stop at the next free camp area even if it was close to the highway. But fortunately, the next free camp area had a track that lead into bushland and when we spotted another caravan there, we thought "this will do us".

It was a lovely little bush camp area that was just set back enough from the roadway and the wayside stop. Soon after we settled in a car pulled in with two men and a lady. They had stopped for a toilet break as we later found out when the young lady, who did not see us, dropped her pants to expose to us all her glory. After that excitement the place settled down to be a perfect little overnight stop.

Day **160**

Although basically just the side of the road it was reasonably quiet here and we both slept exceptionally well. The weather has been superb as the sun has been out most days with the temperature always remaining below 30 degrees and the nights mild to cool. Today is about knocking over a few kilometres while enjoying the scenery as we get closer to the WA border. We have not planned to stop anywhere and will just take the day as it comes.

As we travelled through the Yalata Aboriginal Reserve there seemed to be a lot more tree growth but apart from that the landscape remained reasonably constant. Apparently, the areas that are just low shrubs are like that because of the soil type and its variation between Limestone and Loam. Then towards the end of the Aboriginal land we spotted a sign saying Head of Australian Bight where there was whale watching from the shoreline "in season". Seeing it was a sealed road we decided it would be worth a look even though it was 12 kilometres in. As we headed down that road we began to travel in a more South Easterly direction and encountered what it would be like to travel into the wind. It gave us an appreciation as it had quite a big impact on Lizzie who was struggling and generally not enjoying herself.

When we arrived at the foreshore car park, we were amazed to see that it was going to cost us $5-00 each to see our own coastline. I don't know too many places in Australia that charge Australians to see their own beaches, but as it looked nice, we decided to pay up and take in the scenery. (Not sure how much it cost in season.) The views from the boardwalks were quite amazing, especially the huge sand dunes to the left of the path.

The ocean was stained with the colour of the cliffs as the waves consistently tore away at the bottom of this spectacular country. (Wow!).

We continued our journey and a few minutes after reaching the main highway again we spotted a dingo on the side of the road that quickly darted into the shrubs as we got closer. Fortunately, though we were quick enough to get some shots of him and when he got a safe distance into the paddocks he turned and just looked at us and we took some more photos. Even though he was a mangy looking specimen we are getting a good photo collection of the native wildlife. It was not long after that we spotted another dingo and took even better shots. This Dingo was a lot younger looking than the first one and looked considerably healthier.

Not long after our Dingo encounters the road came within sight of the coastline and we were able to visit a number of lookouts that were all quite spectacular. The first was the best, and although it was a free camp area and we were able to stay there we decided not to as the wind was ferocious. We just cruised up the coastline towards the WA border looking for the most suitable free camp spot and with a choice of six or so before the border we settled on a spot about 50 kilometres east of WA.

The spot we chose had a water tank and Tee was impressed as she wanted to wash her hair tonight and as we had already done two nights on the tank it would empty us out if she did. One of the only things that is inadequate in Lizzie is her water supply which is only 55 litres. But to be honest we have taken every opportunity to fill up and it has not proven to be a problem "as yet". We have 40 litres of drinking water which we think is more important anyway and we closely monitor this.

We wanted to stop short of the border as we had bought a heap of fruit and veggies in Port Lincoln a few days ago and did not realize that we could not take them into WA. So, we took this opportunity to eat as much as we could and Tee made up some yummy potato salad and honeyed carrots so we wasted nothing. I gave her one of my secret recipes called zucchini boats which she insisted on making under my instructions even though I said I would cook them. Tee takes great pride in saying she is the master chef of the household and as I get absolutely spoilt in the process, I have learnt to agree.

Day **161**

We had a great night's sleep and did not leave our campsite until almost 10-00am and on the way out we topped up our water supply. The coastline as we travelled changed again as it went from sheer cliff face to the land tapering off to the waterline. We came across another vantage point to view the coastline and pulled in. From here we could see the waves more clearly but there still did not seem to be much sand. We spoke to an elderly couple from Perth for a while before heading off again. Prior to the border we stopped at one more viewing point and met a couple from Frankston in Victoria who were doing a three-month trip to WA. While speaking to them another couple came over and said "Howdy Neighbour", and Tee said to me later that we had stopped in the same free camps as them two nights running. We all had a chat for a while before all heading on our own way (which was the same way in fact).

When we reached the WA border, we were confronted by quite a checkpoint and these guys were quite serious. We had got rid of all our veggies and I threw the last into a bin they had beside the checkpoint. They inspected the vehicle and we even had to give them our honey, which we did not realize. We saw the Frankston couple at the checkpoint who we had met earlier, and gave them a wave before proceeding into Western Australia.

Our fuel level was about half full and we were unsure where to fill up next as when we got to Eucla the fuel price for Diesel was $1.92.9 per litre. But it would be a risk to try and get to Madura Roadhouse and the prices may be even higher. We say this as the Nullarbor Roadhouse was $2.04.9

per litre. So begrudgingly we filled it up (or close to it) for $75.00, it would normally be closer to $50.00 but as the fellow next to me said – ya gotta have it! (All this time the Brisbane price for Diesel was $149.9 p/l)

A few days earlier I had picked up a tourist brochure that had mentioned Eucla and more specifically the ruins of the Old Telegraph Station. After filling the fuel, we headed off to see it. As we reached the back of the Eucla Roadhouse, we realized that it was perched high above sea level and that there was about two kilometres or so of land before the Old Ruins and about another five hundred metres to the ocean. We travelled out to the Old Telegraph Station that was filled with sand but still in reasonable condition for ruins. We took photos of each other there before deciding to go and see what the beach here looked like. It was a long walk and with the sun getting quite hot the temperature was increasing rapidly.

We reached the beach and were spellbound by its beauty. The sand was brilliant white and soft like talcum powder, with the ocean an optical light blue before getting darker at where the seaweed was. There was an old dilapidated jetty there that we could not get onto, but it made a marvellous backdrop for the stunning photos we produced. On the way back to Lizzie we marvelled at the huge sand dunes and the amazingly different landscape we were witnessing.

Back on the road again and the highway came down the embankment to the lower plains not long after Eucla and followed us on our journey for many many kilometres. We had a pile of luck over the next 50 or so kilometres as we got to see and photograph three emus followed by a group of three Wedge Tailed Eagles that were feasting on some fresh road kill. Tee got a ripper shot of one as it had just broken into flight.

Not long after all this excitement we spotted a shady looking rest stop and we decided to stop for a bite to eat and a short rest. As we arrived Tee spotted something in a tree nearby and I thought she said "look at the Koala" but in fact she had said "look at the Galah's". I grabbed the camera a got a couple of lovely shots of these two lovebirds who were only metres from the Motorhome. Turns out they were Major Mitchell Pink Cockatoos, and neither of us had seen them before, it was really exciting. I tried to slip out of the Motorhome and get some more shots but they fled when they heard the door open.

After lunch I told Tee that I was really tired and that I wouldn't mind staying here the night. As I said that, a weird looking fellow in a hi-ace van turned up and with his thick black beard and odd look he quickly earned the nickname of Creepy Jesus from Tee. We went for a walk after lunch which made me feel a bit better and with a huge amount of inland driving ahead of us, we decided to push on.

We travelled a further 300 kilometres and stopped at a roadside stop about 120 kilometres short of the Balladonia Roadhouse. The roadside stop had a heap of caravans in it and we went out the back of it and camped in bushland about fifty metres from everyone else. We went to bed really early, but I could not tell you what time it really was as we had crossed time zones and all the clocks and watches in the Motorhome showed different times. All I can tell you is that it was dark when we went to sleep and we had a superb sleep.

Day **162**

We awoke before the sun rose this morning and Tee was keen to get some kilometres in before it got warm. The goal for the day was to reach Norseman and stop at a free camp some 70 kilometres south of Norseman on the road to Esperance. I took some photos of the sun rising before we headed on our journey for the day.

The first challenge was to reach Balladonia without running out of fuel as I had passed a few roadhouses late yesterday in the hope that the price would start to drop as we got deeper into WA. I thought I had heaps of fuel but as I got to about 50 kilometres from Balladonia, I started to get quite concerned. In fact, I had made mental plans of getting on one of the pushbikes and locking Tee in the Motorhome while I rode to Balladonia for fuel. Of course, I did not tell Tee this as I felt like such a tight arse trying to run the gauntlet over a few dollars savings on fuel. As we got closer and closer to Balladonia, I imagined my bike ride getting shorter and shorter and it was only when I knew we would make it that I told Tee what was going on.

Even though I admitted to being a tight arse I only purchased $50-00 worth of fuel in Balladonia as I was sure this would easily get us to Norseman which was 190 kilometres away. On the way to Norseman we stopped at a place called Newman Rocks and I stopped there mainly to photograph the sign as my friend Dave's surname is Newman and I could send it to him in an email. It turned out to be a lovely place, and as the area we were now travelling though had recently received heavy rainfall, it was quite green and very pretty (nothing at all like Dave!!).

We made it to Norseman and after exploring the town we filled up with fuel to head to our free camp area. Fortunately for me the fuel price was some thirty cents cheaper than Balladonia and I could again justify my title of "chief tight arse".

The free camp area on the way to Esperance was OK and we looked forward to a relaxing evening.

Day **163**

Turned out we had quite a good night's sleep apart from some late arrivals who started pitching a tent at 10-30pm. That doesn't sound too late but because we have just crossed time zones the sun goes down at about 6-30pm compared to 8-30 in South Australian time. This has thrown us out a bit as we have been used to going to bed when it got dark, but now, we are lucky to have eaten Dinner before the sun goes down.

Today we would be visiting the town of Esperance and I have been really looking forward to this as I have been told it is beautiful. On the way there we stopped at a place called Grass Patch (funny name) where we found some tank water and water for our daily use. We topped up and kept on towards Esperance. On the way the landscaped changed with the paddocks turning brilliant green from all the recent rains and the Banksia's were in full bloom.

When we arrived in Esperance, we found a very busy town which was not too dissimilar to Port Lincoln. I think both these towns have become important shipping towns for the mining industry and in doing so have lost a lot of their tourist appeal. We stopped to buy Petrol and supplies (mainly fruit and veg that we lost at the border) and we went in search of the white sandy beaches. We found a coast road that took us to a lovely lookout and as we arrived there the sun came out just in time for us to capture the 360-degree views. The surrounds of Esperance are stunning with a sheltered harbour and a bay of Islands just off the coast. We went for a short walk and on returning the sun decided to disappear again which seemed to make the wind pipe up and make its mark.

As we started to leave town, we found a Dump Point and I was able to perform my favourite task. While there we met a lovely grey bearded fella (I say he was lovely as he called us Young Un's) who told us that Cape Le Grand National Park was an awesome spot and that they had just come from there. We were tempted to go there but the weather was now turning unpleasant with strong southerly winds and light rain. The clincher as to why we didn't go was that we were now going to travel this whole coast anyway and he had told us that Cape Le Grand was very popular and it was hard to get a camp spot. Tee and I hate crowds and with it being 50 kilometres in and 50 kilometres back out we decided against going there. Turned out to be a good choice as when we started heading off again the Southerly wind go worse and the rain was intensifying.

We continued our journey west and as we did poor old Lizzie was getting hammered by the Southerly wind that was pushing her all over the road. It was so strong that I was getting quite a sore neck and shoulder from battling to keep her on a straight path. To add to the Wind the rain was adding its little bit of annoyance and the pair caused us havoc for about forty kilometres or so.

As the weather started to clear a little, we saw a signpost to Stokes National Park and although the road was unsealed, we decided to have a look as the rain had meant that we would not have too much drama with dust. In fact, the road was quite good and very smooth so it was an easy eight-kilometre drive to Stokes Inlet. On the way in we spotted a number of Emus that we stopped to photograph, as unlike the emus that we had seen before these fellas were on lovely green grass. Stokes Inlet was quite choppy due to the strong winds and with not much to do there unless you had a boat we continued on our journey.

At about 2-00pm we arrived at our free camp spot near the Munglinup Roadhouse and decided this would be our stop for the night. I was happy to stop here as my neck and left shoulder was quite sore and was kind of hoping Tee would massage it for me. We had a couple of beers and I was fortunate to get a massage which seemed to help heaps. Tee cooked up a hamburger for Dinner and I finished off the last of the pre-border potato salad – that was superb I might add.

Day **164**

Earlier this week we had decided not to go to Wave Rock which was about 150 kilometres off our coast road. But on reflection we both really wanted to see it so we decided that we would take our time over the next day or two and visit it along with a couple of lake areas that we could visit either side of our journey there. We woke early this morning and I spent most of the morning writing and Tee did a few chores inside the Motorhome.

We had an early lunch before setting off on our 100-kilometre trip for the day. Basically, we were just going from one free camp to another to get a bit closer to Wave Rock, and feel as though we had done something for the day. Before leaving Munglinup we topped up our daily water and did our usual pre-travel checks. The weather was quite mild and even slightly chilly which was a nice change, and it has made it much more pleasant for sleeping. It was a short drive from Munglinup to Ravensthorpe but the scenery was lovely as the landscape here has become quite undulating and there were a number of areas left to natural bush. Even the natural bush is quite different here to the East of Australia with a lot of Banksia's and other beautiful natives. We saw a huge open cut mine but apart from that the journey was quite uneventful until we got to Ravensthorpe.

Ravensthorpe was a nice little town and we stopped on the outskirts on the way into town to have a cup of tea. The place we stopped at had some old machinery and an old utility rusting away in a paddock; it was an old railway loading dock with the old railway station ruins up a track that you could see on a nature walk. We thought about having a walk and a look, but the recent rain had made everything quite muddy and the soil was a rich red colour and looked very sticky. We slowly drove through Ravensthorpe having a look at the town and were soon on an open road heading for our next free camp.

Within ten minutes we arrived at the free camp which looked OK from the road but was hard to park a Motorhome in, even one our size. The reason for this was that it had a lot of overhanging trees, and the areas without trees had unlevel ground. I have had a number of bad nights sleep trying to sleep on the wrong angle so I am now very fussy to get the levels just right as there is nothing worse than trying to drive and enjoy the next day on a bad night's sleep. We eventually found a good spot and although not far from the main road we set up camp.

After almost six months on the road now we are getting better at sleeping through passing trucks and it is more local noises that wake us now (like late arriver's and Whiz Bangers).

Being only about 1-30pm we had lots of spare time to read and do chores around the Motorhome and Tee gave me another shoulder massage as my neck and shoulder is still causing me grief. At about 6-30pm our nightmares came true with a whiz banger arriving and parking near us and then at 1-30am another vehicle awoke me (a late arrival). Fortunately, the whiz bangers were quiet and the late arriver's made little noise after arriving, and we did go to bed early so we still got a good night's sleep.

Day **165**

Absolutely freezing this morning, only seven degrees when we woke, but the sun was shining and we looked forward to a lovely day. We left the Free camp just outside Ravensthorpe at 7-30am as we are still not tuned to the WA times yet even though it is a lot like our time back home. The evenings here are dark unlike what we experienced in SA and Victoria over the summer months. Both Tee and I prefer the dark evenings when at home as it gives you slow down time before going to bed. But for travelling in a Motorhome the long light evening work fantastic. - Back to our Journey. -

We had planned to get to Wave Rock today and if the accommodation was OK, we would spend the night there. Our first stop was at Lake King which we thought would be a wet lake with the town built around it, but not the case. Lake King is a salt lake that is located six kilometres west of the township and we drove to it for a look. If you are not into salt lakes, I would not recommend going out of your way to see it, but Tee and I thought it was cool and were glad that we diverted off our track to see it. On the way through Lake King Township we checked out the fuel prices as we were starting to get a little low. The first place we stopped at was a 24-hr pump that was located beside the tavern. The price of the fuel was good but with the morning sun screaming on the unprotected display screen of where you pay, I decided to go to the general store to see what price they were offering. Fortunately, this was on the way to Lake King as the price at the General Store was 17 cents per litre higher (worth making the effort to read the unprotected screen). After looking at the lake itself we went back to the self serve 24 hr pump and muddled our way through the sun ravaged screen. I really hate those pumps but I suppose they fulfil a need and they are usually priced well.

As we travelled towards Wave Rock, we saw many works of what we call "Farm Art", which are sculptures made in metal and other quirky things that the farmers put at the front of their properties. The one that stood out in our minds was the farmer who had built a 20-metre-high pile of dirt, complete with a cliff face and had perched a dump truck on it with the front hanging over the cliff. We passed Holt Rock soon after which is another large granite outcrop and not too long after arrived at Wave Rock.

Upon arriving at Wave Rock, we saw that it had become commercialized, something that Tee and I did not particularly like. But because we had travelled 200 kilometres off our original track we were going to have to put up with the touristy shit. It costs $7-00 per vehicle to see Wave Rock which is not a lot of money but still an added expense seeing it is a long way off the track of most tourists. Anyway, we had a walk around and over the huge granite rock and took a pile of photos. I would highly recommend walking around the whole rock as you will get to see the many lizards that call this place home. They are amazing little creatures and run across the rock at a phenomenal speed. But on hot days keep your eye out for snakes who also love this place.

Wave Rock is a quite unique rock but we were only mildly impressed. If we had of known what it was like we may not have travelled all this way to see it. But if it is reasonably close to your journey plans, I would call it a "must see" place. They also need to improve the tracks around the rock as when we visited, there were fallen trees over the pathways, overgrown shrubs blocking the pathway and a lack of signage to mark the pathways. None of these things will bother you though if you are only going to the Wave itself.

The campground at Wave Rock was a dustbowl and we did not feel inclined to pay the $28-00 that they were asking as we had no plans to revisit the Wave so we headed off at about 2-00pm for a free camp spot about 120 kilometres North of Albany. We had a bite to eat at Hyden even though it was after 2-00pm. We did this as we would be lucky to reach our campsite by sunset which occurred about 6-30pm in this neck of the woods. Tee had spotted a free camp that was closer on the map and we considered going there but as it was about 60 kilometres off our planned route we decided to push on.

We soon arrived at the town of Karlgarin where our navigator (NOT TEE) decided to have a brain freeze and sent us on a wild goose chase for about twenty minutes. As we were struggling to make the required distance before sunset this interruption did not go down too well. In fact, Samantha (or Karen if you put her on Aussie voice) was very close to navigating her own way out of the ditch on the side of the road. This would please Tee to no ends as it always seems to talk over her when she is speaking to me.

Finally, on track we travelled while watching the sun slowly fade in the West and it was touch and go if we would arrive in daylight. The one positive out of this late travel was the hordes of Australian Ringneck Parrots (twenty eight) that covered the roadway ahead of us. At 6-20pm we arrived at Louis's Lookout which was the most Northern of three campsites near the town of Borden that we could choose from. Louis's Lookout did not have a toilet but when we arrived there no-one was there. To us a campsite minus people far outweighs having a toilet block. Arriving just in time to see the last of the sun setting we marvelled at the view we were parked next to and the fact that no-one else was here to enjoy it. The view I am talking about was that of the Sterling Range which dominates the landscape in this neck of the woods.

Day **166**

We had a marvellous sleep, totally undisturbed; except for 5-30am when Albie rang me. He had forgotten that we were three hours behind his time and as I had text him last night, he was returning my call. I had text him last night to see if he and his family were OK as they had a Tornado in Yarrawonga yesterday, (according to an email I got from Mum). When I heard the phone ring, I knew it was him but did not get to the phone quick enough to answer it.

After brekkie I rang Albie and he described the Tornado damage to me in great length and in the typical Albie fashion, which includes many AHM AHH's followed by more AHM AHH's. He also told me that it was his 30th Wedding anniversary and that he and Jude were off to Echuca after lunch for an overnight paddle boat ride. After telling him Chopper got less than 30 years and after we took the piss out of each other for another 20 mins I had another cuppa with Tee.

As this spot was so nice, we decided to stay the day and head off on Sunday for Albany. This gave us rest time and time to prepare the route for the rest of our WA experience. Expecting to see a lot of cars during the day, as this was a lookout, we only had about six cars arrive the whole day and by 4-00pm no-one looked as though they would be camping the night either. Fingers crossed we will have another quiet night with mild overnight temperatures.

Day **167**

No other campers joined us last night and we had a marvellous sleep. The place again looked stunning as the sun rose and we looked forward to our day's travel which would take us through the Stirling Range and to Albany. We have picked out a free camp area that is about forty-five kilometres east of Albany and if it is no good Plan B will be to head west along the coast until we found a suitable site.

First things first though and I have to get fuel at the nearest servo as I had driven the day before yesterday in the hope that Borden would have a fuel station. But upon checking on the internet we soon realized they didn't and at first thought we would have to drive forty plus kilometres out of our way to get fuel at Gnowangerup. But fortunately, the town past Borden (Amelup) had a general store with fuel and we set the navigator to the task of getting us there. This sounded like a simple task but our navigator has a mind of its own and when you don't have a specific street in a town that you want to go to and select "centre of town" it picks its own street. In the city this is not too bad but, in the country, that street may be twenty kilometres from where you want to go.

We arrived in the town of Borden and filled up our daily water before continuing on to Amelup, and true to form the navigator tried to take us in the wrong direction. We were fortunate though as we saw an advertisement sign for the Amelup General Store after doing a U-turn on what I was sure was the incorrect direction. BLOODY NAVIGATOR!!!! Back on track and we soon found the General Store at Amelup and put $30-00 worth of petrol in Lizzie's tank, enough to easy get us to Albany where the fuel prices would be kinder.

As we approached and passed Amelup we were being shadowed by the mighty Stirling Range which to us looked very similar to the Grampians in Victoria. But unlike the Grampians in Victoria, WA charge an entry fee into this National Park, even to drive through it. With no desire to visit mountain ranges and quite content to view them from level ground we continued to Albany. We stoped just after the Mt Barker turnoff to have a cuppa and we did consider going to see Mt Barker but decided against it as it was a fair distance off our set route.

Albany looked like a busy and well-organized town and we soon found a Shell Servo where we got super cheap fuel and cleaned all our windows and mirrors that had collected some lovely bug specimens and rolled them in dust for good measure. I asked the guy in the servo where the Coles Supermarket was, to which he replied that they were not open on Sunday. I was amazed by this as some Coles Supermarkets in other states don't close day or night and 7 days a week, but he did help me with directions to the IGA for which I was most grateful. The IGA in Albany was in the older part of the town which is near the water, and upon approaching it we saw how lovely the town really was. In fact, it is what I expected Esperance to look like.

The IGA store was pumping, as you would expect with Coles and Woolworths shut, and we got all our needs before heading back to our "Plan A" free camp. The place we were heading for was a place called Norman's Beach and from Google looked very nice indeed. It was on a section of dirt road that went for about six kilometres, but I had also inspected this on Google Maps and the road looked quite good so we decided to break our "No Dirt Road" rule.

Upon arriving at the dirt section of road we were passed by a vehicle that had been following us for over 20 kilometres and once he hit the red dirt road, I worked out why he had passed us. I simply stopped the Motorhome and waited until the dust settled before slowly travelling the six dirt kilometres. The campsite was not as good as we thought it may be and we thought about turning to "Plan B" but with the budget tight and there not being many people here we chose to have a look at the beach before deciding. The beach was stunning, as was the landscape around it with pristine white sand, rolling Blue Ocean, soaring hills and granite boulders rolling into the ocean. Obviously, this persuaded us to stay and we went back to the Motorhome to set up camp. We had a late lunch before having a quiet afternoon. We thought about going fishing that afternoon but with us planning to stay here for two more days we decided to leave fishing until the morning.

Day **168**

The decision to stay here three nights came out of necessity as we were over budget and with Lizzie's service now due, we had to rein in costs. Norman's Beach looked great this morning and the place that we parked was beside a lagoon which was both to the left and front of our Motorhome. We had brekkie then headed to the beach for a spot of fishing. The beach was stunning and I had brought my camera to capture it beauty, as my skills with a camera are much better than that of a fisherman. We, or more Tee than I, tried our luck at fishing in both the lagoon and the ocean without success but I did get a heap of lovely photos. We went back to the Motorhome and had some lunch before cleaning all the salty gear with fresh water, which took a good couple of hours. The rest of the afternoon we read books before I cooked up a lovely pasta meal for our dinner.

My only complaint for the day was that we were surrounded by bloody young tourists who absolutely ruin these places for everyone else. They have no respect for other people and tonight we had some who parked within three feet of our Motorhome. In fact, if there was a fire or a flood, I would have to crash Lizzie through them to get out of the place. I had a go at him but he pretended not to understand English. I am patient with these things but one of these young bucks is going to push my button soon and pay the price. They are very rude young individuals who should be better behaved in someone else's country.

Turned out that Tee's buttons got pushed before mine and after them saying that they were not sleeping in the car they stayed in it until long after 10-00pm. The earlier annoyances we had to put up with as it was still early evening, but these were things that would not have annoyed us if they had parked a reasonable distance from our Motorhome. To give you an idea how close they were, when they had their car door open, they could not fit between their vehicle and our Motorhome. This would be understandable if the place was packed but it was not with only two other vehicles in a fairly large area. (2000m2)

The annoying things they were doing in the early evening included cooking fish within ten feet of our Motorhome and smoking right beside us. As I said we had to live with this as it was only about 8-00pm but it did annoy us as we could not leave our Motorhome windows open to enjoy the breeze and the fresh air. They had also set up there tents straight in front of us and spent from 9-00pm to 10-00pm going backwards and forwards to their car from the tents. With torches darting everywhere and their car doors banking three feet from where we lay chatting, we listening to the radio with the windows closed trying to drown out their noise.

At 10-30pm though enough was enough and Tee opened the window and told them to consider other people and SHUT UP. They made smart assed comments and I joined in by telling them in no uncertain terms to be quiet or I would make trouble for them in other ways. They seemed to shut up but I did hear one more door bang which woke me a little before midnight. Then proof came to us that there was a God and the wind picked up to a furious pace followed by driving rain. This woke us and we enjoyed the show from the Motorhome of them struggling to keep their tents dry. Sound a bit mean but they had driven us to anger and resentment. I even wondered if Ivan Milat had gone through the same process in the early days!

Day **169**

This morning we still woke early but were extremely tired with our concerns now turned from the horribly selfish tourists to the rising water level of the lagoon and the slippery road surface. One group left very early in the morning and had a hell of a time on the slippery road surface, so our concerns grew. They had also set up a tent but when the rain came ended up sleeping in their vehicle. We decided that if the rain continued, we would just stay here an extra day or until the road surface improved. By this stage we realized that the lagoon was at its peak and that flooding would not force us to leave but a slippery red road may delay our departure. We had all the supplies necessary to last a week but it would mean we would not have a shower as our daily water would only last until the morning in normal use.

The selfish tourists crawled out of their tent at about 10-00am and did not leave until lunchtime. They spent from 10-00am until about 11-00am in their car before coming out to pack up all their gear, by which time it was raining again. They were all giggling which re-enforced our belief that they were smoking dope then and the night before. It also explained their lack of empathy for other people around them. We were so glad to see the back of them but were now concerned that later today they would be replaced by other dickhead tourists.

As the early afternoon progressed, we had patches of sunlight and I went for a walk to see if I could find a parking area that would be higher and not allow vehicles to park alongside us. Lizzie is a great Motorhome and had no trouble getting us out of the soggy ground we were parked on and up the slight hill to higher ground. The spot I parked her in was fabulous and there was no way anyone would be able to disturb us this evening. Later that day Tee described the anxiety that these horrible inconsiderate people caused her and that she was so relieved and relaxed now that I had removed that possibility. I agreed and added further that it was something that the world was creating more and more of – a lack of empathy and a breed of passive aggressives.

Both relieved at the new position of Lizzie we had an afternoon nap and both felt great by the evening. We had a quiet evening as the occasional rain shower passed over us and we chatted while enjoying some radio and music.

Day **170**

This morning we are off to explore some of the southern parts of WA which is so green and pretty at the moment. But first with the overnight rain we have to contend with the six kilometres of greasy red dirt road. We decided to take it slow and easy as the surface looked quite slippery and we wanted to minimize the mud on the sides of Lizzie. The first five kilometres went well and then we came across a number of cars in a row. As we reached within a kilometre of the bitumen, we came up towards a large tractor heading the other way. I moved to the side of the road to keep out his way and that is when Lizzie slipped and went sideways into the ditch. Over a metre of the sides of the road was just slippery soft fill that looked firm but was not. I jumped out of the Motorhome to wave the tractor down and he stopped immediately. I checked the front of Lizzie and she was fine but well and truly stuck in mud. (So much for me trying to keep her clean).

The tractor fellow was a nice guy and he radioed to his mate to bring a chain so he could tow me out. We chatted while waiting for his mate and turns out they all worked for a large local farm here and were on their way to clear a paddock. When his mate arrived, we decided that the best way to tow Lizzie out was from the rear as if we tried from the front it may pull the back down into the ditch. At this point only the front of the vehicle was covered in mud so I much preferred towing it from the rear. They hooked up the chain and as easy as you like the five tonne Lizzie was pulled backwards out of her muddy embarrassment. The truth was I was more embarrassed than anyone, but the fellows were lovely saying that it is a shocking road and poorly constructed by the Albany Shire Council.

(I think they were just trying to make me feel better.) I jumped back in the Motorhome, thanked the guys, and within two minutes we were on the bitumen.

Back on the road we would drop into Albany to top up our supplies as there seems to be no major towns on our route until we reached the Margaret River area. Albany was busy so we wasted as little time as possible there, we both hate being in the city areas. From Albany we headed inland a bit and halfway to the town of Denmark we stopped for a cup of Tea and I wanted to have a good look at Lizzie and how she fared on her mud slide. No damage to Lizzie but a hell of a lot of thick red mud that would take a bit to remove, but most importantly neither Lizzie nor Tee and I were harmed in any way.

We soon reached the town of Denmark which was lovely and we found a water tap where we filled up the house water and also a couple of spare containers that we normally have our drinking water in. Our drinking water is starting to get low so we are planning very soon to book into a caravan park and while there top up the house batteries and do some laundry. In Denmark we stopped off to have a look in a second hand shop where Tee found some good books and I got some curtain clips to replace the broken ones in the Motorhome.

After Denmark we had marked a free camp area on the map that we were going to check out but we forgot about it and drove straight past it. The next thing we knew we were in the town of Walpole and we stopped to have a bit of a look around. The town was quite nice as it was located on a large inlet that was calm and pretty. We pulled up at the jetty and considered staying there the night as there was not any "no camping" signs. But we ended up not taking the risk of upsetting anyone and kept travelling.

Soon after the town on Walpole we found a roadside stop and both agreed that it would be fine to stay here for the night. After being there an hour or so all by ourselves the inevitable happened and a group of travelling tourists arrived, we thought it was too good to be true. There were four of them in a 4wd and they soon had their shit all over the place while setting up a tent. They were carrying on and pissing freely into the bushes in full view of the roadway. Tee and I were annoyed as the roadside stop was about 400 meters long and they had to park almost opposite us.

But we are getting a bit more cunning now and decided to sit tight until they were all set up, and then move the Motorhome well away from them. Another caravan turned up just before dark while I was cooking dinner and to our disbelief the grubby tourists quietened down and we no longer felt the need to move our Motorhome away from them.

Day 171

We actually had a great night's sleep and, in the morning, I took some photos of the overseas tourist's camp spot as I could not believe how much shit they could spread around in such a short time. Back on the road again and we planned not to travel too far today as we had decided overnight to not go to a caravan park in the Margaret River area and instead do some Laundry in Manjimup. We would then find a free camp near Willow Springs that we had marked in our Camp6 book. On the way to Manjimup we passed the town of Quinninup where we were going to stop for a cuppa but it was off the highway so we kept going.

Just shy of Manjimup we saw a wayside stop called Diamond Tree Lookout that we thought sounded interesting so we stopped there for a cuppa. After having a cuppa, we went to explore this Diamond tree and as we walked to it, I said to Tee, "wouldn't it be cool if we could climb it!" As we reached the tree, we realized that in fact we could climb the 171 feet to the top of it. The tree had a series of spikes driven into it that spiralled up the tree to the top where an observation tower had been built, it was quite amazing. Tee was not keen to climb it but I was super keen and off I went. Turns out it is quite a strenuous climb with only one stop on the way up in the form of a steel platform. The climb after the steel platform turned to a vertical climb and if you don't like heights then there is no way you should attempt this climb. The view from the top was amazing and if you can get over the fear of climbing steel pegs over 100 feet in the air you will love it. I took a heap of pictures along the way and more when I reached the top, where I took panoramic photos of the 360-degree views. This one goes on my "must do" list.

While we were over at the tree someone put a flyer on our windscreen advertising Quinninup Eco Caravan Park at $20.00 per night for a powered site. There was a Laundry there so we decided it would be economically viable to go there for a night or two. Before we went to the Diamond Tree, I had emailed a Caravan Park in the Margaret River area that was on a sheep station, to make enquiries. When we got back from my climb, they had emailed back saying they had saved a spot for us and were now booked out. Tee and I decided to go to Quinninup Eco Caravan Park for two nights as it was so cheap and then drive to Margaret River on Saturday and stay there for two further nights. This was a good plan as it was Easter Friday tomorrow and with the long weekend all the parks, free or charged, would probably be booked out. We had some lunch and then we set off for the Quinninup Eco Caravan Park which was about 20 kilometres back.

We arrived at the Quinninup Eco Caravan Park at about 2-30pm and met the owner who promptly told us that it was $30.00 per night as it was Easter. I voiced my disapproval and showed her the price on the flyer again stating that it had just been put on our windscreen today. She said that we could compromise at $25.00 per night. I was very annoyed but as we had driven back 20 kilometres to be here, we were now committed.

After parking the Motorhome Tee organized all the washing that needed doing and we went to the laundry together. As we got there, we discovered a couple of fellows removing one of the washing machines that had just broken down. This left one machine which was currently being used. The good news was that it was only $2.40 per load and with three loads we would make up for the extra $5.00 per day we had to fork out for the campsite.

The water here was disgusting though as it looked like straight creek water and I did not even put it into our house water it was so bad. This meant that our drinking water would get very low in the next few days and I decided to email the Margaret River Camping Park that I had booked to ensure they had tank water. They emailed me back that evening and said that they did; what a relief. This caravan park has nice grounds but the service and services give it a big thumbs down in my book. We spent the rest of the afternoon doing chores on the Motorhome and I took the bikes off the back and gave them a wash before cooking a pasta meal for Tee and I. The clothes would have to stay on the line overnight as they have not dried; in fact, we have had some small sprinkles of rain which ensured their fate until the morning.

Day **172**

Tee was restless last night and woke up not feeling too well this morning. I let her sleep in and sent off a few emails before offering to cook her bacon and eggs for brekkie, to which she eagerly responded "yes please!" After brekkie we had not many plans for the day other than to get Lizzie into shape for the next leg of our journey. As Tee was not feeling all that good, she went back to bed and read a book before falling asleep around midday. While she was reading, I kept checking the washing and continued my outdoor chores. These included washing the bike cover, washing Lizzie and repacking the boot so we had more room in the Motorhome.

That afternoon a couple and their young son arrived at the campsite next door to us and set up. It was not long before the young fellow came around to our side of the Motorhome and said hi. I asked him what his name was and he said in a very polite manner that his name was Jack. Now Jack was a very polite young man who very much reminded me of my own son Luke when he was that age. He had that whole Dennis the Menace look going on. He kept dropping over to see me and was a delightful young fellow who was always so polite and friendly. That is a lot for me to say as I am not a big fan of kids. One time he asked me – "do you have a lady in there?" pointing to the Motorhome, to which I replied "well yes Jack indeed I do". As I said this Tee popped her head out and said hi Jack, and Jack was satisfied with that and off he went. I spent the afternoon reading and the evening writing to complete a productive day and ensure that we were ready to head off early in the morning for Margaret River.

Day **173**

Absolutely freezing this morning with the inside temperature reading seven degrees. But we awoke early as we had no intentions of hanging around Quinninup, in fact we were on our way by 7.45am. On our way out Jack and his family were having brekkie and he waved feverishly as we drove out with a huge grin on his face. Lovely well-mannered boy.

We drove out of Quinninup and headed towards the town of Pemberton enjoying the lovely treed landscape as we travelled. The town of Pemberton was soon upon us and we purchased some fuel before heading again on our journey. Not far out of Pemberton we spotted a roadside stall that was boasting fruit and veggies for sale and we pulled over to see what they had. Turns out they only had apples but the location was so nice that we decided to have a cup of coffee there on the side of the road. To our left we watched a herd of cattle enjoying the pristine paddock that they called home. The whole area was surrounded by a huge Karri tree forest, the trees were massive. We took a number of photos before again heading off on our way, ultimately to Margaret River.

The landscape soon started to change to that of the coast with a huge number of Grass Trees (Black boys) and other less towering gum tree varieties. Before we turned to head to the Margaret River area our plan was to Visit Augusta and more specifically Cape Leeuwin which is the most South Western point of Australia. Arriving in Augusta we were confronted with an enormous crowd of people all over the town making parking impossible for us anywhere near the shopping district with Lizzie. Well it was Easter Saturday, and with that we headed to the inlet where we parked the Motorhome on the foreshore and went for a walk. It was a nice fishing spot but as I heard one of the Asian tourists say, the real sights were at Cape Leeuwin and the "Lie howse".

Cape Leeuwin was lovely but again very crowded so we parked Lizzie in a car park about 300mtrs from the main Lighthouse car park. The spot we parked in was for parking to look at the old Waterwheel which used to supply fresh spring water to the lighthouse. It has long stopped turning but the spring water still flows freely over the structure and due to its limestone content has calcified to create an unusual looking rock formation. We took photos while climbing over a huge rock outcrop which gave us stunning views over the two oceans. This is the spot where the Indian and Southern oceans meet. This spot is a truly remarkable and is a "must see" for the Aussie traveller but as to paying five dollars per head to enter the lighthouse grounds I am not sure. We certainly didn't feel the urge to pay it and were well satisfied with enjoying the beautiful scenery that could be witnessed without the tourist shit.

Again, off we went and we now decided to take the coast road towards Margaret River and stop at a few beaches on the way. The beach road certainly looked quieter than the road on which we came into Augusta on, and we were well pleased with our choice. We took a left turn at the Hamelin Bay Beach exit only to be confronted by another huge crowd at that location also. So, we took a few photos from the Motorhome and we were on our way.

Switching on the Navigator to take us to Margaret River meant that she tried to get us back onto the main highway which ran parallel to the beach road in a Northerly direction. But by ignoring her for a while she reset and took us to Margaret River via our preferred coast road. We passed a number of tourist caves along the way but at $22 per head per site to view we could think of far better things to spend our hard-earned dollars on. Sure, it would have been lovely but our budget just does not allow us these luxuries. So far today has been lovely as we have seen some amazing Karri forest and sensation coastline and we were both looking forward to staying at the Big Valley Campsite being it was a working sheep station and all.

Driving into Margaret River was another shit fight of tourists, and with no place to park we had to move on and go directly to our campsite which was a little disappointing as we could do with topping up our supplies. Big Valley Campsite was about ten or so kilometres out of town and it was not long before we arrived at their front gates (or cattle grid in fact). The road in had been particularly ordinary as it was quite corrugated and of red dirt. We took it slow as it was only yesterday that I had given Lizzie a bath. We drove to the office to check in and by the time we had reached there we did not feel all that good about the place as it was packed and looked a little feral. But we persisted as we needed drinking water and they had told me via email that tank drinking water was provided. I met up with Kylie at the office and told her who I was and she told me that they had a cancellation so we could have a powered site. This made me feel a bit better about the place and I proceeded to check in while their pet goat ate some office paperwork before having a go at their phone line. She also told me that the spot we were going to was quieter than most with not that many children.

Tee and I were not all that impressed with the place but felt as there were no free camps close by it would have to do. Our disappointment turned to anger as we went passed a bunch of kids on our way to the water supply. In fact, I directly asked Kylie where the drinking water was and she had told me that we could drink the water at the site but with recent rain it was stirred up a bit and that the water at the camp kitchen may be better. Now that was a direct lie, along with the no kids shit, both of which we discovered within ten minutes of arriving there. A classic case of "tell them what they want to hear", but by this stage we had no choice but to stay. Now I expect poor treatment and lies in the city but from country folk I did not. Just goes to show this place is more a tourist caravan park than a working sheep station, so don't be fooled by the friendly sheep farmer shit, this place is not worth coming to. We kept to ourselves and mostly in the Motorhome the rest of the day and I cooked up a hamburger for Dinner which was yummy before we retired to the bedroom to watch a pre recorded movie.

Day **174**

Last day of March and this morning I jumped on the internet to plan where we would head next. On the CMCA site I found a local winery that offered free camping to its guests only 20 kilometres up the road. This pissed me off as we would not have stayed here if we knew that. But at least the next leg of our journey would be nicer and cheaper. We did fuck all for the rest of the day as we hated staying at this place and really wanted no part of it. (Can you tell!)

Day **175**

Our first task for the day will be to find some drinking water as we were lied to at Big Valley Campsite and are now down to our last five litres. If we can't find somewhere, we may have to buy it, perish the thought! We left Big Valley Campsite with a rush and were on the road out of there by a few minutes after 8-00am. We slowly drove off the dirt road and breathed a sigh of relief as we reached the bitumen without incident. As we were not keen to do much in the township of Margaret River, we just drove through it and even at 8-30am it was quite busy. We kept or eyes open for a water tap but with hardly anywhere to park it was highly unlikely that we would be successful in finding drinking water here.

We continued towards our next free camp area as it was only 20 mins up the road and we wanted to make sure it was OK before touring the wineries etc for the day. There are not many camping areas in the Margaret River region so it would pay us to check out the site first. The winery that was offering the free camping to self contained RV's was the 3 Oceans Winery near the town of Metricup. We planned not to stop anywhere on the way but we found a little fruit and veggie place and as we needed a few bits and pieces we went in. We got some tomatoes, a pumpkin, free range eggs and a big bunch of spinach that Tee had been hankering for. As we had not had brekkie yet Tee said we should find a park and she would cook me up a fresh omelette. Now how could I say no to that and I said if she threw in a cup of tea, she had a deal. Tee cooked up a ripper omelette before we headed off, finally, to see the 3 Oceans RV section and check it out.

The 3 Oceans Winery was a big concern and the main building had a gift shop, wine tasting section and a café / restaurant. Not on the scale of Brown Brothers Victoria but bigger than most wineries that Tee and I have been to. We went inside and spoke to a young lady there about where the RV's usually parked for overnight accommodation. She was not sure but said that anywhere in the car park would be OK, so with that we were off to explore the area. We drove west towards the coast and our first stop was at a nuts and grain store where the gentleman was so helpful and we ended buying some Lupin. Now I have never heard of Lupin and it is not yet available in Queensland but it is supposed to be an appetite suppressant and good for lowering cholesterol, it is also Gluten Free. More to the point Tee had never heard of it and as we both liked it, we had to buy some, which we did.

We then went to a winery where we sampled some nice whites, but as they were not exactly to our taste, we didn't buy any. They were all either too dry or too sweet, it seems very difficult to get a happy medium like Moselle use to be. Never mind it was nice to try and back on the road we went. The costal town of Gracetown was our next stop on the map and it turned out to be a lovely little spot. By this stage though we were tired and decided to go to the campsite for the day and come back to Gracetown in the morning.

Back at the 3 Oceans Winery I did a few chores around the Motorhome which included cleaning the back of the bus (red dust) and at the same time I pulled the bikes off and dug out our flippers for the following day. We had a little nap after that as we hadn't slept well at the Big Valley Campsite, and the wine and sun of the day had really tired us. After a nap we cooked up a lovely Dinner of hamburgers and fresh veggies and by 8-30pm we were both ready for bed.

Day **176**

The plan for the day was going to be to follow the coast to Busselton and then inland to a free camp near Donnybrook, but we found that our hot water system was leaking and it would now not start. I was really pissed off about this as we were half way though saving for Lizzie's next service, now overdue, and I had just organized it to be done in O'Connor near Perth in the next week or so. This service would cost us around $500.00 and with over $120.00 per week of our budget so far being swallowed up by repairs this latest breakdown was not welcomed. Lizzie was fast becoming an expensive old lady.

So, the plans for today would now change and after I found a repair agent for the Hot water system, we would just go back to Gracetown for a bit of swimming and snorkelling. With the temperature forecast to reach 30 degrees today it was not a bad plan anyway. I got onto a repair agent and the news did not seem all that good with the repairs estimated to be in the vicinity of $750.00. So, our budget would again be tested. After this I was not in the best of moods and Tee copped a bit of my crankiness.

Soon after we headed off to Gracetown and we had a really lovely day of swimming and snorkelling even though the water was a little cold. We left at about 4-30pm and on the way back to 3 Oceans Winery we found some drinking water at a nearby town which capped off a good day after its shaky start. Back at the 3 Oceans Winery we both took an opportunity before Dinner to phone friends and relatives. While making these calls, we were paid a visit by a young lady (Nina I think her name was) who told us she was the caretaker and that we were not supposed to be camping here.

I explained to her that it was marked on the CMCA website as a campsite for self contained vehicles and that I had asked in the Winery yesterday before staying. The discussion went on for ages and it will just suffice for me to say that she was a rude and angry young lady.

Not one to take things lying down I immediately searched for an email address for the 3 Oceans wine company. I did this as it was pointless arguing with this girl and she seemed to me to have no authority to be saying what she did. The 3 Oceans wine company seems to have just got new owners as their website was being rebuilt and finding an email address was difficult. I sent one email which bounced back to me and was lucky enough to find an email address that went through. I got a response within an hour or so from Ben who was the Head Winemaker of the company, he said he was sorry for the confusion and that the 3 Oceans Wine Company had no intentions of entering the camping market. I sent an email back to him explaining the benefits of offering the service to fully self-contained vehicles and that my only issue was that the young lady who spoke to me was plain rude. He sent an email return stating that he would talk to his management about the possibilities I raised and that the young girl who spoke to us "was not" an employee of the 3 Oceans Wine Company. This is exactly what I thought, and I think she was just renting the old farmhouse on the property and decided she could vent her life's anger on a couple of Motorhomers who were harming no-one. We slept at the 3 Oceans Winery but our sleep was light as we were both pretty pissed off by this young lady.

Day **177**

Our hope for today was to have a better string of pleasant events than we have had for the past week or so. It was the start of a new budget week and we had saved $250.00 of our budget money for the service on the Motorhome. This gave us savings of $350.00 towards the Motorhome service and if it wasn't for the hot water service breaking down, we would be flushed with cash again. Never mind at least we had saved almost enough for the Service and we could worry about the hot water costs over the next month or so. If the hot water service was not leaking, I think we could have saved repairing it for a month or so as the weather is still warm here and we are heading north. But with the leak it seems silly to not fix it as it has already cost me an expensive pair of shoes (that were wet and mouldy) and the water damage bill could exceed the repair costs. So, no point delaying the inevitable we will just have to wear the cost and get it fixed.

We set off very early this morning and we planned to cross to the coast before hugging it all the way to Dunsborough and then to Busselton. We had to get fuel and food on the way and either one of those towns should have a good supply of both. The Margaret River area is nice but we have seen a lot of nicer places on our travels and because it is so busy, we liked it even less. I suppose it is good for a weekend trip from Perth but for the Traveller it is a little over commercialized.

Travelling through the landscape to the coast was pretty and a standout feature at 7-30am is the flocks of Australian Ringneck Parrots and the soft morning sun that glistened over the many vineyards and stunning native grass plants. We soon reached the coast and within no time were half way to Dunsborough where we spotted a signpost that we turned at to reach the lovely beach at Canal Rocks. What a stunning place this was; from its creamy soft white sands to its rugged rocky outcrops this place is amazing. It immediately goes on my "must see" list and the early morning visit seemed to be a great time to be there as only fishermen were parked in the area. We spent a few hours here admiring the beauty of the place whilst walking all around and over the rocky capes. WOW! It did get busy, or relatively busy, after nine thirty but not distractingly so.

With such a good start to the day we felt more positive than we have felt for a week or so, and back on the road we soon reached the town of Dunsborough. Travelling from the South we basically drove straight into the main shopping centre where we bought fuel, food and BEER!!! And everyone knows that the only way to fix a bad week is to have a beer or two. From Dunsborough we explored the Cape Naturaliste area which extended west of the township. Firstly, out to the lighthouse and then we veered into a couple of side roads, the first of which took us to Rocky Point. At Rocky Point our tummies told us what time it was (Lunchtime) and Tee made me up a couple of rounds of fresh salad sandwiches, which I devoured while admiring the lovely ocean views. I often think to myself how lucky we are as people pay millions of dollars to have a view like this and as travellers, we not only have it for free, but can change it at any time we like. (No sales commission or stamp duty). Our next stop was at Eagle bay where we saw one of the nicest swimming beaches on our journey so far. Tee said if we were staying around here, she would have gone in for a swim.

Back through Dunsborough and onto Busselton and Tee commented how lovely this whole area was and I agreed. If we ever had to live in WA, we both agreed that we would choose this area as it truly is lovely. Just out of the Busselton area was the first of two areas that had free camping. As we arrived at it though we decided against it as it was covered in litter and was a less than pleasant looking place.

We set the navigator for the inland town of Donnybrook as the second of the free camp locations was on the road to Donnybrook through the town of Capel. But again, the navigator tried to take us the long way and we found ourselves passing the signpost to Capel and having to do a u-turn on the highway. I have no idea why these things are so stupid but we are slowly learning to keep our eyes open and not just blindly follow the stupid things instructions. And mind you, this is a brand-new navigator also. If this writing is ever published, I promise you Navman international I will never mention what brand the navigator is.

We eventually found the second free camp area even though the sign to it had disappeared. The only reason we saw it was because there was a caravan already there and Tee spotted it from the main road. We pulled up in a spot there and tried to keep cool for the remainder of the afternoon as the mercury had hit 33 degrees and it was quite sticky. When the weather cooled down Tee cooked up some marinated chicken wings and a pile of fresh veggies, and after dinner, I had half of that cookie I bought in the nuts and grain store while Tee had a chocolate cookie. We went to bed early so we could turn the lights off and open the windows and we chatted for an hour or so. We also had a laugh at the older couple who were camped in an old caravan not far from us, as they were running a generator that was as old and they were and yelling at each other just to be heard over its offensively loud noise. Fortunately, the generator went off at 8-30pm and we soon drifted off to sleep.

Day **178**

We had a great sleep last night and were in no rush this morning as we have a fair bit of time to kill before we can get our Motorhome into the hot water repairers, and it is only about 200 kilometres from where we are now. Tee said she would be cool to hang around here until lunchtime and that suited me as I had a bit of writing to do. We were both excited about our next destination even though our last winery experience was not all that pleasant. After lunch we headed off to Donnybrook which was only about 30 mins up the road and arrived to find a busy little country town.

Our first job was to find some house water and as luck had it, we drove almost smack bang into the transit park that had all the facilities one would need and plenty of water taps to boot. While I filled the Motorhome with water Tee rang up to see how much the Transit Park would cost per night as we thought it wouldn't be a bad place to spend a night or two. Wow it was $30.00 per night which is way too expensive for a place like this so we quickly canned that idea. And as we had no need for supplies, we decided to drive directly to Thomson Brook Winery and see if we could stay there. Tee rang them to confirm that they were OK with Motorhomes but had to leave a message as there was no answer. We did not want to have to deal with the same sort of shit that we had at the 3 Oceans Winery.

The Thomson Brook Winery was only a few minutes out of Donnybrook and signposted extremely well. As we turned into the road it was on my phone rang and I asked Tee to answer it for me. It was the owners of the Winery who were more than happy to have us. Within minutes we arrived at the Winery which was absolutely beautiful, with a red rose lined driveway that lead up to a rammed earth cellar and working sheds. There was an orchard, dam and of course a lovely vineyard all dotted with cheeky young sheep who were keeping the green grass at bay.

The owners were Terry and Pam who made us feel more than welcome and chatted to us before letting us settle in for the afternoon. The area they had set aside for CMCA members was a lovely grassed area and their three dogs came over for a pat. This made Tee very happy as she so much misses her animals and we both cannot wait to get a new doggie when we get back home. We had a quiet evening and were entertained by the Alpaca's joining the sheep in the apple orchard, who were picking apples off the trees for there short necked friends. At first, we were concerned that they should not be there but Terry told us that he was getting rid of the orchid and that if we wanted any apples then we could help ourselves. It was hilarious to see the sheep scampering every time they heard an apple hit the ground. Tee cooked up another batch of marinated chicken wings and veggies which we devoured before having a quiet evening just chatting.

Day **179**

It was so peaceful here last night but Tee did not sleep all that well and was tossing and turning quite a bit. This meant that I was also awake a fair bit as I am a very light sleeper. Terry and Pam seemed quite busy as they had a market to go to on Saturday and were preparing all their goods for sale. Tee and I felt a little in the way so decided to go over and buy a couple bottles of wine before heading off.

Terry was in the winery but Pam was still walking down from the main house which was a kilometre away. Terry ran through their selection with us and we bought a few bottles from him. We told him that if they needed any help, we would be glad to help as we had nothing much to do. He then asked if we were staying for a few days and I said that we would love too but did not want to impose as they were busy. He said "don't be silly' and that "we were no trouble and were welcome to stay as long as we liked". We were very happy about this as Tee would like a day nap later as she was not feeling too good. When Pam arrived, she suggested we go and look at Gnomes Ville which was only 15 kilometres away. We thought that this would be a lovely little trip and then when we got back, we could have a bit of lunch and Tee could have a nap in the afternoon.

The countryside on the way to Gnomes Ville was superb with rolling hills, large dams and dense native forests. We had no idea what to expect when we arrived there but we were blown away when we saw how many of the little buggers were placed all over the landscape. No joke there was in excess of two thousand, it was bloody amazing. All different themes, all different colours and groups who had their own sponsors. People do some amazing things and this display of Gnomes is just another crazy example.

When we got back to the Winery Pam and Terry had gone to the market with their produce as it was a Friday night market. The place was so quiet which gave Tee an opportunity to have a nap and me an opportunity to ring some friends and relatives. But before I made any phone calls, I decided to take up Terry's offer to pick some table grapes which I did while Tee was sleeping. It was great fun and I must have got about seven kilos of red grapes before sitting under the shade of a gum tree to ring some family and friends.

While I was chatting to my mum Tee woke up and was thrilled to see the lovely red grapes that I had picked and left on the table outside the Motorhome. I wrapped up my call to mum and asked Tee if she wanted to join me in the orchid where I was going to pick some red delicious apples. We picked the apples that were closest to the Winery but Terry had told us that there were some good ones down the back of the orchid. The sheep were very curious to see what we were doing and were keen to pick up the apples that dropped as we picked. But they were still scared of us, so they waited until we moved away before they attacked the fallen apples. They were absolutely hilarious to watch as their mouths don't open wide enough to bite the apples so they use their lips and push their teeth down on the apples resting on the ground. They do this while keeping one eye on us and the other eye on the jealous sheep that don't have an apple and are ready to pounce.

As we made our way across the orchid the alpacas were looking at us funny, and as Pam had just told us a story of how they defend the sheep from foxes we didn't want to push our luck. Tee was already half way back to the Motorhome by the time I turned around to ask her if we should go back. When we safely made it over the fence, I said to Tee that I could walk around the perimeter of the fence to the other apples and she could prepare the grapes to be washed.

With this we went about our prepared plan and as I picked the red delicious apples and dropped the odd one the sheep got more game and were right beside me waiting for the apples to fall. I had a great time with them and as I had a bag of apples already picked, I feed the sheep and the alpacas seemed satisfied that I was not a threat.

The other plan for the day was for me to cook pasta and for us to both enjoy it with the wine that we had just purchased. But as we had eaten a pile of grapes and a couple of apples by dinner time, we were both not that hungry. We decided to save the past meal and wine for tomorrow night and had a couple of beers instead.

Day **180**

Today is my eldest sons' birthday and I have already sent him an ecard and a put some money into his account as a present. A funny fellow is my eldest and very different to his brother. He moved back to Melbourne about twelve months ago and has recently started doing stand up comedy. When he told me what he was doing I didn't think it was too serious and was not prepared for how good he actually was. He really loves it and it has helped him with his confidence. Another thing I could not believe was that I have a 27-year-old son as it feels like only yesterday that I was 27. I rang him and wished him a happy birthday and we had a long chat. Our relationship has been strained over the years as we are very different people, but now I think he is getting harder and I am getting softer and we seem to get along a whole lot better.

It has been a catch-up time for Tee and I as I have been ringing everyone and Tee is making grape jam with the grapes that we haven't eaten, and it is sensational. Tee loves cooking and she is also feeling heaps better after a goods night's sleep, "we both are". I have checked the awning and worked out how to fix the bracket that has come off and can you believe that the hot water service is now starting. The leak will still be there but we will now not have to have cold showers for the week. I have also spent a lot of time on the internet this afternoon checking out how the hot water system works as I can't afford to get ripped off from the Perth repairer. I found that I can buy a brand-new unit for $600.00 and as I had been quoted $487.00 for the tank alone by the repairer, we are booked in to see, obviously I have a few questions to ask when I get there.

Day **181**

It is lovely and quiet here but we have decided to keep travelling as we don't want to overstay our welcome. Before we left though, we went and saw Terry to get another bottle of Rose as it was superb. Terry was tinkering about in his wine cellar and we told him that we were off today and that we would like to buy another bottle of wine before we left. He seemed a bit disappointed that we were leaving but was happy to get us another bottle of wine from the cellar. We chatted for a while and he gave us an extra ¾ bottle of Rose that Pam had used as a tester at a show yesterday. Terry and Pam are lovely people and their Winery is easily the best campsite that we have stayed at for many reasons. It is only open to CMCA members which makes it even better as you don't get any of the feral's, in fact the whole time we have been here we have been by ourselves. It is like owning our own Winery, it has been absolutely fantastic.

We set off at about 9-00am and went into the town of Donnybrook to top up our house water and empty the shiter. Yahoo my favourite job! We did this and went back into the main street of town to get some bread and top up Lizzie's fuel. Our plan for the day was not to travel too far as we have four days on the road until we need to be at Lizzie's service place near Perth. I have marked it out in the Camp6 book and today we would have a choice of two free camp areas to the Northeast of Donnybrook. The road to these free camps was very pretty and the soil around this region looks very fertile with good water supply. Terry had told us that there is a lot of spring water in the area which makes all the dams look extremely healthy. This along with the hilly pastures and gum tree woodlands make for some extremely pleasant scenery and we enjoyed our journey.

Our first free camp spot to look at was just outside the town of Mumballup, whose greatest asset appears to be the tiny pub, which had its door open when we went past. It was at a place called Glen Mervyn Dam and when we arrived, we knew it was not for us as it was full of campers with powerboats and water-skiers. It was far too busy for us and the powerboats were far too noisy to make for happy camping. We continued toward our second option which was not far outside the township of Collie at a place called Stockton Lake.

As we reached the town of Collie, we saw a busy little country town that even boasted a McDonalds store, and it has been quite a while since we have seen one of those. With no desire for a Big Mac we continued until we reached our option two campsite. As we arrived our disappointment for the day was doubled as the second campsite was now a charged site and at $7-00 per person, we expected to see some nice amenities as we drove in. But to our dismay all we saw was a dustbowl filled with a few campers and not a lot of room to park. What a disappointment this place was and with a motorbike park right next door and two power boats already on the water we had no intentions of parting with fourteen dollars to stay at a place like this, it was quite yucky.

So off we set again and we went back into the township of Collie to plan our next move. While in a park at Collie we decided that it would be best to go back to Thomson Brook Winery and stay there until we had to travel to Perth on Thursday. I felt a bit embarrassed going back but Terry seemed genuinely disappointed when we left and it was a stunning place to stay. When we got back, we had a laugh with them about our return and we had a chat before putting Lizzie back on the exact spot that she was in some five hours earlier. That afternoon we helped Pam in trimming the 200 plus rose bushes that lined their driveway. It actually turned out to be a mammoth job as the rose bushes were quite overgrown and in fact as the sun set, we were not even half way through them. We called it quits at about 6-00pm and said to Pam that we would get stuck into it again in the morning. Back at the Motorhome we dusted ourselves off a bit before I cooked the Dinner that Tee had prepared. We both then had a Beer and then a nice glass of Thomas Brook Rose.

Life doesn't get better than this! We watched the sunset over the hills, then climbed into the Motorhome, having a chat before going to bed quite early at 9-00pm.

Day **182**

Today we plan on knocking over the rose pruning and with the temperature set to hit the mid to high 30's we decided to start early. We really appreciate having this place to stay without charge and are helping out so as to feel as though we are not freeloading. We got stuck into the Roses but by noon the temperature was stifling and we decided to call it quits until later in the afternoon. But all day it did not really cool down and we decided to put off finishing the roses until the morning. We went into Donnybrook and Tee did some washing while I filled the house water at the Transit Park in town. I also bought some bracket to fix the water bottle holder in the Motorhome which I did during the course of the afternoon. Tee spent the afternoon drying the washing and having a bit of a spring clean in the Motorhome.

Day **183** - Day **184**

Turns out that yesterday was the hottest April day the Perth region has ever had and it reached about 35 degrees here (37 in Perth). We decided that because it was so hot, we would start early and get the roses mostly done before it got too hot. Tee and I toiled away until about lunchtime and finally completed the Roses. They looked fabulous and all were now uniformly shaped. After lunch we did some reading and writing and we said to Terry & Pam to give us a yell if they needed help with anything. At this stage we plan to leave Thursday.

After pushing them to ask Pam said Terry really needed some help with some Cab Sav grape picking. Tee and I said we would love to help and our Wednesday and Thursday was spent picking grapes. We had a great time doing this and on Wednesday evening we spent a happy hour in the Wine Cellar tasting all their lovely wines. Thursday morning, I woke up with a bit of a hangover but Tee was fine as she had been more sensible that I had the night before.

Day **185**

We competed the Cab Sav grape picking and Terry seemed happy with our work. Picking grapes is not as easy as it seems and it has taught me to appreciate the job of selling Real Estate and how much easier it is to use your brains rather than an older body like mine. I am starting to think that I should continue at Real Estate sales when we return home but to do it on more of a part time basis.

I watched Terry and his son putting the grapes through the de-stemming machine which was quite interesting and spent the rest of the day writing. Tee enjoyed her time by painting her nails and doing girly stuff. I have also booked the Motorhome in for its service on Monday at a place in O'Connor near Perth for Monday morning. We will leave here Sunday morning so we can stay on the outskirts of Perth Sunday night and be at the mechanics first thing Monday morning. I spent this afternoon writing and calculating the rest of our trip around Australia and more specifically where we would get the next 10,000-kilometre service. Turns out that Port Augusta in South Australia will be the logical choice.

Day **186**

Turned out to be quite a warm night last night and this morning it is starting to drizzle so we won't be doing any more grape picking. This comes as a relief to me as I am a bit sore this morning and because of the humidity I didn't sleep all that well either. We decided to head into town and top up our shopping supplies. We have saved a heap of money by staying here and in fact we have got all the funds required to get Lizzie serviced on Monday. This was the original plan but to achieve it has been fabulous. In fact, we have also not spent any of this week's budget yet, and now being three days in we should save a bit of the current week's budget also.

In town we wanted to check the price of a gas refill as we don't want to run out of house gas while exploring the WA coast on the way to Broome. We stopped in at the hardware store but they only did "swap and go". Fortunately, the BP servo did fill and even though the tank was not empty we filled it for peace of mind. The IGA was directly across the road and we did a big shopping and returned to Thomson Brook around lunchtime.

Armed with full supplies Tee cooked up a couple of fresh Enchilada's that we had just purchase. They were very tasty and I don't think I have ever had them before. The rest of the day it rained which gave me a heap of time to read my latest book which is Nelson Mandela's Autobiography, it is a very good book. We have also decided not to get the hot water service fixed as it will cost far too much and I will have a look at it tomorrow to see what I can do about the water leak.

Day **187**

I had a slightly better sleep last night but it was still muggy weather and we had a fair bit of rain also. As it was approaching 10-00am Tee and I were starting to get concerned for Terry and Pam who had not yet arrived to open the Cellar. I had just changed my shorts as Tee said they stunk and was standing there stark naked when Pam popped up at the side of our Motorhome. She asked if I could give Terry a hand to bring their car back as they had got bogged last night on the track to their home. I must explain that they live on the same property as the Cellar but it is about one kilometre away and over a substantial hill and a very ordinary road. No, road is not the word – goat track springs to mind, and they do this in a Kia Pregio that is slowly dying in the process.

I got onto his quad bike and rode through the grape vines and up the mountainside to where he was waiting with his tractor attached to the sad looking Kia. As I had no tractor experience, when Terry asked if I wanted to drive the tractor or the Kia, it was an easy choice for me. We got the Kia out and he pulled it all the way down to the cellar where he rang the RAC, as it had now also broken down.

With all that excitement out the way I concentrated on trying to solve the mystery of the leaking hot water service. The hot water service is located in a very awkward spot as it is under the bed and tucked up in one corner. To get to it you have to dismantle the bed or poke your head through a narrow cupboard door. I decided to do the later and as I probed, I noticed that the insulation around the unit was all wet. As it was only cardboard, I decided to rip it away as I was never going to solve the mystery any other way. As I did the pump to the Motorhome came on and I saw a trickle of water appear from around the outlet valve at the top of the tank. This was great news as it was under less pressure than at the bottom of the tank and I decided to keep taking the cardboard insulation away to see the leak in full. Turned out to be right on the fold of the outlet valve and would have been weakened during manufacturing. Now I know I can patch it up and get away with this tank until we return home to Brizzie. The repairs were going to cost between $790.00 and $1400.00 depending if we replaced just the tank or the entire unit. As I mentioned earlier, I had found a unit on the internet for $600.00 and now that I can nurse the current unit until we get home, I will be able to fit it myself saving me between $200.00 and $800.00.

Later that evening we had a few glasses of wine with Terry and Pam and said our goodbyes. They even gave us a half dozen bottles of their finest to thank us for the help. It has been a pure delight staying here, not to mention the huge savings on the budget.

Day **188**

We headed off this morning and plan to head to Mandurah where there is a Bunning's store and purchase a tube of metal putty that I found on their website. This should enable me to patch up the hot water tank and with a bit of luck we will not have to purchase a new tank for the rest of our trip. As I mentioned earlier this would save us a considerable amount of money. We travelled passed the outskirts of Bunbury and with no plans to visit there we kept on travelling.

After a reasonably uneventful trip, we finally arrived at Mandurah and the Bunning's store that I was looking for. I asked a lady in the store where I would find the metal epoxy putty and after she grunted Isle 20 at me, I thanked her in a sarcastic tone. I love it when people are so happy in their jobs! I soon located the product and was so excited to do so, as to not find it here would mean I would probably not find another Bunning's store for many more kilometres. The alternative would be searching high and wide in town. But fortunately, it was in Isle 20 and with my luck running high I thought I would push it and see if they also had portable toilet chemicals in the plumbing section. Wow another win and it was $1.50 cheaper than I normally pay for it.

The first free camp that I had marked to look at was just outside the town of Serpentine and Northwest of our current location. Plan B was a free camp north of that location. But as luck was working with us today the first site was fine and we arrived there not long after lunchtime and Tee made me up a couple of salad sandwiches that I ate as a late lunch. The area was OK but there were a few young campers there and we thought it may get noisy. There were also a couple of caravans there that looked very permanent. In fact, one of the vans had a full set up and looked as though it had been there for many months; they even had a cat and dog with them.

I cooked pasta for dinner and we ate it early as we both needed to get a shower before I attempted to fix the hot water leak. The hot water service as I have mentioned before is in a very awkward spot but I managed to patch the leak. We would soon see how successful I have been as the curing time was only one hour. We left it for almost two hours before checking my work and unfortunately our luck for the day had run out as we discovered there was a second leak. I had had enough for the day and decided to patch the second leak in the morning.

Day **189**

We awoke very early this morning as we had to be at the Mechanics shop by 9-00am and I still had the second leak in the hot water tank to patch. Turns out we were wrong about the noise here as it had been very quiet all night and I had slept right through. It was 5.45am when we got out of bed and this allowed us plenty of time to do what was needed and travel to the Mechanics workshop that was only 45 kilometres away. I patched the second leak on the hot water tank before we both got ready to leave camp. Unfortunately, I will not know how successful I was until this afternoon as we will be quite busy today. But in a way that will be good as it will allow more curing time.

The trip towards Fremantle and Perth was very busy as you can imagine on a Monday morning at 8-00am. But the freeways here are very good and they even have a train line that runs through the middle of the freeway, a very clever idea. After struggling through the traffic, we finally arrived at the Mechanics workshop at about 8-20am, forty minutes earlier than our appointment time.

I had only wanted an oil change but the owner of the workshop had told me over the phone that they only do services and it would cost between $450.00 and $500.00. We had saved this amount but as I service Lizzie every 10,000 Kilometres and we had spent so much on the last service I really only wanted an oil and filter change. When we got to the Mechanics workshop, we found it to be a very commercial type premise and the owner was not there when we arrived. I spoke to Mark, a mechanic there, and he had no record of us being booked in. This was disappointing to me in one respect but when he said he could do us straight away I thought we may" have hand" here. I told him that we really only wanted an oil and filter change and he said that was fine and that he would do a quick check over at the same time.

There was no waiting room so we sat on a short brick fence at the front of the building while the work was being carried out. Turns out though that Mark was fantastic and he came to us at regular intervals to report the few minor ailments that Lizzie was suffering from. The worst of which was an exhaust leak at the manifold that we should have fixed.

At the end of the work we paid the bill of $266.00 (fantastic) and mark gave us the name and address of a great exhaust repair man. We thanked Mark and Jason for all their help and we headed off to the Muffler guy who was just a few blocks away. Unfortunately, when we got there though, he had moved and I rang his number to see if he was still close by. His name was Warren and he said that his new workshop was only 25 kilometres away in Rockingham.

We thought about leaving this problem but Lizzie has been making a tappet type noise for quite some time, and now that we know what it is, it would be nice to see the noise problem gone. So off we went to Rockingham and soon we had Warren ratting around under Lizzie. At first, he was not so sure he could fix it and said that the manifold may have to be removed, a very expensive job. But then he said it may be clear enough to slip a new bolt in and that he would give it a try. As luck would have it his masterful surgery had worked and upon starting Lizzie the tappet noise was gone. Lizzie now had a clean bill of health except for a minor weep in the gearbox that Mark had said was only very minor.

Off again and as Tee was very hungry, she had set the navigator to a local KFC store, "our favourite fast food". It was located in the main centre of Rockingham and close to the beach. But unfortunately, when we got there the store had been closed down, much to our despair. Rockingham was quite a large place though and we found a Chicken Treat store that seems popular over here in the West. We don't have them in Brissy. We took our chicken lunch back to the Motorhome and got stuck into it as we were both very hungry.

Back on the road we considered going back to the free camp we stayed in last night as it was only about 25 kilometres away, but as it was only a little after 2-00pm we decided to cross Fremantle and Perth and get up the coast a bit. The Highway got us to Perth in no time and with no interest in cities we took a couple of photos on our way through. We found a fuel place at Neerabup way North of Perth and at that stage we had travelled over 60 kilometres along the main road without seeing one fuel station. As our luck has it though the fuel was a terrific price at $141.9 per litre and we were glad that we had got so far and that the tank was so low so we could take advantage of this great price.

We passed the first free camp site and as it was a bit ordinary, we decided to try plan B, which turned out to be much nicer even though it was on the side of the highway. After stopping and settling on the best spot I checked the hot water tank to find it was 99% fixed with only the slightest of weeping. With some luck it will get us home and save us a great amount of money. We ate the rest of the cold chicken from Chicken Treat and went to bed at 8-00pm.

Day **190**

Wilbinga Grove turned out to be a fairly good rest area even thought it was on the side of a Highway. Tee and I seem to be getting use to passing traffic noise and it is now only close by noises that wake us. This is a good thing for our safety and with the way Lizzie is set up we are quite safe, or at least as safe as possible.

We took our time this morning heading off and before we did, I spent some time writing and I also wanted to check the hot water leak and the oil in the Motorhome after its service. The mechanic had been great at Karl's Mechanical Repairs and I had no doubt the oil level would be fine, but one must check. As for the Hot Water leak it was still leaking slightly so I will have to keep my eye on it.

About 10-30am we left Wilbinga Grove Rest Area with the intention of reaching Cliff Head North which is about 100 kilometres short of Geraldton. This is a journey of around 200 kilometres so we thought we would take a gentle pace there and stop at some seaside towns along the way. Our first stop was at Lancelin and we were quite keen to get our house water topped up and also the toilet rinse water was now empty. I also had to perform my favourite of all jobs – Empty the Shitter – Yahoo!

Lancelin was quite a nice seaside spot with a big estuary that dominates the town. There is a lovely park there and right next door to it is a caravan park which would be lovely for families as the lagoon is calm and safe for young kids to swim in. We visited the lookout that gave us great views of the Lagoon and beach area but as for house water we were unsuccessful.

At this point I must add to keep an accurate diary one must not leave it too long before writing down one's thoughts and, in this case, I have as we actually found a shitter dump point before Lancelin and this was our first stop. I don't know how I forgot this place as it was quite a nice free camp area but was home to a bunch of redneck ferals. The dump point had no water supply and I could only dump the toilet waste and not rinse the cartridge like I normally do. It also meant that I was unable to top up the house water or the toilet rinse water. But the most amazing thing about this place was the live entertainment which came in the form of a scrawny prune faced feral woman who was chastising her children at full volume. The comments went like this – "stop that fucking about or I'll give you a flogging" – but mum it wasn't me – "shut the fuck up or I'll give you both a fucking flogging". Actually, I think there was a few more fuckings in there but I lost count. It seemed quite appropriate to dump our shit there and piss off.

Now after that and after Lancelin we stopped at a few more costal towns and were successful at finding water at Green Head where we topped up all our water needs before having a quick look around the place and moving on. The landscape on our journey has been unusual today as the grass plants (black boys) were in huge numbers in some areas and then we had a run of white sand dunes that totally dominated the landscape of that particular area. It was not until we approached the area around Cliff Head North that we got to see a lot of the ocean from the highway.

One disappointment for the day was that we missed the signpost to the Pinnacles and by the time we realized this we were some 50 kilometres past it and it was not possible to turn back and spend decent time exploring them today. I was cranky about this and we had a little tiff about it. When we arrived at Cliff Head North it was about 4-30pm and we hoped that the clouds would clear before sunset and we could see our first WA sunset over the Indian Ocean. But it was not to be and the perfect sunset would have to wait for another day, it was very pretty though. The consolation was that we got a great parking spot right beside the Indian Ocean and it is a great free camp area.

We had left over pasta for Dinner and after that we decided to watch a You Tube movie as I have a bit of remaining credit on my Telstra 4G account. I found a great old horror movie called Amityville Horror 2 and we settled in for the evening to watch it. At the end of the movie as the credits were rolling, we were joined by a house guest in the form of a field mouse who decided to join us for the evening. It was a classic look with Tee jumping up onto the dining chair screaming "a mouse – a mouse". It certainly came in as our senses were heightened by the horror movie we had just watched and I was not able to find the little bugger after an extensive search of the Motorhome.

It was a full and action-packed day!

Day **191**

This spot is so nice that we have decided to stay for a few nights and with the budget week finishing last night we are in great financial shape. In fact, we are almost $400.00 under budget and if we stay here a few days the news will only get better. As we did a fair bit of travelling yesterday, we decided to have a restful day that we spent reading and writing. We did cook up a heap of stewed apples though as we had about 10 kilograms of them from the Winery that need to be eaten. Tee did a great job cooking them and they are so sweet they don't even need added sugar.

Tonight, we got about 50 pictures of the most amazing sunset and Tee cooked me a yummy steak while we sat drinking a bottle of Thomson Brook wine.

Life is very very good!

Day **192**

Today we thought we may try a spot of fishing and we set up a few metres away from the Motorhome on the edge of the Indian Ocean. I spent about an hour fishing before giving up after losing my hook and sinker on a snag. There is a heap of ribbon weed here and everywhere we go we have new conditions to adapt to. This generally means we are not successful catching fish but enjoy the challenge. I think we are suckers for punishment and live in hope of a good catch.

Tee was much more hopeful and spent another hour or so there after I gave up. She got a series of nibbles but unfortunately the result was one that we are most used to – NO FISH FOR DINNER. While Tee was fishing, she was rounded up by the Gatekeeper- this is the nickname that we have given a fellow camping here in a brightly painted Double Decker Bus. He is a total wanker and stops everyone as they enter the campsite and chews on their ears for as long as they are prepared to listen. We have been trying to avoid him since the first we saw him bailing up a couple on their way in. In fact, Tee saw him yesterday after he had caught a fish and he was yelling at his wife to get the camera. When she got there, he told her how to take the photo and started yelling and abusing her with some obscene words thrown in. I was asleep on a power knap at the time and Tee relayed to me one line of his abuse which went like this – "four fucken years on the road and your still cant take a fucken photo"- he then proceeded to toss the fish away storm over to her and snatch the camera from her hands.

Needless to say, this was why Tee and I were so keen not to have contact with him, but she was cornered by him while fishing and with her sharp tongue was able to limit the chat to a minute or so before returning to the Motorhome. We had a quiet day preparing for our next leg of the journey which would take us to Geraldton and beyond. We met a few nice people during the day and had a chat, but apart from that we did little else.

Day 193

Off early this morning and past the wanker in the Double Decker Bus and off to Geraldton. Nice drive to Geraldton from Cliff Head North about 100 kilometres or so and it was quite attractive. We pulled into Geraldton and ended up right in the centre of town, it is Friday morning. But not any Friday morning, in fact it is the day before the Brats school holidays and Geraldton was alive. The place was pumping and so busy that we had trouble finding a place to park the Motorhome (apart from the paid parking areas). We finally found a spot that was big enough for the Motorhome and it was not too far from Woolworths. We decided to go to Woolworths as well as Coles as we were going to get a heap of supplies. Apparently, the food prices start to increase significantly between here and Darwin. Also, it will allow us to get a fuel voucher from each store which will be handy as we travel. In fact, there is no Coles Express fuel station in Geraldton so Woolworths is the only option for discounted fuel for a considerable distance.

I have picked up a lot of handy tools for our travelling on the internet and one is a complete download of Coles store locations Australia wide. We also use yellow pages to text addresses of places to our mobiles and then it is easy to pop them into the navigator. I have also uploaded all the Coles sites directly into our Navigator. There are so many handy tools to use now that make travelling so easy, but we don't get too technology hitched as it would be easy to be stuck on the damn thing all day and never see the real world. But one other good tool I must mention is to Google "things to do in ---------", which gives you some great ideas and helps you not miss points of interest.

At Woolworths we pick up a few things including drinking water as it is so vital, in fact we now carry 70 litres of drinking water on board. It may be a bit of overkill but Tee and I are very fussy about our drinking water and we wait until we can get tank water before filling up. Even then we put it though a filter jug. Armed with our fuel voucher we squeezed in to the discount fuel station that was totally packed and it was a big effort to get in and out of the place (not designed for large vehicles – good one Woollies).

After filling up we headed to Coles to finish up our shopping and once finished there we had another difficult task to perform in the car park. Geraldton is not an RV friendly town and when I got to Coles, I had to park in two car spots, front to back, and because it was so busy there it took us ten minutes to find the spot that would allow this. When we returned to the Motorhome after shopping, I had to wait until someone beside me drove off before I could go as I had to swing Lizzie out wide to get out. As Tee was putting away the shopping in the back, I saw a family who were parked next to us arrive and that was my opportunity to get out. They had three or four little Brats and when they got into the car, they started eating sandwiches for lunch. What a funny situation this was as I had to sit and watch this family finish their lunch before I could get out. To make things worse I had not had Breakfast as we had run out of bread, milk and cornflakes, all of which we now had in abundance. But because I had a window of opportunity to get out of the car park when this family moved, I couldn't even have something to eat. Finally, the family finished eating and I carefully negotiated my way out of the car park and we stopped close by so I could feed my face.

Geraldton was quite an industrial place and although there was a lot of industry there it was quite an attractive town, and as I said before – very busy. We had one more task to perform before we left Geraldton and that was to find house water. This can sometimes be a difficult task and until you find it, quite stressful. But this is the price you have to pay to stay at free camps as most do not have water. We found one tap on the foreshore but it was a long way from the Motorhome and my hoses would not reach it. This would mean filling up the tank 10 litres at a time via a water container, a bit of hard work, and Tee suggested we keep looking.

As usual Tee's suggestion turned out to be a good one as we found a beautiful park not far away which had a tap right next to the roadway. We filled up with water before parking the Motorhome on the foreshore of the park near the toilet block. As the toilet block was so nice, I decided to have a shave there as it is so much nicer to have a shave with free-flowing water. We also met Gerry there, a big Canadian fellow who was admiring our Motorhome. He was a lovely fellow who lived locally and we chatted for a while.

Back on the road with all the chores done – except the shitter – which we could do at the free camp as they had a dump point there. The free camp area that we were going to was just 15 kilometres out of Geraldton and as usual we had a plan B if this place was no good. The road to this free camp took us over a dry range with unusual looking mountains and an ocean view to our rear. As we got on top of the range, we had a stunning view of the valley in which we would be camping and when we arrived at the free camp, we knew we had no need for plan B.

At the free camp we set up and I emptied the shitter before a quiet afternoon and evening. As I was cooking our round English sausage for Dinner, we got talking to a local couple who were originally from England. Brian and Wendy were a lovely couple who knew the WA area very well and did a heap of free camping all the way up the WA coast. They were originally backpackers as youngsters and had seen all of Australia. As it was now dark, they said we could catch up in the morning and they would mark all the great spots they knew of on a map for us. With this we departed to eat Dinner and have a restful night's sleep.

Day **194**

We awoke to a new day and Tee was not feeling all that well although at this stage I did not know it. I had a job that I wanted to do that involved pulling the bed area apart in the Motorhome and I needed a bit of help from Tee. The job I wanted to do was firstly to check if any of the leaking hot water was getting into the boot of the Motorhome as it was on the same level as the hot water service. Then I wanted to further putty up the slight leak that still remained in the hot water tank. Fortunately, the water had not leaked into the boot area although I think it had done slightly before I had discovered the leak a week or so ago. It was ever so slightly damp but none of the gear in the boot had been affected – this was a great relief as I have already lost a lovely pair of shoes to this bloody leaky tank.

I was just about ready to start on the tank repairs when Brian and Wendy popped up for our morning meeting. As promised, they came over to mark our map and show us the best places to see all the way up the WA coast. This lovely couple helped us immensely and their tips have altered some of our destinations as we would have missed some lovely spots. We spoke for a while before they had to head off to their holiday destination of Kalbarri about 150 kilometres north of here.

After they left, I found a couple of weeping spots in the tank which I set about repairing. The epoxy that I am using takes an hour to set but we decided to leave it for much longer than that to give ourselves a better chance of success. We spent the rest of the morning putting the Motorhome back together and then after lunch we were just lazing around and reading.

One of the campers that is staying here is quite a comical looking character and on the first day produced a ukulele that they began to play over the sound of their noisy generator. I said to Tee, "I always wondered what happened to Tiny Tim?" but Tee did not know what the heck I was talking about until I showed her a You tube clip of him. https://www.youtube.com/watch?v=zcSlcNfThUA She laughed and said it well could be Tiny Tim as there were some striking resemblances. This in itself was quite funny but what had us in awe was that HE turned out to be a SHE and the story lost its credibility until we decided that perhaps Tiny Tim had had a sex change!

From laughter to pain and Tee was still feeling quite ill so she decided to look up medical centres and try and book in. As big as Geraldton is though it does not have a medical centre that is open Saturday afternoon or Sunday – amazing. I said to Tee that she should ring the hospital and have a chat to them. It was now 2-30pm and I said to Tee, "Let's just go in there as I could run a few errands while she was waiting to see a doctor". Tee agreed and we quickly packed up and got going. Tee set the navigator and back into Geraldton we went and we soon arrived at the Hospital where I dropped Tee off and went to run some errands. On the way to the hospital I noticed that BCF did gas refills and as we had just run a bottle out, I headed there first. Good call too as the 4 kg we use for cooking had just run out and their refill only cost me $14.50, I paid $23.99 in Lorne Victoria for the same bottle. I found my way to BCF and was served almost immediately. I then wanted some cash as when we head north from here, I have been told that a lot of places charge for, or don't have credit card facilities.

I remembered from when we were food shopping yesterday that there was some ATM's in the mall where Coles was. Now all I had to do was find Coles. Fortunately, Geraldton is well laid out and I had little trouble finding it and I got my cash. Also, I parked the Motorhome in a spot that was much easier to get out of as I did not want to be stuck there like yesterday, especially if Tee was in and out of the hospital quickly and called me to pick her up. I sent Tee a text message to see if she wanted anything else in Coles while I was here and she said no by reply text. But when I was just about to get into the Motorhome she rang back and gave me a couple of items to get. Back on the road to the hospital to wait for Tee and just as I was turning into the street that the hospital was on Tee text me to say she was ready and had just got into the hospital car park – great timing! We picked up her medication from a local pharmacy by the foreshore in Geraldton and headed back to our camp spot.

Although it was not good that Tee was sick at least it happened near a major town and we could get her there quickly, as apparently north of here get a little less civilized. Also, all the chores are done and we can head directly north now and not go back to Geraldton in the morning like we planned.

Day **195**

We were happy to get an early start this morning and with the great advice Brian and Wendy had given us we decided to head to Kalbarri. On our way out we discovered that this camp was not a free camp like it said in the Camps6 book and that it actually was $7.00 per person per night. We had already left so we didn't go back to pay, but on reflection I should have and felt a bit guilty even though you didn't get much for that fee. (No water and no power). Over my guilt quite quickly we settled in to enjoying our journey which started with an inland country drive before joining the coastline again. Inland here was very dry but still uniquely pretty and we enjoyed the sites. We first pulled over at a place called Lynton where we saw a number of old convict buildings.

We then made a stop at the Pink Lake, just outside Port Gregory, where we had a cup of tea and Tee whipped up a yummy salad for lunch. Back on the road and we were soon at the shire of Kalbarri sign where I got Tee to take a photo of me in my Carlton shirt. I was keen to get this as Carlton had just recorded there first win after losing their first three matches under the guidance of Mick Malthouse. It was even more significant as the win was over the Western Australian team – the West Coast Eagles. We then past the camp spot that Brian and Wendy were staying at and decided that if we didn't like the accommodation in Kalbarri, we could always come back to it and surprise them.

On the way to Kalbarri there are many pull in areas including Red Bluff, the Grandstand and the Natural Bridge. Not sure of all the names but they are all worth a look as they are all spectacular in their own natural way. We got to the town of Kalbarri and although it was a lovely spot it was a bit touristy and we thought Wagoe Beach where Brian and Wendy were staying would suit us better. I rang the caravan park from Kalbarri to ensure we could get in as it was WA's school holidays and fortunately, they still had some powered sites.

So, we back tracked the 15 or so kilometres to Wagoe Beach and when I got to the Reception of the Caravan Park, I had the great pleasure of wiping my shoes on their West Coast Eagles door mat while wearing my Carlton shirt. For a Carlton supporter it doesn't get better than that. We pulled into the park itself and were soon spotted by Brian who had a smile on his face as he greeted us. He laughed and said we must be stalking them. It was now after 4-00pm and we said that we would catch up with them after we settled in. We went over and shared a few drinks with them and had a chat and a lovely evening.

Day **196**

Not the best of sleeps for either of us last night as the Motorhome was on the wrong angle sloping down at the back. This makes all the blood rush to your head and you usually wake up with a headache in the morning. The Motorhome looked like it was high enough at the back and was on the chocks but the slope of the pad was more than I thought. We both felt unwell and just took it easy for the morning. As we were here for two more days there was no need to rush out and about. I turned the Motorhome around to work with the slope and because the slope was significant, I didn't need the chocks at all.

Around 10-30am we both started to feel a bit better although I still had a very stiff neck. Shortly after Brian popped around and said that while talking to the fellow on the other side of his caravan, he was told that you could collect oysters off the beach directly below us. This made both of us feel much better almost immediately and as low tide was at 3-00pm we planned our day around that.

When I grabbed a few items at Coles while Tee was at the doctors, I picked up a few kilos of marinated chicken wings that were on special. These were close to their use by date so we decided to cook the whole lot up so they didn't go off. We had a big feed of them and I had a can of coke, after which I started feeling a lot better. We got all the gear ready to pick the oysters including our reef shoes for the rocks. The kilometre or so walk down to the ocean was quite pleasant as it was all down hill and there was an abundance of lovely white sand dunes. But we dreaded the walk back as the sand was soft, the climb was long and if we were loaded up with oysters then it would be a trudge. But we were happy to do this for the abundance of oysters that were promised.

When we arrived on the beach, we were not disappointed as there were oysters everywhere. The area was sandy down to a rock shelf that protected the land from the erosion of the wild ocean beyond. In fact, at the edge of the rocks where the waves met the rocks was a huge channel where fishing for deep sea fish was possible, although the area was quite wild and risky. We quickly got to work at removing the little suckers from their resting place and wow how fresh these little buggers are. Tee was going crazy eating them as quick as one every 10 seconds – she was a machine. We kept watch though as there were many rouge waves that threatened to wash us out to sea. Not long after we started our feast Brian, Wendy and their two girls appeared in their 4wd and told us of the large oysters a bit further along the beach. In fact, they said they were just going to come over and see us at our campsite as they didn't know how to shuck them and had a few to show us. The two girls said they wanted to go back to their van and Brian said he and Wendy would come back down and take us to the bigger oysters.

While they were gone Tee continued her demolition of the oysters and I took some fabulous photos of the waves crashing into the rocks. When they returned, we jumped into their vehicle and headed up the beach. We had a great time with them and we all ate a pile of oysters with Tee leading the way. And wow what a bonus as we now did not have to walk all the way back up to the campsite.

As we had chicken wings for lunch, we didn't want much for dinner so the stewed apples fitted the bill. We had a few glasses of wine and chatted with Brian and Wendy for a while before retiring early to catch up with some much-needed sleep.

Day **197**

This morning was super windy and by the look of the sand dunes in the area it must be like this most of the time. Tee was not feeling to crash hot and we decided to have a quiet day. Tee did some washing and I defrosted the fridge and we again had drinks with Brian and Wendy in the evening.

Nice place Wagoe Beach but we are ready to move on now.

Day **198**

The wind was still crazy this morning but we both had a fantastic sleep and Tee is feeling much better, although not completely right. We are looking forward to our journey today which will take us through Kalbarri and onto the National Park there, with our intended destination being the Murchison River. We got the Motorhome prepared for take-off and popped over to see Wendy and Brian to say our good-byes. They have been great company over the past three or four days and we both promised to keep in touch. Back on the road and we thought we would top up the fuel and headed past the Ampol in Kalbarri to the BP around the corner. I checked and topped up the air in the tyres while Tee checked the price of fuel. With the price being 8 cents per litre higher at the BP than the Ampol when I finished with the tyres, we headed back to the Ampol to fill up. I grabbed a loaf of bread while paying for the fuel and we were on our way.

The Kalbarri National park takes in an area that extends from the coast south of Kalbarri and then East of Kalbarri all the way back to highway one. We had visited a lot of the sites that were on the coast before going back to stay at Wagoe Beach some three days ago, so we were off to see what inland delights this region has to offer. The first turnoff was to Natures Window, a place that appears in most tourist ads for WA. But the road to it was red dirt and 25 kilometres each way and that was far beyond the limitations of our no dirt road policy, so we didn't go there. Again, it was disappointing to miss things but we have to be practical as we have to live in this Motorhome every day and neither of us like living in filth. In addition, getting water to clean the Motorhome out here would be quite difficult and not very environmentally friendly.

We then came to another turnoff which led to a couple of Gorges and this time the road was sealed and we took the turning. Then we found that it cost $11.00 per vehicle to enter and we were not that keen to see them at that price, especially as we will see many more Gorges for free. Now if Natures Window was on a sealed road and $11.00 to get in, we would have not given it a second thought and gladly paid up. The advice for National Parks in WA is light and if we had of known that it cost $40.00 for a monthly pass, we would have purchased one and gone to some of these places. So, if you are going to WA remember to buy a monthly pass and you will not have to worry about which National Park you can visit. Although to add confusion to the plot some National parks are not included in this and you have to pay to enter them regardless – Monkey Mia is an example of this.

A shame but this now meant that we will see nothing today in the Kalbarri National Park except for the roadside scenery on the way to the Murchison River. Outside the National Park where people had created farmland the scenery got extremely dry looking and the red soil made it look quite like a desert in parts. As we approached where the Murchison River free camp should be, I did not hold out much hope that there would be water in it. But to my surprise there was water in it as well as a fair-sized group of black swans. We found a nice spot on the Northern side of the River and set up camp. It was now about lunchtime so Tee made me up my favourite sandwich – the humble peanut butter variety and we ate while looking over the river and watching the black swans at play.

The day really heated up in the afternoon and the temperature inside the Motorhome reached 35 degrees. Tee had a nap while I continued to research our trip and evaluate the necessity to purchase a National Park pass. Now if I had have known about the pass when arriving in WA it would have been worthwhile but as we were only going to enter one more National Park apart from Monkey Mia, we will be better off just getting a day pass. This is annoying to me as we have probably missed a few things because of it. It just goes to show that you should go into the information centres, as if we had we would not have missed stuff – lesson learnt. We had a fairly good sleep except for being woken up by a couple of boys who were walking around after 10-00pm with torches and talking very loudly.

Day **199**

We are not sure what to do today as we are well ahead of schedule but the free camps away from the coast are not that crash hot. After discussions though we have decided to try the next few free camps and if they are no good then we will travel up to the coast to just below Denham. In the end the free camp at Nerren Nerren is OK so we thought we would free camp for the last time in a while here. We will be off to the Monkey Mia / Denham area in the morning and it is quite touristy there so I think we will be up for a few camping fees etc in the area. Fortunately, the budget is good and staying here today will ensure that we stay inside the budget. Did not do too much today but I did manage to finish Nelson Mandela's Autobiography which was superb reading. It has been cloudy all day and threatening to rain but we have only had spits. With a bit of luck, we will be swimming with the dolphins at Monkey Mia tomorrow.

Day **200**

We slept reasonably well last night even though the free camp at Nerren Nerren was quite busy. As usual we got the late arrivals waking us up and the early risers doing the same, but what can you do. Tee said she was looking forward to going to Monkey Mia and it certainly has a reputation of being a great place to visit. At Nerren Nerren we are a fair way inland and with the temperature set to rise above 30 degrees again we were keen to get back to the coast. By 8-00am we were already on the road and cruising towards our first destination of Denham. We had no plans to stop before Denham but thought that if we find some nice places, we would certainly visit them. By a little after 9-00am we had reached the Overlander Roadhouse, a place that we would come to see again soon in less attractive terms. This was the point where we turned west and not long after we did, we saw a turning to the stromatolites, which are formations that date back to some of the earliest times on our planet – some 3.5 billion years.

The beach that boasted the stromatolites was made up of millions of tiny sea shells which they once used in the olden days to make building blocks. There is an example of the building blocks close to the foreshore and just past that is a jetty that allows for viewing of the stromatolites. It is quite an amazing place and well worth a visit, it also gave us our first look at the ocean in this area which is beautiful. On our way back to the car park we bumped into an elderly couple that had been at the Wagoe Chalet Park when we were there. They had also seen us at Neeren Nerren free camp but decided not to stay there and had stayed last night at Hamelin Homestead, which was an old working sheep station. But at $24.00 per night for two people – unpowered, it will not be an option for us; it is also way too far from the action at Monkey Mia. Not much further up the road and we entered the World Heritage listed area and soon after that the coastline became our constant companion on either side. It was lovely to see the pristine colours of Shark Bay and we soon arrived at a place called Shell Beach where we stopped for a quick look. Nice but not too much to do here except swim so we were on the road to Denham again.

Denham is absolutely beautiful and the weather was doing its best to make it look even nicer as it was bright, sunny and not a stitch of wind. We stopped Lizzie on the foreshore where the grass was sooo green and the ocean sooo blue and we decided to stay here for a bite of lunch. During our lunch there was plenty of hustle and bustle behind us as a family of emus decided to cross the main street and onto the nice green grass of the Denham foreshore. It was an amazing sight as I have never seen emus in such a busy place, but they seemed quite casual about it and from what we could see it must be a common occurrence around these parts. We took a pile of photos of the emus in the area, and as it was so beautiful, we would ask about prices in local caravan parks. To our dismay the caravan parks in the area were not that pretty with most being quite dusty and unappealing. We asked at one place and at $41.50 per night they were also not cheap.

Tee suggested that we move on to Monkey Mia and ring about the prices there on the way. The prices were $52-00 for a powered site but only $32-00 for a non powered site and as we are self-sufficient in power, we thought this would be the best option. The next shock was the entrance price of $8-00 per person just to get into the area. But what can you do and as we were so far in front of budget, we decided it was a once in a lifetime experience and we should hang the expense. The Monkey Mia landscape is amazing and without the blue of the ocean it could only be described as desert with deep red soil, shrubs not trees and salt pans at every turn.

The Monkey Mia Dolphin Resort was packed, as you would expect in school holidays, and our unpowered site turned out to be a spot in their car park. It was so exciting to pay $48-00 just for a spot in a dusty car park. But this was going to take an attitude change for us or we were going to have a miserable time here. Tee and I decided that the experience of seeing the Dolphins was going to make up for the impression we had formed. While we were at the Nerren Nerren free camp I overheard a conversation of a guy from Perth who told another couple at the free camp that there was nothing to see at Denham and Monkey Mia and that when he went there, he did not see the dolphins in the four days he was there. We now know that this guy was full of shit as Denham itself was worth the drive-in let alone the fact that we now know the Dolphins come in at least once every day. Confirmation that this guy was a wanker.

To try and break our new positive resolve a black Wicked van pulled in beside us with a young Swedish couple inside. Our experiences so far with these vans has been all bad but we had no choice but to make the most of it as we had paid $48-00 to get to this point and with the dolphin feeding not occurring until the morning, we had to remain positive. The resort itself was quite nice and if not for the huge number of people I am sure it would have been quite pleasant. I said to Tee that we should go down to the beach for a while and maybe have a swim and a snorkel. It was quite hot and I think this worked to keep the beach reasonably quiet and we had a lovely swim, although the snorkelling was average with poor visibility and no rocks or weed. We wandered back to our Motorhome about 4-30pm and set ourselves up for dinner and a relaxing evening.

Not long after, the Swedish couple got back to their van as they also had been down on the beach. I said hello and after a while we started chatting. In fact, we had no choice but to chat as we came face to face each time we exited our respective accommodation. Turns out they were a lovely young couple and we sat around chatting for most of the evening. The Wicked van they had was painted up in Black Sabbath paintwork but in fact they listened to Jazz music that Tee and I really love. We swapped travelling experiences and we learnt a trick or two as they showed us a Wiki app that they had on their ipad which was better than the camp6 book we had as it had the ability to filter information. We also chatted to a German couple next to the Swedish couple who were now Australian citizens and lived in Geelong Victoria. They were on their way to the Ningaloo Reef area (near Exmouth) where they were booked in to snorkel with the whale sharks, at a cost of $360.00 per person. This is something that Tee and I would love to do but at $720.00 for both of us we could not justify the cost, although we are tempted.

To our surprise most of the campers around us were in bed by 9-00pm and the Resort was fairly quiet. We made a deal with Nick and Ulrica (the Swedish couple) that we would awake at 6-30am to see the Dolphin feeding at 7-30am. The only negative incident occurred at 1-00am when a stupid girl bumped into the back of our Motorhome on her way to her cabin from the resort bar. It took Tee and I a while to get back to sleep but we awoke fine at 6-30am when our alarm went off.

Day **201**

Feeding the Dolphins of Monkey Mia is something that is a part of most people's bucket list, and we were actually doing it. After a cup of Tea and a quick refresh we made our way down to the beach with Nick and Ulrica our new Swedish friends. It was about 7-30am and already many people were on the beach looking for the Dolphins who were due in very soon. In fact, it was not long before we saw them in the water a little way off shore. Everyone is instructed to stand back away from the water near the boardwalk until the Dolphins gather and prepare to be fed. As we waited the number of people swelled to around 300 which is quite a crowd but the early morning seems to keep everyone quiet, even the brats.

Around 8-00am a lady with a portable microphone called everyone to the waters edge and four other girls joined her while she described the six dolphins that had arrived for the feeding which included a baby. I spoke too soon, as while we were standing at the waters edge a little Brat in a full buoyancy vest did a superb face plant into the water and started howling. Whah Whah as its mum took it away and the whole family missed out on seeing the Dolphins – Brats, why would ya! We were towards the end of the line of people and with most of the action happening near the jetty Tee and I decided to move closer. As we did, we heard a rahhhhhh scream and behind us near the boardwalk was a bigger brat going crazy chasing Emus. But because it broke the silence it all seemed quite comical and reminiscent of the Home Alone movie. Even though we were now behind other people we had a better view of the Dolphins who had now made their way right up to the five ladies in the water. It was an amazing sight as these wild creatures were lying in two feet of water and less than 10 feet from a crowd of 300 or so people.

I took a heap of great pictures and when the lady in charge asked everyone to move out of the water while the buckets of fish were brought down, I said to Tee "stand still" as we were already out of the water. This meant that everyone in front of us that were in the water had to walk around us. We were now in the front row and if we smiled hard enough, we may get a shot at feeding the Dolphins.

Each Dolphin received five fish and each fish was handed out was by another lucky visitor chosen by one of the five ladies in the water. When the fourth feeding was given to an older gentleman beside us Tee and I both thought we would miss out. But I could not believe it when I was asked to feed the last fish to one of the Dolphins. I handed the camera to Tee (the underwater camera that Tee had never used before) and I fed the fish to the dolphin. It was an amazing buzz as the Dolphin rubbed against my leg after she took the fish. They are lovely gentle creatures and I felt so privileged to have been chosen out of the crowd. We then headed back to Ulrica and Nick before walking back to the Motorhome.

Back at the Motorhome I uploaded the photos and Tee had taken some lovely shots of me feeding the Dolphin, shots that I will cherish forever. Not only that but it made the $48-00 we had spent to stay here seem like peanuts compared to the experience that we had had. THE POWER OF POSITIVE THINKING HEY! We said our goodbyes to Nick and Ulrica before heading back to Denham where I promised Tee, I would make her some French toast and Bacon for Brunch.

Tee was not feeling the best and had an upset tummy so when we went into the IGA to buy some bread we also bought some cultured yogurt to try and settle her tummy. We also bought some fuel before finding a nice parking spot on the Denham foreshore for me to prepare brunch. After I set the table up outside to cook on, I realized that it was too windy and I would have to cook French toast inside the Motorhome. We generally don't cook things like bacon in the Motorhome as it tends to linger but with the stiff breeze outside our choices were limited. I did a great job on the French toast (if I do say so myself) and after eating we relaxed a while before heading off.

With around 140 kilometres to travel before we reached the Overlander Roadhouse and only 51 kilometres after that to reach the next free camp at Gladstone Lookout time was on our side to do some more sightseeing. We stopped at Nanga Station which was quite nice but as the water was choppy and the breeze stiff, we decided to just take a few photos and move on. At Denham I did not fill right up with fuel as we anticipated that the fuel prices in Carnarvon would be much keener and I bought enough to get us there. When we got about 25 kilometres from the Overlander Roadhouse my calculations would be thrown out the window by what would happen next. There on the side of the road were two young girls whose car had broken down and they were madly waving at us to pull over. Now if they were not girls, I don't think I would have stopped as you hear many bad tales of such events, but I could not leave two girls alone there so I pulled up after conferring with Tee. Turns out they were German tourists and that they had only had the car a week. It was a Mazda Ute and in a very rough condition, something you would see a farmer driving in a paddock and not two young girls touring Australia in.

After trying to get the car going, I realized that the clutch had packed in and that I had no chance of fixing it. We thought of the best options and agreed that as there was still plenty of daylight and the road was not isolated, that we would take one of the girls to the Overlander Roadhouse and the other girl would stay with the car. I told the girl who was staying with the car that if we didn't return in two hours then she should flag down another passer by. With the plan in place we set off for the roadhouse and were there in about ten minutes. At the roadhouse I was shocked, as was Tee, as to how the owner there reacted to my request for help. He passed us the phone and gave us a card of a towing mob that we rang. The cost to these girls just to tow the car was going to be over $500.00 at which I was totally shocked.

Up until this stage I had tried to help them by doing the talking but now it was their choice as what to do next as I didn't know their financial position. The girl was in tears and said it may take a week in Denham to get the vehicle repaired. I said to her that they really had little option as they had to get to safety and could not leave the car where it was. The towing guy had told her to get back to the car and that he would be there in an hour or so. I took her back to her friend and the car and I tried to get the car going one more time without luck. The other girl was now crying as her friend had told her the news. We waited with them a while but took off about 30 mins before the towing guy was due to arrive. I felt comfortable to leave them as there was still 3 hours of daylight and the road was quite active. I gave them my phone number and told them to ring me and let us know how they got on.

I think there is a lesson here to be learnt as these girls are really quite silly to travel alone in a poor-quality car with no insurance and no roadside assist policy. They make themselves vulnerable to predators and the tow guy could lure them into sexual favour in lieu of the cost of towing. They had made very poor decisions and they had so with the help of poor service from Wicked vans who had ripped them off on their hire of a van before deciding that buying a car would be a better option. I felt terrible not helping them further but there was nothing more we could do and ultimately, they could pay for the repairs and towing and move on.

Back on the road and with that unpleasant situation behind us we were now short on fuel to make Carnarvon, but we had to stop for these girls and could not think of the cost as it is not important. You would also think that phone service in these areas would be better but we are still a long way behind in Australia in that respect. We soon reached the free camp area of the Gladstone Lookout and it turned out to be a great spot high on a dusty hill that overlooked Shark Bay – this time we were viewing it from the Eastern side and would see a stunning sunset.

Day **202**

Not many campers here and we had a pretty good sleep with one exception being a whiz banger pulling in at 10-00pm to wake us up. Fair dinkum the place is three acres in size and they pull up 20 feet from us. We decided to take a rest day here today and I have been writing all day. Tomorrow we will be off to Carnarvon to fill up on supplies and the next free camp is about 100 kilometres North of Carnarvon where we will stop for the night before heading to Coral Bay the following day.

Day **203**

Wow we got a great start this morning and were on the road by 7.45am, and sure as heck we were not going to make Carnarvon on the fuel we have. The day before yesterday I felt sorry for those two German backpacker girls, but today the whole incident is annoying me. The truth is they are sponging off Australia by expecting to travel around our country for next to nothing. They had no roadside assist insurance and you can bet they had no vehicle insurance either. Most Australians only get to travel all around Australia after working for 30 plus years and paying taxes for all those years. I think what annoys me most is that the backpacker types in shitty vans give travellers a bad name and that is not fair to Australians that have paid taxes for so long and deserve to see their own country in full.

Enough of the whining and we stopped at a roadhouse about 20 kilometres from where we camped for the last two nights. I only put $20.00 worth of fuel in as I thought fuel in Carnarvon would be a lot cheaper. But in fact, the pump price at the Wooramel Roadhouse turned out to be two cents per litre cheaper than at Carnarvon (something that I of course did not find out until I reached Carnarvon). If I had of known this, I would have filled up here as the people at the roadhouse were lovely. As I was chatting to the lady in the roadhouse another French couple in a whiz banger arrived just to use the toilets. But quick as lightning the owner of the roadhouse was onto them and said that the roadhouse toilets were for paying customers only and not public toilets. They pushed to use them so the owner ordered them off his property. Now that may sound harsh but

I agree with him as they don't want to pay for anything and why should this couple have to clean up after them when they are not contributing.

Back on the road and within five kilometres their whiz banger was passing us, and at the next roadside stop we saw them pulled over. This facility had no toilets, but if you see the bush around roadside stops in Australia and all the toilet paper all over the ground you soon get the picture as to what was happening. We shook our heads and kept driving to Carnarvon.

We arrived in Carnarvon with a list of things to get and after familiarizing ourselves with the town we pulled in to a Home hardware store where I found the plumbing gear I needed. While I was doing this Tee went across the road to the Auto Pro and bought the indicator globe that I needed for Lizzie. The plumbing gear was for the hot water system as the putty that I put on the leak was now not stopping the water from weeping out of the tank. But determined not to pay $93.50 per hour labour to have it fixed, as well as $400.00 extra for the unit, I have decided to put a tap in the inlet hose that we can turn off when the unit is not in use. This will cut down the leaking by 90% and hopefully get us home. Armed with all the repair items that we need the next item on the list was food. We decided to go to Woolworths as the fuel voucher would save us about five dollars when we filled up our fuel. The Woolworths store was right in the middle of town and on the way there we found a tap and we filled up our house water. At Woolworths we spent a heap on groceries as apparently food is much more expensive as you travel further north.

When we got back to the Motorhome, I could not believe my eyes to see the front driver's tyre half flat. At first, I thought it may have been kids but when I saw the valve cap still in place, I knew they would not bother to put the cap back on. I started the task of getting the pump out of the boot while Tee continued to put all our shopping away. By the time I had the tyre pumped up, Tee had all the shopping away and we headed to a tyre shop. I had seen a Beaurepairs on the outskirts of town and as I headed there, we also saw a Tyrepower and I stopped there to see if they had our type of tyres there.

I have now learnt a bit of a lesson with these tyres, or at least tyres with tubes in them as they seem to get punctures in them when the tread is low. Both the punctures that I have now got have happened on the tyres that were the next to change. In fact, with this front tyre I was trying to get some more wear out of it and then put a new one on it as well as the passenger front tyre that I already had a new one for. But this puncture beat me to it and I will have to put the new tyre on now.

The Tyrepower store did not have my type of tyre and in fact were really just a passenger tyre place so we headed towards Beaurepairs on the outskirts of town. At Beaurepairs we were also informed that they did not have a tyre like ours so we decided to get a puncture repair. Then I thought to myself that it would be silly to get a puncture repair done if we were getting a new tyre and tube for it very soon. I asked them if they would just put the new spare on for me, and they did, free of charge. So, if you need new tyres in the Carnarvon area – Beaurepairs is the GO! We headed back into town again and to fill up with fuel and after that we shouted ourselves a lunch at Chicken Treat that we ate on the Carnarvon foreshore which is quite lovely. After lunch I looked up Bridgestone Karratha and rang them to order a tyre for me, as we would be there in two weeks and it would be waiting for us when we arrived.

Back on the road and we reached our free camp spot at about four in the afternoon where we settled in and tried to avoid the heat of the day. The place we stopped at was called MacLeod Lake rest area, which sounds quite nice but MacLeod Lake is a salt lake and from the free camp area it could not been seen. In fact, I climbed two red sand dunes to try and find the lake before thinking to myself I am crazy doing this as it's 40 degrees and I'm not going to find anything special anyway.

The free camp was sited right beside the highway and by 6-30pm we were still the only people stopped there. But at 7-00pm a family turned up and parked on the other side of the drop toilets from where we were. They were noisy when they used the toilets but then quietened down to no noise when they settled into their campsite. As not to let their reputation down two groups of French backpacker types arrived after 9-00pm and preceded to bang their doors and rattle their pans until the noodles were eaten and they went to bed – well after 10-00pm. You just have to love them!

Day **204**

Although interrupted in our sleep it was not too bad here and I spent half of the morning writing as I was a fair bit behind and if I don't keep up a bit, I start to forget things. About 11-00am we set off and with one more day left in the budget we wanted to free camp for one more night. Upon checking the map as we set off Tee discovered that the free camp Bullara was in fact a paid site. We now had the option of travelling all the way to Coral Bay or stop just 40 kilometres from where we had just stayed. As Coral Bay would be a paid site and our budget was running on empty for the week, we decided to stop at Minilya.

As we had only left MacLeod Lake at 11-00am it was almost lunchtime when we reached Minilya free camp. But the place was lovely and we enjoyed the tranquillity of the area. To add to its charm, we got a lovely spot, and with five other caravans in the area we would outnumber any noisy late arrivals. I attempted to fit the cut off valve into the hot water inlet pipe but unfortunately it was too big and it will have to wait for another day to fix. We had a nice evening with a bottle of Thomson Brook wine and a very sound and peaceful night's sleep.

Day **205**

Today we will head to Coral Bay and hopefully a bit of snorkelling, and as we were on the road by 8-30am we should arrive in Coral Bay by late morning. When we did arrive in Coral Bay, we were quite unimpressed by the place as it was very touristy and extremely crowded with people. The Caravan Parks were packed solid and there were Whiz bangers all over the foreshore. I am sure the place is quite pretty when it is quiet but Tee and I can't see what the fuss is about this place. We had a look at the boat ramp area and the beach itself and they were quite nice but no more special than Kalbarri, Denham or many other places we have seen.

With all the crowd of people here there was no way that Tee and I were going to stay here overnight, or even for the afternoon. It turned out well that we stopped in Minilya free camp as we now had time to get to Exmouth by mid afternoon. If we had carried through to Coral Bay yesterday it well would have been a long ordinary day.

The road from Coral Bay to Exmouth was dry and if not for the amazing quantity and size of the termite mounds would slip into the classification of a bit boring. We arrived in Exmouth to the sight of a lot of new development most of which were canal estates. But before we got to Exmouth proper, we had a look at a small place called Pebble Beach on the outskirts of town. Our thoughts of the place where numerous new homes had recently been built was "why would you" as it seems to be in the middle of nowhere with a distinct lack of services. All we can put it down to is the "new frontier" mentality. Tee and I were as unimpressed with Exmouth as we had been with Pebble Beach and were starting to get worried that North West Cape was also going to disappoint us.

We filled up with water in Exmouth before heading to the Lighthouse Caravan Park in North West Cape. We filled the water just in case we didn't like what we saw at the Lighthouse Caravan Park. On the way to the Caravan Park we took a wrong turn, or more to the point we didn't turn when we should have and ended up under some Federal Government high wire communication system of some description. It was massive and a real eyesore. We pulled over and rang the Caravan Park for directions and Tee soon had us back on track to where we should have been going.

We soon arrived at the Caravan Park and it looked OK, but we decided to trim our stay here from a week to two nights. Tee got all the washing done which turned out to be a fair bit of work and we got it dry in the hot dry wind. The people there were lovely and as we cooled down after the long hot day the place started to grow on us. We had a few wines in the evening and as the sun set Tee and I walked over to the beach for a look. It was really lovely and we went back to the Motorhome for an early night.

Day **206**

With the air conditioner running all night we had a great sleep and as it was so hot yesterday, we were quite slow to get moving this morning. At first, we had no plans for the day but later we thought it would be good to check out the beaches between here and the North West Cape National Park. We took off at about 11-00am and we were suitably impressed with the beaches we saw. In fact, I think if it was not for the Beach no-one would even be interested in the area. We went all the way to the entrance of the National Park and asked about camping availability there. The lady was really helpful but the camping system seemed all too complicated and we decided against camping there for the two nights that we had planned, instead opting to just visit the place on a day pass tomorrow and perhaps stay another night at the Lighthouse Caravan Park.

On the way back to the Caravan Park we checked out the massive sand dunes at one beach and decided that any beach along this coastline would be good for snorkelling as there was always an amount of coral and rock area in the water. After taking a pile of photos at the sand dunes we took off to explore some more beaches. At Janz Beach we decided that with the calm and crystal water it was time for a swim and snorkel. I met a local bloke there who was emptying the bins and he told me that this beach was totally packed last week as it was the school holidays. He also told us that the water temperature was about 26.5 degrees. Both good news to us as we got our gear ready for snorkelling.

The sand here is soft and very white in contrast to the optical blue ocean and we were soon swimming in the pristine water. We had a laugh as we both tried to get our flippers on while the waves kept knocking us over. Eventually we were all set up and we swam towards the rocky area in hope of seeing some fish. Within minutes of hitting the water we were surrounded by many types of marine and plant life, and the camera was going crazy. There were heaps of different kinds of fish and marine plants as well as sea cucumbers and large clams. We had a great time in the water and with the temperature hitting 38 degrees it was a great place to be.

As we were snorkelling a local redneck was backing his boat down the sand towards our towels and gear on the beach. I quickly swam back to yell at him but he spotted our gear and was already correcting his line. He was accompanied by a young French girl who could not speak much English and he was obviously out to impress her. This became comical when he accidentally dropped his boat on the sand 10 feet short of the water. I said to him that he was lucky the tide was coming in as it would be a long wait for him if he had an outgoing tide. Then as he drove his 4WD up to the car park he got that bogged, it was quite comical. Eventually he let the tyres down on his vehicle and got it out and I gave him a hand to push his boat into the water. I know he was pissed off as he did not even thank me as he took off.

We swam and snorkelled at the beach for a couple of hours before heading back to the Caravan Park for a very late lunch, 2-00pm in fact. But before lunch we had the fun task of cleaning down all the snorkelling gear and re setting up the entire campsite. This is the only problem with a Motorhome as you have to put everything away when you go out for the day and reset up when you get back. We had a great day and again sampled the Thomson Brook wine in the evening before retiring at about 9-00pm.

Day **207**

Today we are off to the Cape Range National Park and the Ningaloo Marine Park for a look around and a snorkel. The entrance to the National Park is about 20 Kilometres from where we are staying and we arrived there in around 30 minutes. The same lady ranger was on the gate and we purchased a day pass from her and headed into the park. The first place we stopped at in the Park was Mangrove Bay where we saw Kangaroo's, Emus and wild birds in the Bird Hide (this place is well worth a look). We visited a few more ocean spots on our way to the Milyering Visitor Centre and all of the costal scenery was quite spectacular.

We had a quick look around the visitors centre but what we had really come to see was all outside. On the way back to the Motorhome we walked directly into the path of a huge goanna that was meandering through the car park. I took a couple of photos and then off we went. We pulled into a number of beach spot but none impressed us more than Turquoise Beach and after we travelled as far south in the National Park as we could we headed back to Turquoise Beach for our snorkelling adventure. The place was full of people but this was good to us as we did not want to snorkel in a remote area in case we got into difficulties. I would class both Tee and I as slightly above average swimmers but by no means strong swimmers so caution was needed. Even at Turquoise Beach the currents were strong but we were able to talk to others who had been in about the conditions.

After our comedy routine (getting into our flippers) we started our swim out to the coral. But we were in less than three feet of water and ten feet from shore when we were surrounded by pan sized Trevally- sorry that is 45cm Trevally. This place is amazing and as we got out to the coral the types and numbers of fish increased significantly. We were having a ball and we drifted in the current and took over one hundred photos in an hour and a half.

It was now past lunchtime and we were both quite hungry so we decided to get out of the water and go back to the Motorhome for something to eat. Tee cooked me up some noodles and she had some rice cakes with various toppings. We were keen to get back in the water but thought it would be wise to wait a while after eating so we relaxed for about 40 mins after lunch. At 2-30pm we could not wait any longer so we took off again to the beach for a second snorkel. We had thought about snorkelling in another location but the wind was picking up and Turquoise Bay seemed reasonably sheltered. But unfortunately, when we got back to the beach it had become quite choppy. Undeterred we got into our snorkelling gear again and jumped back into the water, but it was no good as there were now small waves and the current seemed stronger than this morning.

A little pissed that we didn't leave lunch til later and stay in the water, but at least we did have a great snorkel here and got to see the wonders of this magnificent place. It was close to 3-00pm when we got back to the Motorhome and we decided to call it quits for the day as the conditions were highly unlikely to change. On the way back to the Caravan Park we stopped at the Lighthouse to get our emails and our phone messages, as it is the only spot around here where we get signal.

We got an email from the Swedish couple that we met at Monkey Mia and I got a phone message from the two German girls that we had stopped for outside Denham. I was really happy to hear that the two German girls had their car repaired and that they were safe. Even though when we left them with the tow truck on its way the dad in me felt that we could have done more and perhaps should have stayed until the tow truck arrived. So, it was a relief to hear from them and they were on their way to Coral Bay. I sent them a response suggesting that they may consider breakdown insurance – again the dad in me.

The Swedish couple, Ulrica and Nick, had been in the Ningaloo area when we first arrived and had sent us a sunset picture from the Lighthouse where I was now receiving this email. But now they were heading back down south past Perth then across the Nullarbor to Victoria eventually. I have put them on our mailing list which is growing rapidly now. It is a list of people that I send updates to of our travels, some of whom I send them to return our emails but many don't. I suppose it will help us determine who our true friends are. We went back to the caravan park and quickly got the air con cranked as the temperature had risen to over 40 degrees.

At first, we thought three days here would be long enough but the place is really growing on us and we both want to do some more snorkelling, so we came to the decision to stay a full extra week. It is always hard when travelling to decide how long to stay in an area as you feel as though if you stay too long you will not have time to see other areas. But we are over a week ahead of schedule and there does not seem to be a lot between here and Broome so the decision is made. This place is so beautiful and we may never be back again so three days seems to be far too short. But I have a sneaking suspicion that in years to come we will venture back to this amazing place. This location hits my "must see list" with a bang and I believe every Australian should see it.

Day **208**

Yesterday we decided to stay here an extra week and this morning I went over to the Caravan Park office to pay for that week. It is $38.00 per night here and although that is high compared to places down South, it is relatively cheap compared to other Caravan Parks up North. Water is a huge problem here and most of it comes via desalination, which I suspect is not cheap. The bonus was that if you stayed a week you get one night free so it was $228.00 for a week, not too bad really. The site we were on though had been booked so we had to move the Motorhome down a couple of sites before Tuesday.

Today we would have a rest day and prepare for the week ahead, along with our future travel plans over the next four weeks or so. I had booked a tyre at Bridgestone Karratha but it was an older tyre that the one I got in South Australia and I was not happy that the tread pattern was different, especially as it was going on the front of the vehicle. I looked at the map and as we were not that interested in seeing Onslow or Karratha, perhaps we should head towards Tom Price and Karijini National Park where there was suppose to be some lovely Gorges. This would still allow us to go past Port Hedland where I could order the correct tyre and we could top up our supplies. I discussed my idea with Tee and she was keen so my next task was to order the tyre from Port Hedland.

Ordering a tyre sounds like an easy job, but when you have limited email reception and no phone reception the task gets a little more difficult. The first task was to go online and via Yellow pages dot com I could send the details of the tyre store to my mobile. Then I would also write the phone number onto a piece of paper in case the message did not go through. Then I had to climb the lighthouse hill to get phone reception, and even though it was easier to drive it was less hassle to climb the hill than to pack up all the Motorhome and then drive. Life isn't always simple on the road and today was proof.

The view from the lighthouse hill was stunning as I climbed and it was not too long before I got mobile reception (the message came through from Yellow Pages dot com). I phoned the Port Hedland Bridgestone store and spoke with Phil. At first, he gave me a price of $300.00 for just the tyre which I replied was too expensive – I knew he was trying it on. He then said he was near the office and when he got to the office, he reviewed the price to $240.00 and I asked him to order it for me and confirm the order by emailing me. He seemed quite vague so I will wait until Tuesday for his email. If he does not reply by Tuesday, I will follow him up again. The last thing we want to do is get to Port Hedland and there be no tyre there for us as we would then have to hang around for a week or order again from Broome or Darwin. While I was on the hill and had phone reception, I also rang mum and a few relatives to say hi. I also rang a Real Estate friend back home to pass on a referral. All the time I was on the phone I enjoyed the brilliant ocean views and was kept company by a couple of falcons and a hawk – what a place!

Back down the hill I went, which was much easier than climbing it, and I told Tee that I had ordered the tyre and we were clear to travel to Port Hedland via Tom Price. We did a bit of cleaning during the day and I even washed the Motorhome. That evening we sat outside in the cool and I ended up having far too much wine and wrote myself off.

Day **209**

We had planned to go snorkelling in the National Park today as the weather was forecast to be perfect. But stupid me had got drunk and was in no shape to drive or snorkel. But on a positive note we do have the whole week here and tomorrows forecast was almost as good as todays. I spent the morning recovering and by lunchtime I had enough strength and mental capacity to start writing. I wrote until I caught up and was starting to feel quite OK, so I asked Tee if she wanted to do a bit of snorkelling this arvo around Janzs Beach. Janzs Beach is only a few kilometres from our Caravan Park so after a bite of lunch we took off. We had a gentle swim and snorkel in which we still managed to get a heap of photos and see some amazing sea life.

Coming out today has been a good thing as I was feeling quite off colour and going for a swim has pepped me up. I would have just been sitting around the Motorhome feeling sorry for myself. After a few hours on the beach we went back to the Caravan Park and had leftover pasta for Dinner. It always seems to taste better on the second day.

After dinner I emailed the National Parks department for Karijini National Park to check out park entry and camping costs. This will help us plan our travels and where we will stay each night. Dales Campground in the Karijini National Park seems to be the pick of the spots as it is located near many of the major scenic attractions. After being near the ocean for a few weeks we are looking forward to some inland sites and scenery.

Day **210**

No wine last night and I woke early, so there is no excuse for not having a big day of snorkelling today. Tee was raring to go and we were on the road by a bit after 8-00am, not bad considering we have to pack our whole home up before we drive anywhere. We were soon at the entry to the Cape Range National Park where we paid our $11.00 entry fee and proceeded to drive to Turquoise Beach where we planned to put a full day of snorkelling.

We arrived at Turquoise Beach at a few minutes before 9-00am and the water looked sensational for snorkelling with the sun doing its normal brilliant self in this part of the country. Once parked we got our gear together and made our way to the beach, and as we had been snorkelling on the drift loop side a few days ago we decided to start there. As expected, when we got in the water the visibility was close to perfect and we were soon surrounded by trevally fish that seem to love the sandy shallows. (My pan sized friends, as I like to call them). We made our way out to the reef and Tee spotted a small stingray that was a brilliant rainbow colour. We both thought that stingrays were a muddy green colour, but it was obvious that this was their natural colour which is quite amazing. As we snorkelled, we saw many different types of marine life including eels, sea urchin and dozens of colourful types of fish. After nearly two hours of snorkelling we decided to go on the beach for a while and relax.

During our break on the beach Tee said she needed her big sun hat so I went back to the Motorhome to get it. While there I uploaded the photos that we had taken so far, and as I did realize that there were almost one hundred of them. I quickly uploaded them onto my laptop and grabbed

Tee's hat and a hat for myself as well as a bottle of cold water. When I got back to the beach, I asked Tee if she wanted to go back in again and she was keen so off we went. Tee and I have snorkelled in Vanuatu but it was nowhere near as good as this and the visibility in Ningaloo is brilliant. We again were surrounded by lovely underwater scenery and as we got out of the water for the second time, I had a bit of a play with the trevally that seemed keen to hang around. I got some lovely shots of them before the camera battery seemed to be getting very low.

On shore and Tee suggested that we go back to the Motorhome for lunch, and after over three hours of snorkelling I was very keen to take up her offer. This is the great thing about living like a turtle, your home is where you are and we did not have to drive anywhere to get a cold drink or have a yummy lunch. Tee cooked me up some two-minute noodles, which seemed to take an hour to cook (as I was so hungry) and Tee had some sardines on crackers. I said to her that she may want to brush her teeth before going back in the water as she may get taken by a shark that mistakes her for a seal! I got a quick ha and a bit of a dirty look so I decided to save the humour for some other time.

After lunch the wind had picked up a bit and we decided to go to the bay side of Turquoise Beach as it was more sheltered. We drove Lizzie to the other car park and headed off to the beach again, it was now almost 1-30pm. Turquoise Bay was much more a swimming beach than the Drift Loop side but still had a fair bit of coral reef in it. We got back into the water and took a heap more photos but we were only in for about 40 minutes when Tee said she had had enough for the day. Tee got out of the water and sunbaked while I spent another 30 minutes in the water playing with the trevally. Unfortunately, though by the time they got right up close to me the battery on the camera went totally flat. I got out and sunbaked with Tee for about another hour and just after 3-00pm we decided to head back to the Caravan Park. On the way back we stopped off at the lighthouse to check our mobiles and to send some emails that were full of underwater shots.

Back at the Caravan Park we got stuck into cleaning the sand off everything and Tee cooked up Bangers and Mash for Dinner. We had a quiet evening – no wine – and watched another movie in bed before going to sleep.

Day **211**

The weather is meant to be cloudy today and tomorrow it is forecast to rain. This is why we decided to go snorkelling yesterday and today has been reserved for chores and relaxing. After the sun and snorkelling of yesterday I was glad to see the clouds roll in this morning as expected. The shitter is just starting to smell a little and when I checked with Tee when it was last emptied, she looked it up on her trusty calendar and told me it was day nine. As we usually empty it after a week it was a job that I could not put off any longer. In Caravan Parks we try and use their amenities as much as possible but at night the toilet in the Motorhome is fabulous.

So, it was shitter empty time and time to fill the house water which I am doing manually from the fresh water supply. The water in the Caravan Park is like at Monkey Mia and they desalinate it themselves on-site. This means that the showers are half salty and only the tanks have fresh fully desalinated water. There is no way that I am putting that salty shit into my tanks even if it means lugging water across the Caravan Park. Fortunately, the tank is not far from our site and I have kept us in good supply of fresh water every day. I was reading that this area (Vlamingh Head) was going to be the main town around these parts but because the water supply was purer near Exmouth that became the main town. I did my favourite chore (yes, the shitter) which I had to carry fully stocked for about 100 mtrs to the dump point. This was strenuous and could easily be turned into an Olympic sport – they could call it the shit put

Fortunately Tee had made me Bacon and Eggs for Brekkie and I was strong – like warrior.

After the lovely Shit Put, I now had to climb the Lighthouse hill to get phone reception. This was to confirm my tyre had been ordered (no email reply from Bridgestone Port Hedland yet) and also ring my water supplier to send me a bill that I will pay. I still have trouble believing that I am ringing a company to email me a bill so that I can pay it and that is the best they can come up with. While up here I also rang some family and friend to catch up and only left when the ants in the area decided to make lunch out of me. The ants also reminded me that I was hungry and when I got down the hill, I asked Tee if she would whip me up something. Tee was happy to do this and even more so when I presented her with a full clam shell that I had found on my way down the hill. It was a beautiful shell and we were baffled as to why someone would just throw it away. Tee said she will polish it up and put it on display at home. (That's going straight to the Poolroom ☺)

After lunch I had a chat with some people who turned up behind us in the Park and spent the rest of the afternoon writing and planning the next part of our journey. I had received an email response from the Karijini National Park people which now meant that I could plot our journey with precision. Also, Phil had ordered the tyre for me and I could give him a close date as to when we would arrive in Port Headland to have it fitted. I think I will remove the old tyre before I get there though as they charge $16.00 to dispose of them and I can drop it at a tip along the way and save that money.

Day **212**

Wow! What a storm we had last night. They had predicted storms today but they must have come through early as we were both woken by ferocious winds and then later by lightning and howling rain. It was about three o'clock in the morning when the rain and the lightning happened so it must have been after midnight when the first winds came through. The good news was that Lizzie did not leak and last night I had put everything away at Tee's request. In fact, I was not going to put anything away thinking that it would be the morning at least before the storm hit. But Tee was right and we would have had a lot of cleaning to do if I hadn't put everything away, and probably a broken awning – Good Call Tee!

The Caravan Park though did not fare as well and there was a lot of rutting around the place where the water had run through. The bottom of the Caravan Park was also like a lake. In fact, the two roads in the Caravan Park had nicknames that the locals made for them, the bottom road was called Lakeside and the top road was called Donerootin – apparently named due to the elderly age of the residents who camp there. I have worked out why they call it Lakeside but this Donerootin I don't understand ☺

We have done all the snorkelling that we had planned to do and just as well as the weather does not look all that crash hot for the week. Today as the weather was a little ordinary, we decided to have a rest day of reading and writing and in the early afternoon Grumpy came over to have a chat. Grumpy is his nick name and he prefers it to his real name which is Ivan. Grumpy lives in a retirement village in Perth and has been coming to Ningaloo for the past 20 years and to the same caravan park. Many older people from Perth do the same thing as Grumpy and head north to avoid the Perth winter, much the same as Victorians by going to Queensland over winter. The thing with Perth is that they have the same state all the way from South to North, unlike our Victorian immigrants.

Turns out Grumpy is a really nice fellow with a crusty shell, hence he assumes the nickname Grumpy and even displays it in the form of a personalized number plate. He came and sat with me and we had a long chat and what he said was so typical of older men. It turns out that this is the first time, in twenty years of setting up his caravan here in Ningaloo that he is truly struggling. Earlier today I heard him swearing to himself and I asked him what that was all about, and he told me that he was so frustrated that he could not physically do the things that he once did so easily. At 82 though he was still doing so well and I told him so, but it was of no consequence as he felt cheated. It is sad when one's mind is still so active and yet the body lets you down. I said to him that he should feel privileged that he got 82 years of physical capability when some never have it. I said that to live one's age and capacity is not a crime and that he just needs to find ways around his issues, I also said that if he needed any help over the next few days to call me over.

Tee made a yummy creamy cabonara for Dinner and it was so good that I had seconds. After dinner I could hardly move as I ate far too much but that was not a problem as I didn't have anything to do anyway. But I decided to go for a walk to try and burn it off a bit and relax my tummy.

Day **213**

We were supposed to get another storm last night but fortunately it did not eventuate and today has started with brilliant blue sunshine and a much milder temperature. With only a few days left at Ningaloo we don't plan to do too much and this morning all we did was read and write and chat to some of the other people in the Caravan Park. Grumpy was his normal self and was shouting foul language at his new satellite dish that was not doing what it was suppose to be doing. In fact, all it was doing was going round and round in circles. But to his credit Grumpy called me over to help him fit a sunshade that required me to climb a ladder and I quickly went to his aid. With the job done I returned to Tee and continued reading my newest acquisition – Steve Waugh's autobiography. In fact, that is not really true as I had bought it some time ago but after reading his other book, I was not in a hurry to be disappointed by another poor effort. In fact, I have now read over one hundred pages and it is quite good reading.

After some cheese and crackers for lunch I asked Tee if she would like to take a trip to the sand dunes that we had visited some days ago. Tee was keen as it was a little boring sitting around reading all day and although the weather was not crash hot (wind wise) we took off for a leisurely drive. We did in fact have a few chores to do before we left but we also had all day tomorrow to do them and there was really only a couple of hours work in total.

It was nice to get out a bit and the landscape had changed a bit after the recent rains, in fact it looked fresh and much greener than three days ago. But as we found out when we reached the sand dunes the rain had also made the water murky and there was a lot more seaweed on the beaches. Never the less the sand dunes were beautiful to walk over and we sat for over an hour staring at the amazing scenery, both sea and land, that this pristine place offered. We were also amazed again that we were here on our own and apart from cars passing by about 500 meters away we couldn't see a soul. The only creatures we saw were birds, crabs and a number of Marsh Flies that became the source of my attention for all the wrong reasons. These little buggers really hurt when they get you and I was soon very proud that I had eliminated nine of them in a row as they persisted to try and make a meal out of me.

A number of photos later and we were off back to the Caravan Park and on the way, we stopped again at the Lighthouse hill to check our phones for messages. I had a message from one of my colleges from the real estate game back home who was trying to contact me about a referral that I had given him. I rang him to find out that he had listed the referral that I had given him and that upon sale he would pay me my fee. This would be a nice bonus as I have not really been pushing to get referral clients as I was sure that my ex-boss had continued his spree of discrediting me with my past clients. Sounds like sour grapes but I have witnessed his venom as an employee as he discredits other in the industry and I don't see myself as special enough for him not to extend to me the same.

Back at the Caravan Park I continued to read my Steve Waugh book until visited by a small group of Mickey Birds who seemed hell bent on taking my attention away from Steve and focus on feeding them. Tee saw them and passed me a small handful of cornflakes which caught their eye immediately. These little fellows got so game that I ended up hand feeding them on our outdoor table. They even posed for photos while eating out of my hand.

The evening was filled with me cooking pasta followed by a DVD watched in the bedroom.

Day **214**

Last full day at Ningaloo and the weather although sunny is even windier than it was yesterday; in fact, the prediction is for winds above 20 knots. This does not bother us as we have done all the seaside activities that we want to do, or can afford, as we would love to swim with the Whale Sharks but at $400.00 each it is not realistic for us. But others in the Caravan Park are disappointed as many want to go boat fishing and the couple behind us want to paddle surf, both of these not possible in the conditions. In fact, a few have gone home as the weather is set to be like this for the next three or four days.

Not much happened today but we did have two couples over for a few drinks in the evening and have made some new friends.

Day **215**

The wind last night was amazing and well over 20 knots. We both got woken up to the Motorhome being rocked in the wind. I stuck my head out the door and Ben from behind us was putting a rock on my thongs that had blown under his caravan. Tee's thongs had blown even further and at one stage we had given up the hunt for it. Fortunately, though we found it wedged under the back tyre. Buying a new pair for the cost was not a problem, but out here it is more about finding a place that sells them.

Time to pack up camp and hit the road so we are both busy with that process. We are well stocked for our journey now with 70 litres of drinking water, full house water, all the washing done and a clean Motorhome. A quick goodbye to Ben and V and then we were ready for our travels. We dropped into the office to hand in the amenities key, which had a $30.00 bond on it and I also put $80.00 worth of fuel into Lizzie for our Journey. As we left, I was OK with the wind as we were heading North and the 20 plus Knot wind was blowing South West. But as soon as we hit the corner to head to Exmouth, I realized we had to travel 80 kilometres south before we turned east. This meant that we would have a headwind for about 150 kilometres and a tailwind for only about 60 kilometres. Anyway, nothing we can do about it now as we are on our way, we will just have to deal with it.

We pulled in to the Exmouth IGA to grab a few grocery items and I needed a toilet stop as the Caravan Park toilets were being cleaned as we left. We had not been shopping for almost two weeks and we still had heaps of stuff so we only had to grab a few items. Unfortunately, it still cost us

$50.00 to grab a few items as groceries in these areas are quite expensive. While Tee was putting away the groceries, I checked my phone messages and rang the people I needed to. We stopped off at the information centre for my toilet break and then we were finally fully on our way. The plan for the day was to travel to one of two free camp spots that were about 160 and 200 kilometres from Exmouth. This would be a short trip but as it was now 11-00am we would be on the road until probably 3-00pm. As we left Exmouth the strength of the wind could be felt belting up against Lizzie, and although she is a strong old girl she did not particularly like the headwind. This became very apparent as the fuel consumption got really bad and in fact it seemed like I could see the fuel needle dropping.

The wind did ease when we turned off the Exmouth road and started heading east, but it was still a headwind and Lizzie was still feeling it. We had a cuppa break along the way and virtually drove past the first free camp area when we saw how crappy it was. But this first free camp was on the road that now took us in a northerly direction, so Lizzie was a lot happier and so were we as the needle would now slow down on the fuel gauge. It was not too much further to the next free camp that turned out to be quite a nice-looking spot right on the dry banks of the Yannarie River. It was now about 3-00pm and there was already about five caravans and Motorhomes here. We found a nice little spot, and as the day passed more and more Caravans pulled in. Just on sunset I went for a walk down to the dry river bead with the camera and captured some lovely shot of both it and the sun setting over it. Tee had stayed back at the Motorhome as she wanted to get dinner ready.

On my return we ate and had a lovely evening, chatting and enjoying the cool breeze. It was really nice that the overnight temperature was now getting a lot cooler as we had moved inland.

Day **216**

O ff again today with the plan to get about halfway or so to Tom Price with an assault on Karijini National Park in two days time. On the way out of the free camp I emptied the shitter again and we were on our way. The wind was again against us as it had now shifted to a Westerly and decided that we needed some more headwinds as we had got such a good run so far this trip. The journey was pleasant as far as the scenery went as the Pilbara region is very beautiful and extremely unique. The only unpleasant part was the fuel consumption as Lizzie struggled through the headwind. In fact, it was so strong that we had used up the $80.00 in fuel by the time we reached the Nanutarra Roadhouse. To add insult to injury the price of fuel here was a ridiculous $1.92 per litre and we had only done 305 kilometers on the $80.00 of fuel.

I was suitably unimpressed but we could not reach the next fuel station as it was about another 120 kilometres away. There was a fellow there from Newman who had been at Coral Bay for a week's holiday, and when I grumbled to him about the price he said "well it is the middle of nowhere." I don't think it really was and even if it was the Nullarbor fuel prices were four cents a litre cheaper, so go figure. Sounds like a genuine Roadhouse rip off to me. Another issue I have is that I don't believe the fuel pump at the Nigaloo Lighthouse Caravan Park was correct either. I noticed it did not seem to fill the tank to the level I expected at $1.72 per litre. This suspicion would grow stronger when I reached the next fuel stop.

We continued our journey and arrived at the first of the two free camps that we were considering to stay at. But because it was only 11-30am we continued even though the House Creek Bridge free camp looked lovely and already had a number of caravans in it. We continued on to the Beasley River Rest Stop but could not get in because the recent rains had made it very boggy and there was no way we were going to risk it. This meant that we would have to continue on until we reached the free camp on the outskirts of Tom Price.

It was now after 1-00pm and we decided that we will have to stop at the next parking area and have some lunch and a break, which we did at about 1-30pm or so. We continued our journey after lunch admiring the unique Pilbara scenery until we reached Paraburdoo.

Paraburdoo was very much a mining town but it was quite pleasant even though it was a little tired. We found a Shell servo there that was a Coles Express outlet and decided to check the pump price before purchasing as we did have enough fuel to make Tom Price. To our amazement the fuel price was $1.68 per litre and was even more in the middle of nowhere than the Nanutarra Roadhouse. This dispelled the theory of the gentleman from Newman and confirmed my belief of the Nanutarra Roadhouse ripping people off. Another belief of mine also rang true as it was the same distance from Nanutarra Roadhouse to Paraburdoo as it was from the Ningaloo Lighthouse Caravan Park to Nanutarra Roadhouse, yet I still had more fuel in the tank as I arrived at Paraburdoo as when I arrived at Nanutarra Roadhouse. In addition, the fuel at Nanutarra Roadhouse was 20 cents per litre more expensive. I am now convinced that the fuel pump at Ningaloo Lighthouse Caravan Park is dodgy.

When I went in to pay for the fuel, I also discovered that I could use my 8 cents per litre fuel saver dockets which brought the price to $1.60 per litre, our first win for the day. We arrived at the Halfway Bridge Rest Area at 4-00pm and settled in for the overnight stay.

Day **217**

As usual when you are alone at a free camp on the side of a highway you get the fuckwits who seem to think they are funny by tooting their horn at you in the middle of the night. Last night was no exception and Tee said that she even heard a siren which she thought was from a mining vehicle. We did go to bed early so I am not feeling too tired but Tee said she was awake for a long time after that. I don't see why people cannot live by the simple rule of "live and let live", and the only reason I can come up with as to why they do it is because they are jealous. It doesn't affect us too much but it does make you a little more tired and it is so unnecessary. The free camp here was a great spot apart from the dickheads tooting as they went past, but Lizzie had a steep climb to get us back on the highway as the free camp was down low on a riverbank. Turned out to be no problem for the old girl though, as she has great low gear selection and she just cruised up the incline.

Back on the road and we were off to Tom Price on our way to Dales Gorge in Karijini National Park. Tom Price was an interesting place where the shops and facilities seemed very much an afterthought to the mining. There was a hardware store there so I went in to see if I could get the correct sized valve cut off that I needed to isolate the dodgy hot water service. Unfortunately, though they had the same sized one that I had purchased in Geraldton but none smaller – no good to me – and they didn't even have toilet chemicals. So, if you need bits for your caravan or Motorhome, Tom Price is not much help. There was a pub though and a service station so after waiting until 11-00am (bottle shop opening time)

I bought some well priced XXXX and we topped up our petrol. Tee and I took photos of each other in front of a big mining truck and we were on our way to Dales Gorge.

The Karijini National Park was only about 40 kilometres from Tom Price but Dales Gorge was about 100 kilometres from here. We didn't pick the distance at the time we planned as it was on a fold in our map and we couldn't judge the distance correctly. Not long after we turned onto the road into Karijini National Park we stoped at the RIP rest stop mainly out of curiosity. Turns out the views were nice over the valley and the site was covered in memorials to dead people, which we suspect were both real and fictitious. Regardless of their reality status Tee and I would not spend a night here as it was a little eerie, although it was a designated free camp – certainly an odd place.

Back on the road and we soon spotted a huge thing on the side of the road coming up, and when we got closer, we saw that it was a dead cow that was fully bloated. It was enormous and quite disgusting – the poor creature. The council would need a crane to remove that. A little further up the road we saw a group of wild donkeys and I stopped to photograph them. I had never seen wild donkeys before and neither had Tee. Confusion reined supreme at our next stop as we came to a T intersection (or side road) that we thought we should go straight at but the only reference to Dales Gorge was to the left. To make matters worse the road turned to dirt and Dales Gorge was 52 kilometres away.

Tee was firm in her belief that we went straight as it was East in direction and there was no reference to an unsealed road. Turns out she was completely correct and we put it down to bad signage. Within 30 minutes we were at the entrance to Karijini National Park which now made reference to Dales Gorge, unlike it did back at the T intersection (or more correctly side road). We paid our $11-00 entry fee and entered the park.

This area also had a camping area which we were going to use and it looked quite OK as we passed it on the way to the gorge. We arrived at the gorge car park at about 1-00pm which was far later than we expected and were now both quite hungry. I was so hungry in fact that I had myself a third peanut butter sandwich, an action that I would regret in the not too distant future.

After lunch we set out to explore Dales Gorge along with Circular Pool and Fortescue Falls. Dales Gorge is stunning and we enjoyed the walk which took us over about four kilometres return and took in all three sights. This place is stunning and we took over one hundred photos here. The best feature was that the weather was cool, so cool in fact that Tee wanted to wear a jacket, which I talked her out of as it was not that cool – but close. Which meant walking the distance would be pleasant and with the grey rain clouds behind the red gorge and the green trees the photos were superb. People always comment that it would be better with the sun out but Tee and I disagree as the colours really come to life in these conditions.

We had a great look around and as we had done it all in fewer than three hours, we saw no point in paying to camp here so we decided to head out of the National Park and on to a nearby free camp. If we had a 4WD we would have stayed as there was more to the National Park than just the Dales Gorge area, but we don't enjoy dirt roads and we are well satisfied with what we have seen. On exiting the National Park, I stopped at a huge termite mound at which Tee photographed me and it made me look tiny – they are amazing – and apparently live on grass plants.

Back on the main road and we were still fighting a headwind which seemed hell-bent on putting Lizzie through her paces as it has for the past few days. Fortunately, though when we turned onto the Great Northern Highway Lizzie received a reprieve. Within 20 kilometres we reached our free camp area that was called the Albert Tognolini Rest Area and was a memorial to his work as an engineer on this Highway. As we approached the free camp, we were greeted with stunning gorge views and when I checked on the map, I realized that it was in a direct line with Dales Gorge and it must be part of the same geography.

The place was stunning and we found a parking spot that was away from anyone else and extremely quiet.

Day **218**

Last night I had no idea how tired I was and after about ten hours sleep, I now feel great. Tee was also well pleased as it was so dark and quiet here last night, as well as being two kilometres off the highway. We were planning to move on to the next free camp today but this place is so nice and quiet we decided we should take a rest day here. Just as well as by 9-30am it had started raining and it is bitterly cold, in fact during the entire day the temperature did not exceed 13 degrees – amazing when you consider where we are in Australia and what the temperature was a week ago. The plan for tomorrow is to drive almost all the way to Port Hedland where our new tyre is awaiting and we can top up our supplies.

Day **219**

Today is a great day for me as it is my ex- wife's 50th birthday. Knowing her personality, she will be pretending to be in party mode while secretly feeling like the old bag that she really is. Sounds like sour grapes hey, damn straight it is, as she put me thorough so much grief during our divorce I feel quite entitled. In fact, while I was desperately sinking in debt and trying not to go bankrupt, she was touring the world with her new deadbeat boyfriend. My only solace in those days was that "life is a great leveller" and now it is my time to enjoy life.

The story of my life during those years is huge and if I were to tell it I could not avoid sounding bitter. I think that no matter how I portrayed the situation it would look ugly. But I know in my heart that I did the right thing and that "life would be the great leveller" and it was. I have come out the other side a lot more balanced person and no longer crave 'bigger and better' and have learnt a level of contentment that can only be achieved with a great life partner. In monetary terms my numbers are now smaller but what I can get has grown ten-fold.

After taking some lovely photos of Albert Tognolini Rest Area where we have been for the past two nights it was off to Port Hedland to take care of business. I was going to stop just outside Port Hedland and send the Bridgestone Tyre Centre an email to say I would be there on Thursday but as I have not had email access, either today or tomorrow should not really be a problem for one tyre. So onwards to Port Hedland, and on the way, we passed through a lovely gorge area that was a continuation of where we had been camping. In fact, it was in between that and Dale's Gorge according to the map.

The journey from there to Port Hedland was fairly uneventful but we arrived there in good time at around 11-30am. We went directly to the Bridgestone Tyre Centre so they could fit us in some time today. In addition to this I had stripped the old stuffed tyre off the rim at a roadside stop on the way while Tee made a cuppa. This made the job of fitting the new tyre very easy for them, and increased my chances of speedy service. Tee was impressed that I could change a tyre, and after 30 years of never touching a truck tyre, so was I.

Phil greeted me as I entered the Tyre Shop and said that if I left the rim with him and came back in an hour or so that it would be ready to put on the vehicle. I thought that was great and I asked him about shopping centres in the area and he gave me directions to the local Coles supermarket. As we had only bought $50.00 worth of groceries in the past two and a half weeks you would expect we were quite down on food, but in fact we were not. The list we prepared should only cost us about $60.00 and would last until we reached Broome or even beyond. Unfortunately, though we always seem to fall into the same trap of over shopping and we ended up with $130.00 worth.

The other job that I needed parts for was this darn leaking hot water service and I thought with the size that Port Hedland was, I would have no trouble getting the cut off tap I needed. Port Hedland is all about mining and everything in and around the town is covered in its dusty bi-product to ensure that no one forgets what makes this place tick. At this stage though we were not right in Port Hedland and I was having no luck finding the stop tap I needed. Tee finally spotted a Reece Plumbing store which should be the place I needed. Unfortunately, though the size I need is food grade only and most places need to order it in. The guy at Reece was very helpful and gave me a metal alternative, but it would be too heavy for the pipe that is suspended in mid air. Tee reckoned that with some fiddling, the tap we had would fit and that we should try that next time we were at a free camp for a full day. Truth is we had no alternative and I will try it when we next stop for a while.

We headed back to the tyre shop and Phil had the wheel all ready for me and he put it straight onto Lizzie when I got there. Now into Port Hedland central with a fuel stop on the way, then to the Information Centre to ask where we could get fresh water from. The town of Port

Hedland is amazing and very much a big Tom Price with ocean. The most astonishing thing about the place is the real estate prices, where a three-bedroom one-bathroom home sells for close to one million. To be honest, someone would have to pay me a million to live in this place, it is quite ugly. The girls at the Information Centre were lovely and explained to me where I could fill up our Motorhome with water. After filling up Lizzie with water we shot out of town as quickly as possible as Tee and I really disliked being here. In fact, Tee felt she had a sore throat and when she mentioned it, I also had a funny taste in my mouth, it was not nice.

If I have offended people by being honest about Port Hedland then I am sorry, but I really could not see why anyone would chose to live here, even if you earn a heap. To Tee and I it would simply not be worth it. As we left town, we were hampered in our travels by speeding trucks that carried up to four trailers behind them. To me calling them a train should allow them to only travel on isolated steel tracks and not take over our highways. They are huge vehicles and it feels mighty unsafe to share the road with them. Not their individual fault but a better solution needs to be sought, as if mining is worth so much then it perhaps should run on its own infrastructure.

After clearing the MINE ZONE, we again enjoyed the scenery and within half an hour or so arrived at our free camp for the evening which was called De Grey River Rest Area and turned out to be a superb free camp – no need for Plan B here. The place was full of campers and we found a lovely spot with real grass and river views. That evening we met some of our temporary neighbours (Stan & Val) who turned out to be from Morayfield, where I have worked for the past 10 years or so. In fact, they even knew one of my past clients who I had dealt with only a year or so ago. We had a good chat and a few beers before Tee and I retired to the Motorhome to heat up our Dinner and hit the sack.

As soon as I hit the pillow, I remembered a bill I had to pay that was due tomorrow. This would normally not be a problem but at this campsite we did not have any internet reception. We had thought about staying here two nights which was now out of the question as the penalty for not paying my Visa on time would be about $80.00 in accumulated interest. So, we made plans to leave early in the morning to ensure that we paid no penalty interest on my Visa.

Day **220**

After an almost perfect nights sleep, or as close as we get these days, we awoke at about 6-00am and decided to hit the road as soon as we were ready. In fact, we were off by about 6-50am which is about our best effort to date. We did not get a chance to say goodbye to our nearby neighbours from Morayfield as it was still early and there was no sign of movement from their caravan, so off we went.

Back on the road and within 10 kilometres of De Grey River Tee said she would try to get Internet reception. I said I thought it was a bit early to try as we hadn't gone all that far, but bugger me if we didn't get a signal. I thanked Tee for her decision to check the signal and jumped on line to pay the bill. The main reason I was so keen to get this bill paid early was because of the time difference from here to the west coast and I was not sure whether the cut off time for paying the bill was 4-00pm or 6-00pm. With the three-hour time difference this could have meant we had to pay it off by 1-00pm Western Australia time. This was now not a problem as it was paid and I considered going back to De Grey River Rest Stop as it was very nice, but after discussing it with Tee we decided to move on.

The next rest area was about 350 kilometres down the road and only about 150 kilometres from Broome. There was not much to see either and the travelling was at best monotonous and could be more appropriately described as boring. We could have stayed at Pardoo station on the beachfront but the road to it was 13 kilometres of red dirt. Our past history on these roads has rarely been pleasant and in fact disastrous, so we are maintaining our no dirt road policy. Fuel was the next thing that came to our mind and by the time we reached the Sandfire Roadhouse I knew we would not reach Broome on our tank level. The price of fuel at the Sandfire Roadhouse was $1.84 per litre which is high but what choice do we have. I only put $50.00 worth in, enough to ensure that we would reach Broome on it.

By the time we reached our free camp we were glad to stop driving as it was quite warm and with no air con the heat saps your energy. The Free camp we stopped at was called the Stanley Rest area and was a good free camp as it was set well back off the road with the road being all sealed. We found a great little spot away from everyone else and it was only big enough for Lizzie, ensuring that we would not be annoyed by young backpacker later in the evening. Tee fried up some yummy chicken with vegetables for dinner and we retired quite early to watch a movie. The movie we saw was "Christine", the great classic car horror movie. It had been years since either of us had watched it and we really enjoyed it. It also used up my outstanding megabytes that Telstra pinch back if we don't use them up.

Day **221**

This free camp area was great and we decided to stay a second night here as it would give me a chance to fix up the hot water leak by blocking the water entry pipe. Tee was addiment that the plastic tap that I bought would fit if we soaked the pipe ends in hot water before sliding them onto each end of the tap cock. But first I did a bit of writing while Tee did some Motorhome cleaning by scrubbing the faces of all our storage cupboards.

The time had come to try and fix this hot water system leak and I could put it off no longer, as yesterday afternoon when we arrived here, we had 3/4 of a tank of water and now it was redlining. I must admit I have been putting off doing this job as it is in a confined awkward space and I was not convinced that I had the right part for the job. I pulled the pipe off and drained the last of our water down the outlet pipe. But after numerous attempts to get the pipe onto the tap cock I admitted failure and said to Tee, "I think we need to go to Broome today to get the right parts". Tee was not that keen as it was quite nice here, and we had both been quite tired yesterday, so we could do with the rest. But with tomorrow being Saturday the parts we needed may not be available, with the short trading hours that these country regions have.

It was now 12-00 noon and I punched Broome into the navigator to see what our ETA would be if we left now. Turns out it would be about 3-00pm so I made the decision that we should go now. Tee didn't say so but I think after rushing off yesterday from De Grey Rest area to pay my Visa bill she was keen on a rest day. The road to Broome was again less than interesting and the only thing I wanted to stop for before Broome was to look at the free camp about 60 kilometres out of it on the road we were now on. It would mean back tracking but we heard that the Caravan Parks in Broome were quite expensive and it may be worth coming back. But as we got closer to Broome, we were leaning towards staying in Broome, or Cable Beach, as we were getting sick of driving in the heat. Our decision got a whole lot easier when we saw the free camp in question as it was not too nice at all.

We pulled into the Tradelink Broome car park at 3-00pm sharp and I entered the store to buy the stop cock that I needed. When I got in there, I was the only customer with the lad behind the counter chatting to a lady who was about six feet tall and questionable on gender. To add to her manish looks she was also rude and said to me "when you are ready", indicating that butting in while they were talking was acceptable. As we were to find out during our stay in Broome, people being rude was quite normal. Ended up they didn't have the parts I needed and seemed keen to see the back of me. Perhaps that is because it was not a lot of money I would be spending, I am not sure, but I was as keen to get out of there as they were for me to leave.

We searched around the area and found a Total Eden store that specializes in irrigation and they had exactly what I needed. I decided to fix the pipe in their car park, and lucky for us I did as the barb fitting was too small and my first attempt to fix the leak was a failure with water pissing everywhere. I took the part back in and got the next size up, which was the same price and they just swapped it over for me. Back to the Motorhome and bingo I had the problem fixed on my second attempt. I loaded a 10-litre container into the water tank to check it and the pump worked effortlessly and stopped with a crisp sound. Tee and I had never heard the pump run so well in all the time that we have had the Motorhome. We now have our suspicions that the hot water tank was leaking slightly when we bought the vehicle. (Good one Ken)

While I had been fixing the water problem Tee had been ringing local Caravan Parks for pricing and availability. We settled on the Cable Beach Caravan Park which was $47.00 per night for a powered site. We resented the high cost that gave us little in return but we were also tired, hot and would like a long shower. We decided to leave looking at Broome central until tomorrow and instead to look at Cable Beach. We got as far as the

Cable Beach car park, and as it was so busy, we could not find a spot to park the Motorhome so we decided to head straight to the Caravan Park.

The economic equation that we used to ease the pain of the expensive campsite was that it would cost us $20.00 in fuel to drive back to the free camp and we could get drinking water that would cost us $24.00 in the shop. We almost convinced ourselves that we had got a bargain. The Lady at the Cable Beach Caravan Park was lovely and we were soon settled on our site getting stuck into all the chores that we do when we come to Caravan Parks. They include; filling up the drinking water, hand washing small clothes, preparing meals for future days among many other things. After this we set up the campsite nicely to settle in for a pleasant stay.

I jumped onto my mobile to check my messages and was greeted by a message that set me backwards in my chair. The message was from a mother of one of the ladies who use to work for me when I was running a Raine and Horne sales operation in Burpengary. She left a message that Debbie had passed away on Mothers Day and that her funeral was tomorrow. In fact, tomorrow was yesterday as I had not had phone reception for many days – cheers Optus. This was horrible news as Debbie was about my age and had two young daughters who I am guessing would only just be teenagers, or maybe not even teenager age yet. Tamara's daughter had babysat them about five years ago and would also be very shocked by the news. The part that hit me even harder was that she was also about my age – perhaps a bit younger.

An event like this re-enforces my belief in what we are doing, and the fact is that life is very short and you must take the opportunity to enjoy it as often as possible. I often speak of how fragile life is to the people I talk to when referring to our reasons for quitting good jobs and taking off. I am so sorry for her death and the grief it will bring her young children but I am taking it as a lesson. I am doing this to mask the fear of my own mortality - how easy it is to no longer be on this planet.

But my next message was a text from my younger brother Rod who had followed my lead in searching for his real father. I was in need of some good news and was keen to mix it with some humour as I gave him a return call. Unfortunately, though he did not answer my call and it went to his message bank. I then tried to ring my buddy Albert in Yarrawonga to see how he was doing but I also got his message bank. I then rang mum and had a long chat with her before helping Tee a bit with the cooking. (More like eating the cold chicken from the night before – but I was near the cooking – that counts don't it?)

Fortunately, before you have a chance to answer that Rod rang me back and told me that his real father had got in contact with him. He seemed really emotional, and that is not Rod like. I am sure that I have told you that Rod is my Step Brother who was brought up by his mother and my dad, but if I haven't, consider yourself now told. When Rod told me I said to him, "what's up fella – my dad not good enough for you anymore?" Now to Rod this would seem like quick witted humour but to be honest Cindy had text Tamara the good news a day or so prior. Now Rod when you read this don't pay out on Cindy as she needs to release as well! Rod and I spoke for over an hour and he told me he was going to visit his real dad and before he did that, he was going to tell his mum and my dad.

This is where I now take full responsibility for my advice to Rod and if I offend you dad when you read this, I can't help it – it has to be done this way. I told Rod that it was his journey and there was no need to tell his mum and my dad until after he had met with his real dad. I said this as I had travelled the path some two years earlier with my own dad and know the emotional feelings involved. Rod did not need this amplified by trying to protect the feelings of his mother and my father who had raised him. I totally believe it is Rods journey and Rods alone, and that he is entitled to understand his genetic make up without question.

To Nelson and Leonie, I am fully responsible for Rod deciding to take this path and am proud that he told me he would take my advice, as you should be, for the courage he is showing in pursuing his emotions. To Rod, the bond that has grown between us amazes me as we are not even related. Yet I freely called you my brother and have now just seen where I wrote that. I wrote it without thinking and am glad I did as it allows me to now reflect on why I wrote it. As I have never had brothers or sisters, I could never understand that feeling – today at fifty years of age I have just discovered it.

On a lighter note we have the same surname so I can pretend I was always cool with it – OK bro! That's right – and don't argue with your older brother!

Wow what an emotional evening it has been and my fourth can of XXXX has helped keep me sane. While I was gasbagging to Rod, Tee had been looking for an old movie she wanted to see on You Tube and eventually found it. That is, she found it between her texting Cindy and looking for the movie. We went to bed and as we watched the movie, I realized why it was free and suddenly sleep was a great alternative.

Day **222**

With all the chores finished at the campsite this morning we decided to visit Cable Beach to see what all the fuss was about and then we would go to the Broome markets that were on this morning. We left the Cable Beach Caravan Park around 9-00am and on the way out I did my favourite chore – yes you guessed it – emptied the shitter. Turns out they had a fancy dump point that even had its own flush mechanism and disinfectant on hand. It was so good that when I finished and flushed the mechanism it felt like I had just been to the toilet myself.

On the road and we were soon in the Cable Beach car park and walking towards the beach. When we arrived at the beach, we were mildly impressed but could easily name twenty beaches in Australia that were superior. Needless to say, we did not stay long and were soon on our way to the Broome markets. Broome was packed around the Market area and we had to park Lizzie a fair way from the action. Probably a good thing though as with all the driving we have been doing we have not really been getting enough exercise. I was keen to find myself a mobile phone cover for my new Samsung and the markets are usually the best priced place to get one. We walked around the Market which was quite pleasant but unfortunately there were no stalls with mobile phone accessories. But I did get myself a smart looking straw hat for ten bucks – great bargain.

We left the markets after about an hour of walking around and went to the Shell servo to fill up Lizzie. One more job to do and that was to find a windscreen repair kit. I tried the local Bunning's store with no success but a fellow in the store suggested Auto Pro around the corner. Bingo, they had what I needed right on the front counter and at $40.00 for multiple use it was great value compared to the $99.00 I was quoted from Novus. Fair dinkum if those guys kept their prices real, I would have used them but $99.00 is too expensive when you can do it yourself. Tee said "now let's get the hell out of here", in line with our distaste for built up areas, and we were off to the next free camp about 120 kilometres east of here.

We arrived at Nillibubbica Rest Area and relaxed for the rest of the day with not much really happening. The only real event was when a stray bull walked into the Rest area with Caravans and campers all round him and drank from a large muddy puddle. He was later followed by a group of cows and calves that did the same. We had a few beers in the evening before going to bed and chatting until we fell asleep.

Day **223**

We both slept quite well last night and even though we were close to the highway the big trucks going past don't seem to wake us that often. In saying that I think we still hear them so our sleep is still slightly disturbed. Tee cooked up a feast for breakfast and I decided to have a crack at fixing the windscreen – pardon the pun! If I am successful at fixing the windscreen, I would have saved us $60.00 and still be able to fix another crack if occurs in our travels later.

I read through the instructions twice and it does seem a little difficult and I was very tempted to put the kit away and attempt to fix the crack another day. But I could not turn my back on the fact that the conditions were perfect to do the job and we were in no hurry to get anywhere today. After my huge breakfast the only thing that would stop me fixing this windscreen was all in my head. In actual fact, once I started fixing the screen it all came together nicely and with Tee's help at aligning the tool, I got a great result. In fact, I had a professional repair done a couple of months before our trip and my job was better. I am not bragging or telling porky pies, it really was and Tee was proud of the job I did. Now feeling ten feet tall I got ready for our next leg of the journey that would take us to Derby, and beyond.

On our way and the scenery remained bland, until we started to spot the odd Boab tree. Now I love these trees and as we continued towards Derby, they just got bigger and more unusual in shape. Then on the outskirts of Derby we saw a tourist signpost that said Prison Boab tree. This intrigued us and we went down the dirt road for a look. Turns out the Boab tree was a monster and was used in the 1880s to hold aboriginal prisoners, short term. My goodness we white folk have a lot to answer to, as I cannot believe the things our ancestors did. Apparently, the tree also had aboriginal significance before these horrible events and is protected under the aboriginal historical act of 1972 as a place of significance.

Back on the road and into Derby where we visited the Information Centre to see what was around town. There are a few tourist flights into the Kimberley's from here as Derby is on the Western edge of the region, but apart from that there is only the jetty area and town. The town was very typical of a Northern Australian town and at the jetty area there is no beach and apparently a few salt water crocodiles. We had a look at the jetty area which was very industrial and the water was very muddy, perhaps due to recent rains, I am not sure. We took some photos of the jetty area and then headed back to town where we bought some beer. I can see why the people up here drink a fair bit, with this climate that is all we are thinking about – a cold beer!

With full Optus mobile reception, we made a few phone calls outside the local cop shop and Tee noticed the old Goal that was next to the police station. It was extremely primitive and you would not lock you dog up there these days. After making our calls and receiving in all our emails we took off to our next free camp area that was called The Boab Rest Area. Back travelling and the Boab trees started to thin out again which made the countryside a little more boring. One hundred and thirty kilometres and two dead cows down the road and we arrived at The Boab Tree Rest Area. It was 2-00pm and Tee toasted me a couple of sandwiches while I looked at the huge Boab that the Rest Area was named after. We thought about going further towards Fitzroy Crossing as there were a few more rest areas, but this was OK here and we went with the theory – "Better the Devil you know!"

The temperature was high and the humidity even higher, and there was not much relief with the absence of any breeze what so ever. By four o'clock we turned to the only relief we could provide artificially, and that was a cold can of Carlton Mid. Boy did that first one go down well as Tee had slipped a few into the freezer and of course that made them extra special. The second beer we both had was no where near as nice, but that was not due to the order they were consumed in but for the fact that they were our last two cans of XXXX. Not even the freezer brought them up to Carlton Mid standard.

Tee had by this stage started warming up the risotto that she had made a few days ago and we finished our third can each just before it was ready. The rest of the evening we sat outside due to the extreme in temperature and went inside only to go to bed. Thank goodness we have a fan in our bedroom as it would have intolerable without it. We finally got to sleep about 9-30pm and we were both quite sweaty despite the fan and our nice showers.

Day **224**

This morning our prayers were answered with the coming of rain. Although it would have been more welcome last night to make sleeping more tolerable, it was still very much welcomed. The rain fixed two problems for us, the first being what I have just mentioned and the second being we could collect the rain and top up our supplies. In fact, we were relying on being able to get water from Fitzroy Crossing as we were down to one more nights supply. In addition, we would love to have fresh rainwater instead of Broome town water for our drinking supply. As luck has it the rain set in so I was able to transfer the drinking water we had into the Motorhome and then replace the whole 70 litres of drinking water we hold with fresh rain water. In fact, I had 12 litres left over which will mean I can top up the Motorhome water tonight after our showers.

The budget has also coped a hammering this week and even taking the tyre out of the equation we are $40.00 over budget. With this in mind and the fact that we are currently at a free camp site that has a sealed surface we have decided to stay here until Wednesday morning (a further two nights). With all the rain and us not knowing what the free camps are like around Fitzroy Crossing it seems the smart thing to do. In addition, it will give the roads time to dry out if we head down dirt tracks on side roads. I say this as there a few gorges near Fitzroy Crossing and I know that at least one of them is on a dirt road.

The water collection and distribution has consumed a fair amount of my day today but I have still had time to read my Steve Waugh book while Tee has pre-cooked some dinners for the next few days. The only entertainment for the day was watching some tourists who were living out of a Ford station wagon as they scrambled to try and dry all their soaked items after leaving them out all morning. I suspect if they went to bed before midnight and woke up before 10-30am they would not have this problem. I can only imagine the stench in the car as the four of them (who had not washed) drove off with soggy towels, tents, chairs and other items all blending into one heck of stink. Tee and I would normally feel sorry for people like this but they often keep us awake in the night and have no concept of other people. So, fuck em!

As this site is a sealed road, we have had a lot of campers turn up due to the rain. Last night we only had three vehicles here but by only 5-00pm we already have seven groups here. There are no backpackers here yet, but then again it is still very early for them. Although it rained today it is still quite warm here and the humidity is the biggest culprit, again thank goodness for the fan in our Motorhome bedroom.

Day **225**

The rain cleared last night just as we went to bed so I brought the awning in and sealed the plastic bucket I had the water in. We didn't want any doggies drinking out of it during the night and spoiling our fresh rain water. The rain clearing also allowed us to sleep with the windows open and take advantage of a very tiny breeze. We slept OK but it was still a little uncomfortable.

This morning I topped up the Motorhome water with our new supply of fresh rainwater and even had enough to top up the toilet flush. It has been great collecting all this rainwater as we will have pure drinking water for at least three weeks. Hopefully though this will now be the end of the rain as we need to move on tomorrow and it would be nice for the roads to be dry. The area is also very flood prone so we don't want to be stuck here either. We watched the comings and goings of all forms of tourists during the day and did very little else. In fact, I bowled over another 100 pages of my Steve Waugh book – pardon the pun - and Tee read her Jackie Collins novel. I sat outside reading as it was very warm in the Motorhome yesterday but later in the day, I discovered that Tee had the right idea, as inside the Motorhome today was much cooler. We were not troubled by rain all day and I even copped a bit of sunburn from my outdoor position.

The only event to occur for us happened at about 3-30pm when the people we met at De Greys Rest Area (Stan and Val) turned up behind us. To add to this Don and Dianne from the Sunshine Coast also turned up. It was the first time that we met Don and Dianne but we had seen their Motorhome (which we admired) on numerous occasions at different Rest

Area's. We all sat around together from about 4-30pm til about 8-00pm chatting about our travel experiences and anything else that sprang to mind. The conversation was very pleasant, as was the beer we consumed. The only unpleasant occurrence was when a bug landed between my toes and decided to bite me right on the webbing. The pain was excruciating and as I could not immediately see what had bitten me, I got into a bit of a panic. Turned out to be a non life threatening bug of some description. No, I am not a sook; it could have been very serious.

The weather also started to cool down in the evening as the wind picked up and the breeze even had a slight chill to it. In fact, at about 7-00pm we got another lot of light rain that lasted until almost 9-00pm and gave me time to collect about another 18 litres of water. We had showers at about 9-00pm and then I used the collected rainwater to again top up the Motorhome tank. This was exciting as it would allow us to leave here in the morning with full drinking water and Motorhome water. As the rain had now stopped and the air was cooler, we seemed certain to get a better night's sleep.

Day **226**

A great night's sleep is what we did get and today we planned to move on to the other side of Fitzroy Crossing at a free camp called Ngumban Cliff Lookout Rest Area. It was a nice morning but it looked as though we would get a headwind as the breeze was quite strong and blowing from the East. Stan and Val were going to meet us at the free camp and we personally had planned to stop in Fitzroy Crossing for a look around and also visit the Geikie Gorge on the outskirts of town.

Don and Dianne (of the Darby Derby Fame) who had their plans of visiting Windjana Gorge dashed by the Gibb River Road being closed off from Derby Darby were now going to attempt a back-door entry via Leopold Downs, just West of Fitzroy Crossing. With all of us set for different adventures it would be Tee and I that left the Boab Rest Area first.

With the budget starting its thirty third week we could now buy fuel and a few bits and pieces when we reached Fitzroy Crossing. But our first priority was to get internet reception to catch up with our emails and also to pay a few outstanding bills before they were overdue. About 60 kilometres down the road we reached the Ellendale Rest Area which was quite elevated and looked like a good candidate for internet reception.

We arrived at the Ellendale Rest Area about 9-15am and it was still quite full from the evening before as many travellers were in the throws of leaving. The bonus of this free camp was that it now had a dump point which did not show on our Camps6 book so must have been a recent addition. In fact, many free camps seem to be getting upgraded in this region with a number having been recently sealed in bitumen. Of course, this meant that it was again time to perform my favourite duty – that's right – empty the shitter. Although not full we were five days in to its cycle and no dump points appeared on the Camp6 map for a great distance.

After the performance of my favourite job I moved the Motorhome to higher ground and away from the smelly dump point. The internet reception here was quite good and I jumped online to receive our emails and also paid two outstanding water bills. One of my emails was from my school yard buddy – Mr Tony De Bolfo, who has carved out quite a career for himself as a sports writer and a writer of numerous books. In addition to the fact that he can write, he has turned out to be quite a nice fellow. We spent some time together last year when he invited me to a Carlton – Brisbane game where, against his reputation of being a tight arse, he bought me a pie and got me a look in the Carlton dressing room after the game. Just kidding Tony! (The tight arse line was not true).

A few months ago, he asked me to pen a few lines about our trip around Australia and to drop in a few photos so he could publish it on the Old Paradian website. He was emailing me to tell me it was up and running and sent me a link. He wrote a lovely article and put my writing in almost word for word, proving my theory that he has turned into a nice bloke

The other emails were from relatives and friends in general and some more bills to remind us of the fact that we still needed to conform to the will of society. The most interesting bill comes from AGL who still charge me $30.00 per quarter even though no power is being consumed. I now know what AGL stands for (A greedy Lot).

While online a cyclist couple, who I think are Irish, arrived and sat at the picnic table near our Motorhome. We have seen this couple on the road numerous times, most recently at the Boab Rest Area, where they spent about four hours in the middle of the day resting before heading off in the mid afternoon. I guess this is to avoid the main heat of the day as they are not young and regardless of how fit they are it must be hard on their bodies. They also seem to have trouble carrying enough water as they have had travellers filling up their water supply for them. All I can say is they are really keen as it seems way too dangerous a pursuit to be travelling out here unescorted with those 53-meter trucks whizzing past and no shoulders on the road.

Minutes later Don and Dianne (Derby – Darby) turned up and parked in front of us. They told us that their mission of back-dooring the Gibb River Road looked shaky as they had been told of flooding in the area. After a brief chat we all left for our respective destinations and Tee and I soon arrived at Fitzroy Crossing. As we had experienced a rather harsh headwind our first concern was filling up with fuel. We pulled into the BP servo and soon realized that this place had a huge Aboriginal population. In fact, I would say that close to 80% of the population was Aboriginal and many were congregating around the servo. At first, I felt a little intimidated, but they all seemed quite friendly and it was only my fear of the unknown that scared me. In saying that I asked Tee to stay in the locked Motorhome as I would not like her to be at risk. By the time I had filled up with fuel and paid the cashier, who was Asian, I felt comfortable that this would not be the case and we moved on to get a few supplies. As we drove though town we again ran into Don & Dianne (Derby – Darby) who had just pulled into a glass blowing gallery. They told us that they had been advised not to travel the back road as it would not be safe in their small 4WD. We parted after confirming that we could all now meet at the Ngumban Cliff Lookout Rest Area later that day.

Tee and I went to the local IGA, which was again run by Asians, and I went alone inside to buy a loaf of bread and a dozen eggs. The IGA in Fitzroy Crossing, although expensive, was immaculate and a credit to the owners and operators. Again, there were many Aboriginal people hanging around but not seeming to be causing any trouble. With our few supplies safely stored it was time to head to Geikie Gorge and with only 18 kilometres to get there it would be a nice short journey.

Unfortunately, what should have been a short journey turned into disappointment as we were blocked from entering Geikie Gorge by a huge pool of water covering the whole road and of unknown depth. Truth be known I could have walked the puddle to check its depth but another kilometre up the road we may have come across the same problem again. As it was, we had already crossed a water coarse flowing lightly over the road and with the possibility of rain, and Lizzie's clearance, it was simply not worth attempting.

Filled with a sense of disappointment Tee and I headed back into town and then onto Ngumban Cliff Lookout Rest Area where we hoped to catch up with all our newly acquired friends. Along the way we took a turn to Minimi Caves but were again turned back by poor road conditions in the form of a muddy boggy mess, but not before acquiring some lovely photos of the stunning scenery that surrounded us. Back onto the highway and within minutes we arrived at the Ngumban Cliff Lookout Rest Area where we spotted Don & Dianne (Derby – Darby) who were parked on one side of the Rest Area while Stan and Val were parked on the other. We pulled up next to Stan and Val as they had the spot with the best view and we sat in awe of the fabulous scenery that lay in front of us.

Later that afternoon after some exploring of the area, we all got together for a chat and a drink; it was a lovely evening and another stunning West Australian sunset.

Day **227**

As we were so elevated at the Ngumban Cliff Lookout Rest Area the sun rose very early and as we had gone to bed quite late, I was still very tired. Due to this fact and the fact that the wind was blowing strongly from the East we decided to stay here another night. Don and Dianne (Derby – Darby) left in the morning but Stan and Val have decided to sit put here for two more nights as they really love it. Tee and I did a bit of exploring but little else today as we relaxed into our pattern of reading and writing for the majority of the day. Another evening of drinks and a chat before an early night to make up for the late one last night.

Day **228**

Off this morning and said our goodbyes to Stan, Val and Max (the cutest little dog ever) who have been lovely company. It has been great to meet so many different people from all different walks of life. These guys had sold up everything to call the road their home, and although not for everyone they seem to really love it. We have met a number of people on the road that have done this, and although not something Tee and I would consider, they all seem to enjoy it. I suspect it is like anything else in life – it is what you make it.

On the road and into a savage headwind that threatens to add substantially to our weekly fuel bill. So, I backed Lizzie right off to a travelling speed of 75 Kilometres per hour. Not too much of a problem as the traffic is very light (almost non existent) and we have planned to only travel about 250 kilometres or so today. We stopped about 90 kilometres out of Halls Creek to have a coffee break and soon after getting back on the road we passed the turning to Wolfe Creek Crater. We had been told that the Halls Creek area was the area used in the filming of the low budget Australian horror movie, Wolf Creek. But until we saw the sign, we did not realize that there was a place called Wolfe Creek.

The night before we had looked up the movie on You Tube, in the hope of finding the full-length version to watch. We had been warned by people not to watch it while on the road as we would not feel safe, but us being us we couldn't help ourselves. The plan was to watch the movie when we got to our free camp near the Bungle Bungle Ranges.

After passing the Wolfe Creek Crater turnoff it seemed like no time until we reached the town of Halls Creek. We need a few things here, mainly water and fuel, and as we entered town on our left was a Shell servo so we pulled in. The price of fuel was reasonable and I put $70.00 worth in as we still had almost half a tank. I asked the attendant at the Shell Servo if there was anywhere in town to get water and in very broken English, she pointed to the Information centre that was almost directly across the road. This was handy as we wanted to go there anyway and check out what sights were to be seen in the area.

The fellow (Chris) in the Information centre was extremely friendly and told us that water could be obtained there but it was 20 cents per litre. At first, I thought this was a bit mean but when he told me that the money went to the RFDS (Royal Flying Doctors Service) Tee and I were more than happy to pay it. Realistically though we had to anyway as we were down to one and a half days supply and the next town was well over 200 kilometres away. Again, I think back to what Clem said to me back in Bollon on our first week on the road – "never leave an opportunity to get water and empty the shitter go by!" His voice still rings in my ears.

With our water and fuel filled up, and the only natural attractions being located at distance on dirt roads we decided to press on to our free camp destination. Sooner than we expected we arrived at the first of two free camp options that are located just outside the Bungle Bungle Ranges. It turned out to be a bit yuck so we pressed on to option two. This free camp was located almost directly opposite the entrance to the Bungle Bungle Ranges and was much nicer than option one. The main camp area was located beside Spring Creek and was a very pretty spot. Trouble was though because it was located where it was, it was extremely popular and when we arrived quite full, even though it was only just after lunchtime. Fortunately, there was a second area away from the creek, and although not as pretty did have a nice breeze blowing through it.

We set up next to a very clean picnic table (very unusual with young backpackers around) and I even set up the awning as the breeze was blowing on the opposite side of the Motorhome and would not cause issues. I was able to tie it down to the picnic table and this would ensure no mishaps. I have to get myself some guy ropes as we have heard so many stories of people having their awnings ripped off and they are expensive also, at around $1,000.00 for a decent one.

Once all set up and a feed in our tummies, we decided that now was a good a time as any to watch the Wolf Creek movie. As we were watching the movie another couple pulled up beside us, but as we were so enthralled in the movie, we didn't go out to say hi. The movie was not as scary as we expected and it was great to be able to identify with all the locations that the film showed off. These included Broome, Halls Creek and Kalbarri if only briefly. Although most of the film was shot in a dark feral abandoned mine location, which puts it in line with many other scary movies – minus the mine bit.

After our movie we went out and introduced ourselves to our new temporary neighbours (Graeme & Lynda from Perth) on our way to having a look at the lower car park and Spring Creek. Spring Creek was OK but the free camp area was packed so we were so happy to be up in the top area where we could enjoy a lovely breeze. On the way back to the upper free camp area we ran into a large red Brahman Bull (big ginger) who looked like a prop from the Crocodile Dundee movie. Without a lie his horns were about three feet across. As we got closer to the upper free camp area, we had to get closer to Big Ginger who was just propped in the middle of the road. I said to Tee, who is much more country than I am, "will he do anything?" to which Tee replied "no". As soon as we got within 10 feet of him though he let out a snort, and when I turned to asked Tee what that was about, she was already off and running. I turned back to Big Ginger and he was "coming at me" so I turned and ran also. Big Ginger won the battle and I was happy to give him the crown of "king of the Bungle Bungle free camp", a crown that this fellow will hold for years I am sure.

When we got back to Lizzie, we told Graeme and Lynda of our adventure with Big Ginger and how he ruled the road. That evening we all sat around chatting and having a few drinks that Graeme had provided, as we had run out over the past few nights and not found a place to buy more. During out chat Graeme kindly asked us if we would like to join them tomorrow as they were going into the Bungle Bungle Range. We graciously accepted as it would be a great experience, and one that we could not do without a 4WD. With that we wrapped up the evening and vowed to get an 8-00am start.

Day **229**

Tee and I slept quite well last night, although I must admit that I did wake up in the early hours concerned a bit about leaving Lizzie alone in the free camp all day. It was like a nightmare for me that I should have had from watching Wolf Creek yesterday, but to me the biggest nightmare would be having Lizzie stolen while we were in the National Park. I again woke up at 6-00am and decided to get up as there was some items that I wanted to take with us in case my fear of Lizzie being stolen came true. I jumped onto my computer and transferred a heap of recent files, which I would need if Lizzie got stolen, onto my memory stick and along with some personal items put them into a backpack. This would ease the pain somewhat if the worst of my fears came true – heaven forbid.

By 7-30am Tee and I were ready to go and as I got out of the Motorhome Graeme was clearing out the back seat of his Prado for us. Tee and I liked the Prado and it is one of the vehicles that we are considering purchasing when we return home. There are a number of 4WD's that we are looking at as we have decided that when we return home, we will sell Lizzie and get a vehicle that will take us to the places in Australia that we have not been able to reach. It will be more suitable for future trips as we will only go for weeks at a time not like this whole year. The trips will be to specific areas that we will be able to discover in detail with the aid of an all terrain vehicle.

By 8-00am we were loaded into the Prado and off to the Bungle Bungle Ranges. Any idea that Lizzie may be able to enter the area was quickly squashed by the 4WD vehicle only sign on the entrance gates to the park. Not that we were considering it, and it made the gesture by Graeme and Lynda all the more special to us. In fact, the gates were not an entrance to the National Park but merely to the Mabel Downs Station, who allow access through their property to the National Park. The road into the Bungle Bungles is some 53 kilometres long and we went through five wet river crossings and at least another five dry, something that would have definitely stopped Lizzie dead in her tracks if the sign on the front gate didn't.

Finally, after driving an hour and thirty minutes through the corrugated dirt road and numerous creek crossings of Mabel Downs Station we arrived at the National Parks Visitors Centre. The lady in the information centre was lovely and Tee had a chat to her while the rest of us had a toilet break. She offered some tour advice to us but Graeme and Lynda had been here before and had already planned their trip.

Back in the vehicle and we were off to Mini Palms Gorge which was a five-kilometre return Class 3 walk. The place was absolutely stunning with towering palms and amazing scenery. The walk surface was our only issue as it was hard to walk in the river pebbles (of varying sizes) and keep looking up at the sheer cliff faces. In fact, on the way out I slipped a bit and buggered the LCD screen on our camera. Fortunately, not the entire screen went black and I was still able to capture all the photos for the day. But it does mean that it will have to be replaced soon (bugger!).

Back at the Prado by 11-30 am and we all decided to have lunch prior to heading to Echidna Chasm. As Tee and I had not shopped for a while we only had cheese and biscuits for lunch. This turned out to be great as we had a lot more walking to do after lunch and this gave us sustenance without feeling too full. We ate lunch under the shade sails and picnic area provided, before jumping into the Prado and heading to the Echidna Chasm car park.

Echidna Chasm is a two kilometre walk that also takes in some truly amazing scenery with the Chasm being absolutely amazing. The twist at the end is that when you think you have walked as far as you can go there is a passage to the forward left that takes you further into the narrow depths – Spiritual place and truly amazing. On the way out of Echidna Chasm Tee and I went to Osmand Lookout as Graeme and Lynda returned to the vehicle. They had been there last time they visited the area and in fact had now visited the whole area with Mini Palms and Echidna Chasm being the only two places they hadn't been on their last trip here. Kindly now they would take us to Piccaninny Creek to see the iconic beehive mountains even though they had been before.

The scenery along the way was again stunning and has to be witnessed in real life to fully appreciate. It was fabulous to have Graeme and Lynda take us here and even if we could have accessed the area, we would not have been able to see all of it in one day like we were doing today. Our next journey was to walk to Cathedral Gorge another three-kilometre return walk. This was a journey through the Beehive Mountains, across river beds, under towering cliffs and on to an amazing waterfall that when dry, like today, doubles as a natural amphitheatre. On the way back to the car park we detoured down Piccaninny Gorge for about 500mtrs to get a feel for the marvellous surrounds of that particular area. In fact, we could have walked this track for several days as there are hiking trails this way that extend for that amount of distance.

Wow what an action-packed day and it was not over yet as we still had to drive back 24 kilometres to the visitors centre before the 53-kilometre marathon that includes five wet river crossings and the westerly sun directly in our faces. Graeme did a fantastic job driving and not only did he have all of the above to contend with but the added bonus of cattle, kangaroos and dickheads towing camper trailers that don't understand the concept of other people. Eventually we got out onto the Great northern Highway about 5-30pm and in the great spirit that Graeme possesses he now said – not far to go now. By the time we reached the free camp area we were all pleased to see Lizzie and the caravan still intact. Graeme and Linda were not concerned but it is not something that Tee and I have done before.

We all got into our little homes away from home and started preparing some dinner until Graeme came back over with a beer to finish off the day. In fact, I only had one more beer, unlike Tee who helped Graeme polish off two bottles of Rosé. They were both quite tipsy with Tee falling asleep by 8-30pm while I did the photos and checked my emails etc.

Day **230**

Tee woke up quite seedy today which made me think that Graeme would be really struggling. In fact, he looked quite ordinary at 8-30am when I saw him walking to the bin but by 9-30am when they were leaving, he looked quite OK. We said our goodbyes and exchanged details so we could keep in touch. We could not thank them enough for the day they had provided for us yesterday and wished them well on their travels. We also had planned to move on today but had no plans to leave before midday. But as we got closer to lunchtime and I had not started writing yet we decided to stop here for the day. This not only gave me time to finish my writing but also to research our trip and organizes the purchase of a new camera. Then at about 1-00pm after I had mentioned Stan and Val to Tee who would turn up, you guessed it, Stan and Val. We were glad to see another familiar face on our journey and it now seems that we are getting a network of friend on the road that makes the places feel homier. This visit did slow down my writing but with the decision made to stay here the night – who cares.

For the rest of today we caught up with some reading and writing. In the evening Stan lit a campfire and all the people who were parked in the upper free camp area sat around and swapped yarns. We went back to Lizzie at about 7-00pm and cooked dinner before I got stuck into planning the next week or so of our journey.

Day **231**

We awoke early this morning and were ready to hit the road by 8-00am. We said our goodbyes again to Stan and Val, which is becoming a regular event these days, and we were off. As the camera was going to cost us almost $400.00 to replace the budget for this week has already been blown. This is not too serious but we want to take it easy for the next few days and not blow it out any further. This will slow us down slightly but it is really important to us to stay within our budget, as if we don't, we will have to cut the trip short (not something either of us want). So, the slightly altered plan for today is to travel about 150 kilometres to the next free camp at Dunham River. This will put us about 80 kilometres short of Wyndham and then with tomorrow being the last day of the budget we will be able to head to Wyndham and then onto Kununurra without damaging the budget much more – hopefully not at all.

Another issue that we are trying to take charge of is the house water that is now on its 4th day of use without refill. We have done extremely well so far on the 55-litre tank, but tonight will see it empty. In this part of the country water is not easy to come by unless you stay at caravan parks, which we can now not afford. Never mind as we should be able to get water at Wyndham and the water supply looks better as we get into the Northern Territory. The scenery from the Bungle Bungle Range to Dunham River is very attractive with rocky ranges following the road all the way, or should I say the road following the rocky ranges. We arrived at the Dunham River Rest Area about lunchtime and did very little for the rest of the day. It was a lovely spot and I even slipped in a few ZZZZ's in the mid afternoon. No Internet reception so it was a bit more of the Steve Waugh Autobiography and a little bit more of what you are reading right now. Tee and I are keen to see Wyndham tomorrow as the last few days have been a little uneventful – I do believe we are getting a little spoilt.

Day **232**

Although very hot when we went to bed it did cool off in the early hours of the morning and our sleep was fairly good. The only issue was that we both woke up with sinus and think that some of the local plants are the culprits. Keen to get moving early we got ready very early and were on the road by 8-00am.

The plan for today was to go out to Wyndham and then back track to just before Kununurra where there was suppose to be a free camp just short of town. The side objectives would be fuel and more imminently important – house water. The scenery from Dunham River was again beautiful with huge ranges and rocky outcrops. Tee and I are baffled by the fact that regardless of their beauty people still make time to graffiti the larger rocks. All we can imagine for their motive is that they somehow believe that by spray painting "Ivan was here 2013" that they will progress to a higher status and be immortalized in stone. But the reality is that council workers and Rangers quickly quell their belief by painting over their statements in as close to the rocks natural colour as possible – Wankers!

Our first stop was to a place called 'The Grotto' and both Tee and I had no idea as to what we would see here. The name did not sound that attractive and we decided to visit it for two reasons – one, it being on a sealed road - and two, we were damn curious as to what it was. The place turned out to be a ravine of sheer rock that had formed a swimming hole at one end. It was similar to Circular Pool at Dales Gorge on a far less grand scale. The place would have been very beautiful with a bit of maintenance, but regardless of this fact it was still quite lovely. We journeyed down the rough rock steeps down to the rock pool and were met by a bunch of French youth who were using the place as a bathtub. This now made the name 'The Grotto' make a whole heap of sense. Back up to the Motorhome and off we set on our journey to Wyndham, and our thoughts were that this would be the best place to secure house water. On the drive the scenery was pleasant with one point of interest being a huge Sandalwood plantation that looked as though it was irrigated by the Ord River or perhaps even Lake Argyle that was located to the East somewhere. We later found out that this was owned by the Chinese, amazing how we have sold out in this country.

Soon after the plantation we again past the start / finish of the Gibb River Road as we did on the way to Derby. As we approached the town of Wyndham, we found a water source near the information board. This required a key to use the tap, and fortunately I had acquired one from Bunning's before departing on our adventure some seven or so months ago. This little tool has come in handy on numerous occasions and has more than paid for itself.

When we arrived at Wyndham, we were greeted by the large teeth of a massive replica crocodile that was surrounded by local Aborigines in the nicest looking part of town. We continued through town and onto the port area and soon realized how similar Wyndham was to Derby as both town centres were away from the port area and both port areas were highly industrialized with Wyndham being more so than Derby. With the colour of iron ore staining and dominating the whole port area, Tee and I were keen to get back to Wyndham central and onto the 'Five Rivers Lookout' that we had been advised to visit.

With a quick stop to get fuel, which we were also advised to get here, I put $50.00 worth in. This was in an attempt to control the budget that had been destroyed by the requirement to replace our damaged camera. As I was to find out later this was a poor call on my behalf as the next fuel we would see, would be 20 cents per litre dearer and I would end up paying 40 cents per litre more for fuel when I had no options. After fuelling up we climbed the mountain range behind the town of Wyndham which was accessed through the suburban part of Wyndham and gave us some insight into the living conditions of the locals.

There are many levels of lookouts on the way to the main 'Five Rivers Lookout' and when we stopped at the first level, we thought that it was OK but nothing to get over excited about (we thought this was it). We stopped here long enough to get all our emails in and with Optus reception I rang Mum to let her know that we were OK and what our travel plans were for the next few days. As we sat there admiring the nice but obscured view, we noticed a number of vehicles proceeding past where we were parked and further up the mountain.

After completing my conversation with mum Tee suggested we keep climbing the mountain and see where all these vehicles were heading. We then got to another lookout that was again impressive but too small to have been where all these vehicles had been travelling to. Off again and then we reached the top of the range and there before us lay the panoramic view that other travellers had raved on to us about. It was a stunning view and goes directly onto our "must see list". We took numerous panoramic photos with our dying camera before enjoying a lunch of cheese and crackers while enjoying the view. Not much more to do now other than to head to Kununurra and the free camp which lay on its Western outskirts. Well that was what we thought anyway until we could not find the free camp and ended up in Kununurra.

We now were in a dilemma as the fuel was 20 cents per litre dearer than in Wyndham and we faced the prospect of having to stay in a caravan park. This was an extremely frustrating situation as if we went on to the next free camp, we would have to choose whether or not to go to Lake Argyle as the next free camp was in the Northern Territory and well past Lake Argyle. It was about 2-30pm (WA time) and we could see Lake Argyle and get to the next free camp but it would mean two things. -1) We would rush Lake Argyle a bit and -2) we would be driving in the dark for an hour or so. Neither of these things we liked doing but our options seemed very limited.

By this stage I was very cranky with myself as if I had not damaged the camera in the Bungle Bungle Range, we could have afforded anything. But there was no use whining as it was done now and I needed to make the best of it. A great motivator in this hot weather is beer, so after discussions with Tee we decided to bite the bullet and head to Lake Argyle and beyond to the NT free camp. The motivator came in the form of a cold slab of

Carlton Mid's that we purchased before taking on our marathon journey. This would allow us to celebrate our victory at the end of the long day of driving that I was half way through.

Off and running and heading to Lake Argyle that was 35 kilometres off the main road. Once we left the main highway, we were greeted with stunning landscape that made the decision to come here very worthwhile. All the way into Lake Argyle the landscape was quite exceptional with red cliff ranges and flats with an abundance of Boab trees. Eventually we reached the Lake Argyle Resort (which is more like an old caravan park) and saw the fuel bowser with the Diesel that we now had to have to reach our next free camp in NT. The next shock of the day came when we saw that the fuel price for Diesel here was $2.04 per litre, 40 odd cents dearer than if I had filled up in Wyndham. I was so cranky with myself and considered staying here the night just to spread the costs into next weeks budget. But when I enquired about non-powered sites, I was told they were $30.00 per night. This would not solve the problem of us being over budget but we thought we would have a look at the Lake itself and decide if it was worth staying. After deciding that $60.00 worth of fuel here would see us to Timber Creek, we headed off for a look at Lake Argyle. On the way out I could not believe that I saw a couple of my old clients (Alan & Joye York) from Mallard Court Upper Caboolture. I had their home listed a few years ago and I remember that their plan was to downsize their family home and travel. Well they were living their dream and good on them. They were chatting with another couple and we were time poor (I can't believe I am saying that), so I did not stop and interrupt them.

We climbed the range behind the Lake Argyle Resort and the view from the top was stunning. I am sure that we would have enjoyed a cruise on the lake the next day but the last few days have been so messed up budget wise we decided it would be best to push on into the NT. After taking a pile of lovely photos we descended the range and headed bank along the Lake Argyle road that would come out close to the WA/NT border.

We had been told that the quarantine restrictions going into the NT were not like coming into WA and it wasn't really a problem as we had not shopped in two weeks and our fresh fruit and veg were well gone. As we crossed the border, we were happy that we had at least seen Lake Argyle even though it was now getting dark. The WA side of the border was set up like stalag 13 (Hogan's Heroes fame) and with very little traffic the gentleman on duty looked very lonely. The NT side was a straight drive through with nothing but bitumen in front of us.

Like Hogan's Heroes fame the activity across the border did not come from the obvious source but in the form of the little Queensland menace, the cane toad. As we got into NT, we started to see the little blighters in large numbers and did our best to run over as many as possible. The fellow on the WA Quarantine gate would have his work cut out for him tonight and would be well advised to get out his golf clubs in an attempt to drive them home. In all honesty though what hope has WA got of stopping these little buggers with about 4,000 kilometres of border to protect.

Driving in the dark in the outback is not my favourite pastime as there are stray cattle as well as kangaroos etc. I also hate driving past those 53 metre Road Trains at anytime and at night they are quite scary. With only about seventy kilometres to the Saddle Creek free camp though, we were happy to be on the home straight. But I spoke too soon as about 10 kilometres further up the road I was confronted with headlights coming at me on both sides of the road. I backed Lizzie right off and watched an idiot in a Britz van pull back into his side of the road just in front of me and just in front of the 53 metre – four trailer Road Train that he was passing. Another Wanker!

Still alive and vowing that night driving is stupid we arrived at a packed Saddle Creek Rest Area. After two circles of the camp area we found a site that was OK but quite unlevel. In fact, it took me three goes to get the wheel chocks in the right position that would allow us a decent night's sleep; even then the shower draining would be a problem. But at this stage we cared little and were keen to have a beer after the marathon day we had just encountered. We were both very tired and cranky and a little short with each other. It would take a big effort to stay nice to each other but after a few beers the stress and calamity of the day quickly dissipated.

Day **233**

Although packed with people we still managed to get a fairly good nights sleep at the Saddle Creek Rest Area and I think the fact that we were really tired last night and had a few beers really helped. We were now in a different time zone and had effectively lost one and a half hours, which meant that it was almost 11-00am NT time when we finally departed. This was not a problem though as we had planned to go as far as Timber Creek and to a free camp called Victoria River Scenic Lookout on its Western border.

On leaving Saddle Creek Rest Area we only now noticed how nice the area is, as it was dark of course upon our arrival. In fact, the rear of the area was at the base of a sheer cliff face which contained rock formations of various colours. The journey from Saddle Creek to Timber Creek was again lovely with a blend of flats and rugged mountains. As the distance to Timber Creek was not far (under 100 Kilometres) we soon arrived at the Victoria River Scenic Lookout. To our disappointment and bewilderment as we reached the road leading to the lookout, we were confronted by No Camping signposts. We now faced another dilemma which had faced us to a larger degree yesterday, but unlike yesterday we would look for a local solution as we had no intention of travelling a million miles again. We decided firstly that this lookout was worth looking at, and after we had explored the area a bit, we would head into Timber Creek and work out our options. The view from the top of this lookout was lovely and gave us a bird's eye view of the Victoria River. Tee fired up the kettle and we had a cuppa before going to explore the other lookout on the Eastern side of this range.

On the Eastern side of the range we met a couple from Rockhampton who were travelling in a Winnebago. They did not have the Winnebago with them but were driving a Suzuki 4WD that they towed on the back of the Motorhome. I asked them where they were camped and they told us they were staying at the Big Horse Creek Campground in the Gregory National Park. They said the place was lovely and Tee and I looked at each other with the same thought – "that will do us!" The view from this Eastern side of the lookout was over the town of Timber Creek and nowhere near as nice as the Western view. But this was of no significance to Tee who was totally pre-occupied with patting Sam their old Labrador dog.

Our next step was to check out the fuel prices in Timber Creek and establish if it was worth buying a few groceries. It was a big fat NO to the groceries as they were ridiculously overpriced and total amazement at the $1.95 per litre price tag on the Diesel fuel. This place is less than 300 kilometres from Katherine where fuel prices are $1.60 per litre, or so I have been told, so how do they work that out. This made our decision to stay at the Big Horse Creek Campground all the simpler and we headed off.

The Big Horse Creek Campground was not a free camp but at $3.30 per person it was not bad and it provided water, toilets and lovely separate parking bays. We settled in to a nice spot and relaxed during the heat of another scorching day. For dinner Tee whipped up a special new treat that had not been named yet and she was open to suggestions. I am not allowed to tell you the ingredients through fear of Tee's retribution but I did get to name it and it is now officially known as the Auspattie.

Day **234**

We both had disrupted nights sleep last night with Tee being woken by a barking dog in the middle of the night and I was woken at 10-30pm by a family of campers who decided that 10-30pm was a good time to start packing up their gear before bed. Never mind we both can catch up with our sleep and we were keen to get back on the road as this place is very crowded. As I backed Lizzie out of our free camp spot, I noticed a puddle of oil and I gasped as I pointed it out to Tee. At first, I thought it may be the gearbox as it has a slightly weeping rear main oil seal, but the only way to find out was to get under Lizzie and have a good look around. As this place was so dusty, and there were no rattling noises we decided that it would be best to check the oil level and then drive slowly into Timber Creek where I could get help if needed.

The oil level was only a little low so I was a little less concerned but still concerned, if you know what I mean. It meant that the gearbox was probably OK and that I would now have to locate the source of the engine leak. We drove into Timber Creek, which was only 10 kilometres away and I pulled into the service road near town that would allow me to look under Lizzie on Bitumen and away from traffic. While driving my hope was that the oil was leaking from the oil filter that I had changed at the last service in Perth. This would mean an easy fix once I had the right tools and not be an expensive repair bill.

On the side of the service road I crawled under Lizzie and prayed that the oil filter had oil leaking from it. Sounds crazy but this would be by far the least of all evils, and as luck has it, it was. I topped up the oil and hand tightened the oil filter in the hope of reaching Katherine where I could purchase an oil filter wrench and tighten it properly. We decided that a local mechanic would rip us off so we put $30.00 of fuel (at $1.95 per litre) in and set off for the day's adventure. I felt confident that if I kept an eye on the oil level, we should not have any dramas. As I had not been to the toilet this morning, I had to find a toilet along the way to Katherine. The only one we could see on the map was one that was two kilometres off the main road at Joe Creek Picnic Area. When Tee spotted the turnoff, she also noticed that it was a dirt road and said "are you sure you want to do two kilometres of dirt road?" I replied that I had to go and it looked like a good place for a coffee anyway.

We headed along the dirt road that was badly corrugated, but the stunning scenery made up for it. After a coffee and toilet break, we noticed that although there was no-one here when we arrived there was now six or seven cars and that all of the occupants were off on the walking trail. It was now my turn to talk Tee into a walk as she had done with me at Mt Shank in South Australia, and I only hoped that the place would be as special. Tee relented to the walk even though it was quite warm and this weather is not contusive to being highly active. Once on the walk though Tee began to loosen up with the walk as the scenery was absolutely superb. The area was like "Mini Palms" in the Bungle Bungle Range only smaller. We took a number of photos as we climbed the range into the Victoria Palm forest, with the cliff face providing lovely shade even though the thought of falling rocks was a little scary.

We passed a number of older couples as we climbed along the walk and no wonder as it was quite treacherous under foot with almost the whole path being made up of loose and various sized rocks. As we climbed along the ridge at the base of the cliff, we saw something totally unexpected and something that we didn't think we would see on the whole trip. Tee, who was now leading the walk, yelled out for me to come and look and before my eyes was a series of Aboriginal Rock Art – We were Amazed to say the least. I took numerous photos of them and one I took included a photo of my lovely wife so people would believe that we were actually there. After staring in amazement at these drawings for some time we decided we should start our decent and keep on our journey.

Back to Lizzie and a quick bottle of water before heading towards our next free camp about 100 kilometres shy of Katherine. Now back at Timber Creek I had calculated that the $30.00 of fuel that I gave Lizzie would get us into Katherine, but as we were heading into a slight headwind, I was starting to doubt that we would reach Katherine without a little more fuel. A short distance up the road we came to another side road that would lead us to the old Victoria River crossing. Now we really wanted to have a close up look at the Victoria River as we had only seen it from a large concrete bridge and the Lookout. We were both keen to see a crocodile in the wild and this looked like it may be a good spot to do that.

The road to the Victoria River was soft in parts and about 150 metres short of the river it was marked for 4WD's only. So, we parked Lizzie and decided to take a walk down to the waters edge. At the time I didn't know it but Tee was quite nervous and when she made that fact known, I decided to do the 'boy thing' and give her a scare. I told her that the bushes on her side of the track looked like a great hiding spot for a hungry crocodile. Tee was soon on my side of the track and gave me a fair slap for good measure. The slap proved to be ineffective as when we got to the water's edge, I noticed Tee was well back from the waters edge so I began to splash the water. Tee said "what the heck are you doing you idiot you will get eaten!" I said "don't be silly I can out run them as they only have little legs". I thanked her for her concern for my safety to which she replied, "I only said that because you have the Motorhome Keys!"

With my ego deflated and Tee getting the last word in we started heading back to Lizzie, disappointed that we did not see any crocodiles. Then Tee noticed some unusual footprints that I photographed as we believed them to be small crocodile footprints and what seemed to be a slide mark where their tails had dragged. At this stage of our trip this was as close as we have got to seeing a live wild croc. Soon after rejoining the Highway we got to the Victoria River Roadhouse and decided that even though we should make Katherine with the fuel we had it was a bit of a risk and decided to drop another $20.00 of Diesel in (at the slightly better price of $1.86 per litre).

The first free camp we had to choose from was 104 Kilometres short of Katherine and if it was no good, we had two others to choose from closer to Katherine. Mathison Rest Area was OK and I was nearly going to move on, but Tee said "it has water" and she pointed to a good spot so we decided to stay. Turns out the spot Tee picked provided a lovely breeze and we set up the awning and sat outside for the afternoon. By early evening all the caravans were away from us and with a big gum tree located at the only spot near us our hope was that we would be on our own. Unfortunately, though a couple in a whiz banger decided to call us neighbour and moved in. This was OK as they were on their own and generally young tourists are not noisy on their own. We settled in for the evening with a few beers while Tee prepared a lovely meal with some of the dwindling supplies that we had. We seriously needed to do some shopping.

I had checked the oil filter again and it seemed not to be leaking, but I would wait until tomorrow to really check it over before being totally convinced that it only needed tightening. At about 9-00pm we went to bed and turned off all the lights so we could look at the stars and enjoy the breeze through our open windows. Then the unbelievable happened and two more vehicles turned up and joined the young couple who were next to us. They proceeded to laugh and carry on and keep us awake until almost midnight. We both did our best to refrain from getting angry but we both really were.

Day **235**

ast day before winter today, but you would not know it up here as the temperature has not been less than 30 degrees in the past few weeks. Our tourist friends near us were fast asleep of course as they had had a busy night last night being complete arseholes. We have decided to stay here today to help the budget and do a full spring clean of Lizzie, inside and out, and remove all the red bulldust of WA.

The young couple next to us, when they eventually awoke, decided to do an oil change and dump their old oil into our bush. I said nothing but took photos of the whole episode so I can email it to the police when I get to Katherine. Some may say that this is a bit mean but to Tee and I this is unacceptable. Later that day while I was washing the outside of Lizzie and Tee was cleaning the inside, I spoke to these young travellers in a friendly manner. My reasoning was to not let them know that I would be the one who dobbed them in to the authorities for the illegal oil dumping. Tee overheard me and was cranky with me for being nice to them. I suppose it sounded like I was selling out but I didn't see it that way. I tried to be nice to Tee all day and eventually she spoke to me again. Tee has a far higher morale standard than I do and I really appreciate that. I am now sorry that I did not give them the cold shoulder that they deserved, as far too often in life people pretend and real issues are avoided. I learnt a lesson today and will try to abide to my morale standards without compromise.

We got a heap of work done today, which we should both be proud of and on reinspection of the oil filter I am confidant that tightening the oil filter will solve the problem.

Day 236

First day of winter today and again you would not know up here as even at 7-00am the sun was blazing and the temperature was on the rise. We are off to Katherine today to do all the shopping and purchases that we need. The process of getting ready to hit the road ran quite smoothly this morning and we were on the road by about 8-00am. Once on the road we had to deal with driving directly into the morning sun which proved to be a bit tuff as we started spotting a lot of kangaroos grazing by the side of the road. Not knowing if they were going to stay put or jump out in front of us, I backed off the accelerator and kept my eye out as much as I could in the harsh sunlight.

Eventually we got a bit of a reprieve and stated heading slightly north. This relieved the direct sunlight, and although still in my eyes it was a lot easier to see and we both felt safer so I gained a bit of speed again. The funny thing we have noticed with the wildlife on the road (mainly kangaroos), is that they seem to get confused when two cars are coming from different directions. I am not sure if this is just a coincidence but it has happened three times with us and ended with the kangaroo jumping in front of Lizzie and in a panic.

It was not too long before we reached Katherine and the Repco store that we had put in the navigator had closed down so we would have to source another store to find an oil filer wrench. Tee spotted a spare parts place down the road a bit and we headed for that. When we got there though the place was packed inside and I needed assistance as I was not sure what size wrench I actually needed. I tried to guess while I was in the store but with three sizes to choose from, I did not want to take the risk. I decided to leave it until we got to Darwin as the choice of stores would be better there and I could get some assistance. But with every disappointment comes new possibility and directly across the road from the spare parts place was a camping shop. Upon entering I found Guy ropes at a good price and the toilet chemicals that I needed were priced better than I could get them at home. I went back to the Motorhome where Tee was looking up the Woolworths store location, and soon we were off to do the grocery shopping.

The fuel in Katherine was very well priced and I got a tank full at $1.59 per litre, 45c per litre cheaper than at Timber Creek and Lake Argyle, just down the road. We had trouble finding a parking area near the Woolworths store and we did not know it but it was a sign of things to come. Finally, we found a parking area and in line with my theory that, with every disappointment comes new possibilities, it was right next to a brand-new Repco store. We walked to the shopping complex that Woolworths was in and Tee said she just wanted a quick toilet break. To her horror she was stopped by a security guy and told it was $2.00 to use the toilet. We both could not believe this and there was no way we would pay that and were confused as to why it was being charged. The only thing we could think was that the local Aboriginals who were loitering outside the complex were misusing the facilities. We decided to drop into the chemist and buy some Vitamins and then go back to the Motorhome for Tee's toilet break and drop off the vitamins before returning to shop.

In Woolworths we were like kids in a candy shop as it had been over two weeks since we shopped last and were looking forward to some fresh fruit and vegetables. The shopping was quite pleasant until we realized the size of the que at the checkouts. I had never seen anything like it there must have been 10 or more people waiting in each check out que. Finally, we got out of there and were on our way. When we got back to the Motorhome an Aboriginal fellow came up to the Motorhome and asked us for some money. The amazing thing was that it was not $2.00 or something like that but $20.00. I used my standard line saying that I didn't carry cash and only used my card. Tee couldn't believe how much he had asked for but we were both expecting to be asked as there were 'no loitering' signs everywhere and it is quite common for Aboriginals to ask for money.

While Tee was putting away the groceries, I decided to measure the oil filter under the Motorhome and go and get a wrench from Repco. Again, I was not sure what size to get as the two larger wrenches were sized either side of the size that I had measured my filter at. But when I went to the counter to ask Wally was a fabulous help and said he would get my sized filter off the shelf and we could check it physically. He was a great help and even sold me the wrench at trade price. I returned to the Motorhome, tightened the filter and Tee was still working away with the shopping. I said to her how I had got great service and told her I was now off to buy some more beer. After finishing off all the chores and putting away the beer we decided to have a bite to eat and enjoyed some fresh salad sandwiches.

With us and the stock levels all filled up we were again on our way. As Katherine was on our way back from Darwin when we headed to Port Augusta (SA) there was no need for us to rush and see the Katherine Gorge and planned to do it on our return. Our next stop would be at a free camp that was located not far from Litchfield National Park. On our way there though we had a change of heart and decided to drop into Edith Falls and perhaps stay there the night.

We soon arrived at Edith Falls and as it was quite pleasant, and the weather was so hot we decided to stay. The place was packed and it took us two loops of the campground to find a nice spot to stop. Unfortunately, though I hit a bollard while parking Lizzie and caused a slight bit of damage to her. I was furious and took out some of my frustrations on Tee who was in no way going to put up with my shit and let me know in no uncertain terms. The mood was sombre and quiet for some time before I suggested we go for a walk and look at the falls and rock pools. This turned out to be a good suggestion as the place was stunning and we both really enjoyed the scenery. We went for a walk of nearly five kilometres in all and before descending to the campground we had a swim in the upper pool which really cooled us down – especially me!

Tee had left some hamburger patties out for dinner from our shopping trip and we cooked them up with onion and eggs before joining them with fresh bread, salad and condiments to create a yummy burger that we washed down with cold beer. IT DOESN'T GET MUCH BETTER THAN THIS! After dinner we enjoyed a few more beers under the awning until retiring to bed at about 9-30pm.

Day **237**

The original plan for today was to get up early and get some hand washing done so it would be dry by lunchtime and we could head off to our next free camp about 120klms north of here and just shy of Adelaide River. Well we did get up reasonably early, just shy of 8-00am and I went over to the amenities to check out the water troughs to wash our clothes in. The troughs were fine but they didn't have any plugs for them so we had to find something that would hold the water in by covering the drain. After a bit of searching through rubbish and in the Motorhome, I found a plastic cup that fitted. I then cut it down to size and hoped that the water pressure would hold it in place.

Tee started doing the washing and sent me off to do boy stuff as she was keen to have me away from her while she was working. I went back to the Motorhome and did some writing and after about 30 minutes I went back over to Tee to see how she was doing. Turns out the cut down plastic cup was working a treat and Tee even let me help by wringing out the clothes and putting them on the clothesline (that I also made, with a length of rope between two trees). Tee was wrapped that the cup was holding as it would have been very difficult to wash without it, not to mention a waste of a lot of water. Also turns out that my masculine hands were also very good for wringing out the washing and that I was quite handy to have around. Surprising after yesterdays effort!

With over half of the washing done we decided to change our plans and stay at Edith Falls for one more night so Tee could do the rest of the washing and then we could go for a swim in the afternoon. I again helped by wringing out the washing and hanging it out to dry. My reward for this fine work was a pair of Peanut Butter Sandwiches for lunch, followed by a glass of Bundaberg Ginger Beer – Yum!

After lunch we gained some new neighbours in Bev and Mal from Warragul – country Victoria. We said our hello's and even spent about an hour having a chat or at least I did while Tee finished the second load of washing. My conversation was only broken up when Tee requested that I could now wring out the clothes she had washed and hang them out to dry. I felt privileged as it proved that I had done a good job and was quite helpful around the laundry.

With the clothes almost dried we decided to start bringing them in and getting ready to go for a swim. By the time we were ready to go for a swim all the washing, less the socks, were now dry and while Tee put them away I had another chat with Mal. Turns out Mal was quite a knowledgeable fellow when it came to farming matters and I asked him a fair few questions about life on the farm. I had also heard that to eat wild goat you had to separate the females from the males for a period of time to get the stink out of them prior to eating. He told me that he didn't know, so I asked him no more about goats. In fact, I couldn't have anyway as I had no more questions to ask. He did tell me though that a friend of his who shot wild goats had once had a contract to supply the meat to a major hamburger retailer, who blended it with their beef to make their hamburger patties. Could be a bushies tale but who knows and apparently goat meat is quite tasty.

Tee and I donned on our swimmers and headed to the plunge pool that in fact was about twice the size of Brisbane's Southbank and had a real waterfall to boot. As we were about to enter the water another couple came up behind us and the fellow said "come on, in you get" and I replied "it's not a kids diving board you know". We ended up chatting to this couple when we eventually braved the initial cold of getting in and soon found out they were from Buderim, Sunshine Coast. This is close to where we live and in fact, we had not long ago met another couple from Buderim (Don & Di of the Derby – Darby fame). We mentioned this fact to Greg and Rhonda and said the couple's name, to which they responded that they had just been into the Bungle Bungle Range on a tour with them.

After some conversation Rhonda suggested to Tee that we should all get together when we got back to our respective homes and go out for dinner. We thought that a lovely idea and I decided that when I got back to the Motorhome, I would email Don and Di so we could all stay in contact. The funniest part of the meeting for me is when they told us of Don's story with the mouse, which was the same story he told us when Stan and Val were with us at the Boab Rest Area. Now Don I am really hoping that this is not the only story you have, and that there are other interesting parts to your life ☺

After our swim we went back to the Motorhome and as promised I sent an email to Don & Di. Tee got out the sausages for Dinner and I topped up the water in the Motorhome before deciding it was time to have a beer. We had a couple before Dinner and watched a bunch of school kids from Melbourne Grammar as they set up their tents and kicked a footy around. At first, we thought they would be noisy but they proved us wrong and were very well behaved. In fact, Tee said that this dozen or so boys on school camp were quieter than a group of four Frenchies, and I had to agree.

Day **238**

This morning it was a little cloudy and we managed to sleep in until 7-30am after a great night's sleep. We went about our particular jobs as we prepared to head off to our next free camp destination. We said goodbye to Mal as Bev had already left for a walk and we were on our way. Not much excitement to report on our 120 Kilometre journey to Bridge Creek Rest Area, but when we arrived there it was in fact nicer than we thought it would be. It had toilets and water supply, which were not mentioned in the Camps6 book, as well as green grass and logs for the fireplaces. We set up when we got there and had a quiet afternoon and evening while we planned for tomorrow's adventure which included driving and camping in Litchfield National Park. Oh, I did forget to mention that we did stop off at Pine Creek on our way to this free camp site and it had a rail museum. If you are into trains it is well worth a look and the town is quite nice and very quiet as it is set off the main highway.

Day **239**

Although the free camp last night looked as though it would be fabulous, in fact it turned out to be an echo chamber for traffic going past. We ended up sleeping in until almost 8-00am, not because we had a great night sleep but due to the fact that we were awoken numerous times during the night by passing trucks and couldn't wake in the morning. At previous campsites the noise of passing trucks had not bothered us but at this one it seemed to be much noisier with the sound of the trucks echoing.

Fortunately, we did not have a long way to travel today and the sleep deprivation would not affect that part of our day. On the other hand though, we had a lot to see in the Litchfield National Park and the lack of sleep may cause issues there. We stopped at Adelaide River as we were able to get phone reception as well as Internet access. I received in all of my emails and made a call to my step brother Rod who was in Cairns on a week off with his wife Cindy – AND NO KIDS. They seemed to be having a great time and were off somewhere when I rang, meaning that the conversation was not a long one.

Well now I am not telling the truth here and it bothers me somewhat, as I am only trying to protect my Dad's and my Step mother's feelings. The truth is that Rod was up in Cairns visiting his genetic father in search of his medical history and why he is what he is. I always find myself apologizing for these events when in reality Rod is entitled to know his real father, as I was, and it is "our journey" - no-one else's. Rod was in fact at his father's place when I called him and I was just trying to keep in touch with him as I know the pain and anxiety that such a meeting creates, as it has only been two years or so ago that I was doing the same thing. He is a very level headed fellow though and probably doesn't need my input.

Back on the road and after receiving my emails and ringing Rod, Tee and I went to look at the Adelaide River War Cemetery. The road to the Cemetery was beautiful and we were now getting a taste of how pretty a tropical place can look when it is well maintained. At the Cemetery we were stunned at all the deaths that occurred up here during WWII. The place was so beautifully maintained and it will, as I am sure it has, serve as a constant reminder of how horrible war can be and that Australia is not as far away from the rest of the world as many people think, physically. The town of Adelaide River really impressed us, as even though small it looks like the place is full of pride.

After Adelaide River it was not long before Tee spotted the sign to Batchelor which is kind of at the gateway to Litchfield National Park. We soon found the centre of town and more importantly to us the Information Centre where we could obtain a detailed map of the area. The town of Batchelor was similar to Adelaide River but appeared to be larger in population. In fact, I googled it and it is about four times the population approximately. Even though the information centre was unattended we managed to get a good detailed map of Litchfield National Park and some other brochures on Kakadu and Darwin.

Our first stop in the Litchfield Nation Park was the magnetic termite mounds that were quite fascinating, as was the height of the other termite mounds in the area that topped 4 meters. They say you can do Litchfield National Park in a day but we will be staying here overnight as it is not too far from Darwin where we will be heading for tomorrow morning. Our next stop was Florence Falls and, on the way, we went and had a look at Buley Rockhole which turned out to be an overcrowded swimming hole. If you could see this place without people all over it, I am sure it would be stunning, but unfortunately it was packed when we were there. The scenery was magnificent but some of the people who were here were drinking stubbies of beer and skylarking. I am not sure when would be an off season here as it is Tuesday today and it is not a public holiday or school holidays, so to see it without a crowd would be pot luck or perhaps a cold day (if they have them up here).

Florence falls was not far from here and we were soon there. Again, there were people swimming in the falls area and you had to select your time carefully to take a photo without swimmers in it. It was a nice waterfall but would not be a contender for my "must see list".

It was now after lunchtime and we were quite hungry, but the surroundings in the car park were ordinary and we wanted to eat in a prettier spot. So off we went again and we hoped that Tabletop Swamp may have a nice picnic area. But unfortunately, Tabletop Swamp was on a dirt track and there was no way we would be taking Lizzie down there. The next stop would be Tolmer Falls and it only took us another 10 minutes to reach there. The car park was much nicer and a lot quieter as there was no designated swimming here. We decided to walk to the falls before lunch as the temperature was hotting up and we didn't want to do the walk straight after lunch on a full stomach. The walk to the falls was lovely as there were many unusual rock formations and the path was all sealed.

The Tolmer Falls were lovely and with only two other couples at the viewing platform it was a lot more pleasant than the other areas that were quite crowded. I took a photo of the two couples who were travelling together, from Germany I think, and they were so pleased that I had offered to take it for them. They offered to take our photo but I was in daggy clothes and unshaven so I declined but thanked them for their offer. We walked back to the car park and had some cheese, crackers and other nibbles on a platter for lunch.

As we left for our next destination – The Cascades – we realized that it was now quite hot and we would have to stop travelling soon to set up camp. We arrived at the Cascades to find that it was 1.7 kilometres to the Upper Cascades and 1.2 kilometres to the Lower Cascades. Even though we had not slept well last night, lunch had rejuvenated us and we were keen to go for a walk. We decided to go to the Upper Cascades (the longer walk) in the hope that it would be the nicer of the two. But we didn't realize until we were well into the walk that it was mostly up hill and on large ununiformed stones. This made the walk twice as hard and the 1.7 kilometres would seem like 17 as we finally reached the falls.

When we did get their Tee was totally exhausted and even the slight risk of crocodiles did not stop us stripping off and going for a swim, although we did swim in the shallow flat rock area where the visibility was superb. I braved the deeper rock pool area briefly until my leg brushed a stick and I was out of there like a rocket. Tee found it quite amusing and made some very clever comments about how brave I was!

The walk back was 50 per cent easier as it was mostly down hill but we still had to watch our step on the loose and uneven rock surface. When we reached the junction to the Lower Cascades, we decided it was too much to walk there also so we gave it a miss. I checked it later on the internet and it seems very similar to the Upper Cascades so we probably hadn't missed much.

As it was now almost 4-00pm we decided to head to the camp area at Wangi Falls which is also the only place in Litchfield Park that we have not seen. That is, of the ones we could access or were interested in seeing. We would have loved to see the Lost City (4WD only) but the Bamboo Creek Tin Mine did not interest us, neither did Walker Creek. We arrived at the Wangi Falls campground and after circling the campground twice realized that it was completely full. Perhaps we should have come here and gone to the Cascades in the morning, but that was not the way we planned it and it would have made us late into Darwin tomorrow. After contemplation we decided not to decide anything until we had visited the falls first and had a nice cool swim.

The Wangi Falls were spectacular and we thought that they were by far the nicest falls in the Litchfield National Park. I think for swimming Buley Rockhole would be the best bathing spot but it seemed to be too packed with people to truly enjoy. On our approach to the falls we got a lovely photo of a Kookaburra whose wings were bright blue. Then Tee saw a sign saying that there was as small risk of fresh water crocs in the area and although not aggressive can still bite you if provoked. This was enough for Tee to say no to swimming and as it was now evening and quite cool, I was happy to follow suit. On the way back to the Motorhome we again met Greg and Rhonda from Buderim who said they planned to stay in Litchfield until the 10/06/13 when they were due in Darwin for a wedding. We chatted for a fair while and recommitted to our plans of getting together in October with Don & Di (Derby – Darby) on our return home.

We returned to Lizzie having decided to sleep in the car park on the outside of the campground here. When we were at Edith Falls many people had also done it there as it was also packed. We don't particularly like doing this but as it is now getting dark, we have no intentions of driving around looking for a place to stay.

Day **240**

Turned out to be a great move staying in the car park last night, as it was super quiet and the only noise was the water running over the falls in the distance. I slept all night and we were up by 7-00am and off to Darwin by 7-30am. With the distance only being 145 kilometres, I expected us to be in Darwin by 9-00am. But I forgot that the National Park road was quite windy and it took us a fair while to make it back to Batchelor.

Once we reached Batchelor though the road got heaps better and much straighter and we were at Harvey Normans Darwin by 9-30am. The process of buying online was quite simple and when we got to the store it only took us a few minutes and one signature to get our new camera. I checked with their IT guy when I was there if they could retrieve my photos of Lake Argyle that were on a damaged SD Card, but unfortunately, he could not. I have decided to leave it alone now until we return home and I will try again at places I know. I bought a few USB flash drives for storage of more photos and we were off. We now needed to find a shopping centre as we needed some bits and pieces for our journey. The lady from Harvey Normans had told us that the Casuarina would be the best bet for us as it would be a little quieter than Darwin. As our fresh rain drinking water had now run out a Big W store would be required and also, we could get well priced Butane there.

We arrived at the Casuarina Shopping Centre and had a little bit of difficulty finding a spot to park Lizzie, eventually parking in a back street behind the Shopping Centre. Worked out well though as it was near a Chemist Warehouse store where Tee bought some beauty products and I got some vitamins. We then went on to buy 50 litres of Big W drinking water, butane and a Water filter for our jug. We then bought a new pair of thongs for myself and did a bit more food shopping in Coles – mainly to get the 8c per litre discount voucher. They work those things as we tended to spend more than we planned purely to save on the petrol. It was marvellous to get well priced fuel again and with the discount voucher we saved another $5-00 on the full tank of Diesel.

Off to Darwin and in line with our dislike of cities we drove around for a quick look and then headed out of there as quick as possible. Darwin seems OK but again it is not why we are travelling and we may fly into Darwin on a later trip and hire a car to look around. But driving a Motorhome in a city is no fun especially without air-conditioning and in 36-degree heat.

The free camp we were heading to was on the outskirts of Kakadu NP and right near the Window on the Wetlands Visitor Centre. As we headed there, we decided to top up our Beer supplies at a town called Humpty Doo – very interesting name. The free camp area looked ordinary at best but we had little choice as the next campsite was some 130 kilometres further on. With no intention to travel that far today we went to the Window on the Wetlands Visitors Centre. Wow cold air conditioning what a bonus and the Visitor Centre was also quite interesting – 1) for the display and 2) for the fact that no-one was at the service desk for the whole 50 mins that we were in the building. We had no idea what was going on there.

The viewing platform at the top of the building was superb and from it we could see over a large wetland area that had a number of water buffalo grazing in it. Also, upstairs was an aboriginal artist who was at work on the decking area which was lovely to see. After leaving the Visitors Centre and grabbing a few brochures we decided to travel a dirt road behind the centre that would give us a closer look at the fenced water buffaloes. We took a pile of photos of these lovely creatures and continued down the dirt road to a Jumping Croc tour centre located at the end of the dirt road.

One of the brochures that we got from the Visitors Centre was for the "Original Jumping Crocodile Cruise" which we presumed was the one we were heading to on the dirt road. But when we got there, we were told that the cruise was $35.00 per head and yet the brochure said $25.00 per head. I showed the seedy looking gentleman the brochure and he replied that this was not them. Fortunately, we had got there after the last tour had departed which saved us the embracement of not going with them and left us with an easy departure.

We spent the rest of the afternoon at the free camp area trying to keep the swarms of mosquitoes out of the Motorhome. The mosquitoes here were ridiculous and it was impossible to go outside the Motorhome without getting bombarded. They did though provide us with fabulous entertainment as we watched the whiz bangers rock up, get out of their vans and start doing a traditional German slap dance. It also proved to us that there is a god, as although extremely resilient, all of them took off again. Great entertainment from behind our flywire.

Day **241**

Today would be a slow day with only the Jumping Crocodile Cruise planned for 1-00pm today. Tee rang the phone number on their brochure and spoke to Connie who was extremely helpful and booked us in to the 1-00pm cruise. Tee also got directions to their establishment that turned out to be only 4 kilometres from our free camp. This gave me the whole morning to write and Tee spent the morning reading and doing her beauty regime.

The crocodile cruise was superb and we did actually see heaps of crocodiles, not just one or two. There were two highlights for me on the cruise, the first being watching them jumping out of the water to their back legs and the second, my ultimate favourite, was seeing Agro – a six metre beast. He is apparently the second largest croc in the territory – on record that is. By the time the tour was over it was about 2-30pm and I said to Tee that we should go onto the hill near the 'Window on Wetlands Visitor Centre' and have some late lunch. We did that and the breeze on the hill made it very pleasant while we ate our platter of nibbles. After lunch, and with good internet reception, we watched a Youtube movie. The movie we watched was Cujo, something that neither Tee or I had seen in many years – it was good fun.

By the time the movie was over it was almost 6-00pm and we headed back to mosquito heaven (our free camp). It was full of whiz bangers again but the mosquitoes were much lighter tonight and the tourists braved them even though they were still extremely annoying. We didn't expect to get the best night sleep here as last night was ordinary. But it was a little cooler tonight so we hoped we could get a reasonable sleep.

Day **242**

True to our word we slept OK here but not much more. Today we were off into Kakadu NP and with no expectations as to what it will be like we headed towards Jabiru. We have checked the map and there does not seem to be much between here and Jabiru until we get close to the town itself where we will turn off to Ubirr Rock. The scenery along the way to Jabiru was much like we have seen all the way through the Northern Territory and not particularly anything special. The only spot that we have seen that is what we expected to see in Kakadu was actually outside Kakadu, at the Windows on the Wetland area. Oh, and of course on the Croc cruise on the Adelaide River.

This was true until we got to the South Alligator Picnic Area that was on the banks of the – (yes you guessed it) – the South Alligator River. The pull in to this picnic spot was quite hidden and in fact the whole area was quite neglected. The parking area and boat ramp area looked as though it could cater for at least 50 cars but was much neglected. We had a look at the boat ramp as it would be easy to see the river from the vehicle there. The rivers here are quite muddy and closer to the coast they seem to have significant currents. You would really struggle if you fell into this river and we joked that this Picnic Area was more a picnic area for the crocodiles than us humans. On the banks of the river I photographed a large number of mud skippers but was keen to get back in the Motorhome as soon as that was done. We then pulled up near the toilet block where we were on our own for about fifteen minutes before suddenly car after car pulled in. They must have spotted our Motorhome and decided to investigate the spot as we were soon surrounded by about seven or eight vehicles. Time to move on and after a quick cup of coffee we were on our way again towards Jabiru.

Just before Jabiru we turned towards Ubirr Rock and the scenery did improve a fair bit with frequent creeks and now rocky ranges dominating the landscape. The closer we got to Ubirr Rock the better the scenery got and we stopped on one occasion to photograph a stunning string of rocky mountains. Not long after these rocky mountains we could see a vast area of wetlands but as it was set quite off the road, we could not get decent photos of it. Soon after though we reached Ubirr Rock where we went for a walk to see the scenery and the Aboriginal Rock Paintings that this place is known for.

This place is absolutely amazing and goes onto my "must see list". We viewed the Aboriginal Rock Art that had been produced on the stunning rock outcrops before climbing to a rocky summit that presented us with an amazing view. The view was a full 360-degree view of wetlands, distant ranges and open green pasture that seemed to go on forever. We took so many photos that the battery went flat in our camera and we decided then to descend and proceed back to our Motorhome. This is truly an amazing place and, on the way out we visited the river area that was about five degrees cooler than on the rocks and a very welcome relief.

Back onto the highway and off to Jabiru where we filled up with fuel, house water and emptied the shitter. We were now over halfway through Kakadu NP and although Ubirr Rock was fantastic we were not overly impressed with Kakadu. In fact, the locals have nicknamed it Kakadon't and prefer Litchfield NP as a weekend away from Darwin.

A few days earlier I had rung Stan and Val who we first met at De Greys Rest Area outside Port Hedland in WA. We had organized to meet tomorrow at a free camp just outside Pine Creek as they had just left Katherine and we would probably not cross paths again for quite some time. Tee said she was bored with Kakadu and as it was now after 2-00pm we had a choice to make. We either stopped close to here for the night or we drive all the way to near Pine Creek and met up with Stan and Val this evening. I said to Tee if I stop for lunch, I will not want to drive again so the choice was hers. Tee said she would prefer to drive on as she had a bit of a migraine and just wanted to get out of here. I agreed with her and although we would miss the Yellow Water area, we were both over it.

Unanimous - and we drove for the next two hours to reach Harriet River Rest Area and catch up with Stan, Val and their dog Max. It was great to catch up with them and Max was so excited to see us. We camped close to each other and chatted about where we had been and what we had done. The beer flowed as well as the stories and we all had a great time into the evening. But that all changed late evening with the arrival of the young tourists who threatened to spoil our good time by keeping us awake late into the evening. Just before a group of them started to set up a tent directly behind our Motorhome I told them that I would be off in the morning and that spot would block my exit. They were co-operative and moved to another spot that was a fair way from where we were camped.

Day **243**

Although my chat to one group of these young tourists got them away from us, we still had three girls in a tent that banged their car doors until well after 11-00pm. This woke us up and our sleep was again spoilt by these selfish little shits. We did manage to sleep until 7-30am though and were awoken by the elderly couples in the free camp. Three of the retirement age campers started up their generators in an attempt to pay back some of these selfish little shits who had kept us awake part of the night. In fact, the group that I had chatted to last night had moved, but not far enough to be clear of the three groups that were now running their generators. These older couples were hilarious and were doing all sorts of things as payback which included; banging car doors tooting horns and the old guy over the back even let off a shot gun. I spoke to Stan when I woke (he was one of the retirement age people running the generator) and he told me that these young ones had kept him up until after 2-00am.

These young tourists are so silly pissing people off as unlike your neighbour at home, you don't know who you are pissing off when you pull up. The old guy had a shotgun and if he had a brain snap these young people would be at serious risk. The annoying thing is that there are thousands of kilometres of free land that they could park in and by doing this would not disturb anyone. But the truth is they are scared to be out there and like to camp near others. The other problem with most of these whiz bangers is that they have no toilet and shit in the bush. It is so disgusting walking down to a pristine river and bumping into a turd.

What is even worse is the toilet paper that ends up everywhere as litter. Now I am not saying they are all bad but I have never seen one with a small shovel and I know that when they come into a free camp with no toilet or shower that they are not going to hold on for two days.

The ramifications not only affect them but also the retired and casual traveller who do the right thing and get lumped into being a free camper. We cop all sorts of shit like people bad mouthing us or beeping their horns at us in the middle of the night. A quick note to all those truck drivers who now do this and think it is funny – think about your tired mate in his truck asleep on the side of the highway, don't let him cop the retribution of your bad behaviour.

Of course, this bad behaviour is not confined to campers in free camps but is ripe through all of society in general. Since the absence of war and direct conflict the world has become filled with passive aggressive people who pretend that things don't bother them. They then get back at people in a sneaky manner and no one knows where they stand. I much prefer an honest society who says what they mean, even if I don't always want to hear it. As I have no ability to make the world like this all I can do is only be friends with like minded people who return my honesty and frankness. Australians as a country are afflicted with this same issue as we are a society who says what we mean and attempt to do the right thing with other countries. We try desperately to be diplomatic and not tread on other nations toes. The problem is that many other countries don't play by the same rules and take advantage of countries like Australia and its people's good nature.

Back to our camping (as I dismount my high horse) and we were all quite sapped of energy due to these selfish young ones. We spent the morning chatting with Stan and Val and watching these selfish young campers slowly getting up after 9-00am. One of the girls who were guilty of keeping Tee and I up until after 11-30pm looked absolutely exhausted and had a look of disgust on her face. Now she got a taste of what it was like to be sleep deprived. They had really spoilt our day as we were due to go our separate ways tomorrow morning and today was meant to be a happy day for us.

Although very tired by lunchtime we were all feeling a little better and decided to take Max (Stan and Val's dog) down to the creek for a swim. Max is only a year old and went nuts when he got to the water and Stan took a video of his play. After our walk we all went back to our accommodation for an afternoon nap. Although none of us got much sleep it was nice to relax and catch up with a bit of rest. Tee and I read and wrote for the afternoon while Stan and Val watched a movie.

Val knew that I was dying to have a roast as I had told her how long it had been since I had had one. She got Stan to pull out a frozen piece of pork from their freezer and she would cook it as a farewell meal. We had a great evening, especially me, who got his roast dream. Tee also fared well as she got her favourite thing also in the crackling. We had a few drinks and chatted for the evening. With no young tourists in the free camp tonight it looked as though we would get a good night's sleep, but I was not getting too excited as it was only 9-00pm when we went to bed and anything could happen.

Day **244**

The temperature last night was a few degrees cooler and with no young tourists arriving late Tee and I had a lovely sleep. We chatted to a few of the other campers in the free camp before saying our goodbyes to Val and Stan who have been great company. We vowed to keep in touch and told them to drop in to our place when they are in Queensland where they were welcome to stay whenever they liked. We thought with the caravan being their permanent home they may like to stay in our home for a change.

Stan and Val took off before we did but only by a few minutes and we would only be travelling in the same direction for the 26-kilometre journey to Pine Creek where they would turn right and we would turn left. When we reached the turning though, we saw a sign advertising the Pine Creek Sunday markets so we decided to drop in. The market though turned out to be a very small affair in which we were lucky to find a few bargains that included two DVD's and a book for Tee. Tee reads a lot more than I do as she does not do much writing, plus she reads very quickly, thus the requirements for heaps of good books. The lady at the stall asked us, when she found out we were Queenslanders, if we knew much about Tin Can Bay. I replied to her that I did know a bit about it and asked why. She said that her ex husband now lived there and to tell him what he is missing if we saw him. Well John Jones from Tin Can Bay if you read this consider yourself told! Then out of the blue Stan and Val turned up as they had stopped in Pine Creek for fuel and had also seen the Sunday Market sign. We chatted for a bit before again saying our goodbyes.

Our plan for the day was to head to Katherine Gorge where we thought we would camp for the night and enjoy the area. We had considered stopping at Edith Creek but as it was an NT long weekend, we thought the place would be packed. We would have checked if Edith Falls was near the highway but as it was 20 kilometres in, we thought that a 40-kilometre round trip was not worth the effort, or the fuel consumption. There was a spot near the Edith Creek turnoff that we considered but it looked a little exposed and was not a designated area.

After a total of about an hour and a half driving, we reached Katherine where we stopped for lunch and to check our emails. I also rang my mum to let her know where we were and Albert (my best mate from Yarrawonga) to see if he would like some visitors in about six weeks. We thought if he could get a day off, we could spend time together but if he couldn't we would travel in another direction. Turns out he was glad we were returning and that he would take a day off when he knew our exact travel plans and dates.

With lunch over with I left a message for my brother Rod and we headed out to Katherine Gorge. When we arrived at the Gorge, we proceeded to the Visitors Centre as it was signposted that all camp fees were payable there. As all the National park fees so far have been $6.60 per person, we thought that Katherine Gorge would be the same. No no no – it was $40.00 for a powered site and $36.00 for a non powered. Fortunately, the girl at the counter said that due to a fruit bat infestation we should check out the campsite first before we committed to staying here. When we looked at the campsite though it was stunning and it boasted a huge saltwater pool. Although expensive we decided to stay as after talking to some people already here the bats were now confined to an area away from most of the powered sites. We parked Lizzie in a nice spot away from the bats and walked back to the visitors centre to pay for the site.

We set up camp and then decided to take advantage of the facilities with a swim in the stunning pool. It was really beautiful here and the swim gave us great relief from the heat of the day. Although the bats were around, they were no big deal and we made plans for the rest of the day. The first chore was to take advantage of the free washing machines and we did all the sheets, towels and our clothes. I made up a makeshift clothes line and we hung them out before going for a walk to the Gorge.

The Katherine Gorge is quite stunning and is also now on my list of "must see" places. We first walked to the river area before climbing to the lookout high above the gorge. The view from here was amazing and with only a few hours before sunset the angle of light was fabulous for taking photos. We then walked a further 2.8 kilometres which took us over the mountain range and eventually back to our campground. We then went for another swim before Tee fired up the hotplate to make me a yummy steak that accompanied the potato and veggies on the side. All washed down with a few beers and a chat before heading off to bed to watch a movie in air-conditioned comfort.

Day **245**

We had a great night sleep last night although I must admit I woke a few times as I was too cold. Certainly, something I can live with though after all the hot nights we have endured. Today we planned to stay at Katherine Gorge until midday when our camping permit runs out. This will give us time to enjoy the services and stay plugged into a power source. The batteries have had a full charge and we have done a few more bits of washing and now are fully cleaned. We thought about having a swim in the huge pool but it has not yet got quite warm enough. I have caught up with my writing and Tee has pre-cooked some rice and pasta for future use. The house water has been totally refreshed and by midday we were ready to hit the road again. We would love to stay here for another couple of nights but it is far too expensive for our meagre budget.

With all the Motorhome refreshed it was off to Katherine to fill up with fuel and to buy a couple of grocery items that we need. I would also like to go to Repco to get an oil filter for Lizzie but as it is a public holiday here today it is unlikely to be open. The first stop was for fuel and as we were pretty low, I would expect to not get change out of $100.00 even with the coupon I have. The fuel that I was getting today would go onto next week's budget as we will be staying at the next free camp for two nights to try and slow the spending. With $100.00 of fuel in her belly Lizzie took us to the supermarket car park where she waited while we got our grocery items.

Back and running we headed to our next free camp which is only 46 kilometres down the road to Alice Springs. On the way we looked in to

482

see the price of the Cutta Cutta Cave tours, but at $20.00 per head it was too rich for our meagre budget so we kept on travelling. We soon arrived at the free camp and with 20 or so caravans already here we found a spot in the middle of them which should ensure no young tourists would disturb our sleep tonight.

Day **246**

Although our sleep was slightly interrupted by late arriving young tourists, in general we had a fairly good sleep. The budget for this week has maxed out so we will have to stay here one more night to keep a lid on it. The day is going smoothly and, in the morning, I got a feed of fresh raisin toast that we had bought yesterday. After brekkie I went to work on trying to recover those photos of Lake Argyle that are stuck on the damaged SD Card. What I was told was an impossible task by Harvey Normans in Darwin has turned out well as I managed to transfer the photos from the damaged SD Card to our computer via our new camera that has Wi-Fi transfer capability. Tee was so proud of me as they were good photos and we have now got our complete trip on hard drive, some 6,000 photos.

We spent the rest of the day reading with Tee finishing yet another book – she is a machine – and me getting slowly closer to finishing my Steve Waugh Autobiography. Yes, that's right – I am still going on that, it's a big book! As the afternoon progressed and the temperature soared (35 degrees) more and more caravans rolled in, and with most of them near our Motorhome we are hopeful for a whiz banger free zone at our end of the free camp area. Tee cooked fried rice for Dinner last night and as there was heaps left over it will be fried rice again for Dinner tonight.

Day **247**

Last night cooled off well and we both enjoyed a good night's sleep. We hit the road by 8-00am and our travel plans were light on distance as we had decided to go and stay in the Elsey National Park overnight. We were heading to a free camp some 50 Kilometres past Mataranka but we thought we may catch a few sights in another National Park. With no real exciting scenery between here and Mataranka it was a quiet drive into town. The Elsey National Park is just past Mataranka and about 18 kilometres to the North East. Mataranka's claim to fame is that it was the literary base for Jeannie Gunn's autobiography novel 'We of the Never Never', which was written about Elsey Station on the outskirts of town. There are characters from the novel in the local park along with a huge termite mound and an abundance of birdlife, as the park is constantly watered. The town is not huge but is quite nice and also has a dump point that I need to make use of. Not the most exciting part of my day but the shitter has to be emptied and yours truly is stuck with the task. In fact, emptying the shitter today became one of the highlights of my day as I will explain.

I was quietly going about emptying the shitter when an older fellow turned up. I am not sure what the shitter etiquette is but I always wait for others to finish before I empty mine. It goes back to the standards of waiting your turn I believe. I had trouble in Eden (NSW) with this once but I have had no occurrences since. This old bugger just waltzed in and emptied it right in front of me and not only that but down the stormwater section. I politely told him to pour it down the sewer part and he grunted something at me before doing just that. He then asked me to pour some water, that I was washing my tank with, into his tank. Fact is that it was my hose I was using and there was no way I would have this old dickheads piss on my hose. I use this for my freshwater and had only used it here as there was no hose at the dump point. I told him to wait his turn as I was washing my tank. He then said 'you in a hurry, are you?' which I thought was a very odd thing to say, as it was he who had jumped in and dumped his shitter in front of me. I ignored his comment and kept going about doing what I do to ensure good hygiene. He then said 'you're taking forever' and huffed off. I was so pissed off I told him to fuck off then. What an amazing situation as I have never come across someone so rude and impatient. Yes, you old dickhead you go down as 'Wanker of the Week!'

Surprisingly I was not worked up by the situation as ten years ago I probably would have snotted him and even a year ago I would have been agitated for hours. When I got back into the Motorhome Tee said she could not believe how rude that old bastard was. What was also funny was that he also seemed calm about it, he obviously gets told to go and get fucked quite regularly and I can see why.

Back on the road and we saw a tourist sign to a place called Bitter Springs so we thought we would have a look. It was only a few kilometres up a side road and when we reached the car park, we saw it was quite a popular spot with a number of cars there. We both had no idea what Bitter Springs was all about so we were keen to have a look.

Bitter Springs as we now know is a stream of warm water (in fact 32 degrees), which has been slightly refined by man to be an almost natural swimming hole. We saw a couple of young fellows with snorkelling gear but the majority of the people here were oldies enjoying a dip. Tee and I fit in somewhere in between these two age groups and thought a bit of both would be nice (a swim and snorkel). The young fellows were snorkelling into a cavern that had been created by the vegetation growing back over the stream. Tee and I were not keen to try this proving that we were indeed somewhere in between these two age groups. We walked back to Lizzie and got our snorkelling gear, reef shoes and underwater camera.

On our return it was straight into the water (no cold-water shock here) and within minutes we were exploring the beauty of this place from an underwater perspective. There were little fish and we also spotted a turtle who was keeping well clear of all the swimmers. We took heaps of photos and the clarity was equal to Ningaloo Reef, it was a very nice place. After our swim and snorkel, we headed back to Lizzie and decided to head straight to our camping spot in Elsey National Park as we would be there by lunchtime.

The Jalmurark camping area was a bit rough and ready in its facilities but the grounds were very pretty and its location on the edge of Arnhem Land is quite awesome. It is also close to the Mataranka Homestead, the Rainbow Springs Thermal Pool and the Roper River. We soon find a lovely spot and the only break in our tranquillity for the day came when the automatic sprinklers came on at 1-30pm and gave me a soaking. I called out to Tee to grab the fishing bucket from under the dining seats and woke her in the process. I had been reading my Steve Waugh book outside, which you will be pleased to know I have now finished, and did not know that Tee was having a nap. Tee, with a blank look on her face, passed me the bucket and I covered the offending sprinkler to save us a further soaking on its next rotation.

The last fifteen or so pages of Steve Waugh's Autobiography were written by his wife Lynette and the last few paragraph of this part of the book stood out to me as being the best of the entire book. Don't get me wrong Steve Waugh writes quite well and it is quite a good book but Lynette has captured the essence of a side of life that is truly underestimated and often taken for granted. Lynette's entire adult life was taken up with a supportive role to her partner and children. Not only was she satisfied with this but genuinely fulfilled by it. Society seems to only reward those who achieve what others perceive to be worthwhile goals. I believe that Lynette has found great balance in her life and we could all learn a lot from her. She has captured the meaning of what I learnt and have cherished from a fellow I once worked with (Tili) who said to me – Craig – "the happiest man that he had met in his life was the one that was happy with what he had".

We enjoyed a pasta meal for dinner and lay looking at the stars and chatting in the evening before drifting off to sleep.

Day **248**

We awoke this morning to sunshine and green grass, as sunshine is almost a certainty up here the green grass was a welcome change. I wrote a little bit this morning while Tee prepared me some raisin toast for brekkie. The day we had planned involved a little bit of travelling but mainly of exploring the Mataranka area. After brekkie and doing a few chores I went over to the camp facilities and had a shower and shave to start the day fresh. The mornings over the past few weeks in the north of the Northern Territory have been mild with the heat only hitting after 12-00 noon and steadily climbing until about 3-00pm – 4-00pm in the afternoon. This meant that the best time to go walking and exploring is in the morning or late afternoon.

The road into the Jalmurark camping area was full of warm springs all over the landscape, even on the sides of the bitumen road. In fact, the whole Mataranka area seems to be full of these springs with the largest being used as thermal pools for our entertainment. We had visited Bitter Springs yesterday so we had planned to see Mataranka Homestead and the Rainbow Springs Thermal Pool today. But first we decided to go and have a look at the Roper River which was just a short walk from where we were camped.

The river was beautiful and there was a couple of swimming pontoons set up for people to use. As it was still early morning there was not a lot of people here but there was a family of four having a nice time in the clear water. We took a few photos of the river before heading back to Lizzie and packing up camp. On the way back to Lizzie we bumped into a young

English couple who we had chatted to in the Bungle Bungle Ranges. We swapped stories for a while and then wished them well for the rest of their journey as they were now heading to Cairns and we were off in the South Australia direction.

Back at the campsite and we packed up Lizzie and headed off towards the Mataranka Homestead and the Rainbow Springs Thermal Pool. As we were not far from either it was only 10 minutes or so until we arrived at the Mataranka Homestead Caravan Park. It was a funny set up here as the National Park is located behind the Caravan Park and made you feel as though you had to stay there to get into the Thermal Pools area. We parked in the outside car park and followed the signs which would lead us to the Thermal Pools. Of course, the signs not only led you to the Thermal Pools but also past the souvenir shop and cafeteria. But neither Tee nor I were tempted by this diversion although the new Rocky Road – Heaven ice-cream did turn our heads. After the strategic detour we finally reached the thermal pool that was not the same as the one at Bitter Springs. This one had been formed into a replica of a resort pool without the finer details – Tee and I much preferred the one at Bitter Springs. This one though was full of people, so much so that I could not even get a proper photo of it. The water quality though was fabulous and we kept on walking though the palm forest towards the river.

They must have had a huge flood here not so long ago as the palms were extensively damaged and their fronds were wedged all over the place. The whole place looked as though it needed a good clean up as it was now quite dusty as the disturbed ground had been washed all over the loose palm fronds and the boardwalks. But it would take a team of 50 men to even make a dint in the entire cleanup that was required. We continued our walk to the river area and upon arrival were greeted by a nice river that was also affected by the flooding as it was full of debris. I am sure this place would be stunning when pristine but Tee and I both agreed that Bitter Springs was our choice as the nicest swimming spot. In addition, the river near the Jalmurark camping area was much nicer than here also. As a rating I would say that this is not particularly high on our list but Bitter Springs and the Roper River region are well worth a visit. In addition, if you are a fan of the 'We of the Never Never' book and/or film then Mataranka Homestead has the replica homestead that was built for the filming of this movie right here. If this sort of stuff is right up your alley then this place is a "must see" but not a must see for Tee or I.

On our way back to Lizzie in the car park we did stop in and look through the replica Elsey Homestead and it was quite well done. Tee and I both thought that this place was as close to Bumfuck Shitsville as you could get in 2013 so in 1902 it must have been shear hell, especially for a lady. I suppose I will have to watch the movie or read the book to see exactly what it was like, although I must admit there are many other books and movies that I would rather see first.

Back on the road and after a brief stop on the side of the road near Mataranka to receive and send all our emails we headed towards our free camp some 50 kilometres down the road. We reached the free camp called Warloch Rest area at about 12-30pm and on the way had decided that we would have lunch there when we arrived. Tee whipped me up a couple of toasted cheese and tomato sandwiches while she had some sardines on her favourite crackers. I managed to drop one of my toasted sandwiches onto my foot which both burnt my toes and pissed me off. But under the' 3 second rule' I ate it all the same, albeit less a bit of its content which remained on my toes until my tummy was full.

This place was quite yucky and although our budget usually dictated our terms of travel, we both decided that we would prefer to move on. This would mean that we would probably end up going to the Daly Waters Pub and stay in their caravan park. We were going to do this tomorrow as we had been told that the Daly Waters Barra and Beef was an experience not to miss. They apparently have a special deal where you get two meals and a campsite overnight for $52.00.

Back on the road and emotionally happy, if not financially, we soon came across the town of Larrimah. Now this place is freaksville if I ever saw it, as it boasts a bright pink pub and caravan park along with some other amazing establishments. We noticed that on all the signboards on the way into Larrimah from Mataranka that part of the sign had been covered up. Because we knew that the fuel symbol was generally located where the sign had been covered up, we presumed that the petrol station had shut down in Larrimah. We also saw a sign advertising a home-made cake and pie shop that had far too much writing on it for us to read at 80 kilometres per hour and would be a blur to someone travelling at the speed limit of 130 kilometres per hour. When we arrived at Larrimah the first place we saw was a home with 20 signboards out front, and the equivalent to a novel written on each board. We did not need to be rocket scientists to match this place to the signboard down the highway a bit. And even upon matching the two it did not heighten our impulses to any degree, let alone enough to visit the place.

In the distance we spotted the pink panther pub and caravan park and headed towards it. As we got closer, we thought it a waste of time to drive in there until I saw a giant stubby that I wanted to photograph. This place had a free Zoo and a bunch of freaks sitting in front of it and Tee remarked that perhaps they had escaped from the Zoo or perhaps it may have been a free-range Zoo. We both laughed as we got the fuck out of there.

As we drove out, we saw the reason why the fuel sign was missing from all the highway signs for Larrimah as the fuel station was half demolished. We laughed at how all the advertising signs were still up and even the toilet inside sign was being proudly displayed. At first, we though it had burnt down but with no telltale black markings we were not sure. There were odd things for sure though – we were glad to get the hell out of Larrimah.

Our next stop would be Daly Waters and hopefully we would stay there overnight and take advantage of their $52.00 feed and stay package which included a feed of Beef and Barra. The Daly Waters Pub and Caravan Park is some two kilometres off the Stuart Highway and we turned off at the signpost. As we approached, we started to get a little disappointed with the look of the place and our gut feelings told us we would probably not stay here tonight. The concept of the place was great and it, I am sure, is a great tourist destination as the pub is decked out with bras, hats, and all other nick knacks. But for Tee it was a reminder of her life with her ex-husband with all shit lying around everywhere. I think the best way to describe the place is like a man's back yard shed where he and his mates go to get away from their wives. I think a lot of people who have never seen a place like this would love it as it is quite unique. But with no sign of the special $52.00 deal we were told about we decided just to look around and then head off to the next free camp that is located on the outskirts of Elliot.

The fuel price at the Daly Waters Pub was $1.76 per litre and I thought this a bit steep so with Elliot within our range of fuel we pushed on. As we turned onto the highway, we spotted another fuel station so I pulled in to check their fuel price. At $1.64 per litre I pulled in and filled up. After another hour of driving through a very uninteresting landscape we finally reached the Newcastle Waters Rest Area a little before 5-00pm. We were immediately shocked at how many vehicles were in this small rest area as it must have numbered over 40. We were even more shocked though after we drove through and found no spot to park. I suppose we should not have been shocked though as it was now about 300 kilometres since the last free rest area. During these 300 kilometres I can recall seeing at least five truck rest areas all of which were empty. I will let you draw your own conclusions on this.

The beer that Tee had put into the freezer some 30 minutes ago would have to come out now and we decided that we had no choice but to continue onto Elliot and stay in their Caravan Park. With this Tee went to the fridge to remove the beers from the freezer so they didn't pop. But as she did so I spotted a turnoff that opened up into a large storage area for road gravel. As it was set well off the road and looked quite OK, I told Tee to come back to the front and I would check it out. The place was great and we found a cosy little corner to park Lizzie, who was also happy as she had taken us a long way today and needed a rest.

Day **249**

After an absolutely amazing nights sleep that saw us in bed by 8-00pm and sleep until 6-00am we awoke to a much cooler climate than we have endured over the past couple of months. There were a few cooler days but you could count them on one hand and this morning it was 12 degrees when we got out of bed. In fact, we both felt a bit chilly and it took us a little while to part with the company of our Doona. This gravel spot was better than many designated rest areas that we have stopped in as we were on our own last night and the big trucks on the highway were a fair distance from us as they passed.

We got going by 7-45am with the intention of stopping in Elliot for a while. We should get Internet access there and catch up with our emails while I also wanted to do some writing. We reached Elliot by a little after 8-30am and we pulled up next to the local park. Tee pulled out her novel while I grabbed the computer to check our emails and catch up with things. I went for a walk to find a toilet rather than empty all the chairs and table out of ours, but the ones in the park were locked. I continued my walk into the town itself but even the service stations didn't allow for the use of their toilets to the public. I am not sure why but I can only guess that they get flocked by tourists wanting to use them but don't buy fuel there. I can understand that, as if they don't keep a lid on that sort of stuff, they will end up council workers, without the pay cheque. In the end I had to empty our toilet / shower cubical and go there – oh well I needed a walk.

As the morning progressed more and more Aborigines entered the park and by 10-30am there was over one hundred of them. They were no bother though and Tee and I quietly went about reading and writing. We stayed here until after lunch and in fact left about 1-00pm to travel the 180 kilometres to our next free camp which was just short of three ways and about 90 kilometres from Tennant Creek. The scenery was similar most of the way but we are now seeing Spinifex Grass again and there have been some red rock areas that have broken up the travelling a bit. We also had to battle through a strong South Easterly breeze which Lizzie was less than impressed with but she was cool when I backed off the throttle and sat on 80 kilometres per hour.

We arrived at Attack Creek free camp about 3-30pm and were not surprised to see it was also close to full. This time though we did manage to find a reasonable spot where we set up camp for the evening.

Day **250**

E ven though we were close to the highway and the free camp was full we got a great night's sleep. I think that the main reason for this is that the weather has cooled down as we head south which makes sleeping more pleasant. It also allows us to sleep with the windows closed and thus reducing all the outside noise that is often responsible for our waking up during the night. We soon got ready for our travels and left Attack Creek Rest Area around 8-30am.

The morning air was cool and fresh and provided us with an excuse to put on our jumpers, something that we have not done for quite some time. We soon were passing Three Ways which is the T-intersection that crosses into North Queensland. We stopped and took a photo of a memorial there but continued straight as our journey was taking us towards Alice Springs and beyond to South Australia.

The next stop was just short of Tennant Creek at the old Telegraph Station where we got out and had a look around. We were both so amazed that someone had lived here as the conditions, even in this mild time of year, were harsh so one could only imagine how harsh they would have been in the middle of summer and over one hundred years ago. We also read that they only received supplies every six months by Camel Train from Port Augusta. We had a good look around at this fascinating piece of history before heading off towards Tennant Creek itself.

But again, just short of Tennant Creek we spotted another place of interest, Lake Mary Ann where we stopped for a cup of Coffee and to fill up our house water. The place was lovely as there was green grass and picnic tables everywhere. We have found though that all the toilet blocks are locked up in these areas as we had seen in the town of Elliot also. We are not sure why this is but it is not nice to be ready to go and then are confronted by a locked gate. It is OK for us as we can use our onboard toilet, but for car travellers or people who just want to picnic here it could be a disaster. This place would be a lovely spot to stop for lunch but unfortunately it has just turned 11-00am and neither of us are hungry yet.

We continued into Tennant Creek to find the place swarming with Aborigines. They were well behaved but we were just surprised to see so many of them walking around town. I know that sound derogatory but they do have a reputation for causing mayhem in these sorts of towns and the bars and shutters all over town pay testament to my thoughts. We compared fuel prices at the four service stations in town and were surprised to see the price varied by nine cents per litre. After fuelling up we payed a visit to Battery Hill which is a gold mine and also houses Tennant Creek's Information Centre. It is located about two kilometres East of Tennant Creek central and worth a look. We had lunch in the car park there that afforded quite a nice view over the surrounding mountains and countryside. We were hoping to spend a bit more time in Tennant Creek but the main street was not that nice and walking around it did not appeal to us.

So, it was now off to the next free camp or perhaps we may even camp in the Devils Marbles Campground. With just over 100 kilometres to travel we arrived at the Bonney Well Rest Area about 2-00pm and although it was not a bad rest area it was close to the highway and we thought that the Devils Marbles Campground that is well off the highway would be a quieter place to sleep. With only 10 or so kilometres to the Devils Marbles we arrived in no time and were amazed by the place. This is definitely a "must see" spot and the rock formations are fascinating. After looking at many of the rock formations from the comfort of Lizzie we pulled up at the campground as we wanted to ensure we secured a place for tonight. We did this as the campground was already half full and the last few free camp areas have been packed. We parked next to another T3500 Motorhome like Lizzie that was no where near as pretty as Lizzie but the couple from NSW were lovely and we had a chat with them before I took off for a walk in the Marbles. Tee was not keen to go for a walk as she said she had seen enough and wanted to do her nails and hair. I wondered off by myself and walked through the entire place marvelling at its stunning beauty and taking over 50 photos.

After my walk we cooked up a feed of bacon and eggs for dinner and when it got dark, we retired to our Motorhome and watched one of the movies that we had purchased in Pine Creek.

Day **251**

After a good sleep I awoke at 5-00am to the flapping of our awning which I hadn't bothered to put away the night before. As it was still dark and very cold when I packed up the awning, I snuck back into bed to annoy Tee with my cold toes. Now both awake I made it up to Tee by making her a cuppa and we lay in bed until about 6-30am. Keen to get an early start though we soon got up and packed Lizzie up for our days travel. Neither of us were hungry yet so we took off at a bit before seven for our day's adventure.

On our way out of the Devils Marbles Campground we passed a dingo quietly sitting on the roadway. We stopped and took photos of him/her and presumed that it would quite regularly get fed by the travellers here. We took a few more photos of the Devils Marbles in the morning light before travelling to Wauchope where we stopped for some brekkie and I did some more writing. While at the Wauchope Rest Area, which is right in front of the Wauchope Hotel Tee washed her hair and did her make-up while I had some cornflakes for brekkie. We were taking our time as we wanted to go to Wycliffe Well and look at the UFO Centre there and figured that it would not open before 9-00am or maybe even later as it was a Sunday.

In fact, we didn't leave Wauchope until after 9-30am as I wrote quite a bit and Tee was enjoying her me-time. But with only 20 kilometres to Wycliffe Well we still arrived there before 10-00am. Turns out that this is not a UFO Centre, as such, but a Roadhouse/Caravan Park that is trying to cash in on the supposed UFO sightings in the area. It was quite entertaining though and very much in line with some of the crazy things people do in the bush to keep the tourists coming and I also suspect to keep themselves amused. The whole place is built in this area because it was a water well that the pioneers dug for their stock route and is still keeping the green grass growing today. Green grass is an advertised novelty out here, along with hot showers and shade. After exploring as much of this place as we could tolerate, we were soon back on the road and heading the short 80 kilometres or so that would find us at our next free camp.

With such a short distance to travel we soon found ourselves at the Taylor Creek Rest Area and we knew we were early as a group of young tourists were just packing up to START their days travelling. Mind you it was after 11-00am and we were trying to spread out our weekly travelling as we had already covered 1,000 kilometres. With two days and three nights left in the budget week we were keen to arrive in Alice Springs on Wednesday morning and in a new budget week. This means just over 300 kilometres of driving over the next few days which is a lovely amount at a leisurely pace.

After a little nap to make up for the very early wake up that our awning provided, I spent the day planning our travels over the next few weeks. This included a tour of Alice Springs, a string of gorges and the majestic Ayres Rock and the Olga's. We have decided not to go to Kings Canyon as we had been there a few years ago and it was a fair distance off track for us. But this may change when we are at Ayres Rock as we are pretty good as far as our schedule goes; in fact, we are probably about a week early in our travelling.

During the course of the day the Taylor Creek Rest Area filled up with heaps of caravans, which is to be expected as all the rests stops have been the same through the centre of Australia. The only thing is though that most are travelling north to escape the cold while we are going south to see this fabulous country.

Day **252**

Today is proof that the best made plans can come unstuck and we left the Taylor Creek Rest Area and headed towards McDouall Stuart Memorial Rest Area. On the way we passed through Barrow Creek which is more infamous than famous due to the mystery surrounding the Peter Falconio murder that occurred on its outskirts more than ten years ago. Shame really, as the small township has a fabulous Telegraph Station that looks in very good condition and the area is quite appealing, scenery wise that is.

With only a total of 100 kilometres to travel today we expected to be at the McDouall Stuart Memorial Rest Area by 10-30am and I could catch up with some writing. We also hoped that we could get internet reception there as it was close to the town of Ti–Tree which we know has reception. But when we arrived, we soon realized two things, one; it was not a nice place to stop for the night and two; it did not have internet reception. So, after a very short deliberation we were off towards the town of Ti-Tree and at least we would be able to receive our emails there.

Not much on the emails and all the bills seem up to date so after our cuppa and Tee having a toilet stop, we headed towards our next free camp option which was Prowse Gap another 50 kilometres down the highway. But when we arrived, we found another free camp that was less than attractive and we had to keep travelling. Option three would be Ryan's Well Rest Area and surely it would be a case of third time lucky. Not far before Ryan's Well we saw a turning to the town of Aileron and Tee remembered Val (Stan & Val from De Greys Rest Area) showing her pictures of the Aboriginal sculptures there and telling us to take a look.

Val was right in telling us that these sculptures were well worth a look as they were huge and they must be seen in real life to be fully appreciated. I know this now as the photos that I took of them did them no justice what so ever. We also visited an Aboriginal art shop there and were tempted to make a purchase as the works were brilliant.

But we just could not see how or where they would fit in our home and decided against our purchase even though the storekeeper told us to make any reasonable offer on anything we liked. In Aileron I also had a decision to make as it would be touch and go if I had enough fuel to reach Alice Springs. I was very tempted to run the gauntlet because the fuel was 30 cents per litre dearer here than it was in Alice Springs, but I caved on the risk factor and put $20.00 worth in to ensure we made the distance.

On arrival at option three (Ryan's Well) we were yet again confronted by a dustbowl that was no bigger than a basketball court and right on the highway. This time though we did have Ryan's Well and the Glen Maggie Homestead ruins to look at, so at least it was not a waste of time stopping there. After a brief walk around and a few photos we had almost resolved ourselves to the fact that we may find ourselves in Alice Springs tonight and not Wednesday morning as we planned. We did have two further free camps before Alice Springs though and we should stay positive.

Positive became the word as we passed Connor Well Rest Area which was worse than the last three and we were positively not staying there. And then our last option of the Tropic of Capricorn Rest Area also proved to be less than average. Now don't get me wrong we could have stayed in any one of these free camps but it would have meant a disrupted sleep and we wanted to arrive in Alice Springs fresh for a good walk around town.

You guessed it our plans were all out the window and we continued our journey into Alice Springs. On the outskirts of Alice, we stopped for a few photos at the Welcome to Alice rock sculpture and were soon in suburbia which seemed so strange after all this outback driving. Tee looked through our brochure books and as soon as we got into mobile range, she started ringing Caravan Parks to compare prices. I spotted Anzac Hill and drove Lizzie up the sharp climb that led us to a stunning aerial view of Alice and the surrounding MacDonnell Ranges. Tee got us a reasonably priced Caravan Park and set the Navigator with its address. Now if you have never been to Alice before Anzac Hill is a great place to start as it gives you an idea of the layout of the town and also a great taste of the surrounding landscape.

When we arrived at the Caravan Park, we were given a map of the available sites, told to take our pick and then come back and pay for it. It ended up that there were only three sites left as one had been taken by another couple who must have been given the same option just before us. Two of the remaining sites were in the middle of the permanent residents, which didn't appeal to us, and the last site was quite nicely positioned even though close to a side road. Obviously, we took the last site and I went off to pay for it while Tee sorted out the Motorhome for our stay.

When I got back from paying for the site Tee told me that I had missed all the excitement as when I had left an Apollo Motorhome had pulled in right beside us (in the same campsite) and the Swedish fellow driving had tried to claim the site. He told Tee that it was suppose to be empty and that she should move our Motorhome, to which Tee just smiled and said "too bad – fuck off". They took off in a huff and Tee just kept on smiling at them. Nice work Tee, they didn't expect that response I am sure. After setting up for the night I made a few phone calls to let all my family and friends know where we were and we went out to the local tavern for Dinner.

Day **253**

We always feel cheated when we stay at Caravan Parks as they are never better than most free camps and yet you pay handsomely for not very much. In fact, it is rare to find clean showers and you end up paying $30.00 plus just to plug in a power cord. The Alice Springs caravan Park was no exception and we were sorry that we didn't stay in one of the yucky free camps on the way into Alice as we would have been financially better off. Never mind as we have done it now and we are in Alice Springs and had a reasonable night's sleep.

The plan for today was to do a Heritage walk through Alice Springs, do a bit of shopping, fill up with fuel and head off to the West MacDonnell ranges after lunch. In fact, after we parked Lizzie in Alice we walked to Coles and did the shopping first so that when we got back, I could check the emails while Tee put the groceries away. I thought we had parked close to Coles but in fact it was quite a walk and, on the way, back the shopping bags got quite heavy. On our return to Lizzie Tee put all the shopping away, I checked my emails and soon we were off on our Alice Springs Heritage Walk. Now Alice Springs is an interesting place but not all that large and we completed the walk quicker than we expected. This turned out to be a good thing as we now had more time today to check out the MacDonnell Ranges.

The Mac Donnell Ranges are stunning and start in Alice itself. They extend for hundreds of kilometres to the West of Alice and with recent un-seasonal rain the scenery was very attractive. The first point of interest on our drive was John Flynn's Grave that we stopped at briefly and took a few photos. But it was scenery that we wanted to see and the next stop of Simpson's Gap gave us a taste of things to come. Tee and I had visited Simpson's Gap some seven years ago, not long after we met, and we both commented on how much greener the place was now compared to then. We also noticed a rock slide that we were sure had not been there last time we visited. The only way to know for sure was to check our old photos when we get home as we both remembered taking photos that would reveal our suspicions. Our walk to Simpson's Gap took us along the sandy river bed, which are a feature of the gorges as they are usually filled with White Gums that are of good size and width for the Northern Territory. We took photos all the way in, and on our return, we walked along the main path and admired the sheer cliff faces of the red ranges and the body of water that prevents all from passing through the gap.

After Simpson's Gap we jumped back into Lizzie and headed to Standley Chasm which upon memory of our last trip was a few dollars to enter. We had seen this place before and with a lot of cloud cover today and not being midday we decided if it was too expensive, we would not go in. In fact, it was now $10.00 per adult to get in which we thought was a bit steep as there was many other beautiful places to see that were no charge. As we had been here before we turned around to head for Serpentine Gorge and then our free camp for tonight. But it was after 3-00pm now and we thought it would be best to go directly to the free camp as they seem to fill quite quickly in the NT.

We saw a day area marked on the map that was also a lookout so we decided to have a quick look before heading to our free camp. As luck has it this was actually now a free camp and we found a lovely spot next to a Motorhome from NSW who had the prize spot overlooking the surrounding ranges. Our spot was still quite good though and we set up for the evening. John from the other Motorhome introduced himself and we had a quick chat before Tee and I had Dinner and went to bed early to watch a movie. The main reason we went to bed so early was that it was freezing cold and after Dinner we just wanted to warm our toes.

Day **254**

We finally awoke this morning at 8-00am after a massive ten-hour sleep. The reasons for our long sleep were a combination of the cold cloudy morning and the fact that it was pitch black and super quiet here all night. It is really amazing because for free we had a much better sleep than when we paid $32.00 in Alice the night before. After Brekkie we we're preparing to leave to discover more of the West Mac's when it began to rain. After a brief consultation Tee and I decided to make this a rest day as it would be no fun climbing through wet cloudy gorges.

I tried to write in the morning but I could not get into it and just before Lunch John asked if we wanted to hook into his generator as he was running it anyway. At first, I was polite and said no but thank you, but he said he was running it anyway so I agreed and thanked him again. We ended up having a cuppa (or two) with John and Margery in their Motorhome which was about twice the size of Lizzie and very plush. The rest of the day was very quiet as it drizzled on and off all day. We did have some young tourists turn up late and set up a tent a fair way from our Motorhome. They were fairly quiet in the evening, not out of courtesy but more because it was so cold and drizzly.

Day **255**

We knew it was too good to be true and at 6-00am the young tourists started their door slamming that woke us up and prevented us drifting back off to sleep. So, by 7-30am we decided we might as well get up even though it was only five degrees in the Motorhome. We had a big day planned and as the weather was due to improve by the afternoon, we were keen to get going by a reasonable time. All was running well and we were on track to leave our campsite by 9-00am but as we went to say our goodbyes to John and Margery we just got talking again.

Finally, off by 9-30am our first stop was to Ellery Creek Bighole that was on a dirt road but only a couple of kilometres it. The road was a bit corrugated but we took our time and Lizzie did her thing in her own time. The camp area here is quite nice and the amenities were very clean and did not look all that old. I made use of the toilet and then we made our way down to the waterhole on foot. The pathway to the waterhole was paved and much more sophisticated than the road into the area. It was not far to the waterhole and we took a number of photos of the gorge and waterhole which was bigger than Simpson's Gap in water storage but much smaller as a gorge. It was a lovely spot and well worth a visit.

Off to our next destination of Serpentine Gorge, and we cannot tell you what this is like as the dirt road was five kilometres long and too rough for Lizzie. We reluctantly turned back about 200 metres in and continued to the Ochre Pits, our next planned stop. The road into the Ochre Pits was all sealed and it was a 300-metre walk from the car park to the viewing platform. Nice spot for a quick look as the colours in the cliffs are quite amazing, but don't be tempted to paint your face with the Ochre as there is a $5,000.00 fine for doing so. Shame they don't fine the tourist the same amount for shitting in the bush as I see more harm in that, but anyway.

Again, to the next destination of Ormiston Gorge which has a lot of infrastructure at the base of it, including; a kiosk, an information centre, a modern toilet block and other outbuildings. We decided to take the Ghost Gum walk, and as we climbed the rim of the Gorge, we were glad that we did as the view was stunning. It is a great walk to go on as it loops down into the Gorge and you can walk back inside the Gorge for your return journey. There were a lot of steeps and loose rocks so it would be a difficult walk if you were elderly but for everyone else it is a "must do walk" in a "must see gorge".

Next was Glen Helen Gorge which has a Caravan Park / Accommodation place at its base and they even do well priced Helicopter flights over the Gorges. I think the cheapest was $55.00 which is very cheap for a helicopter ride. We walked to the Gorge which was nice but nowhere near as impressive as Ormiston and others we have seen. Not on the "must see" list but if you are out in the West Mac's you might as well have a look. With lunchtime passing we were quite hungry and decided to keep travelling until we found a quiet spot to eat. This came a few kilometres down the road when we turned into the Mt Sonder Lookout and parked Lizzie in a spot that afforded us a great view to eat lunch by.

Tee prepared a platter of cheese, crackers and many other nibbles while I took some photos, as the sun had now finally cracked through the persistent cloud cover. We ate and enjoyed the view and decided to visit one more Gorge before heading back to the same campsite that we had stayed in for the last two nights. While eating lunch we also noticed campers and caravans on the Finke River below us but the terrain was too sandy for Lizzie even though it looked like a lovely spot. The last Gorge on the road that eventually arrives in Kings Canyon is the Redbank Gorge and we turned off the main highway to reach it even though it was unsealed and five kilometres long. But it beat us about one kilometre in where it got rough and boggy and was really too risky for a girl like Lizzie.

Disappointed with the Gorges we missed but impressed with what we had seen we headed back to our campsite and arrived there about 4-30pm. We had hoped to get the spot that John and Margery had for the last two nights but we were beaten too it by a Caravanning couple from NSW. Never mind we got our old spot back that had served us well and we were glad to be getting another free night. I cooked up a feed of pasta for Dinner and we watched a movie in bed again as the evenings are amazingly cold.

Day **256**

It was inevitable that we would be disappointed with a day here and there in our travels and today would be one of those days. The East MacDonnell Ranges are ordinary compared to the West MacDonnell Ranges and the road past Corroboree Rock is substandard as a tourist destination. I say this as the sealed road is only one car width and you have to pull onto the gravel as cars approach. We were extremely lucky as a tour bus past us at speed and sprayed us with rocks and yet our windscreen was not damaged.

The day started well for us as we woke to -3 degrees outside and busied ourselves to keep warm (that's outside the sheets you perverted buggers). We were keen to get away early as we wanted to reach Alice Springs as the shops opened and do some grocery shopping as planned. We did exceptionally well and got going by 7-45am. The drive to Alice was about an hour and we got there a few minutes before 9-00am. We thought we may be lucky and get a car park near the Woolworths store but Alice is a bustling place and we had to settle for parking on the edge of town near the Todd River. The walk to Woolworths warmed us up and, on the way, I rang mum to let her know where we were. I also received and sent all my emails as we had been out of signal range for the best part of three days now. We did our shopping and went back to the Motorhome where I made some business phone calls while Tee packed away the shopping. By the time we got everything done it was almost 11-00am and we quickly headed off for the East MacDonnell Ranges. The time we left was cool though as we only intended on four stops in this area and in fact there is not a lot more anyway.

Last time we were in Alice (about seven years ago) we had spent a fair bit of time in this area and not much in the West MacDonnell's. On that trip we had seen camels out here and we kept a close lookout for them as they tend to blend into the scenery quite well. Although that may not be true on this occasion as it is so green here at the moment, whereas seven years ago it was as brown as - as – a camel ☺ Our first stop was at Emily's Gap which was quite nice but as I said before nowhere near as impressive as the West Mac's. We did meet a lovely elderly couple from Hervey Bay there who we chatted to for a good twenty minutes. The second stop was to her sister's gap I suppose, in Jessie's Gap which was slightly less impressive. We took a look around and were soon back in the Motorhome and off to Corroboree Rock.

I sound a bit negative about the place and if we had travelled here before we went to the West Mac's we probably would have been happier. But when the road changed to a single strip of bitumen and gravel either side we were not impressed and it made the trip a little ugly. We were so worried about getting a busted windscreen that we could not really relax and enjoy ourselves which added to the negativity. In fact, if it were not for the fact that we wanted to revisit Trephina Gorge we probably would have turned back when we saw the road narrow. On our previous visit we had a great time at Trephina Gorge as the place in our memories was very pretty and we saw flocks of wild Budgerigars while there.

We arrived at Corroboree Rock and did the walk around and took some photos. Tee suggested we have lunch here as it was after 12-30pm, but I said it may be better to carry on as the road may be quieter around lunchtime and it would lower our risk of windscreen damage. This proved to be wrong as a tour bus (the one I mentioned earlier) was the first vehicle we passed on the stupidly narrow road. We contemplated turning back and if it wasn't for our fond memories we probably would have. As it turned out it would have been the correct decision as 30 kilometres further on and within four kilometres from Trephina Gorge the road turned to rough gravel that was too much for Lizzie to handle.

Pissed off and hungry we turned back and headed for Alice Springs which was just over an hour away. What do you do when you are hungry and pissed off? – that's right – off to KFC in Alice for some greasy junk food. It was almost 3-00pm by the time we ate but the KFC made it all worthwhile and we soon laughed off the poor day and concentrated on the next leg of our journey. After fuelling up Lizzie in Alice we set of South toward Ayres Rock with the intention of stopping at the Mt Polhill Rest Area 68 kilometres south of Alice. When we arrived, we found a tiny Rest Area almost on the Highway that was already close to full. With no decent spot to stop I told Tee I wanted to keep on going to the next rest area as I didn't like it here. Tee was cool with that and even though it was almost 5-00pm off we went. For the second time as Tee was down the back getting us a cold water, I spotted a gravel pit that looked perfect for free camping in. With other campers already taking advantage of this much larger area that was well off the road we felt comfortable stopping here for the evening.

Day **257**

Another absolutely freezing night last night and even though we didn't check our temperature gauge when we awoke, we were both sure it was colder than last night, which was -3 degrees. With only a short distance to travel today and no sightseeing to do we stayed in bed until after 8-00am when Tee braved the cold to make us a cuppa. I spent the morning writing while Tee did a few chores before checking out her new novel by Jackie Collins.

We set off for the days travel around 11-00am with the intention of travelling about 70 kilometres to the next free camp area. With such a short distance to travel we did not expect too much of a change in landscape and were pretty much bang on with our prediction with only a subtle change. It was not long before we arrived at the Finke River Rest Area and pulled in for a good look at it. At first, we thought it was OK but after having lunch there we decided to move on as it was too close to the bridge and the thumping as trucks crossed would not be good for our sleep. We can both handle the sounds of trucks passing in the night but the thumping echo noise as they cross a bridge wakes us both up.

So off again to the next free camp, which was another 50 kilometres down the track and not far from the turnoff to Ayres Rock. The Desert Oaks Rest Area did not look too flash at first but when we perched up the back of it, we good a great outlook and felt really comfortable. This Rest Area also had water so Tee thought she would take the opportunity to do some washing. I filled up the house water to keep up with her demands and then made a makeshift clothesline for the finished results. Tee took care of the rest while I wrestled to read my latest book, a hand me down from Tee, called "Men are from Mars and Women are from Venus." OMG, I have never been as confused in all my life as I cannot commit to being a total Martian, and when Tee told me that this is normal, I became more confused. I will have to keep reading this book and hope that it will all become clearer to me.

The washing dried, I got a bit more of my book read and we both enjoyed a cool sunny day in the centre of this fascinating country.

Day **258**

Well I would not have believed it if someone had told me but it was even colder this morning than the last few nights. The proof in this came by the zero reading on our internal temperature gauge and when I peeped out the back window from the warmth of our bed (with 2 doona's and 1 blanket), there to my amazement was frost, settled on our bike cover. With a fair bit of travelling to do today, by our standards, we got ready to hit the road and the quick movement helped to thaw the bones. We were not super early in leaving but did hit the road by 8-30am which is pretty good when bed is so tempting.

Even though we had a fair amount of fuel in the tank we thought it wise to top up at the Dessert Oaks Roadhouse which is still on the main road to Adelaide. The next place would be at Yulara which is the entrance to Ayers Rock National Park where we would 'have to' get fuel if we didn't top up here. And as we have experienced remote fuel prices in Lake Argyle and other places, we know how expensive this could be. We also wanted to stay within the budget this week so a slow crawl to Ayres Rock will be in order.

The fuel price at the Dessert Oaks Roadhouse did my theory no justice as at $1.94 per litre it was a full 35 cents per litre dearer than in Alice Springs. This is unjustifiable to me and constitutes a consumer rip off. I feel for the locals who already have to tolerate large distances and to be slugged at the bowsers must rub salt into the wound. But the chance for us of the prices being lower at Yulara was extremely remote in fact we were sure they would be much higher. It will be interesting to see the price of fuel there. We also stopped here to check our emails and see if any more bills had arrived before heading off again. The Desert Oaks Roadhouse is on the T-intersection of the road to Ayres Rock (Lasseter Highway) and the road to this point has had green grass on its edges all the way from Alice. For some reason we expected the green grass to magically disappear as we turned onto the Lasseter Hwy as this was Ayres Rock we were going to and it was in the middle of the dessert. But contrary to our fanciful imaginations the green grass continued with only the rare patch of red desert exposed and usually where it had been burnt out.

We continued on out journey towards Ayres Rock very mindful of our fuel consumption and not far before the turnoff to Kings Canyon the unbelievable happened. We got a star crack on our windscreen, and on a good sealed road while travelling at slow speed. We could not believe it as we had almost expected it to happen in the East MacDonnell Ranges where the road was almost designed to bust windscreens, but not here. Fortunately, I still have the repair kit I bought in Broome which still has resin in it and I will be able to fix it at our next overnight rest stop. It still pissed us off though and we pulled over to cover the chip with a special patch that is supplied with the kit.

Not long after that unfortunate incident we spotted the Kernot Range Rest Area that looked quite nice and decided it would be a nice place to stop on our way back to Stuart Highway. We passed the turnoff to Kings Canyon and decided to pull over for lunch at the Mt Connor Lookout. Last time we were here I mistook Mt Connor for Ayres Rock which I thought was an easy mistake on my first visit even though people around me on that particular bus tour thought it funny.

We ate lunch at the Lookout which consisted of some leftover dinners that we needed to consume while they were still eatable. While there we met a couple from Jimboomba Queensland which is near where Lizzie comes from and we chatted for a while before heading off to our next camp spot. They had never been free camping before and seemed nervous about doing it, so I said they could join us at our campsite so they could get a taste for it with someone they knew, (if even only slightly). We passed Curtin Springs and saw the Jimboomba's couple's car and van there and immediately thought they had chickened out and decided to stay at the Caravan Park at Curtin Springs.

We reached the Sandy Way Rest Area that is about 45 kilometres from the Rock itself and a fantastic spot to work from to see the area. The campsite itself is not on the road but over the red sand dunes which are on a track that appears from behind the facilities of what we thought was the campsite at first. Sounds tricky but the track is good and as long as you stay off the soft sand and the vegetation any vehicle can get down there. We found a spot that we thought was OK and decided to go for a walk to the sand hills to the West of our campsite, as I had a feeling we would be able to see Ayres Rock from its elevated position.

It was a pleasant walk in which we admired the native flowers and trees and Tee even spotted some Dingo tracks. My thoughts as we approached the sand hill was "please don't let there be a larger sand hill in front of this one", and to our fortune there was not. This gave us a lovely view of Ayres Rock and the bonus of viewing the Olga's also. It was so lovely here as we had the extra added bonus of being alone while viewing this amazing site. Well we thought we were alone until we turned to see the maker of those Dingo tracks who appeared to be chasing food. We took some photos of the Dingo but more of the impressive view and as we returned to Lizzie the Dingo took off with a disappointed look on his face.

When we returned to Lizzie, I told Tee I was not happy with the position of the Motorhome and that I would look for a better spot. When I found this spot, Tee agreed and we moved Lizzie to it before it was taken by another camper. Now settled, Tee started setting up camp while I repaired the windscreen crack. This task should now have been simpler for me as I had done it before but the darn flies made sure my second attempt at windscreen repair would be an unpleasant one. They seem to know when you have both your hands full and take full advantage of it. Soon after the couple from Jimboomba turned up and I directed them to a spot behind us and we chatted for a while. Tee and I then settled in for the evening (away from the flies) and we ended up watching a movie in bed as we anticipated a cold night again.

Day **259**

Last night did not get as cold as it has been as the cloud cover had built up late in the evening. This was good in one way but it now meant that our time at Ayres Rock would not be in bright sunshine like we had hoped. We set off at a little before 9-00am and were both really looking forward to the day. We soon arrived at Yulara which is a small town at the entrance to the Uluru National Park, where we found the Dump Point we needed quite urgently. I emptied the shitter and we were off again to see the wonderful Monolith that we had travelled so far to see.

We soon reached the Park entrance and forked out the $25.00 each to enter. The lady there was very helpful and we took off to enjoy our day. Our first stop was at the Sunset car park as we would have Internet reception here and as a bonus Optus had provided us some phone reception also. We both made phone calls and sent text messages to family and friends while I also received all my emails and checked for more nasty bills.

Off again and we visited the Cultural Centre to have a quick look and have a toilet break. As we drove to these places we stared in amazement at the size and characteristics of this magnificent product of nature. Ayres Rock is simply amazing and even though on our second trip here, it does not take away the thrill of seeing it in all its glory. Rain hail or shine this place is a definite "must see" and no trip around Australia would be complete without a visit.

After the Cultural Centre, which is quite interesting but not what we get excited about, we headed directly to the Rock itself. The climb of the rock was closed due to the chance of rain so we decided to do the 10.4

kilometre walk around it. The weather was still very cold so we rugged up and I took a backpack so we could take water and take off our jumpers if we got too warm. The walk around the rock is on a good level track and it gives the Rock a whole different perspective. We both thoroughly enjoyed it even though we had sore legs at the end of it.

When we arrived back at Lizzie, we had some lunch and as we had no brekkie this morning, we both ate heaps. Just as we were finishing lunch, I noticed that they had opened the rock climb and I was keen to do it. Tee had said earlier that climbing the rock again did not interest her but I was keen. Thing was though, because I had just walked over ten kilometres and had just completed a big feed it was not the ideal time to attempt such a climb.

Never the less I headed towards the start of the climb up Ayres Rock and with a heap of enthusiasm I might add. This was soon knocked out of me as I reached the chain section of the climb and started to feel the effects of my 10 kilometre walk just before lunch. For the first one hundred meters of the climb I had been like a jack rabbit, more out of determination than good fitness. But I soon slowed right down and was glad to see another fellow about my age stopped and sitting down for a breather. I joined him and we chatted about how easy it looks from the bottom but how difficult the climb was once you started it.

By this stage my legs were feeling like jelly and we sat and chatted for about five minutes before another group of climbers needed to pass us. The group was a family from Korea and included two daughters and a mother and father. The daughters were in their 20's and could speak good English but the parents spoke very little English. The girls were climbing well as was the mother but Papa was struggling a bit and I could see it in his face. I said to him 'come sit for a while and join the old farts club!' He repeated what I said to his daughter who translated it to him in Korean. I knew he understood when he came and sat next to me and with a big smile on his face said 'Ha Ha – old farts club – pointing to the three of us. Then his daughter started to photograph us and taught me my first Korean word "Chijeu" which means "cheese". He was doing well on the climb for someone who had bad knees and was 58 years of age but as I kept climbing my two 'old fart' friends decided enough was enough and started to descend the rock.

As determined as I was to climb Ayres Rock, I was only a third of the way up when my new friends turned around, and realistically I should have attempted it tomorrow. But I feared that it would not be open tomorrow as the weather forecast was not favourable. I decided to do it slowly having plenty of rest breaks along the way and this gave me the encouragement to keep going. But when I reached about the halfway mark, I observed a young fellow who seemed to be struggling coming down. He told me it was harder coming down than going up which made me think I should call it quits and hope that the weather stayed OK and I could do it tomorrow. Then I was saved by a French Nurse who was a little younger than me, who said 'that is rubbish, coming down is easy'. Onwards and upwards and with my new walking companion I forgot about the difficulty of the task and the pain in my legs by chatting and being determined to complete the climb.

After many rest stops and a lot of encouragement, I made it all the way and was very pleased that I had. Seven years ago, when Tee and I did the climb it was difficult but we were both smoking then and put it down to that. I suppose I should be well pleased with my efforts, and I am, but I have vowed to improve my fitness when we return home. The decent was easy as my walking partner had said and I was soon back at Lizzie and Tee was proud that I had achieved what I said I would. She was disappointed that she could not get the spare camera to work and did not take any photos of me on the rock. But I had photos from the top of Ayres Rock and that was enough for me. Back on level ground Tee and I headed to the sunset viewing area to get another look at the Rock and tossed up the idea of staying until sunset. But the cloud cover was strong and we had nearly 200 photos of Ayres Rock from just today alone and we decided to head back to our free camp.

We expected the campsite to be full but it was emptier than yesterday and we parked Lizzie in the same spot we had stayed in yesterday. It was now early in the evening so we ate leftovers for Dinner before retiring to bed and watching a movie.

Day **260**

The entry into Uluru National Park is a three-day pass and we always only expected to use two days of the pass. The first day was for Ayres Rock and today would be dedicated to the Olga's which Tee and I feel are extremely underrated. As I was well behind in my writing, I asked Tee if we could start our Olga experience at about 11-00am which would give me a good solid couple of hours to write. Tee was happy with this and all was good until I went to start Lizzie ---- and ------NOTHING! We had had a bit of trouble starting her over the past few days but had changed the charger to charge directly into main battery rather than the House batteries which we thought was the problem. Fortunately, on those two occurrences we started her by diverting to the house batteries via a switch that Ken (the previous owner) had installed under the dash.

But this time we had nothing even when the switch was pressed. This was not good and I was in a bit of a panic as we had no phone reception and were parked in Sand Dunes in the middle of nowhere and all the other vehicles had left for the day. I lifted the lid on the Battery compartment to see a cable had worked loose and on tightening it I was able to get Lizzie started via the House Batteries. This solved the problem for today but it meant that the main battery was stuffed and would need replacing, sooner rather than later.

On the road and I filled the house water at the top section of the free camp before we headed back into Uluru National Park and the Olga's. There is quite a misconception around that Ayres Rock is a short drive from Alice Springs (468 Klm's) and that the Olga's are next to Ayres Rock

(58.8 Klm's). By the time we reached the Olga's I had settled down a bit about Lizzie's battery problem and had come up with a plan on where to buy the replacement battery from. The whole journey we have battled to stay within the budget, not because we have been extravagant or gone on commercial tours, but because of breakdowns.

Lizzie is not a young girl and upon reflection I think we should have had a separate $5,000.00 budget for incidental repairs. This sounds like a lot and you might say we should have bought a new vehicle to travel in. But it would cost $120,000.00 to have a new version of Lizzie and still there would be no guarantees that we wouldn't have problems. In addition, we would have paid more than $5,000.00 in stamp duty, let alone the depreciation. Tee and I still believe that despite the inconveniences and expense that Lizzie has been a very wise purchase and we love her.

Our first stop was at the Dune Viewing area which provided a lovely distant overview of the Olga's and a taste of things to come. After a number of lovely photos, we continued to the Olga's and stopped at a second viewing / picnic area that had toilets and fresh drinking water, both of which we took advantage of. Off again and to our first walk which was to the Valley Of The Winds and with my legs still like jelly we decided to do the 2.2-kilometre Lookout walk and not the full 7.4 Kilometre Grade 4 walk. On our walk we met a lovely couple from Dromana Victoria (Steve and Caroline) who we chatted to while marvelling at the scenery.

When back at the car park we had a platter for late lunch before heading to our second walk which was a little longer at 2.6 kilometres but equally as impressive. We again met up with Steve and Caroline on this walk (Walpa Gorge) and back at the Motorhome I gave him one of my business cards so we could keep in touch. We have met some lovely people on our travel and hope to keep in touch with all of them.

It was now 4-00pm and we decided to head to the Ayres Rock sunset viewing area, not to see the sunset but because it has good phone and internet reception. Once there I made a few calls and priced a new battery for Lizzie. I was glad I did as they are only $200.00 and before I got a price, I had conjured up a price of over $300.00 in my head and was quite disturbed about its impact on the budget. We again decided not to stay for the sunset as it was again cloudy and with over 300 photos taken in the past two days enough was enough. Both Ayres Rock and the Olga's have made our "must see" list and we would include Kings Canyon. The only reason we are not going there is because of distance and fuel costs as fuel here is over \$2.00 per litre, oh and of course we have been there before.

We headed back to our campsite for a third night in a row as light rain began to fall. As we arrived, we were pleased to see that again the campsite was still quite empty. We found a better spot than the previous two nights and enjoyed a great sleep until early the next morning.

Day **261**

At 5-45am we were awoken by the young couple in the Maui Motorhome that was parked next to us. They had moved their Motorhome as heavy rain began to fall in fear that they may get trapped in the sand dunes that was our campsite. Even though warm in bed and not wanting to brave the cold I thought this a very sensible idea and forced myself to get up. I told Tee to stay in bed and that I would just move Lizzie up to the top Car park (bitumen). Lizzie braved the cold and started immediately, which made me think that she also wanted "out of there!" Once at the top car park I rejoined Tee back in our warm bed and slept lightly until about 7-30am.

After getting all organized, we hit the road about 9-00am and planned to reach the SA border by this evening. But first port of call was the Curtin Springs Roadhouse to fill up with fuel or if it was too expensive to buy enough to get us to the Desert Oaks Roadhouse on the Stuart Highway. Well at $2.16 per litre it was the bare minimum of fuel being purchased here by these two little black ducks. We put $30.00 worth in and were on our way as we thought this would be enough to get us there and buy fuel for $1.97 per litre. Tee and I cannot see how they can justify these prices as Alice Springs have fuel at $1.59 per litre and is only 362 kilometres away from Curtin Springs.

What seemed to be the right amount of fuel to get us from Curtin Springs to the Desert Oaks Roadhouse turned out to be a nail-biting experience as we just made it with the gauge reading under empty as we arrived. I told Tee what I had done about 20 kilometres away from Desert

Oaks so she could join in the thrill. Not impressed she said I was putting us at risk for the sake of a couple of dollars and she was not impressed.

Never in doubt! And we filled up before checking our emails, eating lunch and having a chat to a fellow from Victoria who had a Motorhome just like Lizzie. We arrived at the SA / NT border where we relaxed and read our books for the afternoon. You will be pleased to know that I am now starting to understand my book (Men are from Mars – Women are from Venus) and hope that my new skills will keep me in the good books with Tee. Well maybe not with the fuel incident still fresh in Tee's mind.

Day **262**

Another cold night last night and even though the gauge read 5 degrees I was freezing as I had not put the second blanket on. I expected Tee to be the same but she was fine and I had to get up and move around to warm up. Mind you it was after 8-00am when we woke, so by the time I got ready it was well after 9-30am. I got a bit cocky starting Lizzie and tried to do it from the outside of the vehicle. But this proved to be a huge mistake as I must have flooded her or something and she didn't want to start. I must admit panic did set in as the thought of spending a week here waiting for the batteries to recharge flashed through my head. Fortunately, I got Lizzie started and with my heart still in my mouth we headed of to Marla in South Australia where we could get internet reception and I could use the computer and invertor without fear of being stuck with a flat battery.

At Marla I got the news that Kevin Rudd was Prime Minister again and had a chat to some of the locals in the Roadhouse where I heard the news. I then made my way back to Lizzie where Tee had made some lunch and we ate. After lunch Tee read her book and I did two solid hours of writing to catch up.

We left Marla at about 3-30pm with the intention of travelling another 100 kilometres or so where we would have the choice of three camping areas. Nothing much to report scenery wise and we reached the first camping site (Matheson's Bore) a little after 5-00pm. It was nothing flash but there was a lot of room here and it was a fair distance off the highway also. In the past we have pushed on in these situations hoping that the next stop would be better, the end result usually being disappointment rather than joy. This time we decided to stick to this site as it was fairly good and already had a few caravans parked here. We set up camp and looked forward to a good evening and a quiet night's sleep.

Day **263**

L ast night was very quiet when we went to bed and remained that way until we were awoken at 11-30pm by some young foreign tourists. They entered the camp area and did two full circuits with their lights on full beam before stopping behind the caravan on the opposite side of the campsite to us. Then they proceeded to set up camp and with four of them banging their doors shut time and time again we were assured of a disrupted sleep until the early hours of the morning. The couple that they parked next to must have been more annoyed than we were but at night the door banging echoes for a fair distance. I will not keep going on about these inconsiderate individuals but to say that they are very selfish. Even though our sleep was less than ideal we looked forward to visiting Coober Pedy as we had heard a lot of good things about it. Not that the place is suppose to be pretty but that it is very unique. Lizzie was a good girl this morning and started with no major problems via the House Batteries. With 110 kilometres to Coober Pedy we should arrive there around 10-30am and with that we were on our way. As we were leaving the Awful Foursome were also about to head off which surprised us as they had been up until 2-00am.

The scenery from here to Coober Pedy was very flat and quite uninteresting and after about thirty minutes on the road we were passed by the Awful Foursome in their clapped-out Nissan Patrol. Soon after that they pulled into another rest area which had tank water and no doubt were stopping for breakfast. The fuel level in the Motorhome was getting quite low as we had now done almost 500 kilometres since our last fill. As we approached the Breakaways on the outskirts of Coober Pedy we were faced with a difficult decision as to whether or not we should visit them. But when we reached the dirt road and the 11-kilometre signpost we decided against it. Turns out it was a good decision as we only just made it to Coober Pedy and the extra 22-kilometre round trip to the Breakaways would have left Lizzie short.

Short of Coober Pedy you are left in no doubt as to what they do in this town as the 20 kilometres on the northern side of town is loaded with what looks like giant ant hole mounds. In fact, it looks like a pile of one-man operations gone nuts and both Tee and I were surprised as to why it was like that and not a big open cut run by big business. Turns out I never asked that question while in town so I can't give you an answer. When we pulled into town the first stop was to get fuel (obviously) and at $1.68 per litre we were very happy. As we were getting fuel the Awful Foursome pulled up behind us to also fill up. As small as my revenge was, I took a long time filling up and kept them waiting as long as I could.

We pulled up next in front of the Information Centre where I received in our emails and made some family calls while Tee went in and got us some brochures. There are a number of tours around and if you don't know this already, Coober Pedy is famous as an underground town. In fact, some of the facts that we were told by the owners of Faye's Underground Home is that 80% of the townspeople live underground and that the population of 4,000 is made up of 57 different nationalities. I am not sure of the accuracy of this but there you go.

The Aboriginals that were in town seemed pretty spaced out, which is in line with what we had heard and the town itself is very untidy. We decided to walk around town on a self guided tour and had planned to visit one of the underground paid attractions. Our first stop was in an Opal shop (above ground) that was owned by a lovely Greek fellow who talked us into a purchase. Tee picked out an Opal Broach for my mother who has been doing so much for us while we have been away.

We then visited an underground Opal shop and we were both fascinated by the uniqueness of the structures. We ended up visiting a few more underground establishments before heading back to Lizzie for a cuppa and a spell.

After our cuppa we drove to Faye's Underground Home and after paying the $5.00 entrance fee was given a guided tour by its owner. Colin did a fabulous job of describing the history of Coober Pedy and his home was truly unique. In fact, Coober Pedy goes on our "must see" list, not for its beauty but its total uniqueness and if you are interested in seeing how people live underground then Faye's Underground Home is a great showcase for that.

It was now 3-00pm and we headed out of town to our next campsite called Hutchison Memorial, 12 kilometres South of town. On the way we noticed pipes sticking out of the ground some with Satellite dishes next to them and soon realized that these were more underground homes. In fact, there were clusters of them so one could only call it a subdivision. Very Very unique place.

Day **264**

Now today we originally were still going to be in Coober Pedy, but yesterday afternoon we decided we had seen enough and also decided against paying to stay in town. We were then going to head to half way between Coober Pedy and Port Augusta today but realized that this would put us in Port Augusta on a Sunday. This would be no good as we had planned to get Lizzie's new battery in Port Augusta and had to be there on a week day. Never mind we decided to use the day as a rest day and catch up with all our chores. I got a heap of paperwork done and Tee spent the day reading and making cups of coffee. It was like our Sundays at home together and we both really enjoyed it. We plan to head off in the morning and the following day we would be in Port Augusta where we would get Lizzie's new battery.

Day **265**

Well I did a little too much paperwork yesterday as it turns out, and this morning as we got ready to leave for the day disaster struck. No matter how much I begged, Lizzie just would not start as her battery was completely dead and I had run the house batteries down too low yesterday. The morning was very cold and we thought that by 10-00am it would warm up enough to start Lizzie. It was also sunny so the solar panels would give us the charge we needed to get going. That was the plan but by 11-00am we still had not got Lizzie started. Every time we tried to start her; she was just short of the starting line. At 8-00am I was confident that we would be going by 10-00am as it was a clear sunny morning and for this reason, I did not ask for help from other campers who were nearby. At 9-30am I went to ask the last camper still there for help, only to see them driving off and too far for me to yell out to them.

After a failed attempt (about the fifth) at 11-00am I decided to leave it until about 2-00pm before trying again so that the solar panels could put a big charge into the house batteries and Lizzie would have more assistance to start. We were all alone in an open area of near desert and about 12 kilometres from Coober Pedy. I thought of back up options and decided that if Lizzie did not start at 2-00pm that I would ride my push bike into town to get help. We had phone reception and internet so we were not in fear for our lives or anything but it was still a very unsettling situation.

I could not help myself and at 12-00 noon I decided to give Lizzie another crack. This time I pushed the accelerator to the floor as I tried to start the old girl and wallah she started. Tee and I were beside ourselves and we both hugged each other with joy. We let Lizzie warm up a bit and then hit the road. Fortunately, we had a lot of travelling to do today and this would give the house batteries a good charge. But as it was now midday, we did not have enough time to reach Port Augusta in daylight. We could push on and drive at night but we would be rushed and we both felt that the 350 kilometres of driving that we have planned would be enough to fill the house batteries and get Lizzie started in the morning. At this point I decided that we would buy a generator as this would have been all avoided had we had one. In addition, I could ensure that Tee was warm by using it to run the heater on these freezing nights. I would purchase it outside the budget as it was not really only for this trip, and to buy it with budget money would put too much strain on both of us.

Our intended destination for today was the Island Lagoon Lookout Rest Area which sounded like it may be on a hill. This would form the basis of Plan B if Lizzie did not start on battery power as we could roll and jump start her. Fortunately, the landscape was quite bland as we had a fair distance to travel and as we wished to reach Port Augusta on the one tank, we would have to drive Lizzie at about 80 Kilometres per hour. This plan was being tested by the slight southerly wind that was pushing in Lizzie's face and meant that it would be unlikely that we would achieve our goal. The landscape changed dramatically around Lake Hart and the lake itself was quite spectacular. We stopped and took a heap of near sunset photos at the Lake itself that had a fair amount of water in it. We also considered staying here for the night but thought it best to drive on as we were still a fair way from Port Augusta. At the town of Pimba, which we were rapidly approaching, we had a decision to make. Either we bought fuel or took the risk of making Port Augusta on what we had. With the concerns of the batteries not turning over Lizzie we thought we did not need more issues (like running out of fuel). We most probably would have made it but if the headwinds picked up, perhaps we wouldn't, so we pulled into Spud's Roadhouse to buy fuel.

It was a choice that we were both pleased with and I put $20.00 worth in to ensure fuel to Port Augusta would not be an issue. At the Roadhouse they had a free camp and we made another change to our plans by deciding to stay here the night. Our logic was that if we couldn't start Lizzie in the morning we were at a roadhouse and had easy access to help. We pulled up Lizzie next to an old fella (Des O'Shea) and his dog named Red, and yes, he was a red kelpie like the one in the movie. Des told me that he was named before the movie and that he was a full working dog, now semi retired. They were off to a secret location East of Tenant Creek to fossick for gold. I continued to talk to Des as Tee made a new best bud in Red who sat on her feet while she pats him.

Turns out Des was a Real Estate Agent from Shepparton and when I mentioned John from Kyabram, he told me that he had sold Johns family farm. I had also sold property for John in Queensland (his investment properties) as well as some for his sister. It never ceases to amaze me as to who you meet on the road and Des and I had a good chin wag for over an hour.

Day **266**

A new morning, a new financial year and a new battery for Lizzie – today would be a great day. Although a little noisy at the roadhouse Tee and I had a fairly good sleep and when we were ready to go, we thought we may visit Woomera first. First turn and Lizzie was away taking us to Woomera to have a quick look around. Woomera was only around seven kilometres from Pimba and after a quick look we were back travelling towards Port Augusta. The scenery was very lovely and we really enjoyed the morning travels stopping at various points to take photos and have coffee breaks. By lunchtime we reach Port Augusta and the Tyrepower store was very easy to find, just off the main highway. I purchased the new battery for Lizzie and upon fitting it myself broke a terminal clamp and had to buy a new one. Never mind within an hour I had completed the job and Lizzie turned over immediately – it was a joyous sound. We headed into town where we did some shopping at Coles before sitting down to some lunch in the Motorhome at about 2-30pm, we were starving.

Last time we were in Port Augusta we entered from the East and left through the West and did not think much of the place. In fact, we had basically missed all the residential area and had only seen the industrial side of the place. This time we entered from the North and went through the centre of town and the place took on a whole new perspective. In fact, Tee and I agreed that it was quite lovely and we both really enjoyed the area near the main bridge that overlooked the waterway and had the mountain ranges in the distance. After our hot chicken sandwiches, I made a few business phone calls before we headed off to buy fuel and then onto the Flinders Ranges. We travelled about 25 kilometres out of town where we stopped at Woolshed Flat Rest Area just before dark.

Day **267**

The morning proved to be colder than we anticipated and we decided to remain sheltered in our cocoon until the sun rose over the mountains. Even though we awoke at 6-30am it was not until 8-15am that we braved the cold and got out of bed. In fact, if it was not for Tee coaxing me out with a cuppa, I believe I would have stayed there until lunchtime.

Soon after 9-30am we were travelling towards the Flinders Ranges and even after we had started Lizzie a number of times yesterday it was great to hear her tick over this morning. The scenery on the road to the Flinders Ranges is stunning and we enjoyed our travelling there immensely. Our first stop was in the town of Quorn where we first stopped for a toilet break and then found a water tap to top up our house water. We then went for a long walk around almost all the town admiring the magnificent architecture from a bygone era. It never ceases to amaze Tee and I how stunning some homes are in these country towns. After almost two hours in the town of Quorn we were off again and well pleased with our visit to this small town.

Our next stop was at Kanyaka and the very simple but charming rock formations and water hole. We went for a lovely walk there where we were all alone for about an hour, and even when we went back to the Motorhome for lunch no-one else arrived to view this lovely place. The next stop almost never happened as Tee was not keen to travel on a dirt road but I talked her into it under mild protest. The place was the site of the Kanyaka Homestead Ruins and Tee was not convinced that the place was worth the dirt road effort until we spotted it as we came over a rise.

The place was amazing and it reminded me of the ruins on Norfolk Island, although not as big. The Homestead must have been like a small palace in its day and Tee was so apologetic that she had protested at coming to it. Tee was in awe of the place and said it was one of the nicest ruins she has seen on mainland Australia, and I had to agree. We walked around the place for an hour or so until a group of 4WD's turned up equipped with numerous brats who broke the tranquillity of the place with their high-pitched squeals. Both Tee and I are amazed that this site has not been protected as it will decay to nothing in no time in these harsh conditions.

We drove through the town of Hawker and viewed it from the comfort of our Motorhome as it did not have the charm of Quorn and was a fair bit larger. The drive from here to the Flinders Rangers National Park though was lovely and we enjoyed the scenery immensely with many photo stops along the way. When we reached Wilpena Pound we decided we had seen enough and headed back towards our next campsite just outside Peterborough.

It had been a long day and we arrived at our campsite as the sun was setting. I cooked up a couple of hamburgers in the fading light and we ate as it was getting dark. We had a lovely day today and suggest to anyone visiting SA that the Flinders Ranges are a "must see".

Day **268**

Even though we were right next to the main road at the Black Rock South Rest Area we had a fairly good nights sleep as the traffic was light. When we woke it was -1 degree in the Motorhome and it felt every bit that cold. When we looked out of the Motorhome window there was thick frost on the ground so we cuddled up and stayed in bed. In fact, it was 9-30am before we braved the cold and got up, and only when the gas cooker had been on for 15 minutes at that. But with a cuppa in our tummies we soon started to thaw out and plan the day.

We were well ahead of schedule so we decided to stop a while in any place that took our fancy and when we drove into Peterborough, we knew that this would be a whole day thing. The town is full of history and lovely stone buildings which immediately made us warm to the place. Our first stop was to a second hand shop where we found a Tupperware butter container that Tee wanted for the Motorhome and a porcelain figurine that caught Tee's eye. We took them back for Lizzie to look after while we took a walk through the town. We then found another second hand shop where Tee found a couple of hand made beanies that she wanted. I think that the cold weather has made her think that she needs 20 hats and 30 coats while I believe I will have no room in the Motorhome for anything of mine quite soon.

We wandered through the main street of Peterborough marvelling at all the buildings and the old town hall which had been re-painted looked superb. I spotted a Real Estate window and could not help but have a look at the prices in the area for these lovely buildings and to my surprise the old town hall was also for sale. Not only for sale but at $295,000 and I had to see inside it. I asked Tee if she would like to join me in looking inside this building and she agreed – but not to buy it – just out of curiosity. We went into the office and requested an inspection and were well pleased that it was empty and we could view it immediately. If we were looking at this building when we first left home, I would have been very keen on it but I have become more realistic in our plans and realize that our home and our life in Beachmere Queensland is very good. The itch I had to relocate had well and truly subsided and I now feel a lot more settled in our plans to stay in our current home.

The Real Estate lady was lovely and as we entered the building two things entered my mind, the first was how enormous it was, and the second how much work it needed to be spectacular again. If there were any urges prior to entering the building to take on a project like this they were soon quashed by the sheer magnitude of work needed. The project would not have been so unappealing if others had not made half ass attempts at it, but the fact is that it had been quite butchered by poor workmanship. We graciously looked through the building in admiration of its many lovely features and its amazing history. I told the agent that it was too big for me and she was lovely about it. She even told us where to go to see more on the history of the town and we departed for those very places. The first was to the new town hall which was more spectacular than the old and then we went to the Information Centre that was located in a rail carriage. In fact, the town was built around the rail and at one point in history was the busiest rail stop in the world peaking at 102 trains per day. When you see Peterborough (formerly Petersburg) today that is hard to believe. We had a great laugh and chat with the two people in the Information Centre who gave us some great advice on what to see in town.

The Burg was our next stop, which is located inside the newsagency and is a free display. They run a DVD there on the history of Peterborough which is well worth seeing. Tee and I sat through the 30 odd minute show and were totally fascinated with the history of the place. In fact, I had said to Tee that climate change must have affected this place as we saw farmhouse after farmhouse in ruins on our way here. We later learnt that in the first 20 years of settlement around Petersburg, as it was known then, that they had exceptionally favourable weather. It was only when the climate returned to its normal cycle that farms began to fail and this led to one farmer buying out his neighbours to increase his holdings and stay viable. This created an overstock of farmhouses which resulted in them falling apart through lack of maintenance, in line with the oversupply. Tee and I found this all very amazing and gave us insight as to what we had seen.

The town boasts some amazing train displays including the Steam Works Museum, which is apparently very good. It did not overly interest Tee and I though as it was a little pricey to get in and we were well satisfied with what we had been seeing. For those who prefer two wheels to two hundred, there is also a motorcycle museum in town so don't despair. We had a lovely day in Peterborough and would recommend it highly to anyone who likes a layback atmosphere that is shrouded in history. We left town at about 4-00pm and filled up with fuel before driving all of two kilometres to our next campsite called (funny enough) Peterborough Rest Area.

Day **269**

Very exciting that it did not get as cold last night, in fact it did not drop below 8 degrees in the Motorhome. We set off at about 9-30am after taking our time and not sure how far towards Broken Hill we would get today. With about 290 kilometres to Broken Hill we wanted to break the back of the journey but not get all the way into town. There are a couple of pubs along the way that offer free camping if you buy a beer and we thought that perhaps we may do that.

Our first stop was for a toilet break at the small town of Yunta where we also were lucky enough to fill up our House Water. Not a bad little town but we kept moving on as there seemed like very little to see here. A little further down the track we spotted what looked like a renovated railway station in the town of Mannahill. Turns out it was a Railway Station but was now empty. It was a beautiful building and I took a heap of photos of it before hitting the Highway again. We continued our journey even though we had really travelled far enough by now to pull up for the day. Tee was not feeling the best as she had a migraine and I said we should stop for a bite to eat and decide how far to travel for the day. We ate lunch and discussed our options, coming to the decision that we should just carry on and stop when we found somewhere nice. If this failed, we could continue to Silverton where we could stay in the local Caravan Park there.

The free camps around this neck of the woods are not too flash and with very few trees it would be like camping in the desert. Fortunately, though we came to the town of Cockburn (unfortunate name) where we found an extremely well priced Caravan Park. Tee was not well so the decision not to keep driving to Silverton became a very easy one. We pulled in and had a chat to a couple who were from SA and of mixed gender, and this was just the one we met. They were selling gemstones and other items and had been at Cockburn for about six weeks. At $15.00 we did not expect much but the facilities were immaculate, although old, and there was a large degree of pride at work here. Not much in Cockburn to see but that was not why we stopped here and after popping a few Paracetamol Tee had a nap while I read and wrote. She awoke in the late afternoon feeling much better and with Lizzie plugged into power we were assured a good night's sleep with the heater getting a workout. The biggest thrill of the day was still to come with the promise of hot showers and free flowing water. It was not long into the evening before we headed for them. They were unisex showers, which must have been a relief for the couple we had a chat to this afternoon, and with only two showers in the block we had the place to ourselves.

Day 270

Didn't matter what temperature it got down to last night we were as crispy as toast inside the Motorhome with the power connected and the heater cranked. We have put up with a lot of cold nights over the past few weeks and it was great to be warm all night. I am probably making it sound like we have been doing it really tough but I think it is more a case that we were missing our creature comforts. Tee was loving the heater but I must admit it was at times a little too hot for me and I found myself on top of the doona more than under it during the night.

We were off to Silverton today as we did not see it last time we went through Broken Hill. In fact, today will mark a special event in our travels and that is that we will complete a loop of this magnificent country. The loop is not a full loop to the entire edge of this great country but a loop none the less. The next three months of our journey will fill in all the bits around the edge of the east coast that we haven't seen yet. The only part of Australia that will miss out travelling is east of the Gulf, but you can't see everything in only one year. As part of our love of this country we plan to travel to specific places in a 4WD that will allow us access to areas that Lizzie just couldn't reach and I am sure that the Gulf of Carpentaria will be on that list. We would love to keep travelling after our year on the road but finances and other commitments prevent this becoming a reality. We should be well pleased though as we have already covered over 30,000 kilometres of Australia and yet we really have only scratched the surface. As we have travelled, we have noted places that we will return to in a 4WD and these places will fill many of our holidays in the years to come.

Cockburn is right on the border of SA and NSW so it only took us driving to the end of the side road where the Caravan Park is to be in NSW. In fact, the takeaway store in town was in NSW while the pub was in SA. Broken Hill was less than 50 kilometres from here with Silverton being a further 22 kilometres North West of Broken Hill. The journey to Broken Hill was dull, landscape wise, but with such a short distance to travel it mattered very little. From Broken Hill the road to Silverton had more dips than an aristocrat's engagement party, and we felt like the entertainment had already begun as we travelled.

My main reason for wanting to go to Silverton was to visit the Mad Max 2 museum there and also see a smaller version of Broken Hill. We soon arrived in the town, shaken not stirred, and we pulled up outside the old Gaol which was the first historic building we saw. We got out and took a few photos and walked further to photograph other lovely old buildings around the old gaol. We then drove to some craft shops one of which was a led lighting shop and we went in. When we got into the store, we saw a fabulous and huge map of Australia that had been laminated and when I saw that they were being sold here I just had to have one. It would make a great addition to our home and would compliment the running TV screen that I had planned for the thousands of photos we had taken on our trip. Tee thought it was too big and that we would have nowhere to put it as she didn't want it in the main living areas. But when I said we could put it upstairs in our parent's retreat she agreed and we bought the big one.

We then visited an artist's gallery before jumping back into Lizzie and heading for the Silverton Hotel. The hotel was a great place that had been a drinking hole for Mel Gibson during the filming of Mad Max 2, and in fact many other movies had also been made at this location. The walls of the hotel were filled with photos of these various films as well as local history photos. After the hotel we travelled up the road a bit to the Mad Max 2 museum and other various crazy places where we wondered around for an hour or so. It was now lunchtime and we decided that we should head out to the Mundi Mundi lookout and then onto the Umberumberka Reservoir for lunch. A quick stop at the Mundi Mundi Lookout produced some nice photos but we were now both quite hungry and we were soon off to the Umberumberka Reservoir. It was holding a fair amount of water and was one of the prettier sights in the area so we were well pleased with our choice of locations for lunch.

After lunch it was back to Broken Hill where we both decided that the big towns were not for us and that we should head off, after buying fuel, for Wentworth. It was not the way we had planned it but we were both happy with our decision not to stay in Broken Hill as it was quite busy and we had been here before, some nine months ago. It was after 2-30pm when we started for Wentworth and it was unlikely that we would get all the way to Wentworth today. Our new plan was to reach Popiltah Rest Area which was half way between the two towns. With not much to see along the way we soon arrived at the Popiltah Rest Area and prepared for our overnight stay.

Day **271**

Last night we had a visit from a little creature that came tapping on our flyscreen door. It was a little pussy cat who seemed to be keen to join us and by the look and action of this cat it was not a feral one. The only explanation was that it had been dumped at this rest area and the dumper is the feral one. Feral cats in the bush are a big problem in Australia and kill millions of native animals. What needs to be established is the fact that it is not the cat's fault as it is only doing what it does naturally to survive. It is the horrible humans that dump them that need to be put in a cage. But this cat was not totally feral yet as it seemed to be yearning human company and Tee could not help but feed it a can of Sardines. Upon putting the Sardines out for this pussy cat, it miraculously turned into three cats and although they were not fighting over the food, the first cat we saw was not all that keen on sharing it new found luck. We felt sad for these little creatures but had no way of transporting them to an RSPCA depot, let alone catching them.

We departed the Popiltah Rest Area at the respectable time of 8-45am and as the sun had not yet broken through the light cloud cover it was still quite brisk. We have decided to spend four days in Wentworth as it is a lovely little town and our memory of the caravan park there was very favourable. We drove straight through to Perry Sands which was only a few kilometres North of Wentworth where we would go for a walk and have a cuppa. The landscape on our travel this time was greener than last but still a little ordinary compared to some of the amazing places we have now seen. We arrived at Perry Sands within two hours of setting off and found a nice spot to park Lizzie, right next to a picnic shelter that had a

545

rainwater tank attached to it. As they had just had recent rains (puddles all over the ground) we thought this an ideal opportunity to top up our drinking water supply. The taste test by both of us proved the water to be good stuff so we topped up our supply by about 25 litres which brought us back to 60 litres again.

The next task was to check the Caravan Park prices and availability and at $25.00 per night for a powered site we were well pleased. Fortunately, we were here this weekend and not next as the Caravan Park was booked out then for the 150th anniversary of the paddleboat festival. We had a cup of coffee before going for a walk through the Perry Sands Sandhill's which are fantastic. We had visited them nine months ago near the start of our travels but this time I had more experience with the camera and was able to get some stunning panoramic shots. After a lovely long walk and gathering some lovely pictures we returned to Lizzie and headed to the Caravan Park to book in for our stay in Wentworth.

The Willowbend Caravan Park is located at the southern end of town and on the wet side of the towns levy banks. We drove through town to get to it and recalled the fond memories of our visit here some nine months earlier. We were given a lovely spot right on the river and with only one neighbour to the right of the Motorhome if we kept the curtains closed on that side it would feel like we had the river to ourselves. Not bad for $25.00 per night and the amenities were very clean also. Tee was keen to get some washing on as even though it was sunny the sun was weak and drying time would be all afternoon.

The local RSL club here does $8.00 meals and Tee and I decided that after hanging out the washing we would check out town and also the RSL club. The town of Wentworth is lovely and of all the fish and chip shops that we had visited on our journey, this one was the best. As we passed the shop though I noticed new owners and hoped that the standard had not dropped as we planned to visit it tonight. We went into the RSL to check it out and it looked like good value so we may return here later in our Wentworth stay.

Further on our town walk we found the local IGA food store and went in to pick up a few supplies. I bought some lovely fillet steaks; a dozen eggs and Tee bought some meat pies that caught her eye. On the way out we bought a bottle of wine and decided that a BBQ steak and sausages would be great for tonight to accompany our chips from the takeaway shop. Upon our return to Lizzie Tee checked the washing while I read a local paper and we then both enjoyed the fabulous view that we had before us. We were soon visited by the local ducks who had come to see if they to could dine with us also this evening.

Just before dinner time Tee went and removed the washing while I walked down to the local takeaway to buy our chippies. On my return Tee had cooked the sausages but had allowed me the honour of cooking my own T-bone steak. We had a lovely dinner and a wine or two as the sun started to fade over the river view that we were so lucky to share. We had a lovely day today and trust that the next three days here will be just as magical.

Day **272**

Sunday morning and with very little planned we were able to really enjoy the Willowbend Caravan Park and the fabulous spot we had in it. During the day many houseboats and cruise boats went past us at a leisurely rate as we watched from our heated location in Lizzie's cabin. Later in the day I decided to start the dreaded job of my tax return and because we were away from home, I thought it would be a huge task. But as I got into it, I soon realize that it would not be so bad, as I had set up my spreadsheets very well before I left home and I didn't really have all that much to claim. I got it all done by early evening, except for my bank statements that I thought would have to be requested from my bank and sent to me via email. After completing 95% of my tax return Tee and I sat down to a few glasses of wine and a tasty dinner. Not a big day for activities but a very pleasant day in which we both seemed to get a lot achieved.

Day **273**

Yesterday I had organized to have a look at an old historic home in Wentworth and this morning the agent and I spoke and squared up a time to inspect it. It looks like a lovely home and I could not help myself in organizing an inspection. I think I am getting itch feet from being out of the Real Estate business for about a year now. We will be looking at it tomorrow morning at 10-00am and the agent also wants to show us another similar one that he has on his books. We are doing this more out of curiosity these days as we are 99% resolved to the fact that we will stay in our Queensland home.

I rang my bank to ask if they could email my bank statements for the whole tax year. But as it turns out I was able to print it off from the internet via a link that the patient girl from customer service guided me to. After a number of attempts I got the job done and was able to email all the required information to my Tax Accountant back home. That job took me nearly the whole morning while Tee did all the preparations for the day. After my computer struggle Tee and I set off for a walk to visit the junction of the Murray River and the Darling Rivers but this time from the township side. Last time we were here, nine months ago, we actually rode our bikes through the middle ground to the very point where the two rivers meet. This time it was a leisurely stroll along the levy bank near the Caravan Park and into a lovely park area that boasted landscape gardens and an elevated viewing platform.

As we entered the park, we were greeted by a lovely kookaburra that seemed to have no fear of humans and allowed me to take some lovely photos of him. He only flew away when some brats ran past us on there way to the toilet block. We then climbed the viewing platform where we were able to get a great shot of the Rivers meeting and also a series of photos of native birds in an old dead gum tree nearby. From the park we walked to the Loch and then back into town via some suburban streets. The homes in Wentworth vary from lovely to ordinary and quite regularly they are next door to each other. It is amazing how much different a home looks when a bit of effort and a lot of pride is extended.

We eventually ended up back at the Caravan Park as Tee could not get an appointment at the local hairdressers and we could not find any good books in the local second hand shop. We had a bite to eat and after I sent a few emails and paid a bill we decided to walk back into town and buy some supplies for the next few days. The local IGA was only a short walk from the Caravan Park and we enjoyed walking through town to get there. We grabbed a few items that we needed but did not go nuts as we would have to carry them back to the Motorhome and those shopping bags dig deep into your fingers with a bit of weight in them. Claw hands as Tee calls it.

We had a quiet evening and enjoyed watching the birdlife on the river from the warm confines of Lizzie's hull.

Day **274**

We had the heater temp set perfectly last night and I awoke without the dry nose and throat that I get when the heater is too hot. We both slept well and are really enjoying being on mains power which enables the use of this lovely heater. I told Tee that I would make her French toast in the morning and this morning she did not allow me to forget my promise. After Tee had made me a cuppa in bed I proceeded to get up and get cracking on the French toast. When I got outside, I could not believe how cold it was and this was exaggerated by the toasty conditions that we had created inside the Motorhome.

After brekkie we both got ready for our appointment with the Real Estate Agent and by 9-30am we were ready to walk to his agency which was located only a short walk from this Caravan Park. We arrived early for our 10-00am appointment and were pleased to stand around in the office as the heating was lovely. After a chat with John he took us to see the Postmasters old home which was lovely and full of old-fashioned character. We were then early to see the second home so John showed us around town and also showed us a lovely riverfront acre block of land. We then viewed the second property which was nowhere near as nice as the Postmasters old home before heading back into town. The Postmasters home was lovely and would have made a fantastic Bed and Breakfast but Tee and I are still on track to go home to Queensland and make our house homier. In fact, a lot of Northern Victoria is lovely and if we were currently living in Melbourne, I think we would probably move to this area. But South East Queensland is so easy to live in and with fantastic services close to our home along with the tranquillity of our suburb we can now safely say "there is no place like home!" I think – no – I know - that when we get back home, we will be more settled than we have ever been. I explained all this to John who was gracious in defeat and we returned to Lizzie for our last day in Wentworth.

Back at the Motorhome I compiled a list of things that we needed to purchase in Mildura prior to heading towards Yarrawonga via the mighty Murray. The list included Diesel oil that was on special at Autobarn Mildura, LPG from BCF and butane from Bunning's. As luck has it all these three stores were within a kilometre of each other in Mildura which would simplify our shopping trip. We had decided to purchase a Honda Generator which we would have delivered while at our friend's home in Yarrawonga (Albert and Judy). But the hot water system was still busted and we did not know where to get a new one from. But as the weather was so cold now, we both knew that we needed a solution quick.

With my problem-solving cap on I looked on the internet to try and find a replacement Truma hot water system or a replacement tank that I could fit myself. The prices of these things are crazy with a new unit costing $995.00 and a replacement tank and surround coming in at $660.00. Determined to find a better price I drifted off the fixed units and found myself looking at portable hot water units. This soon became a smart option and I settled on a Companion unit that Anaconda had on special for $249.00 reduced from $399.00. With no fixed address it was hard to buy online and I decided to find a store that was located between here and Yarrawonga. Bendigo was the closest and only a slight detour in our travels so I gave them a call. Wow if I thought that at $249.00 for the Companion unit I had maxed out on my luck then think again. Not only did I get the last unit but the store also had a bonus carry bag and shower unit that they threw in. I quickly secured the deal by paying for it over the phone and I would pick it up in about a week's time on my way to Yarrawonga. Well satisfied with the day's achievements so far, we spent the rest of the day planning our travels for our departure tomorrow and the course we would take to reach Yarrawonga in a week or so time.

Day **275**

Whenever we stay in a place for more than two days, we tend to settle right in. Which is not a bad thing but it gives us time to spread out and packing up takes a hell of a lot longer. This morning was no exception and with the added bonus of freezing cold temperatures it was the first time that I wished I had the inside duties when packing up. Everything I touched, especially the metal objects, felt like ice cubes and when I had to wash the table legs the cold seeped into my bones.

It's funny how you forget these things, as when I was living in Melbourne, I now recall how much I despised these mornings. My most vivid memory is of a young 18-year-old in Melbourne who worked in a tyre service in Preston. The part I remember most vividly is the very early mornings when we would start changing tyres and how freezing cold the metal equipment was, especially the tyre levers that had spent their evening on the cold concrete floor. I am amazed at how focused I was as a young fella as it was not the best of jobs, but I seemed to make the best of it. Truth was, I was about to buy my first home and I really had to work here if I was to realize my first big dream.

Twenty years of living in Queensland had me all but forget these memories and how oppressive the cold can be. Tee and I had fantasized about living in a colder climate where she could wear fashionable coats and scarves, and I could chop fire wood for our open fire in the country. We would grow our own vegetables and fruit and keep our own small group of farmyard animals. To some this sounds like a dream but this trip, which was suppose to find us the idyllic location to do this, has had a different

effect on us both. What it has shown us is a newfound appreciation for
what we have got in Queensland and the freedom that our home is able to
provide us with. By that I mean that we can travel without the constraints
of a small farm and animals – we can go fishing almost any day of the year
without the oppression of the freezing cold – we can work in careers that
we have developed over a lifetime when we chose – we can travel to the cold
climates to experience the changing seasons at short notice. In addition,
we have most of our friends and family nearby and the hobbies that we
planned to do in the colder climate can still be done from our lovely home.
As we begin to approach the end of our travels, we now know we are on
the right track as we both feel happy to finish the journey and at the same
time know we will be happy to be back home.

Finally, all of the metal objects on Lizzie have been put away so I
meandered up to the Amenities Block to run my frozen hands under hot
water and to brush my teeth. Last night I met a fellow who was a little
older than me travelling with his wife in a 4WD and flash camper trailer.
He bragged about how good it was and when I said we were considering
the purchase of one he looked down his nose at me and muttered that they
cost more than $50,000. In the past I would have bit back at him but I
am calmer and more content these days and just let the comment slide.
What he said to me had taught me one thing though, and that was that
these things are way overpriced and more of a fashion statement than a
practical unit. This morning as I walked to Amenities Block, I saw the
pair of them standing outside the trailer having a cup of tea in the freezing
cold. I immediately thought that even though they can go anywhere I like
my comforts and Lizzie was a great choice for what we wanted to do on
this trip. Each vehicle and set up has its best applications, but at $50,000
plus these camper trailers are overrated.

We soon left the campsite that had been home for four days and were
glad to be on the road again. Our first stop was in Mildura where I had
organized to get a heap of things. Wentworth is not that far from Mildura
and we arrived at the Centro Shopping Plaza in under an hour. Inside I
bought a couple of pairs of jeans that I desperately needed and on our way
out we also bought some sausages in Woolworths. Just up the road we
found the BCF and Autobarn store right next to each other and I went
into BCF while Tee had a look in the Spotlight store. In BCF I handed

over my gas bottle to be filled while I had a look at the Coleman Hot Water system that I had got on special at Anaconda Bendigo and would pick up in a few days. It was amazing the value I got as it looks like a good unit and when I totalled the cost of it in BCF, including the bonus items I got; it would have cost me just shy of $500.00 here. Instead of hanging around while the gas bottle was being filled, I walked over to Autobarn where Vince helped me choose the oil I needed for Lizzie. Back to BCF where my gas bottle was now filled and as I paid for it Tee turned up from her look in the Spotlight store next door. Our last stop was at Bunning's for Butane and with that purchased we were on our way out of Mildura. It was a painless shopping process as all the stores were on the same street and we were finished well before lunchtime.

Back on the road and we had planned to cross back into NSW where we would say at the Lake Benanee Rest Area on the outskirts of Euston. Euston was a significant point in our travels as it is the last point where we doubled up on our travels. When we arrived at Broken Hill some days ago, we achieved a full lap of Australia and from Broken Hill to Euston we have doubled up. Lake Benanee would be our first night past the double up and would mark a new point in our journey. But first we would have lunch at Euston beside the mighty Murray. Tee toasted me up a couple of sandwiches with cheese onion and tomato which was yummy in this cool weather. We arrived at Lake Benanee at about 2-00pm and had a relaxing day reading before watching a Robert De Niro movie in the evening.

Day 276

We did not think it would get as cold last night as it has been, and with no heater we were well pleased with that fact. But fact turned to fiction during the night and I awoke many times to a frozen nose. In fact, at 8-30am when we woke it was only one degree in the cabin of Lizzie. With a late start we headed off with the intention of driving to Balranald which is north of the Murray and then back towards to the Murray and to a camp spot North West of Swan Hill. The reason we wanted to go to Balranald was because it was near the Yanga National Park and there did not seem to be many points of interest along the Murray between Euston and Swan Hill.

The Journey to Balranald also proved to be a little uninteresting but Balranald itself turned out to be a nice little town. We stopped in town for a coffee break and I jumped out and bought a fresh loaf of bread from the IGA. Tee spotted a second hand shop as we were heading out of town and we pulled up again to do some shopping there. While I was having my coffee earlier on, I also had a look on the internet to see points of interest in the Yanga National Park and came up with the Woolshed and the Old Homestead. I also noticed that they had just opened up a campground near the Woolshed on the Murrumbidgee River and thought it may be a good place to spend the night. Back in the second hand store and I found Tee a Doctor Harry book that I thought she may like and I bought the Latham Diaries which took my fancy. I also spotted a fabulous orange jumper that was pure cotton and wool. I tried it on and Tee said it looked great so I bought it, along with the two books and all for seven dollars – we love these second hand shops.

Soon after our shopping expedition we headed off towards the Woolshed which was practically on the outskirts of Balranald. We arrived to a pile of dilapidated old buildings that looked like they had only been empty for a couple of years. At first, we thought that the place was not all that interesting (a bit like a feral farm of today), but that was only until we entered the main shearing shed. The shearing shed was massive, in fact it was 100 metres long and in its heyday 130 people worked here during the shearing season. The old equipment was still in place and the whole place took on a new meaning to Tee and I as we viewed it through different eyes. The simplicity of how it has been left gave us a real insight into how it must have been (and smelt) to work in a place like this. We were lucky enough to have been here as another local couple were also having a look. The chap had worked in shearing sheds as a young fellow and was able to describe all the equipment to us – it was like a guided tour.

After our extensive look at the Woolshed we went over to the camping area to find two or three other vehicles taking advantage of the lovely spot. Perched on the banks of the brimming Murrumbidgee we found ourselves a lovely spot where we spent a pleasant afternoon and evening. In fact, we were so impressed with the place that we decided that we would stay here again tomorrow night after visiting the Yanga Homestead and revisiting Balranald.

Day **277**

It was mighty cold again last night and we slept in again until about 8-30am. This weather is so conducive to sleeping in and I feel as though we are making a habit of it. Well it is our time and we are entitled to be enjoying ourselves, but we both feel guilty as we have never allowed ourselves such luxuries in the past. We will get over it. I had a bit of work to do in the morning as I had a few bills to pay and a few questions to ask my Body Corp managers about the 33% increase in their fees. After this was completed and we filled the house water nearby we headed off to the Yanga Homestead. It was just down the road about ten kilometres and it was not long before we arrived.

The Homestead was magnificent and viewing it made us appreciate what the National Parks people were trying to do with the Woolshed. In our opinion they were trying to preserve a time in Australian history as naturally as they could and Tee and I were very impressed.

I always saw the work of the National Parks to be preserving the integrity of natural landmarks throughout the country. But this was a twist on that and in our opinion a very welcomed one. What they were saving here was our identity as a nation growing up and although this was more what we expected from the National Trust, I suspect that in the bush it was not being done. Proof of this was in South Australia where we viewed the ruins of a magnificent stone homestead, Kanyaka Homestead. This magnificent building should have never been allowed to get as bad as it is and although the ruins were nice to see it would have been absolutely spectacular in its full form.

We really enjoyed our viewing of the Yanga Homestead which was topped off by a walk by the stunning lake that surrounded it. On the way out we met a couple from Echuca that we chatted to for a while, swapping travel stories. Back to Lizzie and it was now 1-15pm so Tee rustled me up a couple of sandwiches for lunch. Mum rang me to report that our house was still there and that it was still raining so the mower guy hadn't been yet.

After lunch we headed back to Balranald for a better look at the town and to purchase a butter dish in the second hand store that Tee hadn't seen. I described it to her last night and she was hell-bent on getting it before we left town. The walk through town didn't take too long as it is not a huge town and we were soon in the second hand store and purchasing the butter dish. Come to think of it the walk through town was quick due to Tee's cracking pace; that I believe was set by her desire to have that butter dish. It was still there (thank goodness) and with her new purchase safely secured we were on our way back to the campground near the Woolshed. Not a lot done for the day but a very pleasant day indeed.

Day **278**

Before I write about today, I will have to complete the events of last night. Tee and I hit the sack at about 9-00pm and soon we both drifted off to sleep. At 10-30pm we were both simultaneously awoken by the sound of heavy rain and the engine revs of the only other vehicle by the Murrumbidgee with us this evening. At first, we did not realize what was going on as we were still sleepy and then we remembered that we were near the Murrumbidgee River and about two kilometres down a dirt track. The track was a dry weather only track and it soon became obvious to us that it would be smart for us to get back on the bitumen ASAP. This was obviously what the other couple were doing and we soon were on our way.

Tee and I are well drilled for this and we are always ready to hit the road at a moments notice. We pack everything up inside the Motorhome every night and make sure that the awning is in and that the keys are on the edge of the dining table ready to roll. The reason we do this is so that if we get hassled from outside the Motorhome we can take off and be safe. Sometimes we get pissed off with being so organized but being safe while free camping is extremely important to us.

Half asleep I started Lizzie and cleared the windows before heading off down the dirt track that was now getting quite a soaking. We made it out to the bitumen hassle free and although it was horrible to leave such a peaceful spot, it was best we did. We headed towards the Yanga Homestead as we remembered that there was a Rest Area there that was all bitumen and off the highway a bit. As we pulled up there it seemed like a lovely spot but after we had settled right in, we soon realized that there was huge truck traffic on this highway and the lights of the northbound trucks shone in our back window. Too tired to do anything about it we were awoken at least a dozen times during the night.

We permanently awoke this morning at about 7-00am after a dozen or so false starts. With all this rain our plans had been turned upside down as we had decided to camp along the Murray at every opportunity all the way to Yarrawonga. The rain made this an impossibility as most of the river camp areas are slippery when wet. Thing was I also had no Plan "B" so we had to study the Camps6 book and decide what to do. There were a couple of options so we decided to head off towards Swan Hill and see how the day panned out. We had always planned to go to Swan Hill as I wanted to buy some new joggers there and Tee wanted to go into a Sam's Warehouse for moisturizer and other things that she gets in that store back home.

The rain also made the journey less pleasant as visibility was low, and road conditions meant I had to concentrate even harder on driving and was less able to enjoy the landscape. We had quick toilet stop at Tooleybuc, which seemed like a lovely little town on the NSW side of the Murray before spotting a market sign in the town of Nyah on the Vic side of the Murray. We pulled into the Lions park there where the markets had all but been washed out and while I emptied the shitter at the Dump Point Tee strolled over and bought us a couple of hot donuts for morning tea. We had a coffee and the donuts that Tee had purchased before deciding to head off to Swan Hill to do some shopping. The free camp at Nyah was lovely and we were tempted to stay there for the evening or even to come back after shopping in Swan Hill but once on the road we decided that with all the rain it was best to keep moving.

Even though originally I had no intention of going to Bendigo to pick up our new hot water system until tomorrow we also didn't find much to keep us occupied in this wet weather. With that in mind as we entered Swan Hill we thought if we got going from here early enough, we could get the Bendigo leg of our journey completed today and camp at Huntly on Bendigo's outskirts.

As we parked in the back blocks of Swan Hill (due to the lack of suitable parking), Tee reached in under the bed to grab her umbrella for the walk into town. As she did so she discovered water had covered a substantial part of the storage area under our bed. We both hate water leaks, but due to our amazing run of fine weather on our journey we have not had to concern ourselves with the elements causing us grief in this area. The hot water service on the other hand made sure we knew all about water leaks. With a lack of sleep and this new discovery our resolve was tested and tempers did flare a bit. But Tee is so resolute in her ability to smooth things over that it did not get out of hand. We discovered that it was the back window again but this time with the heavier rain it was much worse. It was something that needed a better environment and conditions to work on so with Yarrawonga (Albert and Judy's Place) where we would be in a few days time, we would have to wait until then to repair the leak.

Tee and I left all the gear out and headed into town to shop, and when we got to Sam's Warehouse, I said to Tee that I would meet here back here after I bought my shoes. I thought it would give us both time to cool off and enjoy our own space for a bit. The shop that supposed to have my new joggers on special did not carry its parent companies catalogue specials so I was left emptied handed. But as I left the store, I noticed another shoe store across the road that was have a 50% off sale. As I entered the store my day got a whole heap better as I found the joggers I was after and in my size and on special. Wow!

I raced back to catch up with Tee who had already found most of the items she was after and we picked up a few more things before heading back to the Motorhome. Back at the Motorhome and with clearer heads we cleaned up the water and decided that we would have to soak up the leaks until Wednesday when we would be in Yarrawonga. We headed off and stopped at Lake Boga where we had lunch and decided that Bendigo was achievable and we should pick up the Hot Water System today. Some of these towns that we were stopping in were very worthy of more time but the weather was so miserable that to keep moving was to keep sane and we might as well get all the chores done.

With just short of 200 kilometres to travel I rang the Anaconda store in Bendigo to ensure that we had enough time to reach them today, and with a 5-00pm closing time this was not a problem. We hightailed it to Bendigo, only stopping at the Shell in Kerang to fuel up and arrived at Anaconda with an hour to spare. After picking up the new portable Hot Water System we headed out to Huntly Lions Park and set up for the evening. With no other Caravans or Motorhomes here, we thought we would be in for a quiet Saturday night but at 6-00pm a small Pizza bus turned up and started selling Pizza's out of the free camp. We were amazed at this as it was probably the last thing in the world that we expected to see but if nothing else this journey has taught us to "expect the unexpected!"

The Pizza dude left at about 9-30pm so we thought our noise problems would be over with – think again. The last vehicle to buy a pizza decided it would be nice to stay here until midnight playing duff duff music. When he had finished, the cold night air brought us more duff duff music from a nearby house that continued until 6-30am ensuring that our sleep here was highly interrupted and extremely unpleasant.

Day **279**

We eventually woke at about 9-00am and were both very tired from the last two nights of badly disrupted sleeps. We had thought about going back to Bendigo today for a bit of a look around town but neither of us felt up to it and the weather was still drizzly and very cold. Our highest priority today had become finding a quiet camp spot where we could get a good night's sleep. Scouring through the Camps6 book we discovered a camp area about 40 kilometres from here on the outskirts of Elmore. It was on a back road and we thought this would make it a great option.

We finally got going at about 10-30am and by 11-00am we were in Elmore where we bought a cask of wine and a few veggies in the local IGA. Within minutes of leaving Elmore we found ourselves at the old Elmore Field Day site that had now be renamed Aysons Reserve. The place seemed perfect as it was right on the Campaspe River and the road in seemed extremely light on traffic. We found a spot that wasn't too soggy and settled in for a quiet afternoon, with the hope that our dreams of a quiet night's sleep would not be shattered by some unforseen event.

Day **280**

This place is both super quiet and super pretty with green grass and a lovely river vista. We both had an excellent night's sleep and decided rather than trying to re-invent the wheel we should stay here tonight also. I rang the Cobram Tyrepower (where I had ordered my tyres from) to check if the Toyo tyres had arrived. They had so I booked us in to get them fitted at 1-00pm tomorrow as this would ensure we would not be rushed on the two-hour drive from here to Cobram.

After brekkie we decided it would be nice to spend a few hours in Rochester which was only 10 kilometres up the road. Mind you, brekkie didn't happen until after 10-00am and it was closer to 11-00am when we finally got going. The reason for the late brekkie was that we wanted to pull the bed area apart to check that water had not leaked into the boot from the leaking back window. Unfortunately, it was a little damp and so was the underside of our mattress. Tee stripped down the bed and moved the mattress to the front of the Motorhome which allowed me to pull all of the gear out of the boot.

Fortunately, it was only minimally damp and nothing had been damaged by the small amount of water that had got in there. Never the less we decided to get all of our books out of the boot and swap them with some items that were stored in the overhead cupboards. The items that got the flick into the boot were our bike helmets and my old Akubra hat, none of which would be affected if they got wet. They also took up a lot of room in the overhead cupboard and were an ideal choice. With all the books safely stored we were able to rearrange the boot and the under-bed storage area to ensure that even if a bit of water got in nothing would get damaged. Tee put the mattress back upside down so it would dry out during the day. We sound a bit paranoid but when the hot water service was leaking it ruined a very expensive pair of shoes and we didn't want a repeat of that.

We arrived in Rochester in no time as the sun made some cameo appearances on our journey there. The countryside on the way to Rochester was beautiful with green grass that was dotted with baby lambs and dairy cows. Tee had run out of reading material so we would hit the second hand shops in our quest to keep her occupied. We also had a lot of rubbish to dump as there had been no bins at the Aysons Reserve Rest Area and my printer was also heading to the bin in order to create more damp-proof space in the Motorhome.

When we first parked in Rochester, we found a lovely spot but then realized we would have to find a bin to dump the rubbish first. So, we pushed off in search of a bin with adequate space to accommodate our pile of rubbish. We found a bin and straight across the road from that bin was a parking bay for Motorhomes and caravans so we parked there. We then walked the short distance into town and admired all the old buildings and pubs that the town of Rochester boasts. We found a lovely second hand shop that had a great supply of books of which we bought three for the grand total of $1.20. We then meandered through town and found a hairdresser that could do Tee's hair tomorrow morning.

The dilemma for us though was that this would interrupt our plans to be in Cobram by 1-00pm to buy the four tyres for Lizzie. But in true fashion we took the motto of our trip literally and decided that "as we had no particular place to be, and all the time in the world to get there" we could delay the tyres by a day. Tee was very happy with this and if Tee is happy then I am sure to follow suit.

On continuing our walk through town, we came across a Honda dealer so we went inside to look at the generator we wanted to buy – the Honda EU20i. They had it on display and I asked the owner if the price displayed as 'special' was the best price he could do. He was a nice fellow who gave us a fairly good price but not as good as I can get online, so unfortunately, he would not make a sale today. We continued to have a good chat though and as with most people we talk to he plans to travel like we are. I responded by saying that he should 'just do it' as life is too short to procrastinate and wait for 'the best time'. He also gave us some advice when he found out that we were staying at Aysons Reserve. He told us that lots have things have been stolen from there and to lock everything up overnight, especially generators. We thanked him and made our exit as his phone started to ring.

On our way back to Lizzie we stopped at the local IGA and bought a hot chook and a fresh loaf of bread for lunch which was now way overdue. Back at Lizzie we ate our hot chicken sandwiches before making the short journey back to Aysons Reserve. When back at our new favourite camp spot Tee noticed and older couple who had a generator and went over to share the Honda man's knowledge with them. Turns out they were Victorians who had been here before and had experienced the thefts that other people incurred during their last visit here. Not that we didn't believe the Honda man but now we were very aware of the risk and would ensure everything is locked up overnight.

Day **281**

Tee awoke very excited that she was getting her hair done today and as we were not rushed for time, we slowly got ready to go back to Rochester. We headed off just before 10-00am in thick fog and drizzle to Tee's appointment. Tee had not witnessed fog like this too often and was surprised when I told her that it may stay like this all day.

We arrived back in Rochester in plenty of time for Tee's appointment and parked in the same spot as yesterday. Tee headed off for her appointment while I jumped on the computer to write and look up spare parts for our fridge that has a slightly broken freezer door. Of course, the freezer door only came as a complete unit and at $85.00 plus delivery I would repair it for now and find a better option when we returned home. I had not long done this and emptied our rubbish when Tee arrived back with her hair all done and pretty. Tee's hair was fantastic and it was done at a fabulous price, so ladies if you are in the Rochester area and need (want) your hair done then its Deb's Country Cut'z in the main street. In fact, Tee says that even if you are within 100 kilometres of Rochester then it is worth the trip – yes Tee was very impressed! It turned out we could have made the tyre appointment in Cobram but as it was all sorted, we left the amended appointment stand for 1-00pm tomorrow.

Off we went again back to the Aysons Reserve Rest Area and with the afternoon now free I played around with my new phone downloading apps and working out how the updates worked. I got onto a great app called Wiki Camps which only cost $3.00 and was every bit as good as the Camps7 book.

To Tee's amazement the fog did not lift completely all day.

568

Day **282**

It rained a bit again last night and our concerns for the damp in the Motorhome was growing as Tee believed that after three days of something being damp and unaired mould starts to grow. Fortunately, today we would be heading to Yarrawonga (Judy & Albert's place) where we would be able to attend to the problem in depth. I had rung my friend John in Kyabram last night to see if we could catch up today and even though we made a tentative time of 11-00am at his office I decided this morning not to go. My reason for this was that he sounded really busy and I felt as though it would just be a hassle for him to have me there. When I told Tee that I was not wanting to visit John she was glad as she had picked up on the same vibe while I was having a conversation with John on the phone yesterday.

This now meant that our first appointment for the day would be in Cobram at 1-00pm to have the four new tyres fitted. As we started to get packed up and ready for our journey Tee noticed that the fellow across the way from us, who had his generator chained to a tree away from his van, was not awake yet but his generator was not there. He had been running it last night and because it was so cold this morning, we presumed it would be running now. But it wasn't and it made us think that it may have been stolen last night, as the Honda man told us was occurring in this free camp. But we did not see him before we left and didn't get a chance to answer the little morning mystery that we had created. Truth is he probably brought it in last night and couldn't be bothered starting it this morning. But that would not be as exciting as the story that Tee and I had developed between us and we left thinking that the Aysons Reserve thief was alive and very much active.

We had about 180 kilometres to travel today to reach Yarrawonga and Cobram, where we were booked in to get our tyres, was about 30 odd kilometres short of Yarrawonga. The journey there took us over the Murray into NSW and as we crossed the bridge between Echuca and Moama, we spotted two amazing things. The first was a steam driven paddle steamer on the river (that the bridge sides prohibited us getting a real good look at) and a fruit cake that was yelling at nothing as he entered the town of Moama – lucky Moama. This fellow seemed like he was very angry at someone who was following him, even though no one was there.

We stopped for a coffee and toilet break in Strathmerton which is just short of Cobram and arrived at the Tyrepower store at about 12-30pm. We walked into the store and were immediately struck by a cold and unfriendly atmosphere. The lady at the counter was professional enough but did her job with no feeling or friendliness what so ever. She basically just told us where to take the Motorhome and to then come back and sit in the waiting room until the job was complete. After I took Lizzie around the back, I tried to strike up a conversation with the owner who was in the workshop area. He was also very unfriendly and told us that we had to go and wait in the office while he worked on the tyres. I felt very uncomfortable as I wanted to go over a few things with him, but his attitude was very negative and I left it at that.

We sat in the sterile environment of the front office and even my friendly attempts at light conversation with the lady at the front counter were met with polite but cold one-line answers that went no further. I have no idea what type of bug had crawled up these people's arses but they were now dead and infecting their new home.

The job was completed in under an hour and if it was not for the frosty service we would have been impressed. But because we felt like we were an inconvenience to them by being there we felt as though they had done the job quick to get rid of us. Honestly it was a bizarre atmosphere and you truly would have thought that we had just run over one of their children the way they were acting. Bottom line we got good tyres at a good price and in good time. We would never see them again and even that would be too soon.

With our heads still spinning from that experience we decided to treat ourselves to a feed of Fish and Chips. We spotted a shop in Cobram called Big Momma's Kitchen that looked great so we parked Lizzie and headed in. The people in the store were lovely and Tee and I soon realized that we were not two headed monsters and settled in to a lovely conversation with the owners. The food was lovely as they cooked in rice oil and used a tempura type batter. The portions were also generous and they served it to us on a plate which we ate in the corner of their lovely store.

So – if you are in the Cobram area and need a feed then Big Momma's kitchen is the place to go, and if you need tyres – Well?

After the mixed experience we had in Cobram we were soon heading to Yarrawonga to spend time with our good friends Judy and Albert. We arrived at there place about 2-00pm and did little until Albert and Judy arrived home from work at about 3-45pm. When they got home, we gave each other a hug and proceeded inside where we chatted the night away. Well not the whole evening – as it was the decider of the State of Origin tonight and Albert and I had some serious football to watch. The night ended perfectly with Queensland beating NSW in the decider and we all soon headed off for a good night's sleep.

Day **283**

Plugged into power we had an excellent night's sleep but as it was late when we went to bed, we were a little tired still in the morning. I was amazed that Judy and Albert got off to work so early as we heard them leaving at about 7-00am. Today we planned to get Lizzie all scrubbed up and Coral (Judy and Albert's daughter) would be coming over with Charlotte (Judy and Albert's Grandchild) around lunchtime to pay us a visit.

I thought to myself – Life is amazing and it travels so quick – as I was at the hospital when Coral was born, and now she has a two-year-old daughter – Amazing!

I remember two funny things I said back in the time when Judy was pregnant with Coral. The first was – That the baby, when it was born would certainly not starve as Judy had quite prominent breasts. The second was that they should call the baby Craig. The first comment turned out to be incorrect as Judy actually had a lot of trouble breast feeding and Coral did have trouble putting on weight. The second comment took over 20 years to come true as it was then that Coral married Matthew Craig to finally satisfy my request to have the baby (Coral) named Craig.

It was lovely to see Coral again as she was now a beautiful young woman with a happy cheeky little toddler. Tee, Coral and I chatted for a couple of hours and had a lovely afternoon. Coral had arrived as I had just finished washing Lizzie but Tee had not yet completed cleaning the inside of the Motorhome. So, when Coral left Tee finished off the cleaning and it was all done by the time Judy and Albert got home from work.

Albert made fresh pumpkin soup for dinner and we chatted until 9-00pm when Judy declared that we should watch a comedy DVD that she had got from one of her work colleagues. Tee could hardly stay awake and went to bed about 10-30pm and I followed at about 11-00pm. It was raining so I covered the back of Lizzie with a tarp to stop water getting in to the leaking back window. It seemed to do the trick but I must silicon it up tomorrow as we would not want to do this every time it rained, especially on the road.

Day **284** - Day **287**

The timing of our visit to see Judy and Albert could not have been better, as they were doing it a bit tough with a number of family issues that we all go through from time to time. I spent a fair bit of time with Albert as he had an RDO on the Friday, as did Judy. I was mesmerised by the footy on TV as it had been almost ten months on the road now and we had watched very little TV in that time. Albert and I watched a number of games while the girls chatted about whatever girls chat about.

It was fabulous to be with my good friends and equally as exciting to be able to walk around their lovely big home after being confined to the Motorhome space, especially in the cold climate. The whole long weekend was filled with chatting and laughter which continued late into the evenings. What Tee and I also found amazing was the fact that when we went to our Motorhome in the evening to go to sleep it felt like we were returning home. It was truly an odd feeling as we both never thought we would feel like that.

Day **288** - Day **293**

J udy had organized to have the week off
with us which we thought was very lovely,
but due to family issues her time was more dedicated to her adult children
and things were not as sweet as they started out being. Tee and I felt left
out in the cold and as we had both been through what her daughter Coral
was going through, the only way for us to keep in communication was
to offer advice. All the family seemed to be on tender hooks and Tee and
I were dealing with it as best we could. It was hard not to be involved in
what was going on even though it was really none of our business.

As the week progressed tensions rose and Tee was feeling very
uncomfortable about the whole situation. Albert and I were communicating
but that too was a little strained as we seem to have grown different over the
years. In general conversation this did not appear to be a problem and over
the thirty plus years that we have been friends we have always got along
fabulously. But this was different as now our opinions and beliefs were
being thrown around. I tried to give Albert and his family good advice
that was coming from the heart but it was not getting through as it seems
that their core belief system is different than Tee's and mine.

Albert had a day off on Friday (26th) as he was trying to get a shed
built to hold all his daughter's furniture. His son Roy was also back home
and would also need storage space for all his furniture. This was putting
an enormous strain on Albert and I was unhappy about seeing my best
friend suffering. His way of coping is to bury himself in work and the
shed would take us away from other family members and into his large
garden. We worked for two days on the shed which we got 70% complete

and Albert seemed well pleased. The Sunday was dedicated to the moving of Coral's furniture into temporary storage (Alberts work shed). By the end of the three days I had had enough and although Albert would take Tuesday off to do more work for his family, I was not that keen to keep it up. I did agree to stay until Tuesday to help but I was not happy that it was only Albert and I that were doing all the work.

Day **294**

After moving furniture all day, I decided to stay away from Albert's family after dinner for two reasons. The first was Judy's unwelcoming attitude and secondly, I wanted time with Tee to discuss what we should do. It would also give them space and time without outsider's ears, even though we were supposed to be close friends. Tee and I had had enough of the tension and with our advice seemingly falling on deaf ears we seemed to be more of a hindrance than a help. I say this even though Albert kept wanting us to stay and the fact that I had done three hard days work for him and his family. Tee and I decided this evening that we would leave tomorrow for the benefit of all involved.

Day **295**

With our decision made last night and with the family heading off to work early this morning we had no way of telling them of our decision. This was probably a good thing as if we had of discussed it last night, I am sure the situation would have got heated. Tee and I prepared Lizzie for her journey towards North Queensland and by a little after 10-00am we were off and running. We headed towards Corowa and then diverted away from the Murray in pursuit of arriving in Forbes before nightfall. The journey was reasonably uneventful although the countryside was amazingly green and as we continued North the rain began to fall.

We had lunch at a small town just before Urana but as it does not appear on our map its name has eluded both Tee and I. Not to be deterred I checked my Wiki Camps App and found that it was Urana Dam and in Urana itself, on the outskirts. I was so excited about this lunch as in Yarrawonga, on the way out of town, I bought a couple of fresh loaves of bread and had requested Tee make me my favourite lunch – Peanut Butter Sandwiches – Yummo! I was so excited that I scoffed down three rounds and even had space for a couple of squares of chocolate. The hard part of this lunch stop was the text that I sent Albert to tell him that we had left Yarrawonga.

The rest of the journey was mundane and when the rain came, I felt like stopping short of Forbes as I had been driving for about five hours. But the free camp in Forbes looked great and we really wanted to get there this evening. We arrived just before five and as it was raining, we didn't even get out of the Motorhome. A fellow camper informed me that I had left my lights on and after thanking him I turned them off and got out to do a few set up chores. The rain had slowed by this time and I turned on the gas for cooking and put the chocks under the rear wheels to level Lizzie for a good night's sleep.

After an early light dinner, we decided to ring the lady looking after Whiskey our cat and see how the little stinker was doing. Brenda rang back a short time later to say that Whiskey was fine and that she was eating fabulously in the cooler weather. Tee made a call to Val and Stan who were now near the Gulf in North Queensland and we chatted on speaker phone for about a half an hour. We decided to try and catch up in the Atherton Tablelands as even though coming from different directions we would probably arrive there at similar times. It was great to talk to friends in a less intense fashion as the last week or so had been quite draining, emotionally. They told us that Max (their doggie) had spotted a Motorhome like ours and was whining for an hour or so thinking it was us. We told them that we had not long ago purchased a Golden Retriever puppy (Bo) as we had planned to do and that we would be picking her up when we arrived back home. We said our goodbyes and planned to catch up in the Atherton Tablelands in a week or two.

The rest of the evening was dedicated to working out our new portable hot water system so we could both have hot showers. Fortunately, this worked out well and the new hot water system was a great success. I wrote for the evening and Tee read in bed before we hit the sack at about 10-00pm to the sound of light rain on the roof and a dickhead doing burnouts in the distance.

Day **296**

Today we would be attempting to travel 450 klm's to the town of Walgett, which is just south of Lightning Ridge and not that far from the sunny state of Queensland. As we left Forbes, and more particularly the campsite that we had just stayed at, we noticed that the weather was improving even though it had been raining. The chill in the air had almost disappeared and we were extremely happy that we were heading north.

Our first stop was at the Shell Servo in Forbes where we filled up with Diesel before our days travel. The two gentlemen in the Servo, who were about my age, seemed very interested in my travels and asked where we had been and how long we had been travelling. When I told them they both said how envious they were to which I responded in the advise given to me by the old timer in Hervey Bay - "there are a thousand reasons why you should not do it, but only one why you should" – take the one as life is short and the time to live is now. Now as I said this, I thought of the NOW generation and thought that this advice is already being lived by them on a daily basis. The problem with that is that most of them can't afford it and yet that doesn't seem to stop them. The late baby boomer generation seem to be all work and no play – it is a shame that we can't put the two generations into a big mixing pot and blend them into the correct balance.

Back on the road and it was not long before we were on the outskirts of the town of Parkes – Home of the Dish. On my many visits to Parkes I had never seen it so green and lush. We did not stop in Parkes but we did manage to get a coffee break at the Dish itself. What an amazing structure and it is so hard to believe it was built in 1961. We took a heap of photos and had a cuppa before hitting the road again. We drove through Dubbo and had to stop either side of town for road works as it looked as though the recent rains had caused some havoc with the highway surface. We continued our Journey through the town of Gilgandra, the home of the Cooee, (which I didn't know had a home) and as we left Gilgandra, we also said goodbye to the Newell Highway – famous for its truck traffic. Lizzie was so happy as those trucks spray so much shit off the road in the rain.

As we continued our northward trek the landscape got dryer and dryer despite the rain. Obviously, the soil was not as fertile but it mattered little to us as the temperature was a yummy 21 degrees and it looked as though the bitterly cold weather was now far behind us. The road from Gilgandra to Walgett was in a very poor state and Lizzie was not enjoying the rough surface and crumbling edges. Again, it was probably bad due to the recent rains but Tee and I both felt that it was not that well maintained before that either.

We arrived in Walgett at 5.07pm and soon spotted the Rotary Park that was a free camp area. Tee prepared Dinner for us, steak and veggies, while I did the weekly budget and paid a few more bills (darn things never stop coming). We had driven over 1,000 kilometres in the past week with over 900 kilometres in the last two days alone. We had gone over budget, mainly due to the service I had done on Lizzie while in Yarrawonga ($300.00) and in fact 90% of the budget had gone to Lizzie, if you include the fuel. But we were only $100.00 down on the overall budget and this included that service and the four new tyres we purchased in Cobram a few weeks ago. Pretty good considering, so Tee and I are well pleased with our efforts.

Day **297**

Walgett turned out to be a pretty good rest stop and in the morning we filled up at the local fuel station in a new budget week. With such a big drive yesterday, we could afford to be a bit kinder to ourselves and travel just 300 Kilometres today to the Queensland country town of St George. In fact, we had toyed with two other locations, the first being Dirranbandi (250 kilometres) and Roma (almost 500 kilometres). We immediately ruled our Roma as we felt that it was too far after yesterday's effort and we would see how we felt when we got to Dirranbandi as to what our final destination would be.

Our journey would take us through the town of Lightning Ridge that Tee and I imagined to be similar to Cooper Pedy. In fact, the Castlereagh Highway did not go through Lightning Ridge and we had to travel five kilometres off the highway to reach it. Our thoughts of Lightning Ridge were similar to what reality was as the town was a bit like Cooper Pedy but not as dry and a lot tidier. The fossicking and gemstones did not appeal to Tee and I so we didn't stay long, but did stay long enough to find a lovely fresh fruit and veggie stall where Tee bought silver beet and tomatoes. The veggies looked great even though a bit pricey. We had a quick look at the Artesian Bore Baths on the outskirts of town and were amazed at the housing that some people live in, before getting back to our journey.

It seemed like no time at all until we reached the Queensland border and the town of Hebel. The town was originally called Kelly Point after the brothers of the infamous Ned Kelly were suppose to have settled here after the Glenrowan standoff. We stopped for a coffee break and to admire the pub that was as original as you could get, short of falling down. Off again for the short trip to Dirranbandi, which was one of the rest areas that we were considering, and when we arrived there, we decided at 2-00pm it was too early to stop. We kept travelling to St George which also marked a significant point in our journey as it was here that we had a water leak in Lizzie on day two of our adventure.

This was the second time that we had crossed our earlier travels but this time we were feeling different as we were now not far from home and it felt a little strange. We felt like it would be nice to turn East and back to our new king size bed and full-sized shower. But we had to resist the urge as we only have eight or so weeks to go and we are both keen to see the North Queensland Hinterland and Coast.

Our destination would be the Beardmore Rest stop which was beside a river and promised to be a lovely spot. It was not too far out of St George and we arrived there with twenty minutes of leaving town. Now came the slap in the face, as the campsite was closed and a big fence had been placed over the roadway. We were really pissed off now as the next rest area was over 100 kilometres away near the town of Surat and I was not keen on driving that far today. With no choice but to keep on driving we were just about to turn back to the highway when a 4WD pulled up alongside us. The lady passenger told us that if we were looking for a free camp there was another site about seven kilometres further up this road and to follow them. We did that and ended up at the Beardmore Youth Camp site which was absolutely lovely. When we pulled up, we thanked the couple who had led us here and set up for a quiet evening.

Day **298**

With a great night's sleep and the fact that we went to bed so early we were on the road by 8-00am. This was just as well as we would attempt a 530-kilometre day today which would see us travel all the way to the outskirts of Emerald. This may not seem like much in a car but in an old bus like Lizzie it is quite exhausting. The road conditions were also very poor and with huge two and three trailer trucks passing on a continuous basis the shoulderless roads are quite treacherous.

We passed through the town of Surat on the way to Roma and with the road conditions still ordinary, and continuous roadwork's, we were concerned for our windscreen. We stopped briefly in Roma but only for fuel as we had a long way to travel and the roads were so bad that we were making poor time. Then after Roma our fears were realized when a two trailered cattle carrying truck flying at about 100klm's per hour in a 40klm's per hour roadwork's zone sprayed us with stones. At first, I thought we had survived the onslaught but Tee's words of Fucken Hell soon told me I was dreaming.

After that incident I was in a foul mood as was Tee, and we cursed every truck that we passed for the next two hundred kilometres. Along the way we passed the turnoff to the Carnarvon Gorge and considered visiting it but we were both over the travelling and really looking forward to stopping at a campsite north of Springsure.

The road did improve after the Carnarvon Gorge turnoff and the scenery was also much prettier. This helped us get into a better place mentally and by the time we reached the Virgin Rocks Rest Area we were a lot happier. With the small rest area packed we slipped in between two caravans and the place more resembled a Caravan Park than it did a free camp.

Day **299**

The Virgin Rocks Rest Area is lovely and the view behind the campsite superb, especially at night as the cliff face is lit up. Not sure who or why it is lit up but it looks spectacular. Although the campsite was good, I did not sleep all that well and it is probably because I had a really sore shoulder from driving. I get this sore shoulder as Lizzie has no centre arm rest and my left arm is always unsupported. Fortunately, Val and Stan rang this morning and said that they are going to stay with her brother somewhere near Port Douglas for a few days. This meant that we did not have to rush to catch up with them and with that I decided to have an extra day at this free camp and we could catch up on a few chores.

The first job I tackled was to give Lizzie a bath as we had good access to water and driving in the rain earlier this week had made her filthy. It took me a good two hours to wash her down but it was well worth it as she came up looking super. I then checked all the battery levels, oil and water along with other little jobs I found to do along the way. I was unable to fix the crack in the windscreen as I did not have enough resin in the repair kit. I will have to pick some up in Emerald tomorrow on the way through, along with a wire joiner for the temperature gauge that has broken off in the engine bay.

Tee told me while studying the map that she used to live in Oaky Creek which is just outside Emerald so we plan to go there tomorrow on our way to Clermont. Today has been a good rest day for us and as we have been pushing the kilometres out since leaving Yarrawonga it will also allow us to stay within budget for the week, if only just. I got an email from my tax accountant to tell me of my healthy return that is due to me, so all in all it has been a great day.

Day 300

Something happened yesterday evening that we have not encountered in a few months, we had some tourists arrive late to camp. Pizza face and Grandma (what's going on there) not only turned up but proceeded to park directly in front of our Motorhome and facing us. The nose of their car was less than three metres from the front of our Motorhome, meaning we would have to full lock to get out – amazing. He would be lucky to be 20 and she was well into her forties and yes there was only one tent – eeeehhhhh!!!!!! I am only being mean as these people seem to have no social etiquette and they were right in our face. The door banging finished at 8-00pm and resumed at 7-00am so it was not too disturbing for us.

We got ready quite early and were on the road by 9-00am, in fact we could have got on the road much earlier if it wasn't for the second cup of tea and me dawdling. Our first stop today would be in Emerald to pick up some supplies and buy more fuel. We have been really churning out the K's over the past week and the budget is in danger of going over for the second week in a row.

As we arrived in Emerald Woolies was straight in front of us and we thought it was a good a place as any to top up our groceries. I also needed to get a wire connector for Lizzie as the temperature gauge wire had broken at the engine. Fortunately, there was a Repco store in the same shopping complex and I was able to get a wire connector there. While I was doing that Tee had branched off to look in the Discount Chemist store, which she loves with a passion. After a quick look in the BCF store I met here back at the Chemist store before we headed off to do some grocery shopping.

We only got a few items, fewer than fifty dollars worth, and one of them was a hot chook that we both fancied for lunch.

Back at Lizzie we headed off to the Servo to fill up with fuel before heading towards Capella, the turnoff to Tieri and Oaky Creek. The smell of the hot chook had been luring us since the moment we left Emerald and although we planned to eat lunch in Tieri at about 12-30pm by 11-45am we could resist no longer. We stopped in Capella at a lovely roadside stop in the middle of town and ate that lovely hot chook on fresh bread with mayo – Yummy!!!!!!!!!!!

After our sensation lunch we drove to the Capella showgrounds where I was lucky enough to be able to perform my favourite duty – yes – empty the shitter. With that out the way we drove back to Capella central then headed off to Tieri. On the way we saw many vehicles from the Variety Bash Rally and it was lovely to see these old jiggers in action, and for such a good cause. As we entered the road to Tieri, we were a little concerned as there were numerous mining trucks coming out and we were not keen on being sprayed with stones again. Fortunately, the road is quite good and more to the point quite wide so it was an uneventful 10 kilometres until we passed the mine entrance.

We continued on and soon arrived at the town of Tieri which was a lot nicer than Tee and I expected for a rural mining town. In fact, it was well maintained with good facilities and a feeling that there was good community spirit and pride in the town. But this was not the town that Tee had spent her 10th Birthday in and it was on to the town of Oaky Creek a further 10 kilometres up the road. When we arrived there all we found was a coal mining site with car parks and an administration building. There was no sign of the Caravan Park or the school that Tee had been to all those years ago (shit I mean – a few years ago). Tee was a little disappointed that she didn't find anything that she recognized but was still glad that she had visited the place.

We later learned, via the internet, that the town of Oaky Creek, which was mainly made up of demountables, ended up in Tieri including the school that Tee attended. Tee took a number of photos of both towns as she wanted to send them to her sister Shelley in Sydney.

Off again and with 100 kilometres to travel from here to Clermont we arrived there at about 3-30pm. We stayed at a local park that we thought was a free camp and enjoyed a night stroll along Hoods Lagoon where I climbed a windmill and Tee photographed my stupidity.

Day **301**

Found out later in the evening from another camper that this was not a free camp, but we took our chances as it was a Saturday night and the council workers would probably not be out and about. Turned out to be a good call as this place was a super place to camp, as it was very quiet and we felt safe. We had a superb night's sleep and in the morning Tee and I decided to go down to Hoods Lagoon again and feed the ducks.

While Tee was getting ready, I looked Clermont up on the internet to see if there were any markets on this morning, as it was Sunday. I found that a local market would be on in the centre of town (Rose Harris Park) but we were not sure how far we were from it so we decided we would drive there after feeding the duckies. As soon as Tee opened the bread bag the ducks were flying in from everywhere and nothing was going to stop them getting a feed – even their fear of humans. They were going nuts and stomping on Tee's feet to be the first in line for a feed. If we were not there to ration the feeding frenzy the whole bag of bread would have been gone in under a minute. I told Tee of the geese that were on their way for a feed and she saved a few pieces of bread for them, as they were swimming over and not flying like the other ducks did.

The whole feeding process was different than we imagined as we pictured ourselves sitting on a park bench slowly feeding a half dozen little ducks. What we got was over fifty ducks and geese going nuts and the whole thing was over before we knew it. With this we headed back to Lizzie and with a few final checks and me replacing the Temperature Gauge engine wire we were on our way.

We soon realized that town was not too big and just across the bridge from where we stayed the night. Clermont is a lovely little town and we soon located the Rose Harris Park where the Markets were SUPPOSE to be. BUT No markets - and I thought that everything on the internet was correct. Shattered and bruised (not really – but disappointed) we headed off towards our next destination of Charters Towers. The good side of the Markets not happening was that we saved a few bucks and we got away early. Some more positives were that the Temperature Gauge was working again and that Tee was proud of my mechanical skills (she didn't see how easy the job was) and I was humble ☺

On the road again and with close to enough fuel to reach Charters Towers I was keen to drive slowly and see if we could reach there on the current tank of fuel. It was a bit of a game for me but it would also make good economic sense as the roadhouse fuel prices are obscene. The landscape on our journey this morning was getting prettier the further North we went, with rolling hills and more trees. We arrived at the Plain Creek Roadhouse at about 11-30am and decided that we should stay here for lunch as there were not many wayside stops on this road and it would be good to have an early lunch for a change.

The Plain Creek Roadhouse was packed with travellers, not because it was a nice place but purely for the fact that there was nothing on this road for over 300 kilometres. They also didn't let us down with their Diesel prices either as they were 30 cents dearer than Charters Towers and 25 cents dearer than Clermont. This made me more determined to reach Charters Towers on my current fuel even though it would be marginal. I had faith in Lizzie even though I didn't tell Tee what our fuel status was.

Back on our way after lunch and the first signpost we saw read; Next Fuel 196 Kilometres. Tee asked me if we had enough fuel to which I replied "shit yeah", even though at normal speed we only had about 150 kilometres of fuel. I kept Lizzie at a constant 80 kilometres per hour and as time moved on, I was more confident of our ability to reach Charters Towers. I told Tee of my little game about 10 minutes out of Charters Towers and she was again very angry with me. She said that I was an idiot and I was never to do that again. I agreed that I was silly but told her that when I saw that obscene pump price at Plain Creek Roadhouse, I wouldn't pay that price on principle. In hindsight she was very correct as if I ran out of fuel, not only did we stop but would also, more than likely, have to bleed the fuel lines.

In my life I have done many things on principle, and in most cases, it was not in my best interest. But this is who I am and I do not want to change as I feel it is the right way to be. Perhaps though in this case it was taking things a bit far, as one customer making a stand in the middle of the Queensland outback is unlikely to make a difference. We made it to Charters Towers and I think we were very lucky too, as Tee told me upon our arrival. We had travelled 612 kilometres on one tank of fuel at an average of 8.74 kilometres to the litre – amazing figures for a 4.5 tonne Motorhome fully loaded.

After filling up with fuel we headed off to Fletcher Creek Rest Area that was only 40 kilometres up the road. On the way we rang Val and Stan to try and find a spot to meet up. I found out that they were only about 50 kilometres from the intersection that we would pass through tomorrow but they had booked in for two nights at a Caravan Park in Mount Surprise. Then the phone went dead before we could make a firm date and location to meet.

We soon arrived at the Fletcher Creek Rest Area and were amazed at the huge number of Caravans and Campers there, as the numbers must have topped one hundred. Despite this the place was calm and quiet and we found a lovely place to park Lizzie. It was almost 4-00pm when we arrived and I decided to try and create a plan for us to meet up with Stan and Val. This plan was made more difficult by the fact that we had no mobile or internet service and that there were no towns of decent size between where we were and where we thought we might meet up with Stan and Val.

At first, we thought we may go back to Charters Towers as we wanted to buy a roast and get some beer for our few days with Stan and Val. But we were not sure as it was 42 kilometres back there which meant a loss of 84 Kilometres in total. This was about one hours driving and about $16.00 in fuel. In the end we decided not to make a decision and to do the deciding the next morning after a good night's sleep.

Day 302

Despite the number of people at the Fletcher Creek Rest Area it was a super place to stop and we both had a magnificent night's sleep. So, if you are travelling this way don't be put off if you see the place is packed as it seems to hold numbers well and is a great spot to spend the night. On the way out in the morning we also got to see the lovely creek that ran beside the campsite and with that we were on our way to the Mount Garnett area (known as the gateway to the Atherton Tablelands).

We had a fair amount of travelling to do today but we thought that we should reach the junction of the Kennedy and Gulf Development Roads by a little after lunchtime. You would have probably gathered by now that we decided against going back to Charters towers for Beer and a Roast and decided to take our chances at finding a place on our way where we could buy them.

Our progress to the Atherton Tablelands was severely slowed a short distance into out travels by the beginning of roadwork's and the single lane highway that caused me to be extremely cautious and slow me right down (if that is possible in Lizzie). By single lane I mean single lane that catered for both directions, a single width piece of bitumen with dirt and rocks either side. The control of traffic flow was regulated by size and all smaller vehicles had to stop and pull over as trucks approached. A darn sensible idea when a fifty metre Semi is coming at you at 100 kilometres per hour. Even though this road rule was displayed at regular intervals we still encountered irresponsible drivers pulling into the gravel as we approached and continuing at full speed. Fortunately, we survived the journey without further damage to our windscreens, but I am not sure how.

We reached the town of Greenvale by about 11-30am and if not for my curiosity we would have missed the main part of town completely. This was because the town centre was off the main road and its entrance was over a cattle grid and beside the entrance to the Greenvale Caravan Park. Fortunately for us we found it as the Pub is the Three Rivers Hotel that Slim Dusty made famous and besides that is an extremely pleasant place. The towns claim to fame was that at one time, I believe in the 60s or 70s, was the largest Nickel mine in the southern hemisphere.

Keen to have a look inside the pub we were greeted by a lovely lady who was born and bred in the Mount Surprise area and had lived in the district all her life. She was so friendly and the whole place had a great vibe. Not only that but they sold Carlton Mids at a good price of under 50 bucks. After our beer purchase, we went back to the Motorhome and Tee prepared some crackers and toppings for our lunch. While Tee was doing that, I spotted a signpost that named and pointed to a Sausage Tree which I had never seen nor heard of before. There were actually two of them in town and only a handful apparently exists in the whole of Australia. A native of Mozambique South Africa the huge unusual fruit that resembles a hanging German sausage has no apparent use (apart from its physically amusing appearance). I enjoyed walking around the tree and photographing it until the garden sprinkler got me and I headed back to Lizzie for lunch. We ate lunch and were then on our way after a pleasant short stay in the town of Greenvale.

The roadwork's continued to dog our journey until we reached the intersection of the Kennedy and Gulf Development roads. Now this is where we had to make the second big decision of the day and that was whether to turn to met Val and Stan where they were camped at Mount Surprise or to continue on to Mount Garnett and ring them from there. The decision was not too difficult in the end as (A) it had taken us until 2-00pm to reach here when we thought we would be here by 12-00 noon and (B) we would not have enough fuel to reach the next free camp if we went to Mount Surprise. We obviously continued on but before we did, we stopped and sent Stan and Val an email explaining our plans and that we would meet them at the Archer Creek Rest Area – still no Optus reception.

Onwards to the Archer Creek Rest Area and at Mount Garnett we pulled in to the Servo to buy some fuel for my new generator. After that we tried the local food store but failed to secure a roast, but a little further up the road we did score some terrific free-range eggs at $2.00 per dozen. Not only were these eggs free-range but they were free-house also. Yes, these chickens were able to wonder freely through the lounge, kitchen and anywhere they liked.

On the outskirts of Mount Garnett, we were lucky enough to get Optus reception and I quickly rang Stan and Val to tell them of our plans and how we could meet on Tuesday at the Archer Creek Rest Area, if that was OK with them. They were more than happy with that and Tee and I were pleased that we would meet up with our good friends again soon. I then rang my mum to let her know that we were safe and where we currently were. Mum reported that all was well at home and with that we were on our way again.

We arrived at the Archer Creek Rest Area a little after 4-00pm and found a spot that was OK but hard up against the Highway. We met a lovely couple from Newcastle (Al and Pam) who we shared drinks with and had a chat with until dinner time. The spot we were parked in was quite noisy though and it would be highly unlikely that we would get a very good sleep.

Day **303**

True to form the road noise from the many passing trucks did wake us on numerous occasions but our sleep was OK considering. As promised, I cooked Tee up a yummy brekkie of Sausages and free-range eggs which we thoroughly enjoyed. Unimpressed by our current parking spot in the free camp we decided to keep our eyes out for campers in a quieter part of the free camp area that were leaving this morning. We also had to consider that we needed an area that would cater for Stan and Val as they would be arriving before lunchtime. In addition to this Al and Pam also were on the hunt for a quieter spot and the task seemed to be harder than we thought. But as luck would have it four campers opposite us all left within an hour of each other and we moved in quickly to secure our new home for the next 24 hours.

At lunchtime Val and Stan arrived with Max (their dog) jumping out of his skin to say hello to us. He is a great little dog and he was so excited to see us that he didn't know which of us to jump on first. I had reserved a spot for Stan and Val by spreading gear out all over the grass area beside our Motorhome as they had done for us when we met them again near Kakadu NT some months earlier. It was great to see them again and we chatted all afternoon and evening while making plans to travel together to Cooktown and then back down the North Queensland coast. Pam and Al also joined us in conversation and we all had a great day.

Day **304**

After a better night's sleep on this side of the campground we said our goodbyes to Al and Pam, and joined by Val and Stan we were off into the Cooktown direction. Al and Pam had been great company and gave us some good hints as well as a brochure on camping grounds all the way up to Cooktown. We swapped details and were off, with Val and Stan right behind us.

Our first stop would be the Millstream Falls which is suppose to be the widest water fall in Australia. It was only about 10 kilometres up the road and then down a dirt road of about a kilometre in length. This is the first time on our trip that we have teamed up with another vehicle and it will take a bit of getting use to. Fortunately, we have a two-way radio each and we are in constant contact. We did not know if the falls would be at the end of a dirt road but it was more than likely that they would be as most are.

As we approached the turning into the Millstream National Park the road in was indeed dirt and I went very slowly as Stan, who was following right behind me, had not long polished his car and caravan. We reached the car park to the falls without raising much dust and with four caravans already there the car park was a bit of a squeeze. The walk down to the falls was very pleasant as it was all bitumen and with only about 400mts to walk it was a pleasant stroll. The falls themselves were quite lovely, but as to the title of the widest falls in Australia I am not too sure. We spent a short amount of time looking at, and photographing the falls before returning up the hill to the crowded little car park. Stan and Val left first and all my efforts of keeping the dust off Stan's car were for nothing when an old idiot in a filthy Landcruiser came flying into the National Park and totally spraying Stan with dust. The only positive was that I hadn't left the car park yet and none of the dust had covered Lizzie. This did not stop me from calling the inconsiderate prick some choice names and giving him the finger. What a jerk, as what he did was so unnecessary.

Stan took it well and we continued on towards Ravenshoe where we would start to do some of the chores that we had planned for the day. I set my Wiki Camps navigator to the Ravenshoe Dump Point where we became the first in a que of Vans and Motorhomes that seemed to arrive straight after we got there. No shitter Nazi's here and we got back on the road and headed for a local Park to fill our house water tanks. In the local park we met a few local Aborigines who I asked about the water and they told me it was good to use. While I was filling up the water bottles a little Aboriginal girl was quietly saying hello to me and because she was crouched down, I did not see her. She had a tiny voice that screeched a bit and I thought it was a Cockatoo saying hello. I was studying the closest gumtree to see this Cockatoo without success until I saw this little girl. She was absolutely beautiful with big chocolate brown eyes and a huge smile. I felt so silly looking into a tree but I don't think anyone noticed and I wasn't about to admit my error. I asked her what her name was but she was now shy and I could not make out what she was saying. Her uncle who was a few feet away said hello to me and when I told her how pretty she was her uncle made her say thank you to me.

While I was filling up with water Stan spotted a Mitre 10 store and pointed it out to me. I needed some liquid nails and three screws as I had leant on the dining table this morning and had to fix it today some time. We headed over to the Mitre 10 store while Val and Stan waited for us down the road. I got the liquid nails but they did not have the screws I needed and anyway I had another way to fix it. I needed fuel and even though I may have made it to Atherton I thought it not worth the risk and filled Lizzie up at the Ampol Ravenshoe. (scared of Tee)

Off again with Val and Stan in pursuit as the scenery and the altitude got better and higher. We reached some Wind turbines at the top of a ridge outside Ravenshoe and because we were so close to them and the view was so stunning, we decided to stop again for a few photos and to admire these much hated structures. The wind turbines were amazing as Tee and I had never been so close to them before but the view – well that just took your breath away. To us it was like Maleny (Sunshine Coast Hinterland) on steroids and with a warmer temperature. The rolling hills were so green that it was near impossible to believe where we were on the map.

Back on the road and with Stan having to travel some distance to find an adequate turning space we were well ahead of him on our way to Atherton. The gap did not last long though as we soon hit roadwork's and were stopped for over five minutes as the vehicles heading south came through the single available lane. The road here must have been flooded out or something as we encountered a number of these stoppages on the way to Atherton. But along the way to Atherton the roadworks could not compete with the sheer beauty of this place and with numerous rain forest sections Tee and I were continually impressed.

We arrived in Atherton where I immediately spotted an IGA store of major proportions. And as I entered the car park, I radioed Stan to let him know that there was room here for his vehicle to park and turn safely. We all went into the IGA store, which was massive, and did a large shop. Larger than we intended as the prices were good and the variety excellent. On the way out we bought some wine and Tee and I ate a hot chicken sandwich in the car park while Stan and Val headed to the Rocky Creek War Memorial Rest Area, our destination for the day.

Not long after Stan and Val had arrived, we dawdled in and set up beside them. We spent the afternoon planning our trip together and had a pleasant time until about 5-30pm when Tee and I retreated to our Motorhome for dinner and a quiet evening together. All was good until about 7-30pm when three mini bus loads of French tourists turned up and started pitching tents close to our vehicle. This got us both agitated as we knew they would cause us grief some time in the not to distant future. And true to form they started yelling and giggling and two boys started to take a leak in the grass behind our Motorhome. Fortunately, I spotted them and told them to get the hell out of there and use the toilets with the redheaded one returning "no speak English", a standard line for these smartasses. I then told them I had a tyre leaver here that I would use on them and all of a sudden – wallah! – they understood. After they had set up three tents, they all took off back to Atherton (we presume for dinner) and we braced for the onslaught when they returned. Although not too noisy they were still annoying and through the night they woke Tee a couple of times.

Policy really needs to be created about this sort of behaviour as the Caravan people are currently being treated like second class citizens in their own country. I have now spoken to many couples who now no longer free camp due to the disruption that these young tourists cause. I feel it is unfair that people who have spent their whole life paying taxes in our great country cannot freely live out their retirement dream of touring Australia cheaply. While freeloaders from overseas can not only do it but abuse it by leaving their rubbish and being so disruptive as to spoil other people's enjoyment. Take heed that this will create Camp rage similar to what occurs as road rage. The point is that we as a human race have become so much dog eat dog that it is now affecting our way of life and without legislation and enforcement things will get nasty. The easy fix would be to ban non self-contained vehicles from overnight stays all over Australia. These tourists will then have to either pay for accommodation or buy vehicles that are friendly to the environment. That way the ones that are here will have "skin in the game" and be made more responsible for their behaviour.

If the police would also like some easy targets then they should raid the free camps for roadworthy's and drug testing. This would also create safer roads and safer campsites for our grey-haired brothers and sisters that just want to enjoy their retirement. New Zealand has introduced the Freedom Camping act which is designed to combat the problems associated with this activity and Australia should follow suit as the problem will only get worse in time.

Day 305

We awoke this morning and Tee was still upset with the events of last night. She spoke to the single lady in the van next to us who told Tee she was kept up all night and was very scared as some of the tourists were pissing at the side of her van. This is simply not on and we decided that we would move on today to try and find a quieter spot where these problems were less likely to happen.

There were no such suitable sights in the Camps6 book but I did find a spot at Kairi which was only about 15 kilometres away from here. It did mean that we would have to back track a bit towards Atherton but it was not that far so we were keen to do it. We told Stan and Val that we would like to leave and they agreed even though they were not as affected as we were by the young tourists. They were happy to work in with us and respected our feelings; as well they needed a few items in Atherton that they had forgotten to buy yesterday. It would also be good for us to re-visit Atherton as our butane cooker was on the blink and Tee has been trying to limp it through til when we got home. Another positive was that we could visit Lake Tinaroo which we thought we may miss or catch up with on our way back down the coast.

We were ready in a flash to go but Stan and Val were still packing up. Tee and I decided to leave anyway as we were so pissed off with the place and we just wanted to get the hell out of there. We told Val that we would meet them in Atherton as we were heading off to walk around the town a bit. Stan was walking Max their dog somewhere and we told Val to let him know what we were doing.

We soon arrived in Atherton which was only 10 or so Kilometres from the Rocky Creek War Memorial Rest Area and parked outside the Holden dealership at the northern end of town. We dropped in to look at the Colorado twin cab ute, as I am considering this type of vehicle when I get back home. The sales fellow was not too pushy and we left with a brochure for me to read at a later time. The Bunning's store was close by and we bought the second last butane cooker that was on the shelf, along with some toilet chemicals and some butane canisters. Tee and I then took a leisurely stroll through the town of Atherton which is very charming and quite old fashioned. 90% of the stores are single shop faces along the main street with the multinationals being located off this strip and in the back roads. This gives the town of Atherton great appeal and a lot of individuality.

Tee and I visited a couple of second hand shops and in the second shop she found a couple of teddy bears that would provide good company for Bo (our puppy) when we got home. Tee got this idea from Val as doggie toys are very expensive and we got two lovely teddy bears for three dollars. As we were just leaving the large pet shop in town, we got a call from Stan and Val who had finished all they needed to do in Atherton and were wondering if we were ready to head off. We told them we were on our way towards them and that we too have bought what we needed. We all left Atherton together and after stopping briefly for generator fuel we headed towards Kairi hoping that the campsite there was OK.

With only a little over ten kilometres to travel we soon arrived at the Lions Park in Kairi which was a lovely little spot. Stan thought we were actually going to Lake Tinaroo and was not all that impressed. He soon came round though as the place was lovely and Max enjoyed the lovely green grass. We soon set up camp and decided that this place was worth staying in for a couple of days as it was quiet and central, with both mobile and internet reception.

We didn't do a great deal for the rest of the day other than a few chores and a series of chats that went on all day and into the evening.

Day 306

It was lovely sleeping here last night and Tee had a great sleep as I should have done, but for some reason I was awake for a couple of hours in the early morning. Never mind though as I still managed a good amount of sleep and could catch up tonight by hitting the sack early. I decided that I should dust off the push bike and head out to Tinaroo Dam while Tee and Val did their washing. It was about eight kilometres each way and would be a lovely amount of exercise in a pleasant environment. It started out that way and in the early morning the ride was very pleasant. Unfortunately, though there was a heap of roadwork's and I had to be very careful not to get hit by cars as the road was now very narrow with no shoulders to take refuge on. I negotiated my way through these obstacles unscathed, but I didn't get to enjoy the journey because of them.

Fortunately, the best scenery was yet to come and the rest of my bike ride around Tinaroo Dam and onto the Dam wall was most enjoyable. I took a lot of lovely photos and with a number of taps along the way I got to recover briefly at each and enjoyed the view. I must admit that recently our exercising has been less than minimal and the 17 kilometre ride this morning had me really struggling.

Tee had done all the washing by the time I got back and we just potted around for the rest of the day. I found a spare part that I needed for Lizzie on the internet and ordered it and even found time to change the oil in my new generator. I also rang the electoral commission to find out how we could vote on the 7th of September 2013 as we would still be on the road and probably a long way from home. Later in the afternoon Tee and Val cooked up a roast Dinner for the four of us, which we ate together in their Caravan before retiring to our own Motorhome to prepare for heading off in the morning.

Day **307**

We headed off this morning and our first trip would be to the Tinaroo Dam as Tee, Val and Stan had not been there yet. I had a head start as I rode out there yesterday morning and had a good look around. Our first stop should be the Dam but the roadwork's had already begun and we were stopped twice by the road workers before we reached the Dam itself. Stan and Val would meet us there as they were ready before we were this morning and took off a short time before we did. Finally, through the roadwork's, Tee and I took a peek at the lookout just before the Tinaroo Dam but the view was only average as the trees in the area had covered most of the view. We continued to the Dam where we again caught up with Stan and Val and had a cuppa before all heading to the Dam Wall. It was a bit windy this morning so we all decided not to stay too long, and I was well pleased that I rode here yesterday as I got a heap of photos then and the views of the dam were a lot clearer. We took off after a bit of a walk around and headed back through Kairi towards our next campsite of Granite Gorge, just outside Mareeba.

The landscape as we left Kairi progressively got dryer and we were soon passing the Rocky Creek War Memorial Rest Area which we stayed at a few nights ago. A few kilometres north of there we came to a turning that was the back road to the Granite Gorge Caravan Park. Tee checked the map and it was a sealed road so we decided to turn down here rather than travelling to Mareeba then out to Granite Gorge. We had to wait for Stan and Val on the corner of the back road but as we had the two ways working communication was quite simple. As soon as we headed west down this back road the landscape got dryer and much more country. The surrounding hills were covered in large Granite Boulders and were a promise of things to come.

The entire trip to the Granite Gorge Caravan Park was sealed until we reached the entrance of the Caravan Park that was a dusty corrugated track. When we arrived in the Caravan Park itself, we were suitably unimpressed as the place was a dustbowl and very uninviting. We considered staying here only for the Gorge walks but when I was pulled up by the owner/ caretaker and called darling I was very much against us staying. She treated me in a derogatory manor by yelling "hey Darling, if you want to see the Gorge you have to pay the $28.00 camp fee up front". I was only having a look at the scenery and when I told Stan, Val and Tee of my treatment they all agreed that we should move on. The treatment was not the main reason as the place was an ordinary dustbowl and at $28.00 was not what we expected.

The next possibility for our next overnight stay was the Mareeba Showgrounds that was located about 15 kilometres north of here. We weaved our way through the countryside until we came out in the industrial part of Mareeba. We then drove through Mareeba and at the north end of town we turned left to get to the Mareeba Showgrounds. The campground here was OK but they had a horse show on and the place was packed, so we decided that this was also not going to be the place we stayed tonight. Our next option was another 40 odd kilometres north of here near Mount Molloy at a place called Rifle Creek Rest Area. This was also the junction of either heading north west to Cooktown or east to Cairns. Tomorrow we would be taking the North West option and then after visiting the Cooktown area for two or three days we would be back through here on our way to Cairns. We arrived at the Rifle Creek Rest Area and were happy that it was now third time lucky in our search today for a suitable overnight camping spot.

We settled in quickly and found the place to be a good spot that had great tree cover and a lovely meandering creek on its boundary. As with any place though if you have good neighbours it is fine but there is never any guarantee as to who is going to pull up next to you.

Day **308**

Tee and I had a super night's sleep last night, the best we have had in a week. We put it down to the fact that the weather overnight was much milder here so the cold nights were not waking us up in the early hours. We all headed of at about 9-00am and today it was Stan's turn to take the lead in driving, and he would also choose where we stopped for the night. This was a lot less stressful on me as the driver as I had no decisions to make other than to press the stop and go leavers on Lizzie, I really enjoyed it. Not much really occurred today other than we arrived at the James Earl Lookout Rest Area at about 11-00am after one coffee break along the way. Stan had done a marvellous job of getting us here and we spent a quiet day chatting and enjoying the magnificent view.

Day **309**

The James Earl Lookout was all bitumen and not all that inviting for campers; although with the knockout views we thought it was very nice. For this reason, we were almost alone at this camp spot overnight except for a pair of German girls who turned up in the usual Whiz Bang set up. Amazing that their vehicle even ran as I believe it to be a 1974 Toyota Hi-ace van that is now close to 40 years old. They are also very brave young girls travelling around Australia by themselves and sleeping in open campsites. Fortunately for them though they were extremely ugly and unlikely to fall victim to a predatory male. They befriended Val last night and said they would like to follow us to Cooktown and stay where we were all staying. When Val told me this, I told her that they couldn't as their vehicle was not self contained. She said oh shit and went over to their van this morning to tell them. Val said they still wished to follow us and I was surprised when I saw them take off fifteen minutes later without us.

Stan and Val had a bad night sleep last night as their doggie Max was not feeling too good. They had been kept awake until after midnight, which I knew as they had woken me as they walked though their van at about that time. They were not in the best of moods this morning and when the German girls drove off without them, they were annoyed even further. I said to them that they need not be upset as that was typical of the NOW generation who are only nice when they are getting something. This is a generalization but they are renowned for this selfishness.

It was Tee's turn to be in charge today and I assisted her before we left in choosing our route for journey. We were heading to Cooktown and with only 80 kilometres or so to travel it was not all that difficult. Stan was not in the best of moods and was being a bit grumpy but we hoped he would snap out of it as the day wore on. We pulled out of the James Earl Lookout Rest Area and proceeded to drop in altitude as we headed towards the coast. There was a Motorhome parked on the side of the road on one stretch of straight highway and he was protruding onto the roadway. Normally this would not be a problem as I would just go on the other side of the road and around him. But on this occasion a semi was heading in the other direction and would reach the parked Motorhome the same time as I would. This meant that I had to slow down and, in the end, I nearly had to stop. What a dickhead – and if that was not proof – what he did next proved his claim to the title. After I passed, he pulled straight out in front of Stan who then proceeded to overtake the 'dickhead in the Motorhome'.

I knew this incident would not improve Stan's mood and it would not be too long before I found this out first hand. We did have a quick stop at Black Mountain and not much was said apart from us agreeing that the fellow in the Motorhome was a complete dickhead. Black Mountain was an interesting place and we took a few photos before heading off again to Cooktown.

When we arrived in Cooktown my first point of call would be a servo as our fuel was low and both Tee and I needed a toilet break. Fortunately, the first servo we saw as we entered Cooktown had well priced fuel and we radioed Stan to say that we were pulling in for fuel. Stan also stopped for fuel and both Tee and I got our toilet stop. Funny thing happened though as Tee went to the toilet first and was bringing the key back to the cashier I arrived to pay for the fuel. Even though the toilets were inside the servo shop they still had it locked, I am not sure why. Tee passed me the key and I gave her the Motorhome key as we crossed. I went to the toilet and on the way out I proceeded to lock it, but as I did the attendant came out saying not to as another lady had just gone in and I would lock her in. The reason he was in such a panic as last time this happened the person smashed the door open to get out. Sad really that we live in a society where we have to lock toilet doors inside buildings.

After the servo we headed to the Cooktown Shire Offices to purchase our camping permit. Before we decided on this type of free camp, I had checked the Wiki Camps app to see if Stan and Val could get into it. We were fine as we had a fully self-contained vehicle and were members of the Leave No Trace program but Stan and Val needed an external bucket for their grey water. But I had seen on the Wiki Camps comments that the council would allow external buckets if they inspected the vehicles first. We were first to purchase our camping permit and with our Leave No Trace paperwork we paid our money and were given a receipt. It was a great concept as the campsite was right near town and would keep the riff raff out (or so we thought). But when Stan and Val went to pay, they were told buckets were not allowed and were given a list of local Caravan Parks.

Stan was furious and I tried to calm him down but he was being very negative. The lady behind the counter was trying to be helpful and said that she would send someone down from upstairs to talk to us. They tried to help us by saying that if Stan and Val used our shower, they would let them camp with us. But Stan was furious and would not agree to that even though we said it would be fine with us. In the end we left and even though I agreed with him about the stupid rule I thought he could have calmed down and taken what they had said. It would have meant they got $5.00 per night camping and been next to us.

Fortunately, the Caravan Park they decided on was quite close to where we were and they seemed OK with it. Then it was our turn to be struck with misfortune with us getting a puncture in our front passenger tyre. I set about changing the tyre which involved pulling the bikes off the back of the Motorhome as the jack and tools were in the boot behind them. By the time I had finished I was covered in sweat and quite grubby in this hot Cooktown climate. Fortunately, my darling Tee had taken over some of my duties and found water for the Motorhome which also turned out to be good drinking water. Not only did she find the water but she proceeded to fill the tanks also. After all this work we found ourselves getting covered in dust by passing cars on the dirt road in front of us. I was not impressed with this and decided to move the Motorhome to higher ground a bit further from the road. I set the entire awning up and was just checking my emails when the next unfortunate incident happened – the inverter broke down. Now this is the thing that converts 12 volts into 240 volt and is crucial for my laptop use. Not only that but we were not allowed to use a generator here and it would be two days without writing and communication.

We then got a call from Stan and Val who were inviting us to join them on a trip around town as they had cleared out the back of the 4WD for us to go with them. Stan had had a nap and was feeling better and I think he felt bad about his mood and wanted to make it up to us. They drove to our campsite and were about to head off when incident number three occurred, in the form of a police officer pulling up and calling me over. She told me that I had to move my Motorhome as I was in a public park. I replied that I had a permit from council but she said that the boundary of that permit was eight meters down the hill. I was bewildered and now was starting to feel the way Stan must have felt earlier today. I told her that her time would be better spent slowing speeding drivers on the dirt road in front of us but it was a waste of breath as they rarely back down. By this stage Cooktown was leaving a very bad taste in our mouths and if it was not for its stunning beauty, I would tell travellers to avoid it. But I was just having a bad day and needed to chill out and forget about all the shit that has gone wrong this morning. Truth is that Cooktown Council is on the right track with this self-contained vehicle rule as it is generally the foreign tourists in whiz bang vehicles that spend nothing and take everything. In fact, in all our time on the road I have not seen a Caravan or Motorhome person being irresponsible to the environment.

We took off in Stan's vehicle to explore the amazing Cooktown and were soon at the waterfront admiring the amazing landscape. But it wasn't until we climbed the mountain behind town that we saw the entire beauty of the place. The view from up here is absolutely stunning and has to be seen to be believed. The lighthouse was amazingly small, the smallest we had seen on our travels, but the view OMG!!!!! There was a painter up here painting the picnic tables and I said to him – 'do you get paid for this?' He said he did and that he gives all the furniture up here many extra coats. We took photo after photo before heading back to our campsite to reset up for our stay. That evening we walked over to Val and Stan's Caravan Park and had a few drinks before going back to camp for Dinner and an early night.

Day **310**

With all the shit that happened yesterday morning and the cramped conditions that we were living in both Tee and I were struggling with homesickness. We had to muster all our positive energy to snap ourselves out of it and decided to plan our day before doing anything. The reason for the planning was that over the past week or so we had just drifted along and not enjoyed ourselves as much. We decided to go for a historical walk through town this morning and then do a bit by ourselves this arvo before catching up with Stan and Val in the late afternoon. We would also need time in a park somewhere so we could run the generator for me to do my writing, receive emails and pay a bill.

With this plan of action set in our minds we rang Stan and Val to tell them that we were going for a historic walk at 8-30am and see if they would like to join us. It was 7-45am when I rang and they said that they would like to join us on our walk. So, we got prepared and had a bite of brekkie before walking over to their Caravan Park to pick them up.

We all had a great walk through town and by the waterfront before heading back to our respective camps for the day. Val had washing to do and we decided that we would visit the botanical gardens that were supposed to be nice. As we were driving to the Botanical Gardens, I spotted a nice park that would be perfect for our generator run. It was quiet and away from houses, so I could do my writing without annoying anyone with the generator noise. The car park to the Botanic Gardens was packed and we had a job to find a decent spot for Lizzie, but as we circled for a second time a car came out of a spot that would accommodate Lizzie perfectly. It seemed that now we had taken control of our days we had also created our own luck, and it was all good.

The Cooktown Botanical Garden are lovely and well worth a trip in their own right, but as an added bonus the rainforest opens up onto Finch Bay. Wow what a spot this is and with no-one else on the beach Tee and I felt as though we were on a deserted island. The water was stunning, the granite boulders that spilt onto the beach were breathtaking and the surrounding rainforest that spilt onto the sand was pristine. We basked and enjoyed the moment for quite a while before heading back through the rainforest gardens and beyond to Lizzie.

Back in downtown Cooktown I pulled up Lizzie in the park I had discovered earlier, cranked up the generator and proceeded to write the afternoon away. At about 3-45pm I had finished my writing and it was just before 4-00pm that we got a call from Stan and Val, inviting us over for a few drinks this evening. We dropped Lizzie back at the Council RV site and got ready to visit Stan and Val for a few drinks. We carried our chairs and wine over to their Caravan Park and spent a couple of hours chatting with them before heading off back to Lizzie for the night.

Tee asked me to cook up some bacon and eggs outside that she slipped onto a sandwich and we ate them before retiring for the evening. We went to bed at about 9-00pm to chat and it was not long after that when we saw a police vehicle speed by checking for trouble. It would not have been five minutes later that a red 4WD pulled up with a single white male in it pulled up right beside us. Tee and I both thought this amazing as it was like he knew when the police drove past, as he was not a self-contained vehicle (obviously) and was not meant to be parked here. Not only that but he proceeded to crank up his car stereo while preparing his vehicle for sleep. He was noticeably drunk and still sipping on a stubby as he went about his business. Tee and I were fuming as the music was annoying us but it was not too loud so we stayed in bed and put up with it. Then he proceeded to turn the car radio up even higher and I could hold my tongue no longer. I bounced out of bed, threw on my pants, flung Lizzie's door open and proceeded to give him a verbal bashing. I then told him to turn the bloody music down and shut up or with one phone call I would have him kicked out of here.

He apologized and desperately tried to turn the music down, but he was so pissed that he couldn't work out how to do that. I again told him to turn it down and he responded by saying he was getting the hell away from me. I did not realize that I had scared him so much but I was glad when he drove off. In fact, Tee was watching him from the bedroom window and he only drove to the other side of a few more Motorhomes that were parked in the same area.

We both laughed at the events that had just unfolded and laughed even more when Tee spotted him walking back to pick up the beer bottle that he had left beside our vehicle. He must have been looking everywhere in his vehicle for that beer as it was a full 10 minutes before he came back claim it. Truth is this was no laughing matter as this nuisance was driving a motor vehicle in this state. We finally got to sleep at about 10-30pm and even though disturbed by this drunk we did not feel in danger at any point in time.

Day **311**

From drunks to Whiz Bangers and we awoke at 6-30am to the sound of a slamming car door which belonged to a group of three foreign tourists that must have been moved on by locals or police from another location. The reason I gather this is that we have never seen them up so early and they all looked liked startled rabbits as they exited their vehicle.

I am being so cynical as both Tee and I are amazed at the events that have unfolded over the past two days. Two days ago, we were in the Cooktown Shire Offices trying to get our friends into the $5.00p/n self contained camp with us, and without success as they would not allow Stan to use a bucket under his vehicle instead of a holding tank. The next day I had the Police moving me 8 metres as I was in the wrong area – apparently, to last evening and this morning where we have drunks and whiz bangers using the area freely. To be honest – I now don't give a shit as we are leaving Cooktown and heading south towards home. Cooktown's landscape is stunning but a lot of its locals are feral and the vibe of the place is not too flash.

Stan and Val were at our site by 8-45am even though we had agreed to leave at 10-00am this morning. They caught me on the hop as I was not prepared to leave yet and was in the middle of a phone call with a friend. Tee said to them that we would be about a half an hour before we were ready and they decided to head off to our next campsite and wait for us there. This spot was only 8 kilometres away and on the banks of the Annan River. We got ready as quick as we could and after filling Lizzie up with water and giving her a little wash, we went into town to buy some bread and generator fuel.

We arrived at the Annan River at about 10-00am and Stan told us that we could not camp here and that the fishing was no good either. He had been talking to a fella who was fishing from the old road bridge and they had been there for hours without luck. There was also a no camping sign in place so our only option was to move on. We decided to head back to the James Earl Lookout Rest Area which we were at about three days ago. It was only about 80 kilometres from here and we arrived there at 11-00am which again was too early to stop for the day.

Stan and Val seemed really keen to move on, which suited us as we were now only eight weeks away from the end of our journey and we were yet to explore the whole North East Coast of Australia. This was a part of the Journey that Tee and I were really looking forward to and the quicker we started exploring it the better. We made it all the way to Mount Molloy today which in reality isn't all that far but is much more than we had been doing for the past week or so. On our way to Mount Molloy we picked up another stone chip and decided to wait until we returned home to buy the resin and fix all the chips in our windscreen. In fact, the way we have been getting them lately we could in fact pick up a few more before we get back to Beachmere.

We made it to Mount Molloy by 1-30pm and had a bite to eat before setting up camp again. The Rifle Creek Rest Area was a lovely spot to camp at when we were here about four days ago and although busy it was quiet and very pretty. This would be our last day on the road with Stan and Val as they would be heading to Port Douglas and we would be heading south to Atherton in the morning.

We all chatted for the afternoon and were joined by other campers from time to time which diversified our conversation. Tee made up a yummy egg and bacon risotto and we ate it before borrowing a movie from Stan and Val to watch. The movie was 'Charlie and Boots', an Aussie travel film staring Paul Hogan and that famous toilet bloke. It was quite entertaining and some of the landscape was quite familiar but both Tee and I thought it was not as exciting as our Journey. And 'Yes' we will look at movie offers, but Tee says only if John Travolta plays me.

Day **312**

We said our farewells to Stan and Val and even though we have enjoyed their company it will be good to travel as Cee and Tee again. On the road by 9-30am and with Atherton in our sights we enjoyed our journey back over familiar ground. Even though we had been here before the scenery going in the opposite direction was different again and this time we stopped for a few photos along the way. It was hard when Val and Stan were following us as we could not just pull up anywhere we liked. Mareeba was very busy when we drove through town and I nearly side swiped a little car going through the main street, that I didn't see. Disaster averted, by luck rather than good skills, and we were soon back in Atherton, a town that Tee and I are very fond of.

We were keen to get an inverter here as running the generator is not something we want to do every day, especially late in the evening while watching a movie. We went from store to store and finally picked up a good one in Supercheap Auto even though it was more than I wanted to pay for one. We had a lovely walk through town and after we bought some fuel in Tolga, we headed back to the Kairi Central Rest Area where we stayed about five days ago. We also stopped at a fresh fruit and veggie place where we got a few things including some yummy farm eggs. Kairi was a lovely spot and we looked forward to a good night's rest here.

Day **313**

True to form Kairi provided us with a lovely night's sleep and we were well rested. Today would see us heading to the coast via the Gillies range and Gordonvale, while we were not sure wether or not we would visit Cairns. On the way out of Kairi we took a shortcut through farmland and onto the town of Yungaburra. The soil through this area is superb and we marvelled at how ideal this area was for farming, even the cows in the paddocks seemed to have a smile on their faces. Our first stop of the day was at the Curtain Fig National Park and the centrepiece of this National Park was the amazing Curtain Fig tree that was enormous. We marvelled at its form from all angles and took a load of photos from the boardwalk that surrounds it.

Back on the road again and we soon saw another point of interest that took our fancy, a place called Lake Barrine that was only a short distance off the highway. When we arrived at the lake, we were confronted with a picturesque lake surrounded in rainforest and emerald green grass. The place was absolutely stunning and reminded Tee and I of Lake Baroon in the Sunshine Coast Hinterland near our home. In fact, the whole area around the Atherton Tablelands reminded us very much of the Hinterland near our home. This reinforced the fact to us that we needed to spend more time enjoying the stunning countryside and bays that surround our home. And further enforces the saying – 'there is no place like home'.

As you can tell by now Tee and I are getting excited about home and can't wait to enjoy the comforts that it will bring. We are really enjoying our journey but do miss some things that only a home can provide – like space! Our journey has now taught us many lessons and one of the most important one I think is 'appreciation', as you tend to get stale if you don't do different things and tend to take what you have for granted. We enjoyed a lovely stroll around the Lake before heading off to find a quiet spot for lunch. A bit down the road we saw a signpost to a place called Catch A Barra, and we thought yeah right. A short distance past this we saw another sign displaying a picnic spot beside Little Mulgrave River. We pulled up, had a bite to eat and took a few photos of the surrounding mountain ranges.

The journey from here to Gordonvale was an extremely tight winding road through mountain ranges, but fortunately we were travelling downhill and the road quality was excellent. It took us quite a while to reach Gordonvale as I took it very slowly to nurse Lizzie down the range and not put excessive braking on her. She handled it brilliantly and when we arrived at Gordonvale, we were greeted by the Bruce Highway – a highway that is very familiar to us. It is the same Bruce Highway as the one I crossed every day on my way to work but some 1600 kilometres north. The sight of the highway name brought memories and yearnings as we were both longing to enjoy the comforts and familiarity that our home brought us. At Gordonvale we realized that it was only twenty odd kilometres to Cairns and it would be silly not to have a look, seeing we were now so close. The transformation from country to city was sharp and swift as we were now stopping and starting at traffic lights and seeing the large shopping centres and high-rise buildings. Yet only twenty minutes ago we were winding through thick rainforest with hardly a car in sight.

My memory of Cairns (12 years ago) was not the same as Tee and I were witnessing now, and after all the traffic then finally reaching the beach, we were keen to get the heck out of here. I am not saying that it is a horrible place, but it is not conducive to a pleasant drive especially in a five-tonne bus like Lizzie. I said to Tee; when we do trips in a 4WD later on we will come back and look at it again. With this we were both satisfied with our brief visit to Cairns and were off again.

It was approaching 3-00 pm now and we though it best we decide where we would be spending the night tonight. We had been given a few hints by other travellers but we thought that Babinda would be the best option. With not a great distance to travel we soon arrived in the pretty and quiet town of Babinda. We then thought before settling here for the day we would have a look at the Babinda Boulders a short distance up the road. There was camping here but with limited sites available we really thought we would be back in Babinda itself this evening. The trip out to the Babinda Boulders took us through some lovely rainforest and when we arrived, we were lucky enough to find the last campsite next to a couple from Goulburn NSW. They greeted us and we had a chat before setting up Lizzie for our stay and then going for a walk along the river and to the small water fall. We walked for about two or three kilometres in the pristine rainforest and marvelled at the huge boulders in the fast-flowing stream. In fact, the stream looked very much like the Rocksberg area near our home but with water.

We must be getting homesick as every place of beauty that we now see reminds us of a place of beauty located near our home!

We returned back to Lizzie and had a few glasses of wine while I cooked Tee a lovely pasta dinner. At about 9-00pm in the tranquillity of this lovely spot we hit the sack for an early night's sleep.

Day **314**

We had a superb night's sleep and didn't open our eyes until 7-00am. The couple from Goulburn who were camped beside us were off today and we had decided to spend one more night here as it was a fabulous place and we could do with a day off the road. Tee hand washed the sheets and a few items as we had good water supply, while I relaxed and did some writing. After lunch we went for another walk through the rainforest before spending the afternoon watching the butterflies and reading our books.

Day **315**

Today would see us return to the coast and onto a sandy beach which we had not seen since Cooktown and even then, only briefly. The weather was fine but Tee was not feeling all that crash hot as the cask wine we drank last night was a little ordinary. We checked the map and decided that we would set our sights on Mission Beach today as it was supposed to be a terrific place. When we got back to Babinda on the Bruce Highway, I crossed it to get to the Rotary Park where they had a dump point. Yes, it's Shitter emptying time again – Hooray! After that task –which I might add I will only have to do another five times before we are home (but who's counting), we hit the road towards Innisfail which will be our next major town. But a short distance up the road we came to a tourist signpost that displayed Josephine Falls which we thought was worth a look.

When we arrived at the falls car park Tee noticed that the falls were an uphill 700mtr walk and told me that she was not up to it the way she was feeling. I on the other hand was feeling great and decided to do the looking for both of us. Tee decided to lock up the Motorhome and have a brief nap to try and get herself feeing better. With not wanting to leave Tee alone for too long and the fact that I felt a million bucks, I decided to jog up to the falls. The scenery was similar to the Babinda Boulders where we had just camped for two nights and I jogged merrily up the meandering sealed pathway up to the first swimming hole. Even though similar to the Babinda Boulders in landscape I think the swimming area was prettier with an amazing water fall cascading into the deep swimming pool. Taking photos all the way, for both our collection and to show Tee when I got back, I continued my jog up to the top pool before jogging back to the car park. Although the weather was quite humid and warm, I actually felt great sweating it out. Perhaps it was just a good way to get that toxic cask wine out of my system.

I was soon back at the Motorhome where Tee was having a rest on the floor of Lizzie. I tapped on the door for her to let me in and when I saw her face, I knew she was not feeling too well. But I could not help being a boy and stirring her up a bit. I asked if she would like me to cook her some bacon and eggs, or perhaps we could buy a hamburger. Tee was not impressed but could only muster a death stare so I was saved from a verbal attack.

Back on the road and we were soon on our way to Innisfail where I hoped to get some fresh bread even though it was a Sunday. The scenery in this part of Queensland is stunning and the mountain ranges are some of the highest in the state. When we arrived at Innisfail Tee wanted a public toilet as she was now quite ill and I found a park that so happened to be right next to a Coles supermarket and across the road from a KFC. Tee rushed off to the toilet block while I checked my emails and paid another couple of bills. When she got back, I popped into the supermarket where I bought two fresh loaves of bread. I then asked Tee if she would like some KFC and that she may not feel like it now but at dinner time she may like it as it would be an easy meal. Again, I got the death stare as she looked as pale as a ghost, but it was lunchtime and after my morning jog I was quite hungry.

I went ahead and skipped off to KFC where I bought 10 pieces of chicken and a couple of packets of chips. I was starving now as the smell of KFC is irresistible to me and when I got back to Lizzie I started scoffing into the chips. Tee looked at me in horror and said the smell was making her ill. But after I convinced her to eat a couple of chips to try and settle her tummy down, she changed her tune. The food did in fact end up making her feel better and it was not too long after we hit the road again that she started getting chirpy. In fact, she seemed so much better that I thought it was safe to stir her up a little by telling her that I preferred her sick as the quiet matched the serenity of the scenery. Tee must have been feeling better as she gave me a rye smile and continued on chatting.

Although Tee was now feeling better, I thought it would be best not to travel too far today and I suggested to her that we stop at the next free camp. Tee agreed and it was about 25 kilometres down the road that we found one. We pulled into it but I was not too keen on it and because the budget this week was good, I said to Tee perhaps a Caravan Park would be nice. Tee immediately agreed and said that we had just passed a turnoff to Cowley Beach and it looked quite nice. I looked up for a Caravan Park there and rang the only one I had listed in my Camps6 book. It turned out to be the only one at Cowley Beach a place that could not even boast a shop and held only a couple of dozen homes. I spoke to Tammy (the caretaker) and they had a couple of spots, so I booked one with her. When we arrived at Cowley Beach we were impressed with the serenity and the Beach was very North Queensland with no waves, islands just off shore and coconut palms lining the beach. We checked into the Caravan Park before heading off for a long beach walk and a relaxing afternoon. Tee was now feeling much better and when we returned from our beach walk, she ate a couple of pieces of KFC chicken.

Day **316**

We didn't do much last night so it was early to bed but this didn't stop us having a lovely sleep in. When we finally did get up, we got prepared for the days events which would see us visit Mission Beach. A lot of people rave about Mission Beach so we were looking forward to our day's activities. After we got all the dismantling chores done and were set to hit the road, I went into the Caravan Park Office to pay for our accommodation and thank Tammy for her hospitality. The Caravan Park here was basic but it was quiet and very well run which made our stay very pleasurable. As we left the Caravan Park, we took one last look at the beach that was like a sheet of glass this morning. Very pretty and quiet place that would make a sensational destination for someone who wanted to get away from it all and just chill.

Back on the road and as we passed the farming country between the beach and the Bruce, we commented on how lucky the farm animals were in this part of the country, with plenty of green grass and idyllic surroundings. It was not long before we reached the Highway where the hustle and bustle began as Lizzie was pushed to keep up with the flow of traffic. Fortunately, we did not have to stay on the Bruce Highway for long as it was not too far before we reached the turnoff to Mission Beach, much to the excitement of Lizzie, who likes the gentler pace.

Prior to entering Mission Beach, we spotted many signs asking drivers to slow down and watch out for Cassowaries. The best was a giant sign with a Cassowary involved in a head on with a motor vehicle. That was not the funny part, as the funny part was that the Cassowary seemed to come off better than the motor vehicle. Not far past that sign we saw a National Park sign pointing towards a Rainforest walk, so we pulled in for a look. The walk was a loop walk and at 1.1 kilometres long it was ideal for this time of the morning in these humid conditions. As we got out of the Motorhome Tee spotted a Cassowary right at the start of where we were going on our walk. We were so excited as we had no idea that we would actually see a Cassowary as we thought they were fairly rare. They are a funny looking creature and quite aggressive so we photographed him from a distance and felt privileged to do so. He kept wanting to come towards us and we kept our distance due to their reputation until we realized that he was trying to get past us onto the track that was just across the road. We pulled back a little and he scooted past us and across the bitumen road leading to Mission Beach.

What an amazing start to our little nature walk and I was so excited to have seen a wild Cassowary. Tee was also happy to see it but I could see a look of concern in her eyes and I asked her what was wrong. She said she was concerned about running into another Cassowary on our walk who may get aggressive and with no where to escape we may get injured. I convinced her to come on the walk by doing the track backward and she agreed but was still tentative. We made our way over to the other end of the loop walk and we were on our way.

As we meandered through the rainforest the humidity seemed to increase as there was not a puff of wind and the sound of flies indicated that we should watch our step as Cassowary shit was not far away. I always thought Cassowary Shit was runny and full of seeds until I tripped on one that stood about 20 cm's high, much to Tee's amusement.

We soon came upon a stream and were delighted when we spotted fish swimming in a crystal-clear section of this stream. Our delight turned to amazement when we then witnessed fish the size of a large frypan swimming by. We then spotted the no fishing sign and a group of plaques describing each breed of fish that were found in the area. The ones we spotted were the Jungle Perch – now doesn't that sound tasty.

Our walk finished without further incident and without being attacked by crazed Cassowaries. As we approached Lizzie we were passed by and elderly couple and the man asked 'how many Cassowaries did you see?'

obviously thinking that the answer would be none. When we told him one, he seemed amazed and it put a spring in their step.

It was not long before we reached Mission Beach and we continued along the Esplanade until we reached a lookout sign where we thought we may get a lovely view of the area. The spot was called Clump Point and it did indeed supply us a lovely view from which we enjoyed a Coffee and a biscuit. We then travelled further North to Bingil Bay where Tee and I went for a lovely walk along the sandy beach that was flanked by Coconut palms and rainforest mountains. After returning to Lizzie we turned south again to revisit Mission Beach that boasts a small row of shops and a lovely small-town feel. Continuing south we headed to South Mission Beach that Tee and I thought was a better beach than Mission Beach proper but the Rainforest Area near Bingil Bay was probably our pick of the bunch. We pulled over on the foreshore at South Mission Beach where we enjoyed a cold KFC lunch while admiring the Island views. We have really enjoyed our visit to Mission Beach but have no inkling to stay here the night as the Caravan Parks are quite expensive and Tully is just a short drive away.

In what seemed like a blink of an eye we were back on the Bruce Highway and then into Tully where they had free camping for self contained vehicles at the Showgrounds. We went for a short tour through Tully first before heading to the Showgrounds to find a spot for the evening. When we got to the Showgrounds, we were told by a traveller there that we had to get a permit from the information centre and that it was all free. We shot over to the information centre as the place was nice and the amenities were first class (for campers that is).

When we arrived at the Information Centre the two ladies there were lovely and told me of the issues that they had recently had with the Whiz Bangers. In fact, they had to kick out a large group of them that had taken over the amenities block and were doing all there washing and cleaning in the vanity basins. I told them of some of the issues that we had experienced and was glad that Tee was waiting in the Motorhome or this conversation would have really got her fired up. I showed them our Leave No Trace certification and they issued me with the free permit which allowed us to stay two nights if we wished. We drove back to the Showgrounds where we enjoyed a pleasant evening and a great night's sleep. Good on you Tully as this has been the best handling of campers that Tee and I have seen in the whole of Australia.

Day **317**

After a terrific night's sleep, we had a leisurely morning as I needed to do some writing and Tee did some housework (or Motorhome work). Tully has been good to us and we did consider going to Tully Gorge for the day and then coming back to the Tully Showgrounds for one more night. But the allure of home is starting to bang in our heads and we are keen to keep moving South. A few months ago, Tee dropped her phone into the washing machine and lost all her contacts. She had said to me a few days ago that she wanted to catch up with some friends from her childhood that were now living in Hervey Bay. As we were within a few weeks of Hervey Bay I decided to assist Tee by trying to find her friend's number on the internet, and as luck has it, I got the number on my first attempt. Tee rang Lorelle and sure enough it was her and Tee made plans to catch up with them when we reached Hervey Bay.

After writing until almost 10-00am we headed south with just a quick fuel stop in Tully to top up our tank. As we headed south the landscape quickly started to dry out but not before we got to the town of Cardwell where we got a stunning view of Hinchinbrook Island and the still waters on its approach. They are still now but the evidence of Cyclone Yasi is still present, in a positive way, with construction workers busy rebuilding its foreshore area. We also purchased some chutney and veggies from a local fruit stall before heading off again.

As we were not in any major rush, we thought it may be nice to find a little quiet country beach to spend the rest of the day and tonight at. We searched the maps and came up with a place called Toomulla Beach which was about 45 kilometres shy of Townsville. As we travelled towards our possible campsite the scenery continued to get dryer and dryer until we reached the turning into Toomulla Beach that had been scared by a recent fire. Not a very inviting entrance but we thought we would have a look as it may get better. The campsite was a few kilometres off the highway and when we arrived there it wasn't too bad as there were good shade trees. But the general area was a bit yucky and we could not find the beach so we moved on. We now decided to pump in as many kilometres as possible today as we did not like the region and thought that further south on the coast we went, it would begin to get more attractive.

We were soon passing through Townsville, which took a long time, as the place is massive and with no desire to visit the place, we steered clear of the centre of town. Tee and I could not believe how big the place had grown and was also in amazement as to why people would want to live here. Anyway, Townsville turned to Ayr and after numerous roadwork's stops, we reached a Rest Area in the small town of Guthalungra which looked great (mainly because I had been driving for so long). We set up camp right on Dinner time and Tee made up some stir fry for us while I relaxed with a glass of wine. Tee was not keen on having a wine – I don't know why ☺

The Rest Area had a great feel to it and even though there were a number of young tourists here they were well behaved. We went to bed at about 9-00pm and were just drifting off to sleep when we were awakened by another young tourist backing his Whiz – Banger to within a foot of the back of Lizzie, which is about two feet away from where we were sleeping. Not only that but where he parked blocked off the entrance to the toilet block. I was furious and quickly threw on my clothes and shot out of the Motorhome to confront him. I told him to not park there as it was too close to us and he was also blocking the entrance to the toilet block. He said that there was no sign and that's when I really burred up. I told him to fuck off as he had just woken me up and I was not going to listen to him banging his doors for the next hour or so. He went quiet and said no more so I followed up by saying that if he started banging doors, I would be out there banging his head, and with that I went back inside.

Back inside the Motorhome I saw him talking to the passenger and five minutes later he took off. Good – these young tourists need to be more aware of 'other people'.

Day 318

With no further incidents last night Tee and I had a great night's sleep and apart from the young smartass walking past and eyeballing me this morning our morning was also very pleasant. Today we intended to visit Airlie Beach and Shut Harbour, which is the gateway to the Whitsunday's. We have a couple of options on where to stay tonight while visiting the area with one being near Shute Harbour and the other at O'Connor Creek just short of Proserpine. But first we will be stopping in Bowen about 80 kilometres from where we stayed last night. Within an hour of leaving the campsite we were on the approach to Bowen and surrounded by fields of tomatoes and capsicums. We had never seen so many tomato plants in the open in our lives and the sight of them in huge rows was quite unusual. We ended up in Queens Beach which was the first Beach Access we found and had a toilet break there on the foreshore. (Well actually in a toilet block on the foreshore). The beach here was a little ordinary but the huge fig trees in the foreshore gardens were spectacular. We headed off with the intention of finding Bowen central and having a bit of a look around.

It wasn't too long before we drove into Bowen's central business area that is very pretty, and as you drive in the ocean is at the end of the road. The buildings are well maintained and the main foreshore area is well laid out. We drove around the main foreshore and took a number of photos in the marina and jetty area before deciding to push on to Airlie Beach. Bowen is not a modern beach town as it has maintained its country feel which made it very appealing to Tee and I.

The turning to Airlie Beach from the North is just before the town of Proserpine and the landscape almost immediately changes as we turned left. The whole area on the approach to Airlie beach is much greener and obviously more fertile as there was an immediate lush feeling like in the wet tropics. Tee and I both enjoyed the drive in to Airlie Beach but when we arrived at the town itself, we both immediately knew that we would not be staying here overnight. Don't get me wrong it's a stunningly beautiful place but it's very overcrowded and quite ritzy which is not our bag. This did not stop us driving around and admiring the place but the volume of people and shops made it like many other big towns and not very appealing to Tee and I. We continued on after a bit of a look around and headed in the Shute Harbour direction, just down the road.

Lizzie was not impressed by the mountainous range that divides Shute Harbour and Airlie Beach, but to us it was lovely as it provided superb views over Airlie Beach. Now Shute Harbour to us was much more appealing as the colour of the water was amazing and it was a lot quieter in this part of town. The fact that it was high tide also made it a lot prettier as we would find out on our way out. We both thought that hiring a yacht here and sailing the islands would be superb but that would have to wait for another day as this trip was road only, and mainly blacktop at that. On the way out of Shute Harbour we stopped at a wayside stop with a stunning view and had a bite to eat while making a few phone calls to family and friends. We spent quite a while here and it was almost 2-00pm when we left to head out of the area. On the way out the tide had receded exposing the not so pretty side of the area which reminded me a lot of the River Heads area near Hervey Bay – a cross between mud and sand.

We were soon out of the area and when we passed Proserpine we decided to keep driving for as long as we had daylight as Home was becoming very alluring. An hour or so later we passed through the outskirts of Mackay and then through Sarina before noticing that we were fast running out of daylight. At this point we picked a free camp to stop at near the town of St Laurance but when we saw campers at Clairview and saw that the sun was trying to hide we pulled in there instead. Clairview was not an official rest area but with so many other campers there already we knew it would be OK to spend the night here. The beach at Clairview was more mud than anything else but with a full moon hanging over the horizon the views were not too shabby. We enjoyed a pleasant evening of lamb chops and wine before a good night's sleep.

Day **319**

Last night I had made a phone call to Clem and Betty, who we met on the second or third day of our travels and made plans to drop in and see them in their hometown of Bundaberg. We should be there in a few days and thought it would be great to catch up, and with their agreeance we cemented our plans. We left Clairview after a pleasant night and on the way out we used the facilities next to a lovely community stall that the locals had opened up. What a great idea as by letting people camp in their town they had created a mobile customer base that would change everyday. Shame more small towns don't tap into the potential sales from travelling nomads. Not much point in us buying produce today though as we were now only two or three days from home and I must say quite keen to get there. I had spent a few hours writing this morning as I seem to have more inspiration in the morning and with all the photos we take reminds me of anything that I fail to remember. With this delay we were still able to get going by 9-00am and with a busy schedule and another of Tee's home towns to see, we were off.

Our first stop would be for fuel as we had done a lot of driving yesterday without much stopping. I passed a tiny fuel station that had fuel priced at $1.56 and didn't stop as I remember Stan saying that he got water in his diesel tank in a small well priced fuel stop. We continued to Marlborough – (not sure what this place was named after but it didn't look like Marlborough country) where I stopped at a large BP station and was shocked to see the price of $1.70 per litre on the pump. But by this stage I had no choice and only bought $30.00 worth to get me to Yeppoon where we knew the prices would be better.

The landscape from Clairview to the outskirts of Rockhampton had been less than exciting and extremely dry but as we started to approach Yeppoon it did improve somewhat. We did find fuel at a good price here of $1.55 per litre and filled up prior to entering Yeppoon.

Our first stop in Yeppoon was for a lunch break and we decided that once we saw some ocean we would pull over for lunch. That spot ended up being an estuary containing old boat shacks and many old boats to keep them company. The estuary was at low tide and exposed its muddy base and to many people the whole scene would be quite unattractive. But I did not see it that way and found the place very interesting and quite unique. In fact, Tee and I much prefer this scenery to that of the stark hi-rise apartments that we witnessed at Airlie Beach. I took some lovely photos of the area as Tee prepared me some lunch, and after lunch I topped up our house water before we pushed off again.

We had travelled into Yeppoon on the Tourist route that was numbered 10, and had stayed on this route so far. But we saw a beach sign that veered off our course and thought it may offer good views of the area due to its elevation. The place we stopped at was called Wreck Point Lookout in Cooee Beach and the views were amazing. We stopped and took a few photos while waiting to see if a fellow with a paraglider was going to take off. We did not see him take off but the views from the lookout were superb and well worth a look. We continued along Route 10 through Emu Park and then the road headed inland again where the landscape began to get dryer and less attractive.

As we passed through Rockhampton Tee was starting to get excited about visiting her old schooldays town of Yarwun. We had another quick pit stop at Mount Larcom where I also dropped into the pub to buy a slab of Carlton Mids. We studied our map to see where we could spend the night as it was now 4-00pm and we had yet to see Yarwun, the main reason for us visiting the area. We found a free camp located 14 kilometres from Yarwun and decided that after our visit to Yarwun we would head straight there.

We soon found the entry sign to the town of Yarwun which said "Welcome to Yarwun" and a far cry from what we would receive when we got there. Tee had her radar going trying to remember the place from her childhood but with 33 years under the bridge it was doubtful she would remember much. We located the Yarwun school but Tee said it was nothing like she remembered and we could not see the original schoolhouse, only a number of portables. We went up behind the school on a dirt road but soon realized that the original school building was not there and in fact Tee felt that the school was in a different location. As we began to turn Lizzie around, we saw an older lady approaching from her front gate in a Suzuki Swift. She obviously lived at the end of the street which was a no through road. She stopped beside our Motorhome and said 'can I help you', which was said in a way to make us feel like we were trespassing. I had not yet picked up on her vibe and just pleasantly said, we are just here looking at the school that Tee went to in her childhood. She continued by telling us that this was a no through road and was very standoffish and rude. With this unusual meeting we turned Lizzie around and headed back into the centre of town to see if we could jog Tee's memory.

Back in town (just around the corner) Tee spotted the old shop that one of her friend parents use to own and we decided to head in. Tee told me that the school use to be straight ahead of us and not behind us like the new school now was. We decided to go in and talk to the shop keeper who may be able to confirm or deny Tee's theory. Tee also got to post a letter here and she was thrilled with that as it was something she had also done as a child for her parents. I said to Tee when we walked in 'there is that lady from behind the school in the Suzuki swift' and thought it would be a good opportunity to find out more about the town. The lady (lets call her the lemon sucker – due to her sour looking face) was talking to the shop keeper (lets call her big Ranga – due to her size and colour) and the vibe was very negative as we strolled in (as you can pick up on by my name calling). But this was Tee's memories and I wanted to get as much info as I could regardless of how nasty these people choose to be. The first thing Lemon Sucker said to me was 'do you mind not going down my street and turning on my son's driveway' and I again explained why we were here and that I did not know it was a no through road. She continued by complaining about the council trucks ruining her son's driveway – yarda yarda. I turned my attention to Big Ranga and asked her if the school had always been there. I also told her that Tee went to school here many years ago and knew the people that use to own the store. Then big ol Ranga went off about how it was a Co-op and that no one owned it and asking me if I knew how a co-op worked – yarda yarda. My mind kept focussing on the entry sign of the town that said 'Welcome to Yarwun' and I tried to stay civil so as to get the info Tee wanted to hear.

Eventually she told us that the railway had swapped the land with the school and the old school house was sold off to locals and relocated to where it is now. And guess who was living in the old school house – you guessed it old Lemon Sucker. I thanked them as we left and we got a sarcastic 'See Ya' from Big Ranga. Not worth the effort we didn't react and simply left saying how amazingly rude these two, so called ladies, had been. Outside the shop we saw and photographed the old schoolhouse that Lemon Sucker lived in and then had a look at the old school site. We headed to the free camp with two thoughts keeping us from getting angry with that rudeness – one – Lemon Sucker and Big Ranga get to live in Bumfuck Shitsville for the rest of their lives and – two – Lemon Sucker gets to also live with the Ghost of the Principle that died on the toilet of her home 32 years ago.

Day **320**

The Calliope River Rest Area was a great place to stay and the river was huge, much bigger than Tee and I expected. The Rest Area itself was also huge and just as well as there must have been over 50 Caravans and Motorhomes parked here over night. With the success of yesterday's exploration into Yarwun we would begin the day by exploring the Boyne Island / Tannum Sands area that was also a place where Tee lived and went to school. This time we hoped that the success would come minus the negativity that Big Ranga and Lemon Sucker provided at Yarwun.

We headed off about 9-00am after I did some writing and paid another darn bill. With a bit over 25 kilometres to travel though it was not long before we reached Boyne Island which because of its proximity to the ocean had grown immensely. Tee took photos of the signs as we entered the town of Boyne Island and we quickly located the Caravan Park where Tee had spent part of her childhood. We drove into the Caravan Park and asked the caretaker if it would be OK for us to drive through the Caravan Park so Tee could locate the site where she had lived. Tee noticed that the playground was gone from the front of the park and that a toilet block had been built over the site where she once lived. The original toilet block was still there but this was an additional block and Tee knew it was the right spot due to the orientation of the original toilet block that she used as a child.

We then drove out of the Caravan Park, thanking the caretaker on the way out, and went in search of her old Boyne Island School. We stopped at a local fish and chip shop for directions to the school and a lovely English lady who was more than helpful directed us to the school that she thought was the oldest in town. There were now three schools in town as the place was highly populated and as I said before this is due to its proximity to the beach. We located the school which was only a short distance up the main street but Tee was struggling to recognize it due to the expansion and new buildings. Tee was not that fussed though as this school did not hold as many fond memories for her as did Oaky Creek or to a lesser degree Yarwun and we drove off to have a quick look at Tannum Sands. But as we were leaving Tee spotted her old classroom on the outskirts of the school confirming that we had at least found the right school.

Tannum Sands was nothing like Tee remembered and with only light memories of the place we continued our journey down the East Coast of Australia. Our next stop would be the towns of Agnes Waters and 1770 which have been given great wraps by a number of our friends. The scenery through these areas has been moderately interesting but with winter being the dry season in these parts it was quite brown. We arrived at Agnes Waters and with 1770 being the furthest point we continued towards there and desperately in search of a toilet block. We eventually found a toilet block and with a water tap nearby I also filled up the house water while Tee made us a bite to eat.

After lunch we continued to 1770 which was lovely but didn't set our socks on fire, so we had a brief drive around before heading back to Agnes Waters for a look and then out and onto Bundaberg. On the outskirts of Bundaberg, we stopped to call Clem and Betty who we arranged to visit a few days ago. This is quite an ironic time for us actually as we are now two days from home and about to meet up with Clem and Betty who we met at Bollon on day two of our Journey. A lot has happened in between so we should have a good conversation with them. But when we rang there was no answer so we rang again and still no answer. I tried Clem's mobile but that number had been disconnected so we had no chose but to keep going. We looked up campsites in the area and found one that was about 25 kilometres south of Bundaberg.

Disappointed at not being able to see our friends today we headed towards the campsite and thought at least we would have an early day and a good relaxing evening. But as we were on the outskirts of Bundaberg, we got a phone call from Clem so we turned back to catch up with our old friends. We had a great afternoon of chatting and laughing and apart from my exploding biscuit episode the day went smoothly. After a number of hours chatting, I said to Tee that we better keep moving as it would soon be dark and we would not be able to find the campsite. With that we said our goodbyes and headed off in search of our next night rest stop.

On the outskirts of Bundaberg, we found another campsite and although close to town we thought it looked quite OK so we pulled in. The place we found was Hinkler Lions Park, Branyan which I think is a suburb of Bundaberg. The place is a bit stark but should be fine for the evening and with only one more day until we arrive home, we can always catch up on our sleep IN OUR OWN BED! We had a bite to eat and I had a few beers before heading for bed.

Day **321**

Today we awoke to our last day on the road and with a fairly good sleep we were so pleased to be heading home. Even though it has been an amazing journey it will be great to be settled in our lovely home with all its space and comfort. We are about 320 kilometres from home but we are going to do a stop over in Hervey Bay as Tee would like to drop in and catch up with some of her relatives that she has not seen for a number of years. I calculated that we would be there just after lunch as we have dawdled this morning and it was now almost 10-30am.

Armed with this information Tee gave them a call and as it was Saturday, they were free and looking forward to seeing us. Back on the road a little after 11-00am it was hard to believe that this was our last day of travel, I know I keep saying this but it was a weird feeling. In no time at all we were in the township of Hervey Bay and with Tee's amazing navigational skills ☺ we arrived at her relative's home just before 1-00pm. Tee and I had a lovely time with her relatives and with under four hours to travel we headed off mid afternoon and arrived home (our fixed home) in the early evening.

It was really weird as we opened our front door after so long living in the confines of our Motorhome. The place seemed foreign and absolutely massive, but we were excited to sleep in our big comfy bed so we did little for the evening other than to watch a bit of TV and then have an early night. OMG how friggen comfortable is this bed!

HOME

We had a massive sleep last night, about ten hours, and again it seems weird all this space. My mum had done a bit of cleaning for us while we were away so the home was not too bad and Tee was spared the ordeal of coming back to a huge lot of housework. Although she does have very high standard and wanted to spruce everything up again. The Motorhome was a different story though as it was very dusty and needed a huge clean up, which we planned to do over the next few weeks. There was also the hot water service that needed replacing and a number of other minor repairs that would ensure that we both would not get too bored in the foreseeable future.

But all of this could wait as we had a much more important task to perform and that was to pick up Whiskey (our "NOW" fifteen-year-old black and white cat) from Meo – Meo cat manor. Into the "car" and -----------Nothing ---------------- flat battery, bugger another task. This will not stop us though and we jumpstarted it off Lizzy (who has 3 near new batteries) and we were off.

When we arrived at Meo Meo Manor we were shocked to see Whizzy as she was about half the weight she was when we left on our trip. This was heartbreaking to us and we are trying to tell ourselves that it was from being stressed, but we were not so sure. Well at least she was alive, and at home we could spoil her rotten like she is used to. (It took Whizzy a month or so to come round but she is now doing fine).

Tee and I took some time to re-adjust back into "normal life" (not sure if normal is the correct phrase) as we now have a different approach to what life is all about and look forward to a future that is not what society wants to dictate to us. Anyone that knows us knows that we don't fit the mould, and this is exactly how we like it. We plan to live very differently than what society dictates, and hold the philosophy that in life "you should do everything that you enjoy and want to do – as long as you don't hurt anyone else in the process" (another Nanu quote).

And in parting I quote you the advice I was given by the elderly fellow in Hervey Bay who we met on our practice trip in the Motorhome.

"There are a Thousand reasons why you should not step out of general society for as long as we have – but only One reason why you should!"
I am sure you have guessed the One reason by now –
but if not

*** It's YOU!" ***